Microsoft®

# Office

## 365

### 2019 Brief Edition

Nita Rutkosky

Audrey Roggenkamp
Pierce College Puyallup
Puyallup, Washington

Ian Rutkosky
Pierce College Puyallup
Puyallup, Washington

## PARADIGM
EDUCATION SOLUTIONS

**Vice President, Content and Digital Solutions:** Christine Hurney
**Director of Content Development:** Carley Fruzzetti
**Testers:** Desiree Carvel; Ann E. Mills, Ivy Tech Community College of Indiana, Evansville, IN
**Director of Production:** Timothy W. Larson
**Production Editor/Project Manager:** Jen Weaverling
**Cover and Text Design:** Valerie King
**Senior Design and Production Specialist:** Julie Johnston
**Copy Editor:** Deborah Brandt
**Indexer:** Terry Casey
**Vice President, Director of Digital Products:** Chuck Bratton
**Digital Projects Manager:** Tom Modl
**Digital Solutions Manager:** Gerry Yumul
**Senior Director of Digital Products and Onboarding:** Christopher Johnson
**Supervisor of Digital Products and Onboarding:** Ryan Isdahl
**Vice President of Marketing:** Lara Weber McLellan
**Marketing and Communications Manager**: Selena Hicks

© 2020 by Paradigm Publishing, LLC

875 Montreal Way
St. Paul, MN 55102
Email: CustomerService@ParadigmEducation.com
Website: ParadigmEducation.com

Printed in the United States of America

28 27 26 25 24 23 22 21 20 19    1 2 3 4 5 6 7 8 9 10 11 12

# Contents

# EXCEL

# ACCESS

# Preface

Marquee Series, *Microsoft® Office 365*, 2019 Brief Edition, prepares students to work with Microsoft Office in a business office or for personal use. Incorporating an accelerated, step-by-step, project-based approach, this courseware helps students build competency in the features found in the 2019 versions of Word, Excel, Access, and PowerPoint.

## Proven Instructional Design

The following visual guide shows how you can use this courseware's clear instruction and hands-on practice to achieve success.

Program openers provide an overview of the software's best uses and give students a preview of the software features and how they are used in the workplace. The openers also provide an overview and visual representation of some of the projects that students will complete.

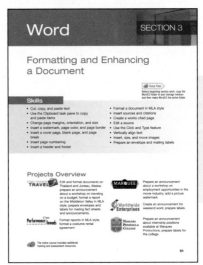

Sections begin with a list of the skills covered and an overview of the projects completed in that section.

Activities begin with a short explanation of selected features followed by streamlined, point-and-click instruction that pares reading to a minimum.

**In Brief** summaries of major commands and features provide instant review and a quick reference of the steps required to accomplish a task.

Magenta color highlights text to be typed.

Screen captures visually reinforce activity steps.

**In Addition** sidebars offer extra information on key features and subfeatures.

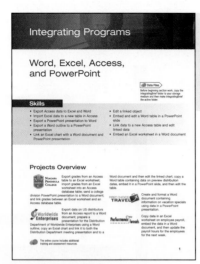

**Integrating Programs** activities devoted to sharing information among Microsoft Office programs highlight the benefits of using the Office suite. Projects include copying, exporting, linking, and embedding data. Students learn how to manage data efficiently in the business office or for personal use.

 # The Cirrus Solution

*Elevating student success and instructor efficiency*

Powered by Paradigm, Cirrus is the next-generation learning solution for developing skills in Microsoft Office and computer concepts. Cirrus seamlessly delivers complete course content in a cloud-based learning environment that puts students on the fast-track to success. Students can access their content from any device anywhere, through a live internet connection. Cirrus is platform independent, ensuring that students get the same learning experience whether they are using PCs, Macs, or Chromebook computers. Cirrus provides access to all the Marquee Series content, delivered in a series of scheduled assignments that report to a grade book to track student progress and achievement.

## Dynamic Training

Cirrus online versions of Marquee Series courses include interactive assignments to guide student learning.

**Student Data Files** for each section provide the files needed to complete each activity.

**Watch and Learn Lessons** explain how to perform the chapter activities, including a how-to video for students to view, content for them to read, and a short quiz that allows them to check their understanding of the content.

**Guide and Practice Tutorials** provide interactive, guided training and measured practice.

**Hands On Activities** enable students to complete the chapter activities in provided data files, compare their solutions against a **Check Your Work** model answer image, and submit their work for instructor review.

## Section Review and Assessment

Section review and assessment activities reinforce and assess student learning.

**Features Summary** lists identify key section features for review.

**Knowledge Check** completion exercises reinforce student comprehension and recall of program features, terminology, and functions.

**Skills Review, Skills Assessment, and Marquee Challenge** assignments, framed within a workplace project perspective, evaluate the ability to apply section skills and concepts in solving realistic problems. Students upload their answers through Cirrus for instructor evaluation.

**Exercises and Projects** provide opportunities for students to further develop and demonstrate section skills. Exercises and Projects are completed live in the Office application and are automatically scored by Cirrus. Detailed feedback and how-to videos help students evaluate and improve their performance.

**Skills Exams** evaluate student ability to complete specific tasks. Skills Exams are completed live in the Office application and are automatically scored.

Multiple-choice **Concept Exams** assess student understanding of the section content.

## Student eBook

The Student eBook makes Marquee Series content available from any device (desktop, laptop, tablet, or smartphone) anywhere. The eBook is accessed through the Cirrus online course.

## Instructor eResources

Cirrus tracks students' step-by-step interactions, giving instructors visibility into students' progress and missteps. With Exam Watch, instructors can remotely join a virtual, live, skills-based exam with students—a helpful option for struggling students who need one-to-one coaching, or for distance learners. In addition to these Cirrus-specific tools, other instructor materials are available. Accessed through Cirrus and visible only to instructors, the *Instructor eResources* for the Marquee Series include the following support:

- Planning resources, such as lesson plans, teaching hints, and sample course syllabi

- Delivery resources, such as activity answer keys and online images and templates

- Assessment resources, including live and annotated PDF model answers for section work and review and assessment activities, rubrics for evaluating student work, and section-based exam files

# Information Technology Essentials

## The Information Processing Cycle

Computers process information in the same way that humans make decisions. We use our eyes and ears to *input* facts and data into our brains. We use our brains to *process* that data and organize it into information. The resulting *output* is a thought or decision that we can display or present by drawing it, writing it, or making a video or audio recording of it. If we decide to keep the results for future use, we can *store* the paper or recording in a file cabinet.

As shown in Figure 1, the information processing cycle can be divided into four segments: input, processing, output, and storage. The cycle relies on computer *hardware* (devices you can physically see and touch in and on the computer) to mimic the human thought process.

### Input

Input involves getting data into the computer so that it can be processed. Some commonly used input devices are described in the following sections.

**Keyboard** Designed based on the layout of keys on a typewriter, the keyboard is primarily used for typing text. Although numbers are found in a row above the letters, most PC keyboards also include a calculator-style number pad for the convenience of bookkeepers, accountants, and others who frequently work with numbers.

Twelve keys labeled F1 through F12, as well as several other named keys, can be programmed to perform special functions in software applications. For example, the F1 key usually displays a help window where you might type a request for instructions on how to print what has just been typed. The Home key might move the cursor to the left side of a line in one program, but to the upper left corner of the page in another. (The cursor, also known as the insertion point, is the flashing bar, dash, or other symbol that indicates where the next character you type will appear on the screen.)

**Figure 1** The Information Processing Cycle

Storage

Input    Processing    Output

A keyboard and mouse are examples of common input devices.

**Mouse** A mouse is a pointing device used for issuing commands and selecting text or files for processing. Moving the mouse on the desktop causes a pointer to move on the screen. If you point to the File tab in the top left corner of the Microsoft Word screen, for example, and then click the left mouse button, the backstage area will appear, allowing you to click the *Open* option if you want to access a file you have previously saved.

If you want to delete several words or lines of text in a file, you can point to the beginning of the first word, hold down the left mouse button, drag the mouse to highlight the text, and then press the Delete key to remove the text from the document.

Most tablets, such as the iPad, utilize a touchscreen as the main mode of user input. Touchscreens have advanced and allow multiple fingers or thumbs to be used simultaneously on the screen.

**Touchpad** Most laptop computers provide a touchpad instead of a mouse as a pointing device. To use a touchpad, move your index finger across the pad to position the cursor and then use your thumb to press the buttons at the bottom of the pad.

**Touchscreen** A touchscreen allows you to select items and input commands by physically touching a specific area of the screen. Most smartphones and tablets utilize touchscreen technology. Touchscreens are also used at information kiosks to provide an easy way to select items of interest, without the necessity of a keyboard. Servers at restaurants use touchscreens to place orders since they are much easier to clean than keyboards and can be used with only one hand.

A scanner is a tool to input either pictures or text.

**Scanner** A scanner works like a photocopier to transfer pictures or text into a computer. If you don't have a digital camera, you can scan hard copies of your photos into a PC and then organize or enhance them with photo-editing software.

**Digital Pen and Drawing Tablet** Although a mouse can be used for drawing designs and pictures, it is very clumsy. Better detail can be achieved with a digital pen and tablet. Some tablets and laptop computers now accept "handwritten" input with a digital pen called a stylus.

Tablets are useful for writing notes by hand when in a meeting or on the road.

Engineers, architects, and designers often use a sophisticated type of graphics tablet to make precise drawings such as those used in building construction and the manufacture of circuit boards for computers. Such graphics tablets are made up of hundreds of tiny intersecting wires that form an electronic matrix embedded in the tablet surface. A stylus or crosshair cursor activates these intersection points, which collectively represent the image.

**Joystick** A joystick (named after the control stick used to fly fighter jets) is an input device consisting of a small box with a vertical stick that, when pushed in a certain direction, moves the cursor on the screen. Most often used to control fast-moving computer games, joysticks can also be used by people who have difficulty using a mouse.

**Digital Camera** Digital cameras can be used to transfer pictures and videos onto a computer. A webcam is a popular example of a video camera that can be used in combination with headphones and a microphone to communicate with people all over the world. Many computers, including all smartphones, now come with built-in cameras and microphones to make this type of communication easier.

A joystick is an input device used to move objects on a computer screen and is a common input device for computer gaming.

**Microphone** With a microphone you can add a "sound bite" to a computerized slide presentation or speak to a friend over the internet. Microphones can stand on a desk or be worn as part of a headset.

**Bar Code Reader** Bar code readers are used for entering the Universal Product Code (UPC) found on items in grocery and retail stores. They also are used to track medication administration in hospitals and parcel being shipped by a carrier company or service.

A digital camera captures images in a digital format and often contains an output device for viewing those images.

A webcam is a digital camera that can be controlled remotely over the internet.

**Dual Purpose Devices** Although usually thought of as storage devices, compact discs (CDs), digital video discs (DVDs), flash drives, and hard drives all allow you to enter data into a computer quickly and easily.

## Processing

A computer's central function is to process data. Processing can involve calculating numbers, editing text, modifying pictures, and other

A bar code reader scans a UPC. The resulting input can be used to check a patient's identity and medication requirements.

information management tasks. The central processing unit (CPU) is the brain of the computer that handles those tasks. The rate at which the CPU can process data is known as the *clock speed*.

**Processors** Most IBM-compatible PCs use a central processing unit made by Intel or AMD. These CPUs process data at clock speeds from 2.0 to 5.0 gigahertz (GHz). (One gigahertz equals one billion cycles per second.) The first Apple Macintosh computers ran on Motorola 68000 processors, but Macs now use Intel processors and can run IBM-compatible PC operating systems.

A processor chip (a CPU) performs the calculations in a computer.

Many CPUs include multiple processors on a single chip. These dual-core or quad-core processors can process multiple instructions simultaneously for better performance. Some CPUs have six processors in one. Single-core processors use a technique called *multitasking*, in which one processor switches between programs so quickly that the user doesn't perceive any interruption, but both programs are actually running more slowly than they would with two separate processors or with one dual-core processor.

**Memory Chips** Memory chips are the hardware that provides the workspace for the data and instructions the computer is processing. The user workspace is called *random access memory (RAM)* because the CPU has quick and easy access to it. Having a large amount of RAM is like having a large work table where you can spread out books, papers, pencils, a calculator, and other tools you need to do your work. RAM is considered volatile or temporary storage because it disappears completely when the power to the computer is shut off.

The amount of RAM a personal computer needs depends on the operating system it runs. A Windows 10 or Windows 8.1 system requires at least 1 gigabyte (GB). A gigabyte equals about one billion bytes.

*Read only memory (ROM)* is sometimes confused with RAM due to the similarity of their names, but ROM is nonvolatile and contains the getting-started instructions that the PC needs when the power is first turned on. As its name implies, ROM can only be used as programmed by the PC manufacturer. You can't make any changes to it; you can only cause its contents to be "read" into the computer.

The motherboard is a container for the computer's CPU and RAM, and contains slots for adding expansion cards. Figure 2 shows a typical motherboard layout.

**Figure 2** Motherboard Layout

## Output

*Output* is processed data that can be used immediately or stored for later use. Output may be produced in either hard copy or soft copy, or in both forms. Hard copy is a permanent version of output, such as a letter printed on paper using a printer. Soft copy is a temporary version of output and includes any output that cannot be physically handled. Soft copy output devices include monitors and speakers.

**Monitor** A monitor is a screen used for displaying graphics and text. New PCs are sold with flat screen, liquid crystal display (LCD) or light-emitting diode (LED) monitors. In an LCD monitor, liquid crystals are sandwiched between two sheets of material. Electric current passing through the crystals causes them to twist. This twisting effect blocks some light waves and allows other light waves to pass through, creating images on the screen. In an LED monitor, the LCD method of light transmission is enhanced by positioning red, green, and blue LEDs behind the liquid crystals. An LED monitor provides a more vibrant, colorful display than an LCD monitor.

Flat screen, LCD monitors are the most commonly used output devices.

**Printer** Traditional printers provide hard copy printouts on paper. Several printing technologies are available, including ink-jet, which places liquid ink onto the paper, and laser, which fuses powdered toner to the paper. In addition to traditional printing, 3-D printing can create 3-D objects by layering melted plastic.

**Speakers and Headphones** Speakers and headphones (both wired and wireless) provide audio output in stereo or surround sound for movies, radio programs, streaming video, online learning courses, and telephone calls.

Computer speakers provide sound output.

## Storage

The storage portion of the information processing cycle involves recording output so that it will be available after the computer has been shut off and RAM has been erased.

Output can be stored for future use on hard drives, CDs, DVDs, and flash drives. A *drive* is a PC device that can read and write data onto the surface of a round platter (disk) as it spins. Hard disk platters are made of metal; compact and digital video discs are made of plastic. Flash drives and solid-state hard drives store data in nonvolatile RAM; they have no moving parts, but they provide the same function as conventional drives.

Portable external hard drives are available in a variety of sizes, styles, and colors.

Hard drives (both internal and external) contain a stack of metal platters (disks), a drive motor, and read/write heads that are positioned to access the top and bottom of each platter. Solid State Drives (SSDs) are made of an array of flash memory and don't contain moving parts. Therefore, they are faster at reading and writing data. Hard drive capacities vary; an average desktop PC might have a hard drive that holds 5 terabtyes (TB).

This flash drive storage device has a USB connector that fits into a standard USB port.

Data CDs are made of the same material that is used for music CDs. In fact, you can play your favorite music CDs using the CD drive of your PC. CDs can hold about 700 MB of data. DVDs can hold from 4 GB to 8 GB, depending on whether they can record on one or two layers. Blu-ray discs are used both for high-definition video and for data; a Blu-ray disc can hold 25 GB to 50 GB.

The flash drives on the market today can hold from 128 megabytes to one terabyte of data on a printed circuit board inside a protective plastic or metal case. They are the size and shape of a person's thumb. Some drives even provide fingerprint authorization. Flash drives connect directly to a USB port and thus do not require the installation of any device driver programs to support them.

Another popular form of data storage is cloud storage. *Cloud storage* is storage space on the internet that can be accessed from any device with an internet connection. Storing on data on the cloud is a good way to back up data, but also leaves it vulnerable to security issues.

## System Unit Ports

*Ports* are the sockets that the input, output, and storage devices plug into (see Figure 3). In the early days of personal computing, serial, parallel, and printer cables and ports were found on all PCs. Today, most external, or *peripheral*, devices use Universal Serial Bus (USB) cables and ports. USB cables and connector plugs are smaller, thinner, and more durable. They transmit data at up to 5 gigabits per second (Gbps) for a USB 3.0 port. As many as 127 devices can be connected to a computer host at once through a daisy-chain-style connection setup.

USB hubs provide extra connection options for computers with only one or two USB ports. You can even make backup copies of your data to an external hard drive connected to your computer via the USB port on your keyboard.

### Exploring Technology 1

Identify the processor, clock speed, and amount of random access memory (RAM) in a computer you often use. ***Hint: On a computer running Windows 10 or 8.1, right-click the Start button and then click* System *at the pop-up menu. In either operating system, if the Control Panel is displayed using Classic view, double-click the System icon.***

### Exploring Technology 2

Identify the hardware you have on your computer and categorize each piece as input, output, or both.

**Figure 3** System Unit Ports

LAN port · USB ports · microphone connection · speaker connection · video port

# Computer Software

*Software* refers to the operating instructions and applications that allow computers to process the numbers, pictures, sounds, and text we enter into them. We can touch the disc that contains the software, but not the lines of programming code that make up the software.

## Personal Computer Operating Systems

The original personal computer operating system, MS-DOS (Disk Operating System), used a command-line interface, which meant that commands were typed into a text prompt and the computer returned text output to the monitor. Today, most operating systems use Graphical User Interfaces (GUIs), in which a mouse is used to manipulate graphic objects such as icons and windows on-screen.

If a PC has an older CPU with a clock speed that is too slow, or if it does not have enough RAM, the PC will run slowly or it won't be able to run the operating system at all. Windows 10 and Windows 8.1 require, at a minimum, a CPU that runs at 1 GHz and has 1 GB of RAM.

The operating system for Apple Macintosh computers is mac OS. Since its initial introduction in 2001, several updates to this operating system have been released, each one with a different code name. Mojave (version 10.14) was released in September 2018. Previous versions included High Sierra, Sierra, Yosemite, Mavericks, Mountain Lion, Lion, and Snow Leopard.

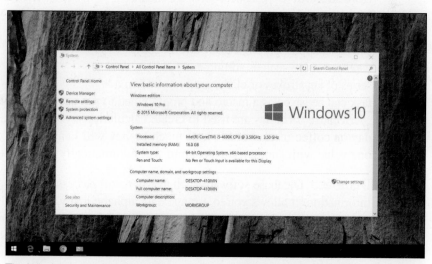

The Windows 10 operating system requires a CPU that runs at 1 GHz.

The Mac OS X operating system can run on IBM-compatible PCs.

## Applications

Applications allow someone with no technical knowledge of how a PC works to use a computer to balance his or her checkbook or to insert a photograph into a personalized greeting card, print it out, and send it to a friend. Thousands of software applications are available to empower users to perform these and other tasks, ranging from mundane to amazing. This section presents the most common types of computer applications on the market today.

**Word Processing** Word processing software was originally designed as a replacement for the typewriter. Now a word processing program such as Microsoft Word can support photos and drawings; mathematical calculations; text in table format; text of varying sizes, shapes, and colors; and even sound bites.

Microsoft Word is a word processing program with several formatting features that can be applied to words, lines, paragraphs, pages, or entire documents.

**Spreadsheet** Spreadsheet software such as Microsoft Excel can be used for both simple and complex calculations. Current versions can also support graphics and perform some database tasks, such as sorting and filtering. A series of keystrokes or clicks used to perform a task can be saved as a macro and programmed to run at the press of a key.

Because formulas are used to create calculations, you can ask, "If I spend only $2 per day on coffee instead of $5, how much money will I save per month?" When you replace one value with another, the program will automatically recalculate your budget.

**Database** Database software such as Microsoft Access is designed to keep track of information. It allows you to arrange data alphabetically, numerically, or chronologically, or you can filter the data to display only those items that match your criteria, such as the names of customers who spent more than $500 at your online music store last year. Database software can easily do simple calculations, such as showing monthly subtotals and an annual total for each of your customers, but complex math is usually best left to spreadsheet software.

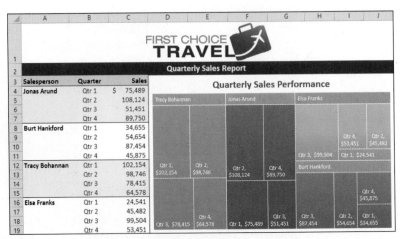

An Excel spreadsheet can calculate elements of a sales report, such as quarterly total sales, and display them in a chart.

| DistID | CompanyName | |
|---|---|---|
| 1 | All Nite Cinemas | 2 |
| 2 | Century Cinemas | 36 |
| 4 | Danforth Cinemas | P. |
| 5 | Eastown Movie House | P. |
| 6 | Hillman Cinemas | 55 |

US_Distributors

## US Distributors

| | |
|---|---|
| DistID | 1 |
| CompanyName | All Nite Cinemas |
| StreetAdd1 | 2188 Third Street |
| StreetAdd2 | |
| City | Louisville |
| State | KY |
| ZIPCode | 40201 |

Information can be entered into an Access database by using a form designed for that purpose.

## Movies

| MovieID | MovieTitle | Rating | Length | ReleaseDate | Genre |
|---|---|---|---|---|---|
| 1 | Ring of Roses | G | 129 | 2/9/2017 | Adventure |
| 2 | The Codebreakers of World War II | G | 183 | 12/28/2018 | History |
| 3 | The Life of Winston Churchill | G | 125 | 1/18/2019 | Biography |
| 4 | Two by Two | G | 95 | 3/13/2020 | Action |
| 5 | Going Global | G | 164 | 9/3/2021 | Documentary |

An Access database report is a selection of data in a database. The user chooses which types of information should be included in the report, and the database automatically finds and organizes the corresponding data.

**Presentation** Presentation software such as Microsoft PowerPoint allows users to create slide shows that can be viewed on a computer monitor or projected onto a large screen. Slide shows can include images, graphs and charts, drawings, video clips, sound, and text. Features such as arrows and boxes that "fly" into the screen and slide transition effects can add interest and emphasis to the content of a presentation.

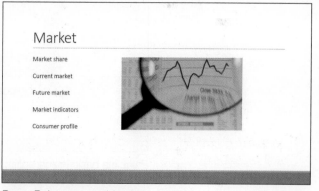

PowerPoint can combine text, graphics, sounds, and videos.

**Audio, Video, and Photo Editing** Photo-editing software is used for organizing, retouching, and editing photographs and videos. Programs such as PaintShop Pro and Photoshop Elements allow you to edit photographs by cropping, removing the red-eye effect, or by making more advanced changes such as putting one person's head on another person's body. You can also create your own slide shows with background audio and then email the results to friends and family or copy them to the cloud and display them on your TV.

Video-editing software such as Adobe Premiere can be used to edit video clips to remove the shots you took of your feet when you forgot to stop recording, or to add music, or to rearrange the scenes to create a more logical flow—or a more creative one. You can also edit the audio tracks. With some relatively inexpensive products, you can fine-tune the sound and achieve a professional level of quality.

The internet provides many options for uploading and sharing videos, music, and photos. YouTube is a popular website that allows users to watch and post videos. Many emerging new musicians use the website SoundCloud to upload their latest tracks and share them with the community. Websites such as Imgur and Flickr are useful for uploading and sharing images.

**Graphics and Drawing** Applications such as Adobe Photoshop, Adobe Illustrator, Microsoft Paint, and Corel PaintShop Pro are popular software packages that provide the tools to design graphical images that can be used for web pages, posters, marketing brochures, and greeting cards. Visio is a graphics application that focuses more on technical and business drawings, flow charts, and organizational charts to illustrate complex processes. Visio is vector graphics–based, meaning that it uses points, lines, curves, and geometric shapes to create images. Raster-based graphics programs use groups of pixels (picture elements) to make an image.

A digital pen and tablet may seem to be a requirement for using drawing applications, but you can do amazing things with a mouse by, for example, picking a circle from a group of shapes and then making it larger or smaller or turning it into an oval. Free graphics and drawing software applications include Inkscape, Skencil, and GIMP.

**Suites** Software applications are often bundled into packages called *suites*. Widely used versions of the Microsoft Office suite contain the word processing application, Word; the spreadsheet application, Excel; the database application, Access; and the presentation application, PowerPoint.

Paint is a basic image-editing program included with Windows.

Adobe Photoshop is a high-end image-editing program used by graphics professionals.

Money management software enables users to manage their money by helping them pay bills, balance checkbooks, keep track of income and expenses, maintain investment records, and more.

Smartphones include PIM software that tracks appointments and stores contact information.

**Money Management** Quicken and Microsoft Money are two software applications with an interface that resembles a checkbook. Users can not only write and print checks, but also track their spending habits, create a budget, generate cash flow reports, download their credit card charges, and keep track of their savings and investments.

TurboTax and TaxCut are income-tax preparation programs that prompt you to enter your tax information and then print duplicates of the state and federal forms with your data on the appropriate lines. They also let you file your tax returns electronically and direct your refund to your bank account.

**Personal Information Management** Microsoft Outlook and Lotus Organizer are examples of personal information management (PIM) programs that keep track of your to-do list, address book, and personal calendar. Many PIMs also contain a scheduler with an alarm to alert you of a meeting, whether it occurs daily, weekly, or only once. Smartphones and tablets can synchronize with your computer's PIM program so you can carry your information everywhere you go.

**Collaboration** Businesses often need several people to collaborate on a project. Collaborative software or groupware, such as Asana, Adobe Connect, and Microsoft Office SharePoint, provides a way to keep track of who has made or suggested changes to documents or plans and to distribute everything electronically. A calendar feature allows

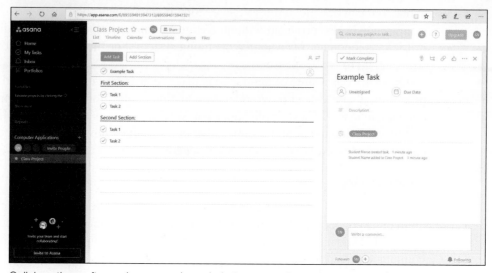

Collaboration software (groupware) can help team members stay connected.

users to schedule meetings at times when others are free. Both email and instant messaging (IM) functions are used, providing real-time communication among team members wherever they are in the world. SharePoint allows direct editing of documents through Word, Excel, or PowerPoint and also provides controlled access to shared documents via the web.

**Gaming** Computer games have come a long way since the Solitaire program included in the first versions of Windows. Today's games contain high-quality 3D animations, sound, and action that are very realistic. Role playing, action, sports, and fantasy games are just a small part of a fast-growing industry. Most users play games over the internet with people in other cities and countries.

Some games, especially those that include realistic simulations, require a lot of computing power. You will need a fast CPU, plenty of RAM, and a dedicated video card for the best performance.

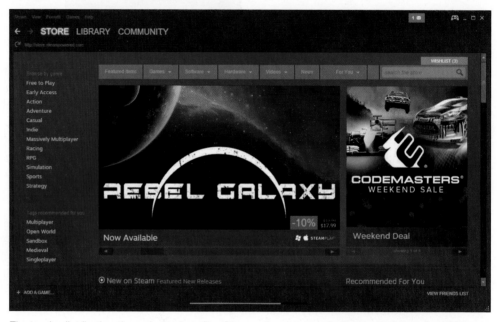

Electronic distribution through services like Steam allow gamers to access thousands of video games that can be downloaded and installed on their computers.

**Open Source** Open source software is the general term for applications that are provided completely free of charge, with no license fees or restrictions and no copyrights to worry about. You can download the software, copy it, and give it to your friends. The programming source code is also provided without charge and anyone is allowed to modify and improve it. Linux is a popular open source operating system. For further details about open source software, go to www.opensource.org.

OpenOffice is a suite of applications that is considered open source and includes a word processor, a spreadsheet program, a presentation application, a drawing application, and a database manager. These applications can save and open data files from Microsoft Office, and they provide many of the same capabilities as the equivalent retail products. OpenOffice can be downloaded for free from www.openoffice.org.

## Networks

Computer networks are created when people want to share something such as a printer, an internet connection, specific information within the confines of their business, or the wide and abundant variety of information found on the web. Networks allow computers to communicate and to share these resources.

## Local Area Networks

The Local Area Network (LAN) illustrated in Figure 4 consists of several computers that are physically connected to one another via a central hub called a *switch*. The network also includes a server (a computer that manages the network) and a shared printer. Most LANs are not stand-alone systems; they connect to the internet as well, so users can take advantage of online resources such as the web and email.

## Wide Area Networks

A company might have several LANs, each in a different location or branch office, and these LANs can be connected to one another to form Wide Area Networks (WANs), as shown in Figure 5. The key difference between a LAN and a WAN is that in a WAN, the company does not own all the pathways between the computers. The data has to go out in "public" to reach its destination, whether that is via a leased optic line or the internet. Leaving the protected local area carries security risks but also provides connectivity benefits.

**Figure 4** Local Area Network

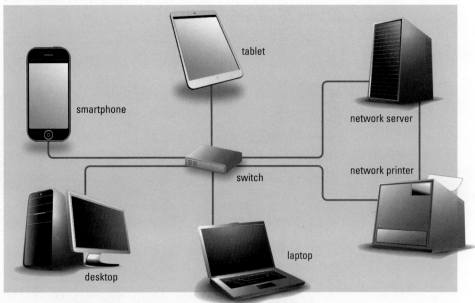

**Figure 5** Wide Area Network

Large companies lease dedicated telephone lines (T1 or T3 lines) or satellite connections to connect their LANs. Many smaller companies find it more affordable to connect their branch offices via the existing internet infrastructure.

## Network Components

Computer networks require specialized hardware and software designed to share information and for other collaborative functions. The various components are explained in this section.

Clients  Clients are the computer workstations where end users run the various applications necessary for them to do their jobs. In a client-server network, clients request information from the servers. Figure 6 shows an example of a client-server architecture. In this type of network structure, the networking paths allow a client computer to send information to a server, which can then relay the information back to that client computer or to another client on the same network. In this network, devices such as network hard drives and printers can be shared resources, available through their respective servers. In addition, the file server can provide access to a shared hard disk.

**Figure 6** Client-Server Architecture

Servers  Servers are data providers that are often larger and more powerful computers than clients. They house the network operating system software that organizes data sharing among the end users' PCs. They can hold large databases of information that users access to compile the reports that keep their organizations running smoothly. Servers might also be used as the storage location for everything every user creates, so that everyone else has easy access to it.

For small networks, the same computer can function as both client and server in a peer-to-peer network where all computers are equal and each one is both data requester and data provider (see Figure 7).

**Figure 7** Peer-to-Peer Architecture

Switches and Routers Within a LAN, all the computers and other network-enabled devices (such as printers) must have a way of communicating with one another. Switches and routers serve as central hubs for that communication.

A switch is a box into which each computer connects via a cable. A switch that connects devices via radio frequency (RF) rather than via cables is called a *wireless access point*. A router is a more sophisticated version of a switch. A router can pass data from one LAN to another and throughout the internet. Routers can be wired, wireless, or both.

Connectivity The PCs that make up a network have to be connected to each other in some way. The original method of connecting PCs used physical cables containing several strands of wire. The latest method is wireless and uses radio frequencies to carry data over short distances from a PC to a switch or router. All the devices are often located in the same room, but the signals are strong enough to penetrate the walls in homes and offices.

The most commonly used type of network cable is unshielded twisted pair cable (UTP). UTP cable is rated by category, and higher categories are needed for faster networks. Standard home networks use Cat 5 or Cat 5e cables; for business use, Cat 6 cable is the norm. Cat 7 and Cat 7a are the newest cable standards that provide up to 10 gigabits per second.

Wireless connections are used where cables are difficult to install or where the users are mobile or not close to a switch or router. Commonly called Wi-Fi, these connections are known by their technical 802.11 protocol specifications.

A switch provides a central connection place for cables from multiple computers.

A router enables you to join two or more networks, or to join your LAN to the internet.

**Protocols** A *protocol* is a generally accepted agreement on how to behave in a certain situation. For example, in many countries it is considered proper protocol to stand during the playing of the national anthem. Computer protocols are international agreements on how to manufacture hardware and software, and how to send data from one computer to another.

Now that wireless connectivity is becoming more common in the home computer market, more people are becoming aware of its associated technical labels. The following is a list of common protocols:

- 802.11ac or Wi-Fi 5 is the current Wi-Fi standard. It has a maximum data rate of 3.46 Gbps and a range of about 70 meters indoors or 250 meters outdoors.

- 802.11n or Wi-Fi 4 is the most common Wi-Fi standard; many 802.11n devices are still in use today. It has a maximum data rate of 450 Mbps and a range of about 70 meters indoors or 250 meters outdoors.

- 802.11g is an earlier Wi-Fi standard. It has a maximum data rate of 54 Mbps and a range of 38 meters indoors or 140 meters outdoors.

- 802.11b and 802.11a are now obsolete Wi-Fi standards, with maximum data rates of 54 Mbps and 11 Mbps, respectively.

- TCP/IP (Transmission Control Protocol/internet Protocol) defines the rules for sending and receiving data between network devices. Each device has a unique IP address, which is a series of four numbers between 0 and 255, separated by periods, like this: 192.168.0.1.

- HTTP (HyperText Transfer Protocol) defines the rules for sending and receiving web pages (hypertext) on the internet. For example, you might see http://ParadigmCollege/myschool.edu on the uniform resource locator (URL) or Address line of your internet browser. Figure 8 shows how data travels across the internet.

**Figure 8** Internet Infrastructure
Data moves across the internet by traveling through a collection of physical devices.

http://www.senate.gov/

http://www.senate.gov/

**Step 1**
You issue a request for information from the US Senate's home page.

**Step 2**
Your request is sent from your computer across a telecommunications medium such as a wireless tower, telephone lines, cable lines, or satellite.

**Step 6**
Your request arrives at the US Senate's web server. The information is sent back to your internet address.

**Step 3**
Your request passes through one or more routers.

**Step 5**
Your request passes through one or more national ISPs.

**Step 4**
Your request passes through your local internet Service Provider's (ISP's) computer. The address you entered is converted to an IP address, which is a series of numbers that uniquely identifies the location of the web page.

- HTTPS (HyperText Transfer Protocol Secure Sockets) encrypts data before sending it over the web. You can see the letters *https* on the URL line when you reach a web page asking for your credit card number or when you are paying your bills online, such as https://emcp/mybank.com/myaccount.

- POP3 is the current version of Post Office Protocol for receiving email. POP is a store-and-forward system in which your email waits on the mail server until you pick it up via an email application such as Outlook; then it forwards it to that application.

- IMAP (Internet Message Access Protocol) enables you to send email online and offline. The message is transferred to the recipient's machine only when a specific request is made to read it.

- FTP (File Transfer Protocol) provides an efficient, fast way to transfer files between computers. It is commonly used for files that are too large for email attachments and for large repositories of files.

HTTPS is a protocol that protects your personal data. Note the padlock at the left side of the Address bar and the website name in green at the top of the screen.

**Connectors and Ports** Wired network connections commonly use RJ-45 connectors. These are similar to telephone connectors (which are RJ-11 or RJ-14) but they use eight wires instead of the usual 2 or 4. An RJ-45 connector is slightly wider than its telephone counterpart.

### Exploring Technology  5

If you have Windows 10, display the Start menu, type **network**, and then click *View network connections* in the list that appears. A list of the computers and other devices in your LAN appears. Open the Network and Sharing Center and explore the icons and links there to learn more about your network. What protocols are installed? What is your connection speed?

### Exploring Technology  6

Ask your instructor if your school has wireless connectivity. If yes, find out where wireless is active and then go to that area to see if you can locate the wireless access point(s) (antennas) that are installed. For example, if the school cafeteria has wireless connectivity, you may be able to see the hardware that provides the access to the internet mounted on the ceiling or walls.

## The Internet

The internet is a global network of computers that allows data of all types and formats to be passed freely from one computer to another (see Figure 9). The web, email, and FTP are different parts of the internet.

**Figure 9** The Internet Network
Communications systems include computer hardware and communications software that allow computer users to exchange data around the house or around the world.

## World Wide Web

The World Wide Web is a collection of hypertext files containing graphics, audio, and video that can be accessed on the internet. The web is only a part of the internet, albeit a very large part.

## Electronic Mail

Electronic mail (email) uses its own protocols (such as SMTP, POP3, and IMAP) to route a message between computers on the internet and hold it at a destination mail server until the recipient picks it up.

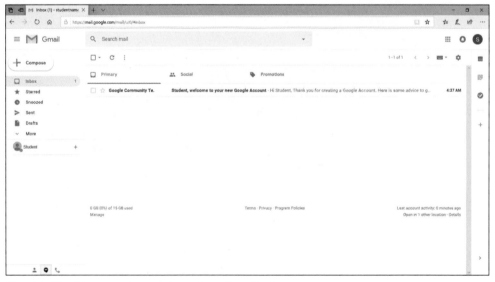

Google's Gmail is a popular web-based email application.

## File Transfer Protocol

Like email and the web, File Transfer Protocol (FTP) is an information workspace on the internet. It was originally used for exchanging data between incompatible mainframe systems, such as those made by IBM and those made by UNIVAC, but is now used to transfer files. A FTP server can be accessed through a web browser or a dedicated FTP application such as FileZilla.

FileZilla is a commonly used application for transferring files through an FTP site.

## Web 2.0

When the World Wide Web became popular in the mid 90's, content hosted on websites was relatively static and created by publishers. Users didn't have much of a chance to interact and be active members in creating and managing the content. Websites were only updated when the content creators felt the need to do so.

As the infrastruture of the internet grew and became more capable of delivering users more bandwidth and speed, the way users interacted with the World Wide Web changed. Websites began allowing users to interact more and add content to websites. For example, the video-sharing website YouTube relies entirely upon users uploading videos and providing feedback in the form of comments. A service such as YouTube would have not been viable in the past because of the bandwidth requirements for watching a video on the internet. A few key elements of Web 2.0 are mass user participation, user created and shared content, social connectivity, and web-integrated applications.

Social Networking  With the advent of Web 2.0, social networking websites became very popular. Facebook and MySpace were the pioneers of social networking, which consists of users creating and maintaining a profile with which other users can view and interact. When Facebook and MySpace were first introduced, they had very limited features that expanded over time. MySpace's popularity waned as Facebook became an

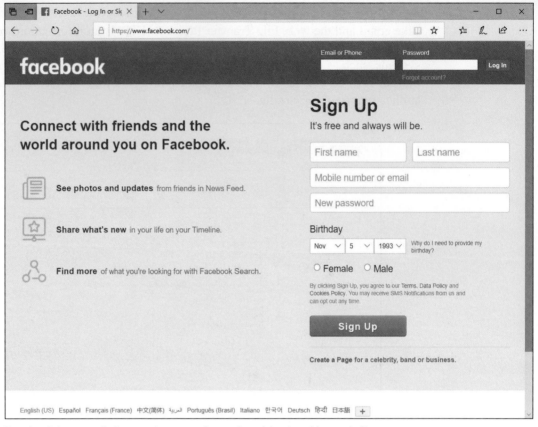

Facebook is currently the most commonly used social networking website.

easier-to-use, more streamlined platform. Facebook allows users to interact with their friends and families by sharing pictures, videos, stories, hyperlinks, event information and so on.

Currently, the most widely used social networking sites are Facebook, Instagram, Twitter, and Reddit. Other social networking sites tend to be based on certain interests. For example, Pinterest is a social networking website that allows users to share ideas through media, primarily pictures. Users can go on Pinterest and find an activity or craft another user has "pinned" on his or her profile.

**Media Sharing** Increased bandwidth and user interaction led to websites being designed to provide users a place to share media such as pictures, music, and videos. These websites generate money by providing users a platform to share their media and then placing advertisements on the website. Imgur, Tumblr, SoundCloud, and YouTube are all examples of media-sharing websites. While these websites allow you to upload media, you must be the rightful owner of the media in order to share it online. Websites like YouTube will take down any content that contains copyrighted materials.

Since so much user-created media is available on the internet, finding specific content can be difficult. Fortunately, there are websites dedicated to providing you with links and information to find content. For example, the website Reddit allows users to post links to pictures, videos, music, articles, and so on in an online bulletin board system. Once a link to content has been posted on Reddit, every user can either "up vote" or "down vote" the post. This voting system allows users to control the content that other users may or may not see.

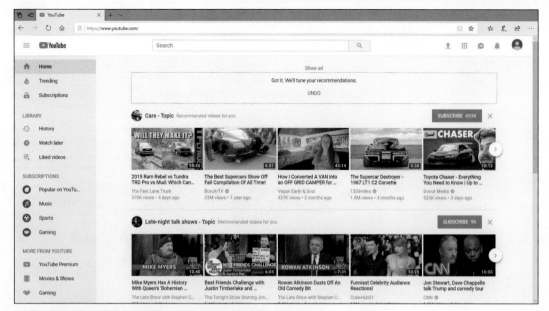

YouTube is the most commonly used video-sharing website.

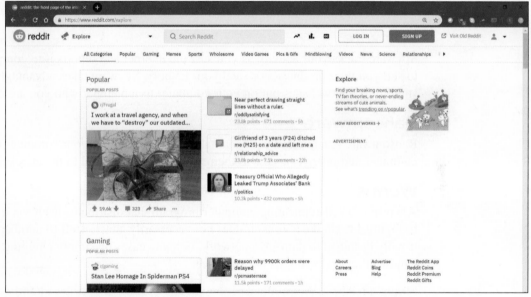

Reddit is a website where users post links to content and other users can vote on it.

## Security Issues

*Malware* is a term describing computer programs that have malicious intent. Viruses, spyware, ransomware, worms, and adware programs all fall into this category.

### Viruses

A computer virus is a string of code written to hurt others by damaging or destroying their computer files or making their computer experience difficult. Viruses are stored in executable (program) files; when the program runs, the virus code executes, causing damage and copying the virus into the computer's memory, where it infects other programs (see Figure 10). A virus is typically spread via an email attachment. Some viruses send themselves out via automatically generated emails to everyone in your address book.

**Figure 10** How a Virus Attacks

When you forward an email with an attachment such as a picture, you may be spreading a damaging virus.

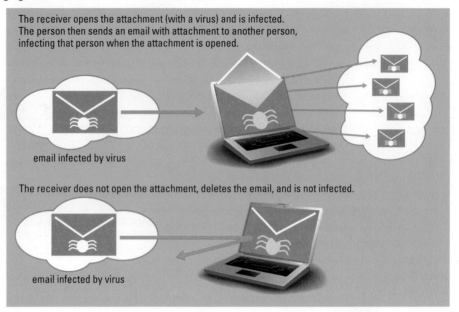

## Spyware

Spyware tracks your activity as you surf the internet and reports it to companies that want to sell you their products—or steal your identity. Spyware takes advantage of cookies, the small files that websites put on your computer to remember who you are on your next visit.

## Ransomware

Ransomware is malicious code that takes control of either your computer or files on your computer and restricts access to them until a ransom is paid to the attacker.

## Worms

A worm is a self-replicating computer program that distributes itself via a network, as shown in Figure 11. Unlike a virus, it does not necessarily attach itself to another file. Worms are usually designed to damage a network, in many cases by simply clogging up the network's bandwidth and slowing its performance.

**Figure 11** How a Worm Attacks

A worm reproduces itself and attacks all the computers on a network.

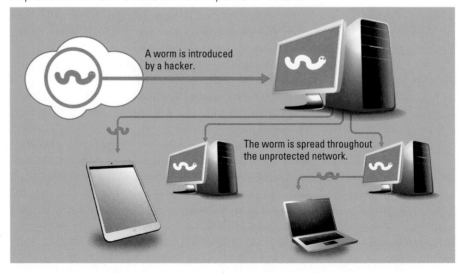

**Figure 12** How a Trojan Attacks
A Trojan pretends to be a useful program but instead opens your system to hackers.

## Trojan

Named after the infamous Trojan horse of the Greek legend, a Trojan is malware that masquerades as a useful program. When you run the program, you let the Trojan into your system (see Figure 12). Trojans open a "back door" to your system for malicious hackers.

## Adware

Adware looks at files on your computer and then sends pop-up advertisements that try to sell you products and services. Although annoying, adware is not usually destructive, but it can slow down your processor and internet speed significantly.

## Privacy Threats and Information Theft

Spyware programs can steal your personal information and tell it or sell it to other people who might be able to impersonate you and take money from your bank account or charge large purchases to your credit card.

*Phishing* is a method of convincing people to reveal their passwords, credit card numbers, social security numbers, and other private or confidential information. Phishers pretend to

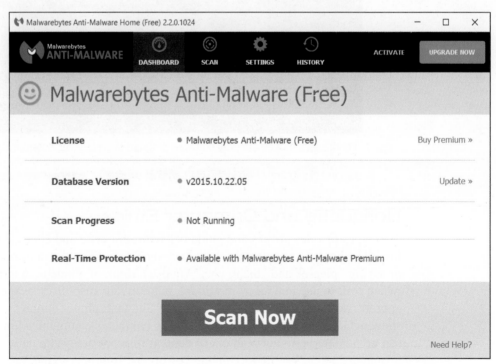

Products such as Malwarebytes scan your computer for malware and help prevent it from downloading in the first place.

be representatives of the victim's bank or a government agency by sending official-looking emails with obscure links back to websites that look exactly like the real website. The information they gather is then used in schemes involving identity theft that allow them to gain access to the victim's bank account, which they empty of its funds.

## Protection Software

Several computer programs are available to protect against virus attacks and the installation of spyware or adware on your computer. Some examples of anti-virus applications are McAfee VirusScan and BitDefender AntiVirus. Spybot Search & Destroy, SpySweeper, AdAware, and Spyware Detector are used for spyware and adware. Windows 10 and Windows 8.1 include an anti-spyware program called Windows Defender.

To minimize infection, always update your computer with the latest security patches as they become available. Keep your protection software up to date by downloading the latest "signature" files of known viruses.

### Exploring Technology  7

Explore the programs on your computer and identify what protection software is installed. Verify that the protection software is up-to-date and active while you are working, and that a regular scan of all files takes place.

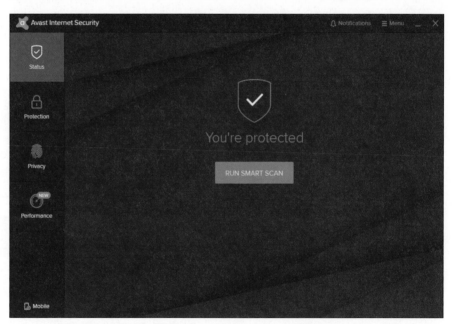

The installation of an antivirus software program such as Avast Internet Security is essential for computers connected to the internet. Keeping the virus definitions up to date will significantly help in the fight against viruses.

## Netiquette and Computer Ethics

Two types of rules govern and guide behavior: etiquette and ethics. *Etiquette* refers to the rules that govern courteous behavior, such as holding the door open for someone, or saying "please" and "thank you." We often think of etiquette in terms of knowing which fork to use in a fancy restaurant, but etiquette also involves the rules for language appropriate in a businesslike environment. Showing proper etiquette is a way of showing a person respect. When applied to computer communication, where words can be misinterpreted or read out of context improper etiquette can result in serious misunderstandings or ill will among coworkers. Improper etiquette can even lead to the loss of a lucrative business contract or even a job.

*Ethics* are the moral principles that govern behavior. In the news, we often see reports about corporate executives who have been charged or convicted of funneling company money into their own personal bank accounts. Politicians are accused of taking bribes from lobbyists in return for a favorable vote on a piece of legislation that will be profitable for the lobbyist's organization. Taxpayers claim tax deductions they are not entitled to. Students submit reports that were written by someone else. People offer to copy the latest music or software program they just purchased and give it to their friends. Where do you stand on these ethical issues?

Both etiquette and ethics have direct application to computers, especially in relation to email and copyright issues.

## Netiquette

Everyone—friends, relatives, schoolmates, coworkers, employers, teachers, businesses, government officials, and sales and marketing departments—is sending email these days. Speedy communication with other people all over the world can be fun, exciting, and productive. However, it can also cause problems. What you write in an email message can hurt someone's feelings, be misinterpreted, or be accidentally sent to the wrong person. You can cause yourself embarrassment or even get yourself fired.

Here are 10 rules of email etiquette. You might want to add a few of your own.

Ethics are the rules we use to determine what is right and wrong, and these rules help guide our choices and actions, both in our personal and business lives.

1. Be brief and to the point. Emails are supposed to be a fast way to communicate. Don't slow down the process.
2. Don't use ALL CAPITAL letters. It looks and feels like you're shouting or angry.
3. Remember to attach the attachment. Mentioning what you are "attaching" in any type of email is a good idea. Get in the habit of stopping as soon as you type the phrase "I am attaching…" and immediately clicking the button for attaching the file.
4. Use spell check (even if you're a great speller). Using the spelling check feature only takes a few seconds and it shows that you care about quality. But watch out! It is easy to click "Change" instead of "Ignore" and change a person's name to a common word and that, whether humorous or not, is an embarrassing mistake.
5. Reread what you wrote from the perspective of the receiver. Ask yourself how the recipient is likely to interpret your words. Did you leave out or misspell a word that completely changes the meaning?
6. Double-check the address in the *To* box. Confirm that you clicked the correct name in your address list. Once you click the Send button, there is *no* way to stop the message or undo an address mistake.
7. Watch your language. Profanity can come back to haunt you.
8. Assume your email will be read by *lots* of other people. Emails are often forwarded so others can take action or to inform a supervisor. Avoid cute or friendly asides and comments that you only want a close friend to see.
9. Always put something in the *Subject* line. A well-written subject will help the receiver decide where to file your message and whether to read it now or wait until later.
10. Privacy does not exist in emails, especially those in a corporate environment. The email

administrator can potentially see the contents of any email. Company policy may allow checking emails to ensure that no company secrets are exposed, or to stop harassing or abusive email.

## Software Piracy and Copyright Infringement

When you install a software application, you must accept the license agreement that describes the legal contract between the user (you) and the software developer. If you do not accept the agreement, the installation process will stop. By accepting the agreement, you agree to everything it says. The contract often covers the number of people who may use the program at the same time. That would usually be one person, but organizations can purchase agreements that cover a specific number of users.

Most software is copyrighted, with the exception of open source software, mentioned earlier. Copyright laws in the United States and most (but not all) other countries state that authors, music composers, TV show and movie creators, artists, and publishers own the works they create and distribute and that no one is allowed to use or copy their work without specific permission. Software license agreements might specify that you can make one backup copy, but you cannot give that copy to a friend. The same rules apply to all copyrighted material including music CDs, DVDs, and songs available on the web. Infringing on a copyright is illegal, and this law is enforced.

Formerly known as the Software Publishers Association, the Software & Information Industry Association (SIIA, www.siia.net) encourages people who witness software piracy to inform them so that they can investigate the situation. Once they gather enough evidence,

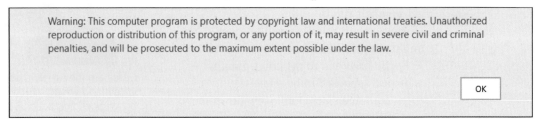

Software manufacturers usually obtain a copyright that prohibits the illegal copying and distribution of software. Warnings such as this one are designed to remind users of the copyright law.

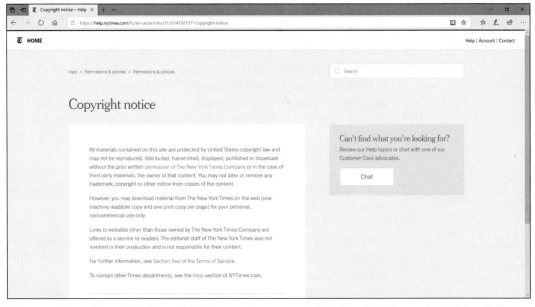

The copyright notice on *The New York Times* web page reminds visitors that the content of the site is copyrighted.

they will contact the organization's executives, ask them to prove they have enough licenses, and encourage them to purchase the software legally. In most cases the pressure works, but if necessary, the SIIA may take legal action.

Software piracy is a felony, but even if it were not, other compelling reasons exist for why you should not copy programs, music, or DVDs. For one, doing so hurts the people who spend a lot of time and money creating products for your enjoyment. They do research. They buy computers, musical instruments, or video cameras. They pay money for studio time to record their songs, and then more money to advertise them and ship them to music stores. They may sell their creations to publishing companies who agree to pay them royalties based on sales. Will you send money to your favorite band every time you give a friend a copy of their latest CD? If graphic artists and musicians can't pay their expenses and cover the cost of making the songs, movies, computer games, and other software you enjoy, how can an individual artist, or even a large company, continue to create more?

### Exploring Technology  8

Check to see who is the registered user of each of the applications on your computer by running it and watching for the name on the startup screen. If it isn't registered to your organization, your department, or yourself, consider asking your supervisor about the registration. Your action could actually help save your organization from costly litigation and potential fines.

### Exploring Technology  9

Navigate to www.riaa.com and click the Report Piracy tab. Read about what you can do to help stop software piracy.

### Exploring Technology  10

Use your word processor to write the explanation you could use when you decline to give or receive an unauthorized copy of a music CD, software program, DVD, or any other copyrighted material.

# Glossary

**802.11 protocol** a protocol for wireless LAN technology that specifies an over-the-air interface between the wireless client device and a server, or between two wireless devices, approved by the IEEE in 1997; also called *Wi-Fi*

**802.11ac protocol** approved in January 2014, this protocol for wireless LAN technology is built on 802.11n but has approximately three times the transfer rate; also called Wi-Fi 5

**802.11g protocol** approved in June 2003, this protocol for wireless LAN technology operates in the same frequency range as 802.11b but with transfer rates similar to 802.11a

**802.11n protocol** this protocol for wireless LAN technology provides for speeds of up to 150 Mbps at a range of up to 250 meters (820 feet); also called Wi-Fi 4

**adware** software that tracks the websites that a user visits to collect information for marketing or advertising

**bar code reader** an electronic device that uses photo technology to read the lines in a bar code; the lines and spaces contain symbols that the computer translates into information

**central processing unit (CPU)** the part of a computer that interprets and carries out instructions that operate the computer and manage the computer's devices and resources; consists of components, each of which performs specific functions; also called the *microprocessor* or *processor*

**client** a smaller computer, terminal, or workstation capable of sending data to and from a larger computer (host computer) in a network

**client-server architecture** a type of network architecture in which a personal computer, workstation, or terminal (called a *client*) is used to send information or a request to another computer (called a *server*) that then relays the information back to the user's client computer or to another computer (another client)

**collaboration software** programs that enable people at separate computer workstations to collaborate on a single document or project; also called *groupware*

**compact disc (CD)** a plastic disc 4.75 inches in diameter and about 1/20th of an inch thick; uses laser technologies to store information and data

**connectivity** refers to the ability to link with other programs and devices

**copyright** the legal protection of an individual's or business's original work, such as software applications, music, and books, that prohibits others from duplicating or illegally using such work or products; an artist or author whose work is copyrighted has the right to charge others for its use

**database** a computer application in which data is organized and stored in a way that allows for specific data to be accessed, retrieved, and used

**digital camera** a type of camera that records and stores images, including people, scenery, documents, and products, in a digitized form that can be entered into and stored by a computer

**digital versatile disc (DVD)** an extremely high-capacity optical disc; also called a *digital video disc (DVD)*

**digital** the process of converting analog information to digital information; sometimes referred to as "going digital"

**digitizing pen** an electronic pen device, resembling a standard writing pen, used with a drawing tablet to simulate drawing on paper

**drawing tablet** a tablet with wires under the surface that, when used with a digital pen, allows the user to create and capture drawings that can be entered and stored on a computer

**dual-core processor** a central processing unit (CPU) chip that contains two complete processors along with their cache memory

**electronic mail (email)** a text, voice, or video message sent or received remotely or over a computer network, or the system by which such a message is sent

**ethics** rules used to determine the right and wrong things to do

**etiquette** rules governing courteous behavior

**File Transfer Protocol (FTP)** a transmission standard that enables a user to send and receive large files, such as reports, over the internet

**flash drive** storage device with a USB connector

**gigabyte** unit of memory equal to 1,073,741,824 bytes

**graphical user interface (GUI)** a computer interface that enables a user to control the computer and launch commands by pointing and clicking at graphical objects such as windows, icons, and menu items

**graphics** computer-generated pictures produced on a computer screen, paper, or film, ranging from a simple line or bar chart to a detailed, colorful image or picture; also called *graphical images*

**graphics tablet** a flat tablet used with a pen-like stylus or a crosshair cursor to capture an image; the user grasps a stylus or crosshair cursor and traces an image or drawing placed on the tablet surface

**hard copy** a permanent, tangible version of output, such as a letter printed on paper

**hard drive** a device for reading and writing to the magnetic storage medium known as a hard disk; consists of one or more rigid metal platters (disks) mounted on a metal shaft in a container that contains an access mechanism

**Hypertext Transfer Protocol (HTTP)** the communications standard used to transfer documents on the World Wide Web

**information processing cycle** a cycle during which a computer enters, processes, outputs, and/or stores information

**ink-jet printer** a nonimpact printer that forms images by spraying thousands of tiny droplets of electrically charged ink onto a page; the printed images are in dot-matrix format, but of a higher quality than images printed by dot-matrix printers

**input** data that is entered into a computer or other device, or the act of capturing such data

**input device** any hardware component that enables a computer user to enter data and programs into a computer system; keyboards, point-and-click devices, and scanners are among the more popular input devices, and a desktop or laptop computer system may include one or more input devices

**internet** a worldwide network of computers linked together via communications software and media for the purpose of sharing information; the largest and best-known network in the world; also called *the Net*

**internet service provider (ISP)** an organization that has a permanent connection to the internet and provides temporary access to individuals and others for free or for a fee

**joystick** an input device (named after the control lever used to fly fighter planes) consisting of a small box with a vertical lever that, when pushed in a certain direction, moves the cursor correspondingly on the screen; often used for computer games

**keyboard** an electronically controlled hardware component used to enter alphanumeric data (letters, numbers, and special characters)

**laser printer** a nonimpact printer that produces output of exceptional quality using a technology similar to that of photocopy machines

**light emitting diode (LED)** a small light that is used in an LCD to improve color and image appearance

**liquid crystal display (LCD)** a display device in which liquid crystals are sandwiched between two sheets of material

**local area network (LAN)** a computer network physically confined to a relatively small geographical area, such as a single building or a college campus

**malware** malicious software

**megabyte** a unit of memory that stores approximately 1 million bytes

**memory** a chip-based data storage system in which each bit of data is represented by a binary on/off state; a series of 1s and 0s

**monitor** the screen, or display device, on which computer output appears

**motherboard** the main circuit board inside a personal computer to which other circuit boards can be connected; contains electrical pathways, called *traces*, etched onto it that allow data to move from one component to another

**mouse** an input device that, when moved about on a flat surface, causes a pointer on the screen to move in the same direction

**multitasking** the ability of an operating system to run more than one software program at a time; the use of different areas in Windows RAM makes this possible

**network** a group of two or more computers, software, and other devices that is connected by one or more communications media

**nonvolatile** storage that retains its data even when there is no power being supplied to it; a hard disk and a flash drive are both nonvolatile

**open-source software** software whose programming code is owned by the original developer but made available for free to the general public, who is encouraged to experiment with the software, make improvements, and share the improvements with the user community

**operating system (OS)** a type of software that creates a user interface and supports the workings of computer devices and software programs that perform specific jobs

**output** information that is written or displayed as a result of computer processing; also the act of writing or displaying such data

**peer-to-peer architecture** a network design in which each computer or workstation comprising the network has equivalent capabilities and responsibilities

**personal information manager (PIM) software** software that helps users organize contact information, appointments, tasks, and notes

**phishing** an activity characterized by attempts to fraudulently acquire another person's sensitive information, such as a credit card number

**photo-editing software** an application that allows users to create and modify images and output them in one of the various image file formats.

**port** a plug-in slot on a computer to which you can connect a device, such as a printer or, in the case of accessing the internet, a telephone line; also called an *interface*

**Post Office Protocol (POP) server** a special type of server that holds email messages until they are accessed and read by their recipients

**presentation software** an application that allows a user to create a presentation of slides

**printer** the most common type of hard-copy output device that produces output in a permanent form

**processing** the manipulation of data by the computer's electrical circuits

**processor** the part of a computer that interprets and carries out instructions that operate the computer and manages the computer's devices and resources; consists of components, each of which performs specific functions; also called the *central processing unit (CPU)*

**protocol** a set of rules and procedures for exchanging information between network devices and computers

**quad-core processor** a CPU that contains four complete processors in a single chip

**random access memory (RAM)** a computer chip or group of chips containing the temporary, or volatile, memory in which programs and data are stored while being used by a computer

**read-only memory (ROM)** a computer chip on the motherboard of a computer containing permanent, or nonvolatile, memory that stores instructions

**router** a hardware device that connects two or more networks

**scanner** a light-sensing electronic device that can read and capture printed text and images, such as photographs and drawings, and convert them into a digital form a computer can understand; once scanned, the text or image can be displayed on the screen, edited, printed, stored on a disk, inserted into another document, or sent as an attachment to an email message; also called an *optical scanner*

**server** a computer and its associated storage devices that users access remotely over a network

**Simple Mail Transfer Protocol (SMTP)** a communications protocol installed on the ISP's or online service's mail server that determines how each message is to be routed through the internet and then sends the message

**soft copy** a temporary version of output, typically the display of data on a computer screen

**software** programs containing instructions that direct the operation of the computer system and the written documentation that explains how to use the programs; types include system software and application software

**software piracy** the act of copying or using a piece of software without the legal right to do so

**software suite** a combination of application programs (usually integrated) bundled as a single package; may contain applications such as word processing, spreadsheet, database, and other programs

**spreadsheet software** a productivity program that provides a user with a means of organizing, calculating, and presenting financial, statistical, and other numeric information; used to manipulate numbers electronically instead of using a pencil and paper

**spyware** software that tracks the activity of internet users for the benefit of a third party

**stylus** a sharp, pointed instrument used for writing or marking on a graphics tablet or other device

**switch** a small hardware device that joins multiple computers together within one local area network (LAN)

**T1 line** a high-speed telephone line that allows for both voice and data transmission and can carry data at a speed of 1.544 megabits per second

**touchpad** an input device that enables a user to enter data and make selections by moving a finger across the pad; also called a *track pad*

**touchscreen** an input device that allows the user to choose options by pressing a finger (or fingers) on the appropriate part of the screen

**Transmission Control Protocol/Internet Protocol (TCP/IP)** protocol that governs how packets are constructed and sent over the internet to their destination

**trojan horse** malicious software that creates a "back door" to gain access your computer

**Universal Product Code (UPC)** a type of code printed on products and packages consisting of lines and spaces that a computer translates into a number; the computer then uses this number to find information about the product or package, such as its name and price, in a computerized database

**Universal Serial Bus (USB) port** a type of port that is widely used for connecting high-speed modems, scanners, and digital cameras to a computer; a single USB port can accommodate several peripheral devices connected together in sequence

**video-editing software** software that allows users to edit sound and video and output it in various digital formats

**virus** a program that is designed to harm computer systems and/or any users, typically sent via email

**volatile** storage that loses its data when power is lost; the RAM on a motherboard is volatile, for example

**webcam** a digital video camera that captures real-time video for transmission to others via a web server or an instant messaging tool

**wide area network (WAN)** a network that spans a large geographical area

**Windows** a Microsoft-developed GUI operating system for personal computers

**word processing software** a type of computer application that allows the user to create, edit, manipulate, format, store, and print a variety of documents, including letters, memos, announcements, and brochures

**World Wide Web (www)** a global system of linked computer networks that allows users to jump from one site to another by way of programmed links on web pages; also called *the web*

**worm** a program that actively transmits copies of itself over the internet, using up resources and causing other problems; also called a *software worm*

# Getting Started

# Adjusting Monitor Settings, Copying Data Files, and Changing View Options

## Skills

- Set monitor resolution
- Modify DPI settings
- Retrieve and copy data files
- Change view options

This textbook and the accompanying eContent were written using a typical personal computer (tower/box, monitor, keyboard and mouse) or laptop. Although you may be able to perform some of the activities in this textbook on a different operating system or tablet, not all the steps will work as written and may jeopardize any work you may be required to turn in to your instructor. No matter what computer you use, you can access the content using the virtual Office experience in Cirrus. If you are unable to access Cirrus or a compatible computer, explore what options you have at your institution such as where and when you can use a computer lab.

One of the evolutions of the Microsoft Office product is that it is offered in a subscription-based plan called Microsoft Office 365. An advantage of having an active Microsoft Office 365 subscription is that the subscription includes and incorporates new features or versions as they are released. This method of providing the Microsoft Office product may impact section activities and assessments. For example, new features and adjustments made to Office 365 may alter how some of the steps discussed in the Marquee Series are completed. The Marquee eContent and online course will contain the most up-to-date material and will be updated as new features become available.

In Activity 1 you will customize your monitor settings so that what you see on the screen should match the images in this textbook. In Activity 2 you will obtain the data files you will be using throughout this textbook from your Cirrus online course. Activity 3 includes instructions on how to change the view settings so that your view of files in a File Explorer window matches the images in this textbook.

Before beginning activities in this textbook, you may want to customize your monitor's settings. Activities in the sections in this textbook assume that the monitor display is set at 1920 x 1080 pixels and the DPI is set at 125%. Adjusting a monitor's display settings is important because the ribbon in the Microsoft Office applications adjusts to the screen resolution setting of your computer monitor. A monitor set at a high resolution will have the ability to show more buttons in the ribbon than a monitor set to a low resolution. Figure GS1 at the bottom of the page shows, the Word ribbon: at the screen resolution featured throughout this textbook and in the virtual office experience (1920 × 1080).

**What You Will Do**   Adjust the monitor settings for your machine to match the settings used to create the images in the textbook. If using a lab computer, check with your instructor before attempting this activity.

**1** Right-click a blank area of the desktop and then click the *Display settings* option at the shortcut menu.

**2** At the Settings window with the *Display* option selected, scroll down and look at the current setting displayed in the *Resolution* option box. If your screen is already set to 1920 × 1080, skip ahead to Step 5.

Screen resolution is set in pixels. *Pixel* is the abbreviation of *picture element* and refers to a single dot or point on the display monitor. Changing the screen resolution to a higher number of pixels means that more information can be seen on the screen as items are scaled to a smaller size.

**Figure GS1** Word Ribbon Set at 1920 x 1080 Screen Resolution

**3** Click the *Resolution* option box and then click the *1920 × 1080* option. *Note: Depending on the privileges you are given on a school machine, you may not be able to complete Steps 3–7. If necessary, check with your instructor for alternative instructions.*

> If the machine you are using has more than one monitor, make sure the proper monitor is selected. (The active monitor displays as a blue rectangle in the Display pane of the Settings app.)

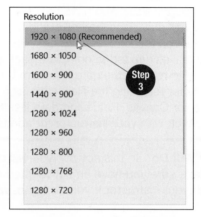

**4** Click the Keep changes button at the message box asking if you want to keep the display settings.

> Some monitor settings will render the computer unusable because objects on the desktop or in a window will become inaccessible and hidden. In this case, Windows will automatically revert the settings to the previous configuration after 30 seconds.

**5** At the Settings window with the *Display* option active, look at the percentage in which the size of text, apps, and other items currently display (also known as the DPI setting). For example, items on your screen may display at 100%. If the percentage is 125%, skip to Step 12.

> The computers used to create the images in this textbook uses the 125% DPI setting, which slightly increases the size of text, applications, buttons, and options.

**6** Click the option box below the text *Change the size of text, apps, and other items*, and then click the *125%* option in the drop-down list.

**7** The message *Some apps won't respond to scaling changes until you sign out.* appears in the *Scale and Layout* section of the dialog box. You may need to sign out of Windows and restart your computer for the scaling options to apply.

# Activity 2   Retrieving and Copying Data Files

While working through the activities in this book, you will often be using data files as starting points. These files need to be obtained from your Cirrus online course or other locations such as your school's network drive. All the files required to complete the coursework are provided through Cirrus. You have the ability to access all of the data files from the Course Resources. You may download all of the files at once or only download the files you need for a specific section (described in the activity below). Cirrus online course activities also provide the individual files needed to complete each activity. Make sure you have internet access before trying to retrieve the data files from Cirrus. Ask your instructor if alternate locations are available for retrieving the files, such as a network drive or online resource such as D2L, BlackBoard, or Canvas. Retrieving data files from an alternate location will require different steps, so check with your instructor for additional steps or tasks to complete.

---

**What You Will Do**   In this activity, you will download data files from your Cirrus online course. Make sure you have an active internet connection before starting this activity. Check with your instructor if you do not have access to your Cirrus online course.

**1**   Insert your USB flash drive into an available USB port.

**2**   Navigate to the Course Resources section of your Cirrus online course. *Note: The steps in this activity assume you are using the Chrome browser. If you are using a different browser, the following steps may vary.*

**3**   Click the Student Data Files link in the Course Resources section.

> A zip file containing the student data files will automatically begin downloading from the Cirrus website.

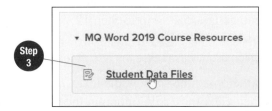

**4**   Click the button in the lower left corner of the screen once the files have finished downloading.

> Clicking the button in the lower left corner of the screen will open File Explorer and the StudentDataFiles folder displays in the Content pane.

**5** Right-click the *StudentDataFiles* folder in the Content pane.

**6** Click the *Copy* option at the shortcut menu.

**7** Click your USB flash drive that displays in the Navigation pane at the left of the File Explorer window.

**8** Click the Home tab and then click the Paste button in the Clipboard group.

**9** Close the File Explorer window by clicking the Close button in the upper right corner of the window.

You can change the view of the File Explorer window to show the contents of your current location (drive or folder) in various formats, including icons, tiles, or a list, among others. With the Content pane in Details view, you can click the column headings to change how the contents are sorted and whether they are sorted in ascending or descending order. You can customize a window's environment by using buttons and options on the File Explorer View tab. You can also change how panes are displayed, how content is arranged in the Content pane, how content is sorted, and which features are hidden.

**What You Will Do**   Before getting started with the textbook material, you need to adjust the view settings so that items in the File Explorer window appear the same as the images in the textbook.

**1** Click the File Explorer button on the taskbar.

> By default, a File Explorer window opens at the Quick access location, which contains frequently-used folders such as Desktop, Documents, Downloads, Pictures and so on. It also displays recently used files at the bottom of the Content pane.

**2** Click the drive letter representing your storage medium in the Navigation pane.

**3** Double-click the *ExcelS2* folder in the Content pane.

**4** Click the View tab below the Title bar.

**5** Click the *Large icons* option in the Layout group.

> After you click an option on the View tab, the View tab collapses to provide more space in the File Explorer window.

**6** Click the View tab.

**7** Click the *Details* option in the Layout group.

**8** With files now displayed in Details view, click the *Name* column heading to sort the list in descending order by name.

**9** Click the *Name* column heading again to restore the list to ascending order by name.

**10** Close the File Explorer window by clicking the Close button in the upper right corner of the window.

## In Addition

### Changing the Default View for All Folders

You can set a view to display by default for all folders of a similar type (such as all disk drive folders or all documents folders). To do this, change the current view to the desired view for the type of folder that you want to set. Next, click the Options button on the View tab and then click the View tab at the Folder Options dialog box. Click the Apply to Folders button in the Folder views section and then click OK. Click Yes at the Folder Views message asking if you want all folders of this type to match this folder's view settings.

### Turning on File Extensions

By default, file extensions do not display. Turning on file extensions is helpful in identifying the type of file. Turn on file extensions at the File Explorer window by clicking the View tab and then clicking the *File name extensions* check box to insert a check mark.

# Microsoft® Word

# 365

## 2019 Brief Edition

Nita Rutkosky

Audrey Roggenkamp
Pierce College Puyallup
Puyallup, Washington

Ian Rutkosky
Pierce College Puyallup
Puyallup, Washington

PARADIGM
EDUCATION SOLUTIONS

St. Paul

**Vice President, Content and Digital Solutions:** Christine Hurney
**Director of Content Development:** Carley Fruzzetti
**Testers:** Desiree Carvel; Ann E. Mills, Ivy Tech Community College of Indiana, Evansville, IN
**Director of Production:** Timothy W. Larson
**Production Editor/Project Manager:** Jen Weaverling
**Cover and Text Design:** Valerie King
**Senior Design and Production Specialist:** Julie Johnston
**Copy Editor:** Deborah Brandt
**Indexer:** Terry Casey
**Vice President, Director of Digital Products:** Chuck Bratton
**Digital Projects Manager:** Tom Modl
**Digital Solutions Manager:** Gerry Yumul
**Senior Director of Digital Products and Onboarding:** Christopher Johnson
**Supervisor of Digital Products and Onboarding:** Ryan Isdahl
**Vice President of Marketing:** Lara Weber McLellan
**Marketing and Communications Manager**: Selena Hicks

© 2020 by Paradigm Publishing, LLC
875 Montreal Way
St. Paul, MN 55102
Email: CustomerService@ParadigmEducation.com
Website: ParadigmEducation.com

Printed in the United States of America

28 27 26 25 24 23 22 21 20 19    1 2 3 4 5 6 7 8 9 10 11 12

# Contents

# Word 365

Microsoft Word is a word processing program used to create documents such as letters, reports, research papers, brochures, announcements, newsletters, envelopes, labels, and much more. Word is a full-featured program that provides a wide variety of editing and formatting features as well as sophisticated visual elements. While working in Word, you will produce business documents for the following six companies.

First Choice Travel is a travel center offering a full range of traveling services from booking flights, hotel reservations, and rental cars to offering travel seminars.

The Waterfront Bistro offers fine dining for lunch and dinner and also offers banquet facilities, a wine cellar, and catering services.

Worldwide Enterprises is a national and international distributor of products for a variety of companies and is the exclusive movie distribution agent for Marquee Productions.

Marquee Productions is involved in all aspects of creating movies from script writing and development to filming. The company produces documentaries, biographies, as well as historical and action movies.

Performance Threads maintains an inventory of rental costumes and also researches, designs, and sews special-order and custom-made costumes.

The mission of the Niagara Peninsula College Theatre Arts Division is to offer a curriculum designed to provide students with a thorough exposure to all aspects of the theatre arts.

# *In Section 1 you will learn how to*

## Create and Edit Documents

Use Microsoft Word to create, edit, and format a variety of business documents and use Word's powerful editing and formatting features to produce well-written and visually appealing documents. Some powerful editing features include checking the spelling and grammar in a document and using Thesaurus to find appropriate synonyms for words; using AutoCorrect to improve the efficiency of entering information in a document; and creating a document using a predesigned template.

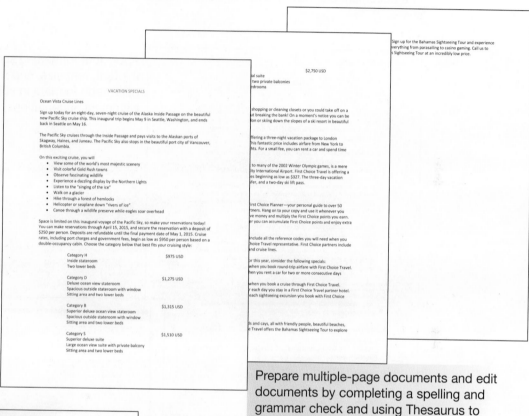

Prepare multiple-page documents and edit documents by completing a spelling and grammar check and using Thesaurus to find appropriate synonyms for words.

Download online templates from and create a variety of documents including letters, faxes, certificates, or awards.

# In Section 2 you will learn how to

## Format Characters and Paragraphs in Documents

Word contains a number of commands and procedures that affect how the document appears when printed. The appearance of a document in the document screen and how it looks when printed is called the *format*. Formatting can include such tasks as changing the font; aligning and indenting text; changing line and paragraph spacing; setting tabs; and inserting elements such as bullets, numbers, symbols, and special characters. The readability of a document can be improved by setting text in tabbed columns and by formatting using styles.

Apply font formatting such as changing the font, font size, and font color. Apply paragraph formatting such as changing alignment, indentations, and line spacing.

**OSLO, NORWAY**

*History*

The founding of Oslo took place in the turbulent period between the *Viking Age* and Norway's *Catholic Middle Ages*. Many remnants and ruins from ancient Oslo can be found in Memorial Park. The city has a fascinating, interesting, and dramatic history.

Oslo's population was substantially reduced during the time of the Black Death in 1348, which claimed over fifty percent of the inhabitants. This epidemic also had political consequences for Norway, which was reduced to a province of Denmark. During this period, Copenhagen was the actual capital of Norway. Oslo was also greatly affected by the Lutheran Protestant Reformation of 1537, with religious conflicts, political separation from the Catholic Church, and the foundation of a Protestant National Church. Many ruins of churches and monasteries bear witness to this process.

Oslo was completely destroyed by fire in 1624. Following intense renewal and advanced city planning in the spirit of the Renaissance, a completely new city was created and named Christiania. In 1814 Norway was united with Sweden, and Christiania experienced strong economic and political growth. In 1905 the union with Sweden was dissolved and Norway gained its independence. The original name of Oslo was reinstated in 1924.

*Population*

Oslo is the capital of Norway and has more than 500,000 inhabitants. Approximately 900,000 people live in the Greater Oslo area, representing twenty percent of the total population of Norway.

*Commerce and Industry*

The working population of Oslo distributed according to occupation includes: industry, 16%; building and construction, 6%; transport, 9%; trade, services, and tourism, 69%.

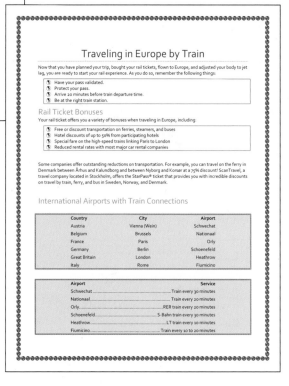

Apply formatting such as inserting bullets and special characters, setting text in tabbed columns, applying paragraph shading and lines, and inserting a page border. Use style sets to apply predesigned formatting such as bolding and centering text, changing fonts, and applying border lines to headings.

# *In Section 3 you will learn how to*

## Enhance Documents

Improve the formatting of a document using features to rearrange text in a document, add special elements, or change the appearance of text. Use buttons on the Home tab to move, copy, and paste text in a document. Improve the appearance of documents by inserting page numbering, headers, and footers; changing margins and page orientation; and changing vertical alignment. Add visual appeal to documents by inserting and customizing images.

Enhance the visual appeal of a document by inserting an image related to text in the document, and a page border and background color.

Enhance the appearance of a document by applying a theme, which is a set of formatting choices that includes a color, a font, and effects; inserting a cover page; inserting a watermark, which is a lightened image that displays behind text; and inserting a header and footer.

Create envelopes and mailing labels quickly and automatically.

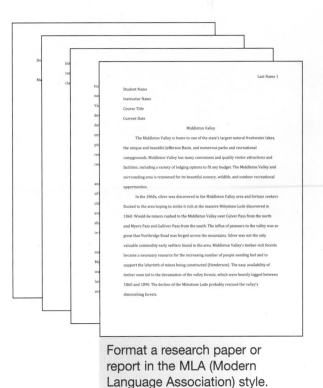

Format a research paper or report in the MLA (Modern Language Association) style.

# Word

# Creating and Editing a Document

> **Data Files**
>
> Before beginning section work, copy the WordS1 folder to your storage medium and then make WordS1 the active folder.

## Skills

- Create, save, and print a document
- Close a document and close Word
- Move the insertion point
- Insert and delete text
- Scroll in a document
- Select, replace, and delete text
- Use Undo and Redo
- Check the spelling and grammar in a document
- Use AutoCorrect
- Use the Thesaurus
- Change document views
- Hide and show white space
- Change the display percentage
- Navigate and find text using the Navigation pane
- Find and replace text
- Use the Tell Me feature
- Use the Help feature
- Review and print a document
- Create a document using a template
- Create, rename, and delete a folder
- Copy and paste a document
- Save a document in a different format

## Projects Overview

Prepare a document describing a special vacation package and edit and format two documents describing various vacation specials offered by First Choice Travel. Prepare a certification of appreciation for an employee.

Customize a sample employee incentive agreement and prepare a fax cover page for the agreement.

Edit a letter to Marquee Productions regarding costuming for a film.

Write a letter to Josh Hart at Marquee Productions explaining the catering services offered by The Waterfront Bistro and then prepare a fax sheet for the letter.

 The online course includes additional training and assessment resources.

1

# Activity 1.1 Creating, Saving, and Printing a Document

Microsoft Word is a word processing program that can be used to create, save, edit, and print documents. To create a document in Word, open the Word program and then click the *Blank document* template. This opens a blank document with the insertion point positioned at the beginning of the document. The document screen contains a variety of features for working with a document, such as the Title bar, Quick Access Toolbar, ribbon, and Status bar. Type text in a document and press the Enter key, and the insertion point moves down to the next line with extra spacing above the line. To create a new line without including the extra spacing, use the New Line command: Shift + Enter. When entering text, Word includes an AutoCorrect feature that will automatically correct certain words that are entered incorrectly. After creating a document, save the document so it is available for future use. Save a document at the Save As dialog box.

**What You Will Do**   As an employee of First Choice Travel, you have been asked to create a short document containing information on a travel package. You will save and then print the document so you can send it to other employees for review.

Opening a Blank Document

**1** At the Windows desktop, click the Start button and then click the Word tile.

> Depending on your system configuration, these steps may vary.

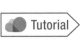
Exploring the Word Screen

**2** At the Word opening screen, click the *Blank document* template.

**3** At the blank Word document, identify the various features by comparing your screen with the one shown in Figure 1.1.

Entering Text

> Refer to Table 1.1 for a description of the screen features.

**Figure 1.1** Word Document Screen

Undoing an AutoCorrect Correction

Saving with a New Name

Printing a Document

**Table 1.1** Screen Features and Descriptions

| Feature | Description |
| --- | --- |
| Collapse the Ribbon button | when clicked, removes the ribbon from the screen (redisplay the ribbon by clicking a tab [except the File tab] and then clicking the Pin the ribbon button [previously the Collapse the Ribbon button]) |
| File tab | when clicked, displays the backstage area that contains options for working with and managing documents |
| horizontal ruler | used to set margins, indents, and tabs |
| I-beam pointer | used to move the insertion point or to select text |
| insertion point | indicates location of next character entered at the keyboard |
| Quick Access Toolbar | contains buttons for commonly used commands |
| ribbon | area containing tabs with options and buttons divided into groups |
| Status bar | displays number of pages and words, view buttons, and Zoom slider bar |
| tabs | contain commands and buttons organized into groups |
| Tell Me | used to look up a feature and provide options for using the feature |
| Title bar | displays document name followed by program name |
| vertical ruler | used to set top and bottom margins |
| vertical scroll bar | used to view various parts of the document beyond the screen |
| Windows taskbar | divided into three sections—the Start button, the task buttons area, and the notification area |

**4** Type Moment's Notice Travel Package as shown in Figure 1.2 and then press the Enter key.

Pressing the Enter key begins a new paragraph in the document.

**5** Type First Choice Travel, press and hold down the Shift key, press the Enter key, and then release the Shift key.

Shift + Enter is the New Line command. Use this command to keep lines of text within the same paragraph, which creates less space between one line and the next.

**6** Type Los Angeles Office and then press the Enter key.

**7** Type the remainder of the text shown in Figure 1.2.

Type the text as shown. When you type *adn* and then press the spacebar, the AutoCorrect feature will automatically correct it to *and*. When you type *teh* and then press the spacebar, AutoCorrect corrects it to *the*. Do not press the Enter key to end a line of text within a paragraph. Word will automatically wrap text to the next line.

**8** Click the File tab to display the backstage area.

The File tab is in the upper left corner of the screen at the left of the Home tab.

**Figure 1.2** Steps 4–7

Moment's Notice Travel Package

First Choice Travel
Los Angeles Office

Are you spontaneous adn enjoy doing something on a moment's notice? If this describes you, then you will be interested in the First Choice Travel Moment's Notice Travel Package. For teh low price of $599 you can fly from New York to London for a four-day stay. The catch to this incredible deal is that you must make your reservation within the next week and complete your London stay within 30 days.

**9** Click the *Save As* option.

**10** At the Save As backstage area, click the *Browse* option.

If you are saving to your OneDrive, click the *OneDrive* option. Click the specific folder in the right panel, click in the *File name* text box at the Save As dialog box, type the document name, and then press the Enter key.

**11** At the Save As dialog box, click the drive in the Navigation pane that contains your storage medium.

Press the F12 function key to display the Save As dialog box without displaying the Save As backstage area.

**12** Double-click the *WordS1* folder in the Content pane.

**13** Click in the *File name* text box, type 1-FCTTravelPkg, and then press the Enter key (or click the Save button).

Word automatically adds the file extension *.docx* to the end of a document name. By default, file extensions do not display. File extensions can be turned on by clicking the File Explorer button on the Windows taskbar, clicking the View tab, and then clicking the *File name extensions* check box in the Show/Hide group. This textbook will show file names without the extensions, since that is the default.

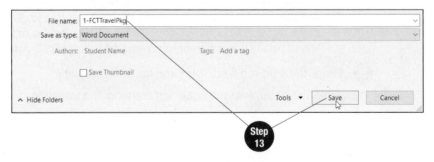

**14** Print the document by clicking the File tab, clicking the *Print* option, and then clicking the Print button at the Print backstage area.

When you click the File tab, the backstage area displays with options for working with and managing documents. Refer to Table 1.2 for descriptions of some common options and information you will find in each option's backstage area.

**Save Document
to Removable Disk**
1. Press F12.
2. At Save As dialog
   box, click drive in
   Navigation pane
   containing removable
   disk.
3. Double-click folder in
   Content pane.
4. Click in *File name* text
   box.
5. Type document name.
6. Press Enter key.

**Print Document**
1. Click File tab.
2. Click *Print* option.
3. Click Print button.

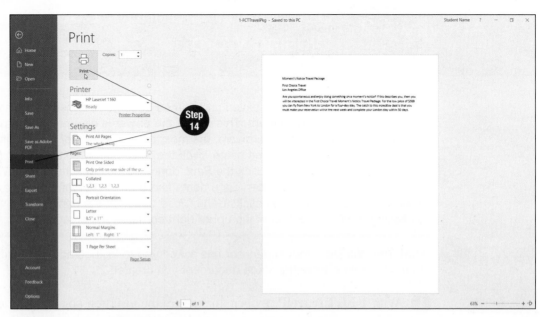

**Table 1.2** Backstage Area Options

| Option | Information |
|--------|-------------|
| Home | templates, recently opened documents, and any pinned documents (Word 365 only) |
| New | available templates such as Blank document as well as online templates |
| Open | options for opening documents; list of recently opened documents |
| Info | permissions, possible issues with sharing the document, document versions, properties (for example, number of pages, number of words), date created, date last modified, date last printed, author |
| Save | saves previously saved document or displays Save As backstage area with options and locations for saving a document |
| Save As | options and locations for saving a document |
| Print | number of copies, printer, settings (for example, one-sided pages, letter size, normal margins, one page per sheet) |
| Share | share document with specific people; share document using email, present document online, and share as a blog post |
| Export | export document as PDF or XPS document; change file type |
| Close | close currently open document |
| Account | user information, connected services, product information |
| Feedback | opens window with options for providing feedback to Microsoft on Microsoft products |
| Options | Word Options dialog box with options for customizing Word |

 **Check Your Work** Compare your work to the model answer available in the online course.

# In Addition

## Understanding Default Document Formatting

A Word document is based on a template that applies default formatting. Default formatting refers to formatting automatically applied by Word. Some of the default formats include 11-point Calibri as the font, line spacing of 1.08, and 8 points of spacing after each paragraph (added when the Enter key is pressed). You will learn more about fonts and paragraph spacing in Section 2.

## Correcting Errors

Word contains a spelling feature that inserts wavy red lines below words it cannot find in the Spelling dictionary. Edit these words or leave them as written. The wavy red lines do not print.

When working in a previously saved and named document, consider saving any new information entered in the document. This way, if the power is disrupted or some other issue occurs with the software or hardware, the most recent version of the document is saved. To save a document with the same name, click the Save button on the Quick Access Toolbar or click the File tab and then click the *Save* option at the backstage area. When finished working in Word, close any open documents and then close Word. Close a document by clicking the File tab and then clicking the *Close* option at the backstage area. Close Word by clicking the Close button in the upper right corner of the screen.

**What You Will Do**  Your supervisor has asked you to include additional information in the Moment's Notice Travel Package document you created.

Saving with the Same Name

Closing a Document and Closing Word

**1** With **1-FCTTravelPkg** open, make sure the insertion point is positioned at the end of the paragraph and then press the Enter key.

**2** Type 3588 Ventura Boulevard.

**3** Press Shift + Enter and then type Los Angeles, CA 90102.

Moment's Notice Travel Package

First Choice Travel
Los Angeles Office

Are you spontaneous and enjoy doi
will be interested in the First Choice
you can fly from New York to Londo
must make your reservation within

3588 Ventura Boulevard
Los Angeles, CA 90102

Step 2

Step 3

**4** Save the document with the added text by clicking the Save button 🖫 on the Quick Access Toolbar.

Step 4

**5** Add additional text to the document by pressing Shift + Enter and then typing 213-555-7800.

**6** Save the document with the added text by clicking the File tab and then clicking the *Save* option at the backstage area.

If you are working in a document that has not been saved, clicking the Save button on the Quick Access Toolbar or clicking the File tab and then clicking the *Save* option will cause the Save As backstage area to display.

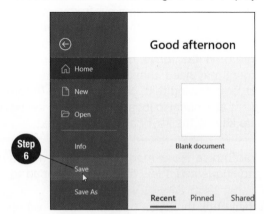

**7** Close the document by clicking the File tab and then clicking the *Close* option at the backstage area.

**8** Close Word by clicking the Close button  in the upper right corner of the screen.

The Close button displays with a red background when the mouse pointer is positioned on the button.

**Check Your Work** Compare your work to the model answer available in the online course.

# In Addition

## Naming a Document

Document names created in Word and other applications in the Office suite can be up to 255 characters in length, including the drive letter, folder names, server name, and spaces. File names cannot include any of the characters in the table at the right.

| Symbol Name | Symbol |
|---|---|
| forward slash | / |
| backslash | \ |
| greater-than symbol | > |
| less-than symbol | < |
| asterisk | * |
| question mark | ? |
| quotation mark | " |
| colon | : |
| pipe symbol | | |

# Activity 1.3  Opening and Editing a Document

An existing document can be opened from the *Recent* option list at the Open backstage area, the Recent list at the Home backstage area, from a folder in OneDrive, or from the computer's hard drive or removable disk. (In this activity, you will open a document from the WordS1 folder on your USB flash drive. If you saved your student data files in a location or folder other than a USB flash drive, check with your instructor for specific steps.) A previously saved document may need changes or edits made to it that might include adding text, called *inserting*, or removing text, called *deleting*. Before inserting or deleting text, position the insertion point at a specific location using the keyboard or the mouse. Use the Backspace key or Delete key on the keyboard to delete text.

FIRST CHOICE
**TRAVEL**

**What You Will Do**  First Choice Travel marketing staff members reviewed your document on vacation specials and suggested a few changes. You need to create a revised version.

Tutorial

Opening a Document from a Removable Disk

Tutorial

Moving the Insertion Point and Inserting and Deleting Text

1 Open Word and then click the *Open* option at the Word opening screen.

2 At the Open backstage area, click the *Browse* option.

3 In the Navigation pane of the Open dialog box, click the drive where your USB flash drive is located (such as *USB Drive (F:)*).

> Press Ctrl + F12 to display the Open dialog box without displaying the Open backstage area.

4 Double-click the *WordS1* folder in the Content pane.

5 Double-click **FCTVacSpecials** in the Content pane.

6 With the document open, click the File tab and then click the *Save As* option.

7 At the Save As backstage area, click the *Browse* option. (This should display the Save As dialog box with the WordS1 folder active on your storage medium.)

8 At the Save As dialog box, press the Home key to move the insertion point to the beginning of the file name in the *File name* text box, type 1-, and then press the Enter key. (The document name in the *File name* text box should display as **1-FCTVacSpecials**.)

> To open the Save As dialog box without displaying the Save As backstage area, press F12. Another method for saving a document with a new name is to click in the file name text box at the top of the third panel at the Save As backstage area, type the document name, and then press the Enter key.

9 Position the mouse pointer at the beginning of the second paragraph and then click the left mouse button.

> This moves the insertion point to the location of the mouse pointer.

**In Brief**

**Open Document from Removable Disk**
1. Press Ctrl + F12.
2. In Navigation pane, click drive containing removable disk.
3. Double-click folder in Content pane.
4. Double-click document in Content pane.

**10** Practice moving the insertion point by pressing the Up, Down, Left, and Right arrow keys to the right of the regular keys on the keyboard.

Use the information shown in Table 1.3 to practice moving the insertion point.

**11** Press Ctrl + Home to move the insertion point to the beginning of the document.

**12** Click at the beginning of the paragraph that begins *Sign up today for* and then type Ocean Vista Cruise Lines announces the inaugural voyage of the Pacific Sky ocean liner. Press the spacebar after typing the period.

Text you type is inserted in the document and existing text is moved to the right.

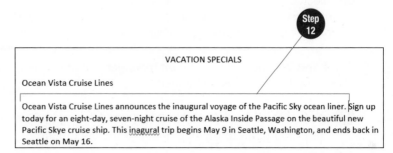

Step 12

VACATION SPECIALS

Ocean Vista Cruise Lines

Ocean Vista Cruise Lines announces the inaugural voyage of the Pacific Sky ocean liner. Sign up today for an eight-day, seven-night cruise of the Alaska Inside Passage on the beautiful new Pacific Skye cruise ship. This inagural trip begins May 9 in Seattle, Washington, and ends back in Seattle on May 16.

**13** Press Ctrl + End to move the insertion point to the end of the document and then click in the last sentence in the document (the sentence that begins *Let First Choice Travel take*).

**14** Press the Backspace key until the insertion point is positioned at the left margin and then press the Delete key until you have deleted the remainder of the sentence.

Pressing the Backspace key deletes any characters to the left of the insertion point. Press the Delete key to delete any characters to the right of the insertion point.

**15** Click the Save button on the Quick Access Toolbar.

Clicking the Save button saves the document with the same name (**1-FCTVacSpecials**).

**Table 1.3** Insertion Point Keyboard Commands

| Press | To move insertion point |
|---|---|
| End | to end of line |
| Home | to beginning of line |
| Page Up | up one screen |
| Page Down | down one screen |
| Ctrl + Home | to beginning of document |
| Ctrl + End | to end of document |

**Check Your Work** Compare your work to the model answer available in the online course.

## In Addition

### Adding Buttons to the Quick Access Toolbar

Buttons can be added to the Quick Access Toolbar that represent commonly used features. For example, an Open button can be added to save steps when opening a document or the Quick Print button to save steps when printing a document. To add a button to the Quick Access Toolbar, click the Customize Quick Access Toolbar button ⯆ at the right of the toolbar and then click the button name at the drop-down list.

In addition to moving the insertion point to a specific location, the mouse can be used to move the display of text in the document screen. Use the mouse with the vertical scroll bar, which displays at the right of the screen, to scroll through text in a document. Scrolling in a document changes the text that appears on the screen but does not move the insertion point. Delete text by pressing the Backspace key or the Delete key. Text can also be selected and then deleted, replaced with other text, or formatting can be applied to selected text. If changes are made to text, clicking the Undo button on the Quick Access Toolbar will undo the change; clicking the Redo button will reverse the previous action.

**FIRST CHOICE TRAVEL**

**What You Will Do** The assistant manager, Jordan Keyes, has reviewed the document and asked you to make a few changes.

Tutorial
Scrolling

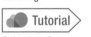
Tutorial
Selecting, Replacing, and Deleting Text

Tutorial
Using Undo and Redo

**1** With **1-FCTVacSpecials** open, press Ctrl + Home to move the insertion point to the beginning of the document.

**2** Position the mouse pointer on the down scroll arrow on the vertical scroll bar and then click the left mouse button several times.

Step 2

> This scrolls down the lines of text in the document. Scrolling changes the display of text but does not move the insertion point.

**3** Position the mouse pointer on the vertical scroll bar below the scroll box and then click the left mouse button two times.

> The scroll box on the vertical scroll bar indicates the location of the text in the document screen in relation to the remainder of the document. Clicking below the scroll box on the vertical scroll bar scrolls down one screen of text at a time.

**4** Position the mouse pointer on the scroll box on the vertical scroll bar, click and hold down the left mouse button, drag the scroll box to the top of the vertical scroll bar, and then release the mouse button.

**5** Position the mouse pointer anywhere in the word *Behold* (located immediately after the first bullet) and then double-click the left mouse button to select the word.

> Selected text displays with a gray background. You can also drag through text with the mouse to select it. When you select text, the Mini toolbar displays. You will learn more about the Mini toolbar in Activity 2.1.

Step 5

On this exciting cruise, you will
- Behold some of the worlds most
- Visit colorful Gold Rush towns
- Observe fascinating wildlife
- Experience a dazzling display by

**6** Type View.

> When you type *View*, it replaces *Behold*.

**7** Move the insertion point to the beginning of the word *Glacier* (located in the second paragraph under the heading *Ocean Vista Cruise Lines*) and then press the F8 function key on the keyboard. Press the Right Arrow key until the words *Glacier Bay and* are selected.

Step 7

> Pressing the F8 function key turns on Extend mode. Use the insertion point movement keys to select text in Extend mode.

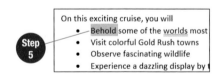
The Pacific Skye cruises through Glacier Bay and the Inside ports of Skagway, Haines, and Juneau. The Pacific Skye also Vancouver, British Columbia.

**8** Press the Delete key.

**9** Press and hold down the Ctrl key, click in the first sentence of the first paragraph (begins with *Ocean Vista Cruise Lines announces*), and then release the Ctrl key.

> Holding down the Ctrl key while clicking the mouse button selects the entire sentence.

**10** Press the Delete key to delete the selected sentence.

**11** Click the Undo button ↶ ⌄ on the Quick Access Toolbar.

Step 11

> When you click the Undo button, the deleted sentence reappears. Clicking the Undo button reverses the last command or deletes the last entry you typed. Click the Undo button arrow and a drop-down list displays the changes made to the document since it was opened. Click an action to undo it and any actions listed above it in the drop-down list.

**12** Click the Redo button ↷ on the Quick Access Toolbar.

> Clicking the Redo button deletes the selected sentence. If you click the Undo button and then decide you do not want to reverse the original action, click the Redo button.

**13** Position the mouse pointer between the left edge of the page and the first line of text in the second paragraph until the pointer turns into an arrow pointing up and to the right (instead of the left) and then click the left mouse button.

> The space between the left edge of the page and the text is referred to as the *selection bar*. Use the selection bar to select specific amounts of text. Refer to Table 1.4 for more information on selecting text.

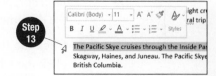

Step 13

**14** Deselect the text by clicking in the document.

> Deselecting cancels the selection of text.

**15** Save the document by clicking the Save button on the Quick Access Toolbar.

**Table 1.4** Selecting with the Mouse

| To select | Complete these steps using the mouse |
|---|---|
| a word | Double-click the word. |
| a line of text | Click in the selection bar at the left of the line. |
| multiple lines of text | Drag in the selection bar at the left of the lines. |
| a sentence | Press and hold down the Ctrl key and then click in the sentence. |
| a paragraph | Double-click in the selection bar next to the paragraph or triple-click in the paragraph. |
| multiple paragraphs | Drag in the selection bar. |
| an entire document | Triple-click in the selection bar. |

**Check Your Work** Compare your work to the model answer available in the online course.

## In Addition

### Resuming Reading or Editing a Document

When closing a multiple-page document, Word remembers on what page the insertion point was last positioned. When the document is reopened, Word displays a Welcome Back message at the right side of the screen near the vertical scroll bar. The message identifies the page where the insertion point was last located. Click the message and the insertion point is positioned at the top of that page.

# Activity 1.5 Checking Spelling and Grammar

Use Word's spelling checker to find and correct misspelled words and find duplicated words (such as *and and*). The spelling checker compares words in the document with words in its dictionary. If a match is found, the word is passed over. If no match is found for the word, the spelling checker stops, selects the word, and offers possible replacements. The grammar checker will search a document for grammar, punctuation, and word usage errors. Start checking the spelling and grammar in a document by clicking the Review tab and then clicking the Check Document button in the Proofing group. The spelling checker and the grammar checker can help create a well-written document, but these features do not replace the need for proofreading.

**FIRST CHOICE TRAVEL**

**What You Will Do**   Continuing with the editing process, you are ready to check the spelling and grammar in the First Choice Travel vacation specials document.

**Tutorial**

Checking Spelling and Grammar

**1** With **1-FCTVacSpecials** open, press Ctrl + Home to move the insertion point to the beginning of the document.

**Step 2**

**2** Click the Review tab and then click the Check Document button in the Proofing group.

> When you click the Check Document button, Word displays the Editor task pane (Proofing task pane in Word 2019) at the right side of the screen with information on how many possible spelling and grammar errors are found in the document

**3** Click the Results button (contains the text *8 Results*) that appears near the top of the Editor task pane.

> The Editor task pane displays the number of possible spelling and grammar errors in the *Corrections* list box. To check all spelling errors, click the *Spelling* option and to check all grammar errors, click the *Grammar* option.

**4** When the word *inagural* is selected in the document, the correct spelling, *inaugural*, displays in the *Suggestions* list box in the Editor task pane. Click *inaugural* in the task pane to change the word to the correct spelling in the document.

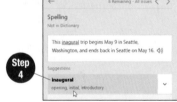

**Step 4**

> Refer to Table 1.5 for an explanation of the options in the Editor task pane.

**5** When the word *worlds* is selected in the document, click *world's* in the *Suggestions* list box in the Editor task pane.

> Click the option box arrow at the right of an option in the *Suggestions* list box and a drop-down list displays. Refer to Table 1.6 for an explanation of the drop-down list options.

**Step 5**

**6** When the word *Your* is selected in the document, click *You* in the *Suggestions* list box in the Editor task pane.

**In Brief**

**Check Spelling and Grammar**
1. Click Review tab.
2. Click Check Document button.
3. Ignore or change as needed.
4. Click OK.

**7** If the text *April 15, 2021,* is selected in the document, click the *Ignore Once* option below the *Suggestions* list box in the Editor task pane.

**8** When the word *the* is selected (this word occurs two times in sequence), click the *Delete Repeated Word* option below the *Suggestions* list box in the Editor task pane.

**9** When the word *of* is selected in the document, click *off* in the *Suggestions* list box in the Editor task pane.

**10** When the word *utah* is selected in the document, click *Utah* in the *Suggestions* list box in the Editor task pane.

Step 7

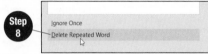

Step 8

**11** If a sentence containing the words *First Choice* is selected in the document, click the *Ignore Once* option in the Editor task pane.

**12** Click OK at the message box stating that the spelling and grammar check is complete.

**13** Click the Save button on the Quick Access Toolbar to save the changes made to the document.

**Table 1.5** Editor Task Pane Options

| Option | Function |
| --- | --- |
| Ignore Once | skips the currently selected text |
| Ignore All | skips the currently selected text and all other occurrences of the text in the document |
| Add to Dictionary | adds selected text to the main spelling check dictionary |
| Delete Repeated Word | deletes one of two repeated words |
| Don't check for this issue | ignores the currently selected text that may break a grammar rule and no longer checks for the specific grammar rule in the document |
| Options for "Grammar" | displays the Grammar Settings dialog box with grammar checking options that can be enabled or disabled |

**Table 1.6** Editor Task Pane Drop-Down List Options

| Option | Function |
| --- | --- |
| Read Aloud | pronounces selected text (speaker necessary) |
| Spell Out | spells out selected text (speaker necessary) |
| Change All | replaces selected text and all other occurrences of the text, with selected text in list box |
| Add to AutoCorrect | adds selected text to AutoCorrect |
| AutoCorrect Options | displays the AutoCorrect dialog box with AutoCorrect tab selected |

 **Check Your Work** Compare your work to the model answer available in the online course.

## In Addition

### Changing Spelling Options

Control spelling and grammar checking options at the Word Options dialog box with the *Proofing* option selected. Display this dialog box by clicking the File tab and then clicking *Options*. At the Word Options dialog box, click *Proofing* in the left panel of the dialog box.

Use options in the dialog box to tell the spelling checker to ignore certain types of text, create custom dictionaries, show readability statistics, and hide spelling and/or grammar errors in the document.

The AutoCorrect feature automatically detects and corrects some typographical errors, misspelled words, and incorrect capitalization. In addition to correcting errors, the AutoCorrect feature can be used to insert frequently used text. Use the Thesaurus to find synonyms, antonyms, and related terms for a particular word.

**What You Will Do**   You need to insert additional text in the First Choice Travel vacation specials document. To speed up the process, you will add an entry to AutoCorrect. You will also use the Thesaurus to find synonyms for specific words in the document.

Adding and Deleting
an AutoCorrect Entry

Using the Thesaurus

**1** With **1-FCTVacSpecials** open, click the File tab and then click *Options*.

**2** At the Word Options dialog box, click *Proofing* in the left panel and then click the AutoCorrect Options button in the *AutoCorrect options* section.

**3** At the AutoCorrect dialog box, type bst in the *Replace* text box and then press the Tab key.

**4** Type Bahamas Sightseeing Tour in the *With* text box and then click the Add button.

**5** Click OK to close the AutoCorrect dialog box.

**6** Click OK to close the Word Options dialog box.

**7** Press Ctrl + End to move the insertion point to the end of the document, make sure the insertion point is positioned a double space below the last bulleted item, and then type the text shown in Figure 1.3. (Type the text exactly as shown. AutoCorrect will correct *bst* to *Bahamas Sightseeing Tour* when you press the Enter key or the spacebar.)

**Figure 1.3** Step 7

bst

The Bahamas consist of over 700 islands and cays, all with friendly people, beautiful beaches, and magnificent dive spots. First Choice Travel offers the bst to explore these exciting and breathtaking islands. Sign up for the bst and experience the bustling city of Nassau, which offers everything from parasailing to casino gaming. Call us to discover how you can join the bst at an incredibly low price.

**In Brief**

**Add AutoCorrect Entry**
1. Click File tab.
2. Click *Options*.
3. Click *Proofing*.
4. Click AutoCorrect Options button.
5. Type text in *Replace* text box.
6. Type text in *With* text box.
7. Click Add button.
8. Click OK.
9. Click OK.

**Use Thesaurus**
1. Click in word.
2. Click Review tab.
3. Click Thesaurus button.
4. Right-click word in Thesaurus task pane list box.
5. Click *Insert*.

**8** Click in the word *breathtaking* (located in the second sentence in the paragraph you just typed), click the Review tab, and then click the Thesaurus button in the Proofing group.

**9** At the Thesaurus task pane, right-click the word *spectacular* in the task pane list box and then click *Insert* at the drop-down list.

> You can also hover the mouse pointer over the word in the task pane list box, click the arrow at the right of the word, and then click *Insert* at the drop-down list.

**10** Close the Thesaurus task pane by clicking the Close button ⊠ in the upper right corner of the task pane.

**11** Position the mouse pointer on the word *bustling* (located in the third sentence in the paragraph you just typed) and then click the right mouse button. At the shortcut menu, point to *Synonyms* and then click *lively* at the side menu.

**12** Click the Save button to save the document with the same name.

**13** Click the File tab and then click *Options*. At the Word Options dialog box, click *Proofing* in the left panel and then click the AutoCorrect Options button.

**14** At the AutoCorrect dialog box, type bst in the *Replace* text box.

> This selects *bst* and *Bahamas Sightseeing Tour* in the list box.

**15** Click the Delete button and then click OK to close the dialog box.

**16** Click OK to close the Word Options dialog box.

 **Check Your Work** Compare your work to the model answer available in the online course.

## In Addition

### Using the Thesaurus Task Pane

Depending on the word being looked up, the words in the Thesaurus task pane list box may display followed by *(n.)* for *noun*, *(v.)* for *verb*, *(adj.)* for *adjective*, or *(adv.)* for *adverb*, and preceded by a collapse arrow (down-pointing triangle). Click the collapse arrow and the synonyms below the word are removed and the collapse arrow changes to an expand arrow (right-pointing triangle). Click the expand arrow to redisplay the list of synonyms.

# Activity 1.7 — Changing Document Views; Hiding and Showing White Space

By default, a document displays in Print Layout view. This view shows the document on the screen as it will appear when printed. Other views are available, such as Read Mode, Web Layout, Outline, and Draft. Change views with buttons in the view area on the Status bar or with options in the Views group on the View tab. Change to Draft view and the document displays in a format for efficient editing and formatting. Read Mode displays a document in a format for easy viewing and reading. Change to Web Layout view to display a document as it would appear as a web page. In Print Layout view, a page displays as it will appear when printed, including the white space at the top and bottom of the page representing the document's margins. To save space on the screen, the white space can be removed using the hide white space icon. Redisplay white space using the show white space icon.

**What You Will Do**   Several people will be reviewing the First Choice Travel vacation specials document on screen, so you decide to experiment with various views to determine the best one for on-screen reviewing.

Changing Document Views

Hiding and Showing White Space

**1** With **1-FCTVacSpecials** open, press Ctrl + Home to move the insertion point to the beginning of the document.

**2** Change to Draft view by clicking the View tab and then clicking the Draft button ▤ in the Views group.

> Change to Draft view to display the document in a format designed for efficient editing and formatting. In Draft view, margins and other features such as headers and footers do not display.

**3** Change to Web Layout view by clicking the Web Layout button ▤ in the view area on the Status bar (see Figure 1.4).

> Change to Web Layout view to display the document as it would appear as a web page.

**4** Change to Read Mode by clicking the Read Mode button ▤ in the Views group.

> Read Mode displays a document for easy viewing and reading. You can also display a document in Read Mode by clicking the Read Mode button in the view area of the Status bar.

**5** Display the next two pages on the screen by clicking the Next button (right-pointing triangle in a circle) at the right side of the screen.

**6** Display previous pages by clicking the Previous button (left-pointing triangle in a circle) at the left side of the screen.

**7** Continue navigating in Read Mode using the keyboard commands shown in Table 1.7.

**Figure 1.4** View Buttons in View Area on Status Bar

**8** Return to Print Layout view by pressing the Esc key.

Pressing the Esc key displays the document in Print Layout view. You can also return to Print Layout view by clicking the View tab and then clicking *Edit Document* at the drop-down list.

**9** To save space on the screen, remove the white space at the top and bottom of each page as well as the gray space between pages. To do this, position the mouse pointer on the gray space above the page until the pointer turns into the hide white space icon ⊞ and then double-click the left mouse button.

**10** Scroll through the document and then redisplay the white and gray space at the top and bottom of each page. To do this, position the mouse pointer on the gray line at the top of the page until the pointer turns into a show white space icon ⊞ and then double-click the left mouse button.

**Table 1.7** Navigating in Read Mode

| Press this key | To complete this action |
|---|---|
| Page Down or spacebar | Move to next page or section. |
| Page Up or Backspace key | Move to previous page or section. |
| Right Arrow | Move to next page. |
| Left Arrow | Move to previous page. |
| Home | Move to first page in document. |
| End | Move to last page in document. |
| Esc | Return to previous view. |

## In Addition

### Using Learning Tools

Read Mode view contains options for reading a document out loud as well as increasing text spacing and displaying syllable breaks. These options, along with other reading options, are available on the Immersive Learning Tools tab. The learning tools on the Immersive Learning Tools tab are designed to help with reading fluency and comprehension. Click the View tab and then click the Learning Tools button ⊞ in the Immersive group and the Immersive Learning Tools tab displays. Click the Column Width button ⊞ on the Learning Tools tab and a drop-down list displays with the options *Very Narrow*, *Narrow*, *Moderate*, and *Wide*. Choose a column width option to focus on specific text to improve comprehension. Use options from the Page Color button ⊞ to change the page background color to make text easier to read and to reduce eye strain. The Page Color button options include *Sepia* (a light reddish-brown background color) and *Inverse* (white text on a black background color). Focus on one, three, or fives lines of text using options from the Line Focus button ⊞. Click the Text Spacing button ⊞ on the Immersive Learning Tools tab and spacing is increased between words, characters, and lines. Improve word recognition and pronunciation by clicking the Syllables button ⊞ to turn on the display of syllable breaks in words. If a speaker is connected to the computer, click the Read Aloud button ⊞ and the text in the document is read out loud and each word is highlighted as it is being read. When text is being read, a playback toolbar containing buttons for controlling the narration displays in the upper right corner of the document.

# Activity 1.8 Changing the Display Percentage

By default, a document displays at 100%. This display percentage can be changed with the Zoom slider bar at the right side of the Status bar and with options in the Zoom group on the View tab. To change display percentage with the Zoom slider bar, drag the button on the bar to increase or decrease the percentage, or click the Zoom Out button to decrease the display percentage or the Zoom In button to increase the percentage. Use buttons in the Zoom group on the View tab to return to the 100% display percentage, display one page or multiple pages, expand the document across the screen, and display the Zoom dialog box.

**What You Will Do** Several people will be reviewing the First Choice Travel vacation specials document on the screen so you decide to experiment with various views and zoom percentages to determine the best view for on-screen reviewing.

Changing the Display Percentage

**1** With **1-FCTVacSpecials** open, press Ctrl + Home to move the insertion point to the beginning of the document.

**2** Click the Zoom Out button ⊟ at the left of the Zoom slider bar to decrease the display percentage to 90%.

> Figure 1.5 identifies the Zoom slider bar along with Zoom Out and Zoom In buttons.

**3** Click the Zoom In button ⊞ at the right of the Zoom slider bar to increase the display percentage to 100%.

**4** Position the mouse pointer on the Zoom slider button on the Zoom slider bar, click and hold down the left mouse button, drag right to increase the display percentage, drag left to decrease the percentage, and then release the mouse button.

**5** Click the View tab.

**6** Click the 100% button in the Zoom group to return to the default display percentage of 100%.

**7** Click the One Page button in the Zoom group to display just the first page on the screen.

**8** Click the Multiple Pages button in the Zoom group to display all of the pages on the screen.

**9** Click the Zoom button in the Zoom group to display the Zoom dialog box.

> You can also display the Zoom dialog box by clicking the Zoom level button (the percentage at the right of the Zoom slider bar).

**In Brief**

**Display Zoom Dialog Box**
1. Click View tab.
2. Click Zoom button.

**10** Click the *75%* option in the *Zoom to* section of the dialog box.

**11** Click OK to close the Zoom dialog box.

The document displays at 75%.

**12** Click the 100% button in the Zoom group to return to the default display percentage.

**Figure 1.5** Zoom Slider Bar

## In Addition

### Working with Windows

The Window group on the View tab contains a number of buttons for working with windows. Click the New Window button ⬜ to open a new window containing the same document. This is useful for viewing a portion of the document while editing in another location. If more than one document is open, the documents can be arranged so that a portion of each is visible. To do this, click the Arrange All button ⬜ in the Window group. Click the Split button ⬜ in the Window group to split the open document in two with a split bar and another horizontal ruler. Splitting a window is useful for viewing different parts of a document at one time. Compare the contents of two documents by opening both documents and then clicking the View Side by Side button ⬜ in the Window group. Both documents display on the screen arranged side by side. By default, synchronous scrolling is active, which means that scrolling in one document results in the same scrolling in the other document. Turn off synchronous scrolling by clicking the Synchronous Scrolling button ⬜.

### Changing Page Movement

Paging through a document occurs, by default, in a vertical (up and down) manner. This default page movement can be changed to side to side, which displays a document more like a book with two pages that are side by side and visible at one time. If the document contains more than two pages, additional pages display in a cascaded manner behind pages. Change to side to side page movement by clicking the Side to Side button ⬜ in the Page Movement group on the View tab. Use the horizontal scroll bar or the mouse wheel to scroll through pages. To use the horizontal scroll bar, click the Next button ▶ at the right side of the scroll bar to display the next page or click the Previous button ◀ at the left side of the scroll bar to display the previous page; drag the scroll box on the scroll bar; or, click to the left or right of the scroll box. The mouse wheel can also be used to scroll through pages.

Use the Navigation pane to browse in a document or search for specific text or items. Display the Navigation pane by clicking the Find button in the Editing group on the Home tab or by clicking the *Navigation Pane* check box in the Show group on the View tab to insert a check mark. The Navigation pane contains three tabs—Headings, Pages, and Results. Click the Headings tab to display in the Navigation pane titles and headings with styles applied. Click the Pages tab to display in the Navigation pane thumbnails of each page. Click a page thumbnail to move the insertion point to that page. Search for text by clicking in the search text box and then typing the search text. With the Pages tab active, each occurrence of the search text is highlighted in the pages. Click the Results tab to display each occurrence of the search text along with the text that displays before and after each occurrence.

**What You Will Do**  Review the First Choice Travel vacation specials document by using the Navigation pane to navigate and search for specific text in the document.

Navigating Using the Navigation Pane

Finding Text

**1** With **1-FCTVacSpecials** open, display the Navigation pane by clicking the View tab and then clicking the *Navigation Pane* check box in the Show group to insert a check mark.

> You can also display the Navigation pane by clicking the Find button in the Editing group on the Home tab.

**2** Click the Pages tab in the Navigation pane.

> Clicking the Pages tab displays thumbnails of each page in the Navigation pane.

**3** Click the page 2 thumbnail in the Navigation pane.

> Clicking the page 2 thumbnail moves the insertion point to the beginning of page 2.

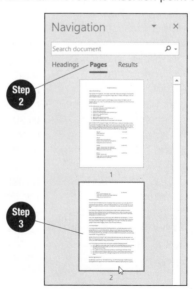

**In Brief**

**Display Navigation Pane**
1. Click View tab.
2. Click *Navigation Pane* check box.
OR
1. Click Home tab.
2. Click Find button.

**4** Click the page 1 thumbnail in the Navigation pane.

**5** Click in the search text box in the Navigation pane (contains the text *Search document*) and then type Pacific Skye.

After you type *Pacific Skye*, each occurrence of the text is highlighted in the document.

**6** Click the Next Search Result button (displays as a down arrow) in the Navigation pane to select the next occurrence of *Pacific Skye*. Click the button again to select the next occurrence.

You can click the Previous Search Result button (displays as an up arrow) to display the previous occurrence of the search text.

**7** Click the Results tab to display in the Navigation pane each occurrence of the search text *Pacific Skye* along with the text that displays before and after each occurrence.

**8** Select the first occurrence of *Pacific Skye* in the document by clicking the first item in the Navigation pane.

**9** Click the X at the right side of the search text box.

Clicking this button ends the current search, removes the search text in the Navigation pane, and selects the current search result in the document.

**10** Close the Navigation pane by clicking the Close button in the upper right corner of the pane.

You can also close the Navigation pane by clicking the *Navigation Pane* check box in the Show group on the View tab to remove the check mark.

## In Addition

### Displaying Ribbon Options

Control how much of the ribbon displays on screen with the Ribbon Display Options button ▣ in the upper right corner of the screen. Click this button and a drop-down list displays with options for hiding the ribbon, showing only the tabs, or showing tabs and commands. The dis- play of the ribbon can also be turned off by clicking the Collapse the Ribbon button ⌃ above the vertical scroll bar or with the keyboard shortcut Ctrl + F1. Redisplay the ribbon by double-clicking any tab or by pressing Ctrl + F1.

# Activity 1.10 Finding and Replacing Text

In the previous activity, the Navigation pane was used to find all occurrences of specific text in the document. To find text and then replace it with other text, use options at the Find and Replace dialog box with the Replace tab selected. Display this dialog box by clicking the Replace button in the Editing group on the Home tab.

**What You Will Do**   As you review the vacation specials document, you discover that the name of the ship is spelled incorrectly and that the ship's cabins are divided into categories rather than classes. You decide to use the Find and Replace feature to correct these errors.

Finding and Replacing Text

Using the Help Feature

**1** With **1-FCTVacSpecials** open, press Ctrl + Home to move the insertion point to the beginning of the document.

**2** The name of the ship is the *Pacific Sky*, not the *Pacific Skye*. To change the name, display the Find and Replace dialog box by clicking the Home tab and then clicking the Replace button in the Editing group.

**3** At the Find and Replace dialog box with the Replace tab selected, type Skye in the *Find what* text box and then press the Tab key.

> Pressing the Tab key moves the insertion point to the *Replace with* text box. You can also click in the *Replace with* text box.

**4** Type Sky in the *Replace with* text box.

**5** Click the Replace All button at the bottom of the dialog box.

> Clicking the Replace All button replaces all occurrences of the text in the document. If you want control over what is replaced in a document, click the Replace button to replace text or click the Find Next button to move to the next occurrence of the text.

**6** At the message stating that four replacements were made, click OK.

**7** Click the Close button to close the Find and Replace dialog box.

**8** The word *class* is used to designate cabins, when it should instead be *category*. To make this change, click the Replace button in the Editing group on the Home tab.

**9** At the Find and Replace dialog box with the Replace tab selected, type class.

> When you open the Replace dialog box, *Skye* is automatically selected in the *Find what* text box. When you begin typing *class*, the selected text is automatically deleted.

**10** Press the Tab key and then type category in the *Replace with* text box.

> When you type the find text and the replace text in all lowercase letters, Word will find and replace all occurrences regardless of the capitalization. For example, Word will find *Class* in the document and replace it with *Category*.

**11** Click the Replace All button.

**12** At the message stating that six replacements were made, click OK.

**13** Click the Close button to close the Find and Replace dialog box.

**14** Click the Save button on the Quick Access Toolbar to save the document.

 **Check Your Work** Compare your work to the model answer available in the online course.

# In Addition

## Exploring Options at the Expanded Find and Replace Dialog Box

The Find and Replace dialog box contains a variety of check boxes with options for completing a find and replace. To display these options, click the More button at the bottom of the dialog box. This causes the Find and Replace dialog box to expand as shown at the right. The options are described in the table below.

| Option | Action |
|---|---|
| Match case | Exactly match the case of the search text. For example, if you search for *Book*, Word will stop at *Book* but not *book* or *BOOK*. |
| Find whole words only | Find a whole word, not a part of a word. For example, if you search for *her* and did not select *Find whole words only*, Word would stop at the*re*, *here*, *hers*, and so on. |
| Use wildcards | Use special characters as wildcards to search for specific text. |
| Sounds like | Match words that sound alike but are spelled differently, such as *know* and *no*. |
| Find all word forms | Find all forms of the word entered in the *Find what* text box. For example, if you enter *hold*, Word will stop at *held* and *holding*. |
| Match prefix | Find only those words that begin with the letters in the *Find what* text box. For example, if you enter *per*, Word will stop at words such as *perform* and *perfect* but will skip over words such as *super* and *hyperlink*. |
| Match suffix | Find only those words that end with the letters in the *Find what* text box. For example, if you enter *ly*, Word will stop at words such as *accurately* and *quietly* but skip over words such as *catalyst* and *lyre*. |
| Ignore punctuation characters | Ignore punctuation within characters. For example, if you enter *US* in the *Find what* text box, Word will stop at *U.S.* |
| Ignore white-space characters | Ignore spaces between letters. For example, if you enter *F B I* in the *Find what* text box, Word will stop at *FBI*. |

Word includes the Tell Me feature that provides information and guidance on how to complete a function. To use Tell Me, click in the *Tell Me* text box on the ribbon to the right of the Help tab and then type the function. Type text in the *Tell Me* text box and a drop-down list displays with options that are refined as the text is typed. The drop-down list displays options for completing the function, displaying information on the function from sources on the web, or displaying help information on the function. The *Tell Me* text box drop-down list will display the last five functions entered.

**What You Will Do**   To enhance the appearance of the document, you decide to use the Tell Me feature to change the font color of the title *VACATION SPECIALS*. You will also use the Tell Me feature to access the Help task pane and find articles on AutoCorrect.

Using the Tell Me
Feature

**1** With **1-FCTVacSpecials** open, select the title *VACATION SPECIALS* by positioning the mouse pointer in the title and then triple-clicking the left mouse button.

**2** Click in the *Tell Me* text box.

> The *Tell Me* text box is on the ribbon to the right of the Help tab and contains the text *Tell me what you want to do*. When you click in the text box, the last five functions entered will display in a drop-down list.

**3** Type font color in the *Tell Me* text box.

> A drop-down list displays with options such as *Font Color, Font Size, Border Color,* and *Font*.

**4** Position the mouse pointer on the arrow at the right of the *Font Color* option in the drop-down list.

**5** At the side menu, click the *Blue* color option in the *Standard Colors* section.

> The Blue font color is applied to the selected title. The Tell Me feature guided you through the process of applying font color without you having to learn how to apply font color using a button on the ribbon or an option at a dialog box.

**6** The Tell Me feature also includes access to the Help feature. To display help information on AutoCorrect, click in the *Tell Me* text box and then type AutoCorrect.

**7** At the drop-down list, point to *Get Help on "AutoCorrect."*

Pointing to the option causes a side menu to display.

**8** At the side menu, click the first option.

Clicking an option in the side menu will display the Help task pane at the right side of the screen.

**9** Read the information in the Help task pane.

The Help task pane contains a Back button to display a previous window in the task pane and a search text box for searching for help on a specific topic or feature. The Help task pane also contains a button with three dots. Click the button and a drop-down list displays with options to display the Help task pane home information; to get help from the Office help center; and to contact Microsoft for help on an issue.

**10** Close the Help task pane by clicking the Close button in the upper right corner of the task pane.

 **Check Your Work** Compare your work to the model answer available in the online course.

# In Addition

## Accessing Smart Lookup

The Smart Lookup feature provides information on selected text from a variety of sources on the web such as Wikipedia, Bing, and the Oxford dictionary. The first time you use Smart Lookup, a message displays indicating that Intelligent Services must be turned on. Click the Turn on button and the Smart Lookup task pane displays at the right side of the screen. The Tell Me feature is one way to access Smart Lookup. To use Tell Me for Smart Lookup, click in the *Tell Me* text box, type the function, and then click the *See more search results for* option in the drop-down list. Clicking this option displays the Smart Lookup task pane at the right side of the screen with information on the function from a variety of locations on the internet. Smart Lookup can also be accessed with the Smart Lookup button in the Research group on the References tab or by selecting text, right-clicking the selected text, and then clicking *Smart Lookup* at the shortcut menu.

Display help information in the Help task pane through the Tell Me feature, by clicking the Help tab and then clicking the Help button, or by pressing the F1 function key on the keyboard. Help is also available from a dialog box or the backstage area. Open a dialog box, click the Help button in the upper right corner of the dialog box (displays as a question mark) and the Microsoft Office support website displays with information related to the dialog box. Click the Help button in the upper right corner of a backstage area and the Microsoft Office support website displays with information related to the specific backstage area. The Print backstage area provides options for previewing the document before printing, indicating the number of copies, specifying the pages for printing, and customizing the document.

**FIRST CHOICE TRAVEL**

**What You Will Do**   You are ready to print the First Choice Travel vacation specials document, but first you want to learn more about printing a document. You decide to experiment with getting help related to the Font dialog box and the Print backstage area.

Previewing and Printing

**1** With **1-FCTVacSpecials** open, press Ctrl + Home to move the insertion point to the beginning of the document.

**2** Click the Font group dialog box launcher 🔲 to display the Font dialog box.

> The Font group dialog box launcher is in the lower right corner of the Font group and displays as a small button containing a diagonal arrow.

**3** Click the Help button in the upper right corner of the dialog box.

**4** Look at the information at the Microsoft Office support website, click a hyperlink that interests you, read the information, and then close the website by clicking the Close button in the upper right corner of the window.

**5** Close the Font dialog box by clicking the Close button in the upper right corner of the dialog box.

**6** Click the File tab to display the backstage area.

**7** Click the Help button in the upper right corner of the backstage area.

**8** Look at the information at the Microsoft Office support website and then close the window by clicking the Close button.

**9** Click the Back button in the backstage area to return to the document.

**10** Click the Help tab and then click the Help button ⑦ to display the Help task pane.

**11** Type print in the Help task pane search text box and then press the Enter key.

**12** Click a hyperlink in the Help task pane pertaining to printing a document.

**13** Read the information and then close the Help task pane.

**14** Click the File tab and then click the *Print* option to display the Print backstage area.

> At the Print backstage area, your document displays at the right side of the screen as it will appear when printed. The left side of the Print backstage area displays the Print

## In Brief

**Print a Document**
1. Click File tab.
2. Click *Print* option.
3. Click Print button.

**Print a Specific Page**
1. Click File tab.
2. Click *Print* option.
3. Click in *Pages* text box.
4. Type page number.
5. Click Print button.

**Print Current Page**
1. Position insertion point in page.
2. Click File tab.
3. Click *Print* option.
4. Click top gallery in *Settings* category.
5. Click *Print Current Page* at drop-down list.
6. Click Print button.

button and *Copies* measurement box along with two categories—*Printer* and *Settings*. Click the Print button to send the document to the printer. Specify the number of copies to print with the *Copies* measurement box. Use the *Printer* gallery to specify the printer. The *Settings* category contains a number of galleries, each with options for specifying how the document should print.

**15** Click two times on the Zoom In button at the right of the Zoom slider bar.

Click the Zoom In button to increase the size of the preview page or click the Zoom Out button to decrease the size of the preview page.

**16** Click the Next Page button below and at the left of the preview page to display the next page in the document.

**17** Click the Zoom to Page button at the right of the Zoom slider bar.

**18** Print only page 2 of the document by clicking in the *Pages* text box (in the *Settings* category), typing 2, and then clicking the Print button.

**19** Move the insertion point to any character in page 3, click the File tab and then click the *Print* option.

**20** At the Print backstage area, click the top gallery in the *Settings* category and then click *Print Current Page* at the drop-down list.

**21** Click the Print button.

**22** Save and then close **1-FCTVacSpecials**.

**Check Your Work** Compare your work to the model answer available in the online course.

## In Addition

### Specifying Pages to Print

Identify a specific page, multiple pages, and/or a range of pages for printing at the Print backstage area. Print specific pages by clicking in the *Pages* text box and then typing the page numbers of the pages to be printed. To print specific multiple pages, use a comma to indicate *and* and use a hyphen to indicate *through*. For example, to print pages 2 and 5, type 2,5 in the *Pages* text box. To print pages 6 through 10, type 6-10. Both commas and hyphens can be entered when specifying page numbers.

### Getting Help on a Button

Hover the mouse pointer over certain buttons and a ScreenTip displays that includes a Help icon and the text *Tell me more*. Click this hyperlinked text and the Help task pane opens with information about the button feature.

# Activity 1.13   Creating a Document Using a Template

Word includes a number of templates formatted for specific uses. Each Word document is based on a template, with the Normal template as the default. With Word templates (and Microsoft online templates), a variety of documents can be created with specialized formatting, such as letters, reports, and awards. Display available templates by clicking the File tab and then clicking the *New* option. At the New backstage area, click in the search text box, type a category, and then press the Enter key and Word displays templates matching the category. Open a document based on a template by clicking the template and then clicking the Create button or double-clicking the template. To download online templates, the internet must be available.

**What You Will Do**   Each month, the president of First Choice Travel, Terry Blessing, awards a certificate of appreciation to a company employee. This month, she is awarding the certificate to Alex Torres and has asked you to prepare the certificate. You decide to create the certificate using a template.

Creating a Document
Using a Template

1 Click the File tab and then click the *New* option.

2 At the New backstage area, click in the search text box (contains the text *Search for online templates*), type certificate of appreciation, and then press the Enter key.

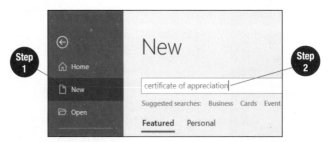

3 Click the first *Certificate of recognition for administrative professional* template in the backstage area. (Refer to Figure 1.6 to view the certificate.)

If the certificate shown in Figure 1.6 does not display, open **FCTCertificate** from your WordS1 folder.

4 Click the Create button.

5 At the certificate, click the word *Name* below the text *AWARDED TO*.

In the certificate, the word *Name* is a placeholder, which is a location for entering specific text. When you click *Name*, the placeholder is selected.

6 Type Alex Torres.

7 Click the *day* placeholder and then type 30th.

8 Click the *month* placeholder and then type September.

In Brief

Create Document
Using Template
1. Click File tab.
2. Click *New* option.
3. Click template.
4. Click Create button.

⑨ Click the *year* placeholder and then type 21.

⑩ Click the *Presenter Name and Title* placeholder and then type Terry Blessing, President.

Your certificate should display as shown in Figure 1.6.

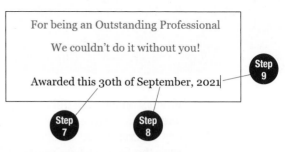

For being an Outstanding Professional

We couldn't do it without you!

Awarded this 30th of September, 2021

Step 9

Step 7

Step 8

⑪ Click the Save button on the Quick Access Toolbar.

⑫ At the Save As backstage area, click the *Browse* option.

⑬ At the Save As dialog box, navigate to your WordS1 folder.

⑭ Click in the *File name* text box, type 1-FCTCert, and then press the Enter key (or click the Save button).

⑮ Print the certificate by clicking the File tab, clicking the *Print* option, and then clicking the Print button.

⑯ Close the document by clicking the File tab and then clicking the *Close* option.

**Figure 1.6** Certificate of Appreciation

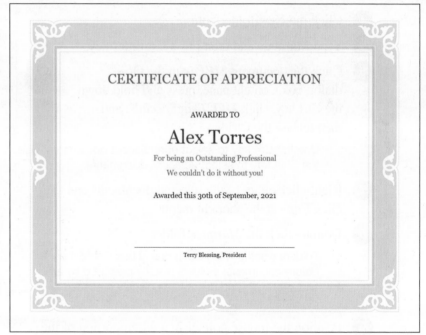

Check Your Work  Compare your work to the model answer available in the online course.

## In Addition

### Specifying a Template Category

When searching for online templates at the New backstage area, a *Category* list box displays at the right side of the screen. The list box displays the category and the number of templates that fit within the category. Click a specific category in the list box, and only templates matching that category will display in the New backstage area.

When working with documents, consider document management tasks such as creating a folder and copying, moving, and deleting documents. Many document management tasks can be completed on one or more documents at the Open dialog box or Save As dialog box. With the *Save as type* option at the Save As dialog box, a document can be saved in a different format such as rich text or an earlier version of Word, or as a web page or plain text file.

**What You Will Do** First Choice Travel does business on a regular basis with Marquee Productions, a movie production company, so you decide to create a folder into which you will insert Marquee Productions documents. You will also save a document in an older version of Word.

Tutorial

Managing Folders

Tutorial

Managing Documents

Tutorial

Saving in a Different Format

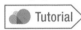

1. Click the File tab and then click the *Open* option.

2. At the Open backstage area, click the *Browse* option.

3. At the Open dialog box, navigate to your WordS1 folder.

4. Click the New folder button.

5. Type Marquee and then press the Enter key.

6. Click the document *MPFax* in the Open dialog box Content pane, press and hold down the Ctrl key, click *1-FCTVacSpecials*, and then release the Ctrl key.

    Use the Ctrl key to select nonadjacent documents. Use the Shift key to select adjacent documents.

7. Right-click either of the selected documents and then click *Copy* at the shortcut menu.

8. Double-click the *Marquee* folder.

    Folders display in the Open dialog box Content pane before documents. Folders display preceded by a file folder icon and documents display preceded by a document icon.

9. Position the mouse pointer in a white portion of the Open dialog box Content pane, click the right mouse button, and then click *Paste* at the shortcut menu.

    The copied documents are inserted in the Marquee folder.

10. You need to send **1-FCTVacSpecials** to a colleague who uses Word 2003, so you need to save the document in that format. At the Open dialog box with the Marquee folder active, double-click *1-FCTVacSpecials*.

11. Click the File tab and then click the *Save As* option.

**In Brief**

**Create Folder**
1. Press Ctrl + F12.
2. At Open dialog box, click New folder button.
3. Type folder name.
4. Press Enter key.

**Save Document in Different Format**
1. Press F12.
2. At Save As dialog box, type document name.
3. Change *Save as type* option to new format.
4. Click Save button.

**12** At the Save As backstage area, click the *Browse* option.

**13** At the Save As dialog box, make your WordS1 folder active and then type 1-FCTVacSpecialsWd2003 in the *File name* text box.

**14** Click the *Save as type* option box and then click *Word 97-2003 Document* at the drop-down list.

**15** Click the Save button in the lower right corner of the dialog box.

If a compatibility checker message displays, click the Continue button.

**16** Close the document.

**17** Press Ctrl + F12 to display the Open dialog box. If your WordS1 folder is not already the active folder, navigate to the WordS1 folder.

**18** At the Open dialog box, rename the Marquee folder by right-clicking the folder name and then clicking *Rename* at the shortcut menu.

**19** Type MarqueeProductions and then press the Enter key.

The new folder name replaces the original folder name. You can also rename a folder by clicking the Organize button, clicking *Rename* at the drop-down list, and then typing the new folder name.

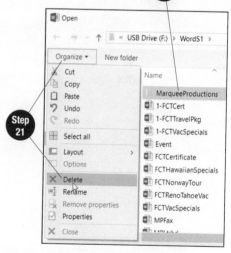

**20** Delete the MarqueeProductions folder by first clicking the folder to select it.

**21** Click the Organize button and then click *Delete* at the drop-down list.

**22** If a message displays asking if you are sure you want to delete the folder and all of its contents, click the Yes button.

**23** Close the Open dialog box.

**24** Close Word by clicking the Close button in the upper right corner of the screen.

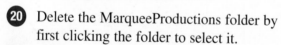 **Check Your Work** Compare your work to the model answer available in the online course.

# In Addition

## Editing a PDF File in Word

PDF stands for Portable Document Format and is a common format for sharing files. A PDF file can be opened and edited in Word. When a PDF file is opened, Word converts the file to a Word document, and the data in the file may not display in the exact format as in the PDF file. Converting a PDF file to a Word document works best with text-based documents.

# Features Summary

| Feature | Ribbon Tab, Group | Button | Quick Access Toolbar | File Tab Option | Keyboard Shortcut |
|---|---|---|---|---|---|
| AutoCorrect dialog box | | | | *Options, Proofing, AutoCorrect Options* | |
| close document | | | | *Close* | Ctrl + F4 |
| close Word | | ☒ | | | Alt + F4 |
| Draft view | View, Views | ▤ | | | |
| Extend mode | | | | | F8 |
| Help | Help, Help | ? | | | F1 |
| hide white space | | ⊞ | | | |
| Learning Tools | View, Immersive | 📖 | | | |
| move insertion point to end of document | | | | | Ctrl + End |
| move insertion point to start of document | | | | | Ctrl + Home |
| Navigation pane | View, Show | | | | Ctrl + F |
| New backstage area | | | | *New* | |
| New Line command | | | | | Shift + Enter |
| Open backstage area | | | | *Open* | Ctrl + O |
| Open dialog box | | | | *Open, Browse* | Ctrl + F12 |
| Print backstage area | | | | *Print* | Ctrl + P |
| Print Layout view | View, Views | ▤ | | | |
| Read Mode | View, Views | 📖 | | | |
| redo (repeat) an action | | | ↷ | | Ctrl + Y |
| replace text | Home, Editing | ᵇ⁄c | | | Ctrl + H |
| Save As backstage area | | | | *Save* OR *Save As* | |
| Save As dialog box | | | | *Save As, Browse* | F12 |
| save document | | 💾 | | *Save* | Ctrl + S |
| show white space | | ⊟ | | | |
| spelling and grammar | Review, Proofing | abc✓ | | | F7 |
| Tell Me feature | *Tell Me* text box | | | | Alt + Q |
| Thesaurus | Review, Proofing | 📖 | | | Shift + F7 |
| undo an action | | | ↶ | | Ctrl + Z |
| Word Options dialog box | | | | *Options* | |

# Word

## Formatting Characters and Paragraphs

**Data Files**

Before beginning section work, copy the WordS2 folder to your storage medium and then make WordS2 the active folder.

### Skills

- Apply fonts and font effects
- Apply formatting with Format Painter
- Repeat a command
- Align text in paragraphs
- Indent text
- Change line spacing
- Change paragraph spacing
- Find and replace formatting
- Create bulleted and numbered lists

- Insert symbols
- Insert special characters
- Set tabs on the horizontal ruler
- Set tabs with leaders at the Tabs dialog box
- Apply borders and shading to text
- Apply a page border
- Apply styles and style sets
- Apply themes

### Projects Overview

Edit and format documents on Oslo, Norway, and Petersburg, Alaska; format a document on traveling by train in Europe; and format documents on vacation packages in Oregon and Nevada and cross-country skiing vacation packages.

Prepare a letter to the chair of the Theatre Arts Division at Niagara Peninsula College requesting 20 theatre interns.

Prepare a movie distribution schedule.

The online course includes additional training and assessment resources.

# Activity 2.1 — Applying Formatting with the Font Group and the Mini Toolbar

Formatting specifies how a document displays and prints. Character formatting can be applied to text with buttons in the Font group on the Home tab. The top row of the Font group contains options and buttons for changing the font and font size of text as well as changing text case and clearing formatting. The bottom row contains buttons for applying formatting to text such as bold, italics, underlining, strikethrough, subscript, superscript, text effects, highlighting, and font color. Microsoft Word has taken some commonly used commands and placed them on the Mini toolbar. When text is selected, the Mini toolbar displays above the selected text. The Mini toolbar disappears when the mouse pointer is moved away from it.

**What You Will Do** You have been asked to improve the appearance of a document on Oslo, Norway, by applying a different font and various font effects to the text.

**Tutorial**
Applying Font Formatting Using the Font Group

**Tutorial**
Applying Font Formatting Using the Mini Toolbar

**Tutorial**
Highlighting Text

1. Open **FCTOslo** and then save it with the name **2-FCTOslo**.

2. Select the words *Oslo, Norway* and then click the Bold button **B** in the Font group on the Home tab.

3. With *Oslo, Norway* still selected, click the Change Case button **Aa ▾** in the Font group and then click *UPPERCASE* at the drop-down list.

   Use options at the Change Case button drop-down list to specify the case of selected text.

4. With *OSLO, NORWAY* still selected, click the Text Effects and Typography button **A** and then click the option in the fourth column, first row (white fill with a shadow outline) at the drop-down gallery.

5. Select *History* and then click the Underline button **U ▾** in the Font group.

6. Select and then underline the remaining headings: *Population*; *Commerce and Industry*; *Climate*; *Holiday, Sport, and Leisure*; and *Sightseeing Tours*.

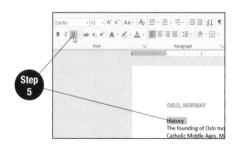

7. Select the words *Viking Age* in the first paragraph below the heading *History* and then click the Italic button **I** on the Mini toolbar above the selected text.

   The Mini toolbar displays above selected text. The toolbar disappears when you move the mouse pointer away from it.

8. Select the words *Catholic Middle Ages* in the first paragraph and then click the Italic button on the Mini toolbar.

**9** Select the entire document by clicking the Select button ⬚ in the Editing group on the Home tab and then clicking *Select All* at the drop-down list.

**10** Click the *Font* option box arrow in the Font group. Hover the mouse pointer over various typefaces in the drop-down gallery and notice how the text in the document reflects the selected font.

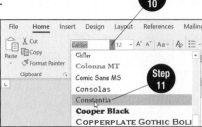

> This feature is referred to as *live preview*. It provides you with an opportunity to see how the document will appear with text formatting applied before you actually apply it.

**11** Scroll down the gallery and then click *Constantia*.

**12** Click the *Font Size* option box arrow and then click *11* in the drop-down gallery.

**13** Click the Font Color button arrow ⬚ and then click the *Dark Red* color option (first option in the *Standard Colors* section).

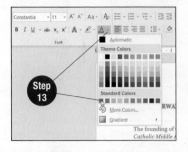

**14** Deselect the text by clicking in the document.

**15** Highlight text for review by colleagues. Begin by selecting the first sentence in the second paragraph (begins with *Oslo's population was substantially reduced*) and then click the Text Highlight Color button ⬚ in the Font group.

> This applies yellow highlighting to the sentence and then deselects the sentence.

**16** Change the highlighting color by clicking the Text Highlight Color button arrow and then click the *Bright Green* color at the drop-down list.

> Clicking the Text Highlight Color button when text is not selected causes the mouse pointer to display with a highlighter pen attached. Highlighting stays on until you click the Text Highlight Color button again.

**17** Select the first sentence in the *Population* paragraph to highlight it and then click the Text Highlight Color button to turn it off.

**18** Remove the text highlighting by pressing Ctrl + A (this selects the entire document), clicking the Text Highlight Color button arrow, and then clicking *No Color* at the drop-down list.

**19** Save **2-FCTOslo**.

**Check Your Work** Compare your work to the model answer available in the online course.

## In Addition

### Using Typefaces

A typeface is a set of characters with a common design and shape. It can be decorative or plain and either mono-spaced or proportional. Word refers to typefaces as *fonts*. A monospaced typeface allots the same amount of hori-zontal space for each character, while a proportional type-face allots a varying amount of space for each character.

Typefaces are divided into two main categories: *serif* and *sans serif*. A *serif* is a small line at the end of a character stroke. Consider using a serif typeface for text-intensive documents because the serifs help move the reader's eyes across the page. Use a sans serif typeface for headings, headlines, and advertisements.

In addition to buttons in the Font group, font formatting can be applied with options at the Font dialog box. Display the Font dialog box by clicking the Font group dialog box launcher. Use options at the dialog box to change the font, font size, and font style; change the font color; choose an underline style; and apply formatting effects. Once formatting is applied to text, the formatting can be copied to different locations in the document using the Format Painter button. The Repeat command provides another method for repeating formatting in a document. Use the Repeat command by pressing the F4 function key or the keyboard shortcut Ctrl + Y. The Repeat command will repeat only the last command executed.

**FIRST CHOICE**
**TRAVEL**

**What You Will Do**   The changes you made to the Oslo document have enhanced the readability and appearance of the text. Now you will turn your attention to the headings.

Tutorial

Applying Font Formatting Using the Font Dialog Box

Tutorial

Formatting with Format Painter

Tutorial

Repeating the Last Command

**1** With **2-FCTOslo** open, press Ctrl + Home to move the insertion point to the beginning of the document and then select the entire document by pressing Ctrl + A.

**2** Click the Font group dialog box launcher.

**3** At the Font dialog box, click *Cambria* in the *Font* list box (you will need to scroll up the list box to display this option) and then click *12* in the *Size* list box.

**4** Click the *Font color* option box arrow and then click the *Dark Blue* color option (ninth option in the *Standard Colors* section).

**5** Click OK to close the dialog box.

**6** Select the heading *History* and then click the Font group dialog box launcher.

**7** Click *Candara* in the *Font* list box (you will need to scroll down the list box to display this option), click *Bold* in the *Font style* list box, and then click *14* in the *Size* list box (you will need to scroll down the list box to display this option).

**8** Click the *Underline style* option box arrow and then click *(none)* at the drop-down list.

**9** Click OK to close the dialog box.

**10** Click in the heading *History* and then double-click the Format Painter button in the Clipboard group on the Home tab.

> When Format Painter is active, the mouse pointer displays with a paintbrush attached. Click the Format Painter button to apply formatting to one location only. Double-click the Format Painter button to apply formatting to multiple locations.

**Applying Font
Formatting at Font
Dialog Box**
1. Click Font group dialog box launcher.
2. Choose options in dialog box.
3. Click OK.

**Apply Formatting
with Format Painter**
1. Apply formatting.
2. Double-click Format Painter button.
3. Select text.
4. Click Format Painter button to turn it off.

**11** Select the title *OSLO, NORWAY.*

With Format Painter active, selecting text applies formatting. Selecting the title removed the text effect and applied the same formatting that you applied to the heading *History*.

**12** Scroll down the document and then click in the word *Population.*

When using Format Painter, apply formatting to a single word by clicking in the word. To apply formatting to more than one adjacent word at a time, select the text.

**13** Select individually each of the headings: *Commerce and Industry*; *Climate; Holiday, Sport, and Leisure*; and *Sightseeing Tours.*

**14** Click the Format Painter button to turn off Format Painter.

**15** Select the last sentence in the document (the sentence that begins *All tours by boat*) and then click the Font group dialog box launcher.

**16** At the Font dialog box, click the *Small caps* check box in the *Effects* section to insert a check mark.

**17** Click OK to close the dialog box.

**18** Select the text *Tour 1: Mini Cruise* and then press F4.

Pressing F4 repeats the previous command and applies the small caps effect to the selected text.

**19** Select the text *Tour 2: Fjord Cruise* and then press F4. Select the text *Tour 3: Fjord Cruise with Dinner* and then press F4. Select the text *Tour 4: Selected Oslo Sightseeing* and then press F4.

You can also repeat a command with the keyboard shortcut Ctrl + Y.

**20** Press Ctrl + Home to move the insertion point to the beginning of the document, select the heading *OSLO, NORWAY,* and then change the font size to 16 points.

**21** Save **2-FCTOslo**.

**Check Your Work** Compare your work to the model answer available in the online course.

## In Addition

### Applying Font Formatting with Keyboard Shortcuts

Along with buttons in the Font group and the Font dialog box, character formatting can be applied with the following keyboard shortcuts:

| Font Group Button | Keyboard Shortcut |
|---|---|
| Font | Ctrl + Shift + F |
| Font Size | Ctrl + Shift + P |
| Increase Font Size | Ctrl + Shift + > |
| Decrease Font Size | Ctrl + Shift + < |
| Change Case | Shift + F3 |

| Font Group Button | Keyboard Shortcut |
|---|---|
| Bold | Ctrl + B |
| Italic | Ctrl + I |
| Underline | Ctrl + U |
| Subscript | Ctrl + = |
| Superscript | Ctrl + Shift + + |

# Activity 2.3  Aligning Text

Paragraphs of text in a document are aligned at the left margin by default. This default alignment can be changed to center, right, or justified. Change paragraph alignment with buttons in the Paragraph group on the Home tab, with the *Alignment* option at the Paragraph dialog box, or with keyboard shortcuts. Text alignment can be changed before typing a paragraph or the alignment of an existing paragraph or group of paragraphs can be changed.

**What You Will Do**   You will improve the appearance of the Oslo document by changing the text alignment of specific paragraphs in the document.

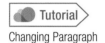

Changing Paragraph
Alignment

**1** With **2-FCTOslo** open, position the insertion point in the title *OSLO, NORWAY.*

**2** Click the Center button in the Paragraph group on the Home tab.

**3** Select from the middle of the first paragraph of text below the heading *History* to somewhere in the middle of the third paragraph of text.

> Entire paragraphs do not have to be selected to change the alignment, only a portion of each paragraph.

**4** Click the Justify button in the Paragraph group.

**5** Press Ctrl + End to move the insertion point to the end of the document.

**6** Click the Align Right button in the Paragraph group.

**7** Type your first and last names, press Shift + Enter key, and then type First Choice Travel.

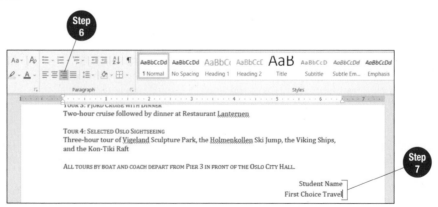

**8** Click in the sentence above your first and last names (the sentence that begins ALL TOURS BY BOAT AND COACH...).

**9** Click the Paragraph group dialog box launcher.

Clicking the Paragraph group dialog box launcher displays the Paragraph dialog box with the Indents and Spacing tab selected. Use the *Alignment* option box in the *General* section to change text alignment in the document.

**10** At the Paragraph dialog box, click the *Alignment* option box arrow.

**11** Click the *Centered* option at the drop-down list.

The *Alignment* option box at the Paragraph dialog box provides another method for changing paragraph alignment.

**12** Click OK to close the Paragraph dialog box and apply center alignment to the sentence.

**13** Move the insertion point to the beginning of the document.

**14** Select the three paragraphs of text below the heading *History*.

**15** Click the Align Left button ≡ in the Paragraph group and then deselect the text.

**16** Save **2-FCTOslo**.

Check Your Work  Compare your work to the model answer available in the online course.

## In Addition

**Aligning Text with Keyboard Shortcuts**
Align text with the following keyboard shortcuts:

| Alignment | Keyboard Shortcut |
|-----------|-------------------|
| Left | Ctrl + L |
| Center | Ctrl + E |
| Right | Ctrl + R |
| Justified | Ctrl + J |

A paragraph of text in a document can be indented. For example, the first line of text in a paragraph can be indented, all lines of text in a paragraph, or the second and subsequent lines of a paragraph (called a *hanging indent*). Several methods are available for indenting text, including buttons in the Paragraph group on the Home tab and the Layout tab, markers on the horizontal ruler, options at the Paragraph dialog box with the Indents and Spacing tab selected, and keyboard shorcuts.

**What You Will Do**  You will improve the appearance of the Oslo document by changing the indent of specific paragraphs of text.

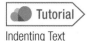

Indenting Text

**1**  With **2-FCTOslo** open, select the three paragraphs of text below the heading *History*.

**2**  Position the mouse pointer on the Left Indent marker on the horizontal ruler, click and hold down the left mouse button, drag the marker to the 0.5-inch mark on the ruler, and then release the mouse button.

> If the horizontal ruler is not visible, click the View tab and then click the *Ruler* check box in the Show group to insert a check mark. The ruler indent markers are shown in Figure 2.1. To precisely position a marker on the ruler, press and hold down the Alt key while dragging the marker.

**3**  Position the mouse pointer on the First Line Indent marker on the horizontal ruler, click and hold down the left mouse button, drag the marker to the 1-inch mark on the ruler, and then release the mouse button.

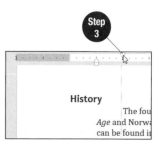

**4**  Position the mouse pointer on the Right Indent marker on the ruler, click and hold down the left mouse button, drag the marker to the 6-inch mark on the ruler, and then release the mouse button.

**5**  Click in the paragraph below the heading *Population* and then click the Layout tab.

**6**  In the *Indent* section of the Paragraph group, click in the *Left* measurement box and then type 0.5.

**7**  Click the *Right* measurement box up arrow until *0.5"* displays.

**8** Click in the paragraph below the heading *Commerce and Industry*.

**9** Click the Paragraph group dialog box launcher.

**10** At the Paragraph dialog box, select the number in the *Left* measurement box in the *Indentation* section and then type 0.5. Select the number in the *Right* measurement box in the *Indentation* section and then type 0.5.

**11** Click OK to close the Paragraph dialog box.

**12** Click in the paragraph below the heading *Climate* and then press F4.

**13** Click in the paragraph below the heading *Holiday, Sport, and Leisure* and then press F4.

**14** Select the text below the heading *Sightseeing Tours* except the right-aligned text and then press F4.

**15** Select the three paragraphs below the heading *History* and then click the Paragraph group dialog box launcher.

**16** At the Paragraph dialog box, click the *Special* option box arrow in the *Indentation* section and then click *Hanging* at the drop-down list.

**17** Click OK to close the Paragraph dialog box.

**18** Save **2-FCTOslo**.

**Figure 2.1** Ruler Indent Markers

First Line Indent    Left Indent    Hanging Indent    Right Indent

**Check Your Work** Compare your work to the model answer available in the online course.

## In Addition

### Indenting Text with Keyboard Shortcuts
Indent text with the following keyboard shortcuts:

| Indentation | Keyboard Shortcut |
| --- | --- |
| Indent text from left margin | Ctrl + M |
| Decrease indent from left margin | Ctrl + Shift + M |
| Create a hanging indent | Ctrl + T |
| Remove hanging indent | Ctrl + Shift + T |

# Activity 2.5 Changing Line and Paragraph Spacing

By default, line spacing is set at 1.08. This default line spacing can be changed with the Line and Paragraph Spacing button in the Paragraph group on the Home tab, keyboard short-cuts, or with the *Line spacing* and *At* options at the Paragraph dialog box. Control spacing above and below paragraphs with options at the Line and Paragraph Spacing button drop-down gallery, the *Before* and *After* measurement boxes in the *Spacing* section in the Paragraph group on the Layout tab, or with the *Before* and *After* measurement boxes in the *Spacing* section of the Paragraph dialog box with the Indents and Spacing tab selected.

**What You Will Do**   The Oslo document project deadline is soon. However, you have time to make a few spacing changes in the document before printing the final version.

Changing Line Spacing

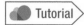
Changing Spacing Before and After Paragraphs

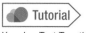
Keeping Text Together

1. With **2-FCTOslo** open, select the entire document by pressing Ctrl + A.

2. Click the Line and Paragraph Spacing button in the Paragraph group on the Home tab and then click *1.5* at the drop-down gallery.

3. Deselect the text and then scroll through the document.

4. After viewing the document with 1.5 line spacing, you decide to decrease the line spacing to 1.2 (which is not an option available at the Line and Paragraph Spacing button drop-down gallery). To begin, press Ctrl + A to select the entire document.

5. Click the Line and Paragraph Spacing button and then click *Line Spacing Options* at the drop-down gallery.

> You can also display the Paragraph dialog box by clicking the Paragraph group dialog box launcher.

6. Type *1.2* in the *At* measurement box in the *Spacing* section of the Paragraph dialog box.

> The Paragraph dialog box also contains a *Line spacing* option box. Click the *Line spacing* option box arrow to display a drop-down list with spacing choices.

7. Click OK to close the dialog box and then deselect the text.

8. Select the line of text beginning *Tour 1: Mini Cruise* through *Tour 4: Selected Oslo Sightseeing* and the two lines that follow.

9. Click the Line and Paragraph Spacing button and then click *1.0* at the drop-down list.

> Choosing this option changes the line spacing to single for the selected paragraphs of text. Line spacing can also be changed with keyboard shortcuts. Press Ctrl + 1 to change to single spacing, Ctrl + 2 to change to double spacing, and Ctrl + 5 to change to 1.5 line spacing.

10. Click in the last sentence (the sentence that begins ALL TOURS BY BOAT).

11. Click the Line and Paragraph Spacing button and then click *Add Space Before Paragraph*.

> This inserts 12 points of space above the sentence.

**12** Press Ctrl + Home to move the insertion point to the beginning of the document, click in the heading *History*, and then click the Paragraph group dialog box launcher.

**13** At the Paragraph dialog box, click the *After* measurement box up arrow.

> Clicking the up arrow changes the measurement to 6 points.

**14** Click OK to close the dialog box.

**15** Click in the heading *Population*, click the Layout tab, and then click the *After* measurement box up arrow in the *Spacing* section of the Paragraph group.

> Clicking the up arrow changes the measurement to 6 points.

**16** Click in the heading *Commerce and Industry* and then press F4.

> Pressing F4 repeats the paragraph spacing command.

**17** Click in each of the remaining headings (*Climate*; *Holiday, Sport, and Leisure*; and *Sightseeing Tours*) and then press F4 after each click.

**18** You decide that you want to remove the hanging indent from the paragraphs in the *History* section. To do this, select the three paragraphs of text below the heading *History* and then press Ctrl + Shift + T.

> Ctrl + Shift + T is the keyboard shortcut to remove hanging indent formatting.

**19** Scroll down the page and notice that the heading *Climate* displays at the bottom of the first page while the paragraph that follows the heading displays at the top of the second page. You want to keep the heading with the paragraph of text. Begin by clicking in the heading *Climate* and then clicking the Paragraph group dialog box launcher.

**20** At the Paragraph dialog box, click the Line and Page Breaks tab and then click the *Keep with next* check box to insert a check mark.

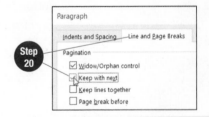

**21** Click OK to close the Paragraph dialog box.

**22** Save **2-FCTOslo**.

**Check Your Work** Compare your work to the model answer available in the online course.

---

## In Addition

### Changing Spacing Above or Below Paragraphs

Spacing above or below paragraphs is added in points. For example, to add 9 points of spacing below selected paragraphs, click the Layout tab or display the Paragraph dialog box with the Indents and Spacing tab selected. Select the current measurement in the *After* measurement box and then type 9. The up or down arrows can be clicked to increase or decrease the amount of spacing before or after paragraphs.

Use options at the Find and Replace dialog box with the Replace tab selected to search for specific formatting or characters containing specific formatting and replace it with other formatting or characters. Click the More button to expand the options in the Find and Replace dialog box. Use the Format button at the expanded dialog box to specify the type of formatting to find and also the type of replacement formatting.

**What You Will Do**   After reviewing the Oslo document, you decide that the headings would look better set in a different font and font color. You decide to use the Find and Replace dialog box to find text with specific formatting applied and replace the text with different formatting.

Finding and Replacing Formatting

**1** With **2-FCTOslo** open, press Ctrl + Home to move the insertion point to the beginning of the document.

**2** The headings in the document are set in 14-point Candara bold and dark blue color. You decide to replace that formatting with 14-point Arial bold italic and orange color. To begin, click the Replace button in the Editing group on the Home tab.

**3** At the Find and Replace dialog box, press the Delete key. (This deletes any text in the *Find what* text box.)

**4** Click the More button. (If a check mark displays in the *Find all word forms* check box, click the check box to remove the check mark.)

**5** Click the Format button at the bottom of the dialog box and then click *Font* at the drop-down list.

**6** At the Find Font dialog box, click *Candara* in the *Font* list box, click *Bold* in the *Font style* list box, click *14* in the *Size* list box, click the *Font color* option box arrow, and then click *Dark Blue* in the *Standard Colors* section.

**7** Click OK to close the dialog box.

**8** At the Find and Replace dialog box, select and then delete any text in the *Replace with* text box.

**9** With the insertion point in the *Replace with* text box, click the Format button at the bottom of the dialog box and then click *Font* at the drop-down list.

**10** At the Replace Font dialog box, click *Arial* in the *Font* list box, click *Bold Italic* in the *Font style* list box, click *14* in the *Size* list box, click the *Font color* option box arrow, and then click *Orange, Accent 2, Darker 50%* (sixth column, bottom row in the *Theme Colors* section).

Step 10

**11** Click OK to close the dialog box.

**12** At the Find and Replace dialog box, click the Replace All button.

**13** At the message stating that the search of the document is complete and six replacements were made, click OK.

**14** With the Find and Replace dialog box open and the insertion point positioned in the *Find what* text box, click the No Formatting button at the bottom of the dialog box.

**15** Click in the *Replace with* text box and then click the No Formatting button.

**16** Click the Less button to reduce the size of the Find and Replace dialog box and then close the dialog box.

**17** Save, print, and then close **2-FCTOslo**.

☁ **Check Your Work**  Compare your work to the model answer available in the online course.

---

## In Addition

### Revealing Formatting

Display formatting applied to specific text in a document at the Reveal Formatting task pane. The task pane displays font, paragraph, and section formatting applied to text where the insertion point is positioned or to selected text. Press Shift + F1 to display the Reveal Formatting task pane. Generally, a collapse arrow (black, down-pointing triangle) precedes *Font* and *Paragraph* in the task pane and an expand arrow (white, right-pointing triangle) precedes *Section* in the *Formatting of selected text* section. Click the collapse arrow to hide any items below a heading and click the expand arrow to reveal items. Some items in the Reveal Formatting task pane are hyperlinks. For example, click the FONT hyperlink to display the Font dialog box. Use these hyperlinks to make changes to the document formatting.

### Comparing Formatting

Along with displaying formatting applied to text, the Reveal Formatting task pane can be used to compare formatting of two text selections to determine how they are different. To compare formatting, display the Reveal Formatting task pane and then select the first instance of formatting to be compared. Click the *Compare to another selection* check box to insert a check mark and then select the second instance of formatting to compare. Any differences between the two selections will display in the *Formatting differences* list box.

# Activity 2.7 Creating Bulleted and Numbered Lists

To draw the reader's attention to a list of items, consider inserting a bullet before each item using the Bullets button in the Paragraph group on the Home tab. If the list of items is in a sequence, consider inserting numbers before each item with the Numbering button in the Paragraph group. Create multiple-level bulleted or numbered lists with options at the Multilevel List button drop-down list in the Paragraph group.

**What You Will Do** First Choice Travel has created a new document on traveling in Europe by train. After reviewing the document, you decide to insert numbers and bullets before selected paragraphs to make the information easier to read.

Creating Numbered Lists

Creating Bulleted Lists

Creating Custom Bullets

Applying Multilevel List Formatting

**1** Open **FCTRailTravel** and then save it with the name **2-FCTRailTravel**.

**2** Select text from the paragraph *Have your pass validated.* through the paragraph *Be at the right train station.* and then click the Numbering button in the Paragraph group on the Home tab.

**3** Position the insertion point at the end of the second numbered paragraph (the paragraph that displays as *2. Protect your pass.*) and then press the Enter key.

> Pressing the Enter key automatically inserts the number *3.* and renumbers the third paragraph to *4.*

**4** Type Arrive 20 minutes before train departure time.

> Numbering before paragraphs changes automatically when paragraphs of text are inserted and/or deleted.

**5** Select text from the paragraph that begins *Free or discount transportation* through the paragraph that begins *Reduced rental rates with* and then click the Bullets button in the Paragraph group.

> Clicking the Bullets button inserts a solid, round bullet before each paragraph. Other bullet options are available by clicking the Bullets button arrow.

**6** With the text still selected, replace the round bullet with a custom bullet. To begin, click the Bullets button arrow and then click *Define New Bullet* at the drop-down gallery.

**7** At the Define New Bullet dialog box, click the Symbol button in the *Bullet character* section.

**8** At the Symbol dialog box, click the *Font* option box arrow, type w, and then click *Webdings*.

**9** Scroll to the end of the symbol list and then click the Earth symbol in the bottom row (as shown at the right).

> Each symbol has a character code. If you know the code, enter it in the *Character code* text box in the dialog box.

**10** Click OK to close the Symbol dialog box.

**11** Click OK to close the Define New Bullet dialog box.

**12** Select the text from *Rail Passes* through *Greece-Italy*.

**13** Apply multiple-level numbering by clicking the Multilevel List button in the Paragraph group and then clicking the middle option in the top row of the *List Library* section.

**14** With the text still selected, change to bullets instead of numbers by clicking the Multilevel List button and then clicking the first option from the left in the middle row of the *List Library* section.

**15** Deselect the text.

**16** Save **2-FCTRailTravel**.

**Check Your Work**   Compare your work to the model answer available in the online course.

## In Addition

### Creating Numbered and/or Bulleted Text

Type *1.* and then press the spacebar and Word indents the number approximately 0.25 inch and then hang indents the text in the paragraph approximately 0.5 inch from the left margin. Press the Enter key after typing text and *2.* is inserted 0.25 inch from the left margin at the beginning of the next paragraph. Continue typing items and Word will continue numbering them. Press the Enter key two times to turn off numbering or click the Numbering button in the Paragraph group. Bulleted lists with hanging indents are automatically created when a paragraph begins with the symbol *, > , or -. Type one of the symbols, press the spacebar, and the symbol bullet is inserted in the document. The type of bullet inserted depends on the type of character entered. For example, type the asterisk (*) symbol and a round bullet is inserted.

### Turning Off Automatic Numbering and/or Bulleting

Automatic numbering or bulleting can be turned off in a document. Turn off the features at the AutoCorrect dialog box with the AutoFormat As You Type tab selected. To display this dialog box, click the File tab and then click *Options*. At the Word Options dialog box, click the *Proofing* option and then click the AutoCorrect Options button. At the AutoCorrect dialog box, click the AutoFormat As You Type tab. Click the *Automatic numbered lists* check box and/or *Automatic bulleted lists* check box to remove the check mark(s).

Insert special symbols such as é, ö, and Å with options at the Symbol palette or the Symbol dialog box. Display the Symbol palette by clicking the Insert tab and then clicking the Symbol button in the Symbols group. Click a symbol to insert it in the document. To display additional symbols, display the Symbol dialog box by clicking a Symbol button and then clicking the *More Symbols* option. Click a symbol at the dialog box, click the Insert button, and then click the Close button. At the Symbol dialog box with the Symbols tab selected, change the font to display different symbols. The Symbol dialog box contains a *Character code* text box. Each symbol has a character code that can be entered in the text box to select a specific symbol. Click the Special Characters tab to display a list of special characters and the keyboard shortcuts to insert them.

**What You Will Do**   You have identified a few city names in the train travel document that need special letters in their spellings, as well as a special character you need to insert in the document.

Inserting Symbols

Inserting Special Characters

**1** With **2-FCTRailTravel** open, move the insertion point to the end of the document and then select and delete the multiple-level bulleted text.

**2** With the insertion point positioned at the end of the document a double space below the bulleted text, type the text shown in Figure 2.2 up to the Å in Århus.

**3** Display the Symbol dialog by clicking the Insert tab, clicking the Symbol button Ω in the Symbols group, and then clicking the *More Symbols* option.

**4** At the Symbol dialog box with the Symbols tab selected, click the *Font* option box arrow and then click *(normal text)* at the drop-down list. You may need to scroll up to see this option. Skip this step if *(normal text)* is already selected.

**5** Scroll down the list box to somewhere between the seventh and ninth rows and then click the Å symbol.

**6** Click the Insert button and then click the Close button.

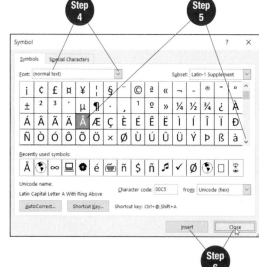

**Figure 2.2** Steps 2–16

> Some companies offer outstanding reductions on transportation. For example, you can travel on the ferry in Denmark between Århus and Kalundborg and between Nyborg and Korsør at a 75% discount! ScanTravel, a travel company in Stockholm, offers the StarPass® ticket that provides you with incredible discounts on travel by train, ferry, and bus in Sweden, Norway, and Denmark.

## In Brief

**Insert Symbol**
1. Click Insert tab.
2. Click Symbol button.
3. Click *More Symbols*.
4. Click symbol.
5. Click Insert button.
6. Click Close button.

**Insert Special Character**
1. Click Insert tab.
2. Click Symbol button.
3. Click *More Symbols*.
4. Click Special Characters tab.
5. Click character.
6. Click Insert button.
7. Click Close button.

7 Continue typing the text in Figure 2.2 up to the ø symbol. To insert the ø symbol, click the Symbol button and then click *More Symbols*.

8 At the Symbol dialog box, make sure (*normal text*) displays in the *Font* option box, select the current number in the *Character code* text box, and then type 00F8.

9 Click the Insert button and then click the Close button.

10 Continue typing the text up to the ® character.

11 To insert the ® character, click the Symbol button and then click *More Symbols*.

12 At the Symbol dialog box, click the Special Characters tab.

13 Click the ® character in the list box.

14 Click the Insert button.

15 Click the Close button.

16 Type the remaining text in Figure 2.2. Press the Enter key two times when you are finished typing.

17 Save **2-FCTRailTravel**.

Step 12

Step 8

Step 9

Step 13

Step 14

**Check Your Work** Compare your work to the model answer available in the online course.

# In Addition

## Inserting Symbols with Keyboard Shortcuts or Character Codes

Another method for inserting symbols in a document is to use keyboard shortcuts. Click a symbol at the Symbol dialog box and the keyboard shortcut might display at the bottom of the dialog box. For example, click the ø symbol and the keyboard shortcut Ctrl + /,O displays at the bottom of the dialog box. To insert the ø symbol in a document using the keyboard shortcut, press and hold down the Ctrl key and then press the / key. Release the Ctrl key and then press the O key. Not all symbols have a corresponding keyboard shortcut. Each symbol has an identifying character code. Click a symbol at the Symbol dialog box and the symbol code displays in the *Character code* text box. To specifiy a symbol by its character code, type the code in the *Character code* text box in the Symbol dialog box.

## Inserting Symbols Using the Palette

Click the Symbol button in the Symbols group and a drop-down palette displays with symbol choices. The palette displays the most recently used symbols. If the palette contains the necessary symbol, click the symbol to insert it in the document.

# Activity 2.9  Setting Tabs on the Horizontal Ruler

Word offers a variety of default settings, including left tabs set every 0.5 inch. Tabs can be set, moved, and deleted using the horizontal ruler. With a left tab, text aligns at the left edge of the tab. The other types of tabs that can be set on the horizontal ruler are center, right, decimal, and bar. The small button above the vertical ruler is called the Alignment button. Each time the Alignment button is clicked, a different tab or paragraph alignment symbol displays. To set a tab, display the desired tab symbol on the Alignment button and then click the specific position on the horizontal ruler.

**What You Will Do**   You have completed some additional research on train connections in Europe. You will add airport names to the train travel document.

Setting and Modifying Tabs on the Horizontal Ruler

① With **2-FCTRailTravel** open, make sure the insertion point is positioned a double space below the last paragraph of text in the document.

② Type International Airports with Train Connections and then press the Enter key two times.

③ Make sure the left tab symbol ⌊L⌋ displays in the Alignment button above the vertical ruler. (If the left tab symbol does not display in the Alignment button, click the button until it does.)

> If tabs display on the horizontal ruler, clear the tabs by clicking the Clear All Formatting button ⌊A₀⌋ in the Font group on the Home tab.

④ Position the mouse pointer at the 1-inch mark on the horizontal ruler and then click the left mouse button.

⑤ Click the Alignment button to display the center tab symbol ⌊⊥⌋.

⑥ Position the mouse pointer at the 3.25-inch mark on the horizontal ruler and then click the left mouse button.

⑦ Click the Alignment button to display the right tab symbol ⌊⌟⌋.

⑧ Position the mouse pointer at the 5.5-inch mark on the horizontal ruler and then click the left mouse button.

**In Brief**

**Set Tab on Horizontal Ruler**
1. Display alignment symbol in Alignment button.
2. Click position on horizontal ruler.

**9** Type the text shown in Figure 2.3, pressing the Tab key before typing each tabbed entry. Make sure you press the Tab key before typing the entry in the first column and that you apply bold formatting to the text in the first row.

> If your columns of text do not look similar to those in Figure 2.3, check to make sure you inserted the tab symbols at the correct locations on the horizontal ruler and that you pressed the Tab key before typing each entry in the first column.

**10** After typing the last entry in the third column (*Fiumicino*), press the Enter key two times and then click the Clear All Formatting button in the Font group on the Home tab.

> Clicking the Clear All Formatting button removes paragraph and character formatting. You can also remove paragraph formatting by pressing the keyboard shortcut Ctrl + Q and remove character formatting by pressing the keyboard shortcut Ctrl + spacebar.

**11** Save **2-FCTRailTravel**.

**Figure 2.3** Step 9

| Country | City | Airport |
|---|---|---|
| Austria | Vienna (Wein) | Schwechat |
| Belgium | Brussels | Nationaal |
| France | Paris | Orly |
| Germany | Berlin | Schoenefeld |
| Great Britain | London | Heathrow |
| Italy | Rome | Fiumicino |

**Check Your Work** Compare your work to the model answer available in the online course.

## In Addition

### Moving a Tab
Move a tab on the horizontal ruler by positioning the mouse pointer on the tab symbol on the horizontal ruler, clicking and holding down the left mouse button, dragging the tab symbol to the new location on the ruler, and then releasing the mouse button.

### Deleting a Tab
Delete a tab from the horizontal ruler by positioning the mouse pointer on the tab symbol, clicking and holding down the left mouse button, dragging the tab symbol into the document screen, and then releasing the mouse button.

### Setting a Decimal Tab
Set a decimal tab for column entries to be aligned at the decimal point. To set a decimal tab, click the Alignment button above the vertical ruler until the decimal tab symbol ⊥ displays and then click the position on the horizontal ruler.

Left, right, center, and decimal tabs can be set with leaders. Leaders are useful for directing the reader's eyes across the page. Leaders can be periods, hyphens, or underlines. Set tabs with leaders using options at the Tabs dialog box. To display the Tabs dialog box, click the Paragraph group dialog box launcher and then click the Tabs button at the Paragraph dialog box. At the Tabs dialog box, enter a tab position measurement, choose the type of tab, and then choose the type of leader.

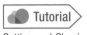

**FIRST CHOICE TRAVEL**

**What You Will Do**   The information you found listing airports with train connections also includes schedule times. You will add this data to the train travel document.

**Tutorial**

Setting and Clearing Tabs at the Tabs Dialog Box

① With **2-FCTRailTravel** open, move the insertion point to the end of the document.

② Click the Alignment button above the vertical ruler until the left tab symbol displays.

③ Position the mouse pointer at the 1-inch mark on the horizontal ruler and then click the left mouse button.

④ Click the Alignment button above the vertical ruler until the right tab symbol displays.

⑤ Position the mouse pointer at the 5.5-inch mark on the horizontal ruler and then click the left mouse button.

⑥ Type the headings shown in Figure 2.4 by pressing the Tab key, clicking the Bold button in the Font group, and then typing Airport.

⑦ Press the Tab key and then type Service.

⑧ Press the Enter key and then click the Clear All Formatting button to remove the bold formatting and the paragraph tab formatting.

⑨ Set a left tab and a right tab with leaders at the Tabs dialog box. To begin, click the Paragraph group dialog box launcher and then click the Tabs button in the lower left corner of the Paragraph dialog box.

> You can also display the Tabs dialog box by double-clicking any tab symbol on the horizontal ruler.

⑩ At the Tabs dialog box with the insertion point positioned in the *Tab stop position* text box, type 1. If necessary, select the *Left* option in the *Alignment* section of the dialog box and then click the Set button.

**Figure 2.4** Step 6, Step 7, and Step 14

| Airport | Service |
|---|---|
| Schwechat ......................................... | Train every 30 minutes |
| Nationaal ........................................... | Train every 20 minutes |
| Orly ................................................. | RER train every 20 minutes |
| Schoenefeld .......................... | S-Bahn train every 30 minutes |
| Heathrow ...................................... | LT train every 10 minutes |
| Fiumicino ................................... | Train every 10 to 20 minutes |

11 Type 5.5 in the *Tab stop position* text box, click the *Right* option in the *Alignment* section of the dialog box, and then click the *2.....* option in the *Leader* section of the dialog box.

12 Click the Set button.

13 Click OK to close the dialog box.

14 Type the remaining text shown in Figure 2.4, making sure you press the Tab key before typing the text in each column.

> If your columns of text do not look similar to those in Figure 2.4, check to make sure you inserted the tab symbols at the correct measurements and that you pressed the Tab key before typing each entry.

15 Press Ctrl + Home to move the insertion point to the beginning of the document.

16 Select the four numbered paragraphs.

17 With the paragraphs selected, click the Bullets button arrow in the Paragraph group and then click the Earth bullet in the *Bullet Library* section. (The Earth bullet is the bullet you selected in Activity 2.7.) If this bullet is not available at the drop-down list, complete steps similar to those in Activity 2.7, Steps 6 through 11, to select and apply the Earth bullet.

18 Save **2-FCTRailTravel**.

 **Check Your Work** Compare your work to the model answer available in the online course.

## In Addition

### Clearing Tabs at the Tabs Dialog Box

At the Tabs dialog box, an individual tab or all tabs can be cleared. To clear all tabs, click the Clear All button.

To clear an individual tab, specify the tab position and then click the Clear button.

# Activity 2.11 Applying Borders and Shading

Insert a border around text and apply shading to text in a paragraph or selected text with the Borders button and the Shading button in the Paragraph group on the Home tab or at the Borders and Shading dialog box. At the Borders and Shading dialog box with the Borders tab selected, specify the border type, style, color, and width. Click the Shading tab and the dialog box displays options for choosing a fill color and pattern style. Click the Page Border tab and the dialog box displays options for applying a page border. The Borders and Shading dialog box with the Page Border tab selected can also be displayed by clicking the Design tab and then clicking the Page Borders button in the Page Background group.

**What You Will Do** To highlight certain information in the First Choice Travel train travel document, you will apply a border to selected text and apply border and shading formatting to the column text. You will also apply a page border to add visual interest.

**Tutorial**
Applying Borders

**Tutorial**
Applying Shading

**Tutorial**
Inserting a Page Border

**1** With **2-FCTRailTravel** open, make sure the first four bulleted paragraphs are selected, click the Borders button arrow ⊞⋁ in the Paragraph group on the Home tab, and then click *Outside Borders* at the drop-down gallery.

**2** Select the second four bulleted paragraphs of text and then click the Borders button in the Paragraph group.

> This applies the outside border since that is the last border option you selected.

**3** Select from the column headings *Country*, *City*, and *Airport* through the line of text containing the column entries *Italy*, *Rome*, and *Fiumicino*.

**4** Click the Borders button arrow and then click *Borders and Shading* at the drop-down gallery.

**5** At the Borders and Shading dialog box with the Borders tab selected, click the *Box* option in the *Setting* section.

**6** Click the *Style* list box arrow until the first double-line option displays and then click the double-line option.

**7** Click the *Color* option box arrow and then click the *Blue, Accent 1, Darker 50%* color option (fifth column, last row in the *Theme Colors* section).

**8** Click the *Width* option box arrow and then click ¾ pt at the drop-down list.

**9** Click the Shading tab, click the *Fill* option box arrow, and then click the *Blue, Accent 1, Lighter 80%* color option (fifth column, second row in the *Theme Colors* section).

**In Brief**

**Apply Borders**
1. Select text.
2. Click Borders button arrow.
3. Click option.
OR
1. Selext text.
2. Click Borders button arrow.
3. Click *Borders and Shading*.
4. Choose border(s).
5. Click OK.

**Apply Shading**
1. Select text.
2. Click Shading button arrow.
3. Click option.
OR
1. Select text.
2. Click Borders button arrow.
3. Click *Borders and Shading*.
4. Click Shading tab.
5. Choose shading and/or pattern.
6. Click OK.

**Insert Page Border**
1. Click Borders button arrow.
2. Click *Borders and Shading*.
3. Click Page Border tab.
4. Choose options.
5. Click OK.
OR
1. Click Design tab.
2. Click Page Borders button.
3. Choose options.
4. Click OK.

**10** Click OK to close the dialog box.

**11** Add the same border and shading to the other columns of text by selecting from the column headings *Airport* and *Service* through the line of text containing the column entries *Fiumicino* and *Train every 10 to 20 minutes* and then pressing F4.

**12** Apply shading to the title by positioning the insertion point in the title *Traveling in Europe by Train*, clicking the Shading button arrow , and then clicking the *Blue, Accent 1, Lighter 60%* color option (fifth column, third row in the *Theme Colors* section).

**13** Insert a page border in the document. To begin, click the Borders button arrow and then click *Borders and Shading* at the drop-down list.

**14** At the Borders and Shading dialog box, click the Page Border tab.

**15** Click the *Shadow* option in the *Setting* section, click the *Width* option box arrow, and then click *3 pt* at the drop-down list.

**16** Click OK to close the dialog box.

**17** Change the page border to an art image. To begin, click the Design tab and then click the Page Borders button in the Page Background group.

**18** At the Borders and Shading dialog box with the Page Border tab selected, click the *Box* option in the *Setting* section.

**19** Click the *Art* option box arrow, scroll down the list until the globe art images display, and then click the first set of globe images as shown at the right.

**20** Select the number in the *Width* measurement box and then type 10.

**21** Click OK to close the dialog box.

**22** Save **2-FCTRailTravel**.

 **Check Your Work** Compare your work to the model answer available in the online course.

## In Addition

### Applying Borders

The Borders and Shading dialog box with the Borders tab or the Page Border tab selected contains a Preview area that can be used to insert borders at specfic locations. Click the sides, top, or bottom of the diagram in the Preview area to insert or remove a border line. Buttons display around the diagram that can also be used to apply borders.

# Activity 2.12  Applying Styles, Style Sets, and Themes

A Word document is based on a template that applies default formatting such as 11-point Calibri font, line spacing of 1.08, and 8 points of spacing after each paragraph. These default formats can be changed with buttons and options on the ribbon and also with styles. A *style* is a set of formatting instructions that can be applied to text. To apply a predesigned style, click the style in the styles gallery in the Styles group on the Home tab. Click the More Styles button at the right of the styles gallery to display a drop-down gallery of additional styles. Word groups styles that apply similar formatting into style sets. Style sets are available in the Document Formatting group on the Design tab. If a different style set is applied to a document, the styles in the Styles group on the Home tab change to reflect the style set. In addition to a style set, formatting can be applied to a document with a theme. A *theme* is a set of formatting choices that includes a color theme (a set of colors), a font theme (a set of heading and body text fonts), and an effects theme (a set of lines and fill effects). Apply a theme with the Themes button in the Document Formatting group on the Design tab. Customize a theme with the Colors, Fonts, and Effects buttons.

**What You Will Do**   To further enhance the train travel document, you decide to apply styles, a different style set, and a theme to the document.

Tutorial
Applying Styles and Style Sets

Tutorial
Applying and Modifying a Theme

1 With **2-FCTRailTravel** open, press Ctrl + Home to move the insertion point to the beginning of the document.

2 Click in the title *Traveling in Europe by Train* and then click the *Heading 1* style in the styles gallery on the Home tab.

> The Heading 1 style in the default style set changes the font size and font color and adds 12 points of spacing above the title. Applying the heading style also removes the shading you inserted in the previous activity.

3 Click in the heading *Rail Ticket Bonuses* and then click the *Heading 2* style in the Styles group.

4 Click in the heading *International Airports with Train Connections* and then click the *Heading 2* style.

5 Apply a different style set by clicking the Design tab, clicking the More Style Sets button at the right of the style sets gallery in the Document Formatting group, and then clicking *Lines (Stylish)*.

6 Apply a paragraph spacing option so the text fits on one page by clicking the Paragraph Spacing button in the Document Formatting group and then clicking *Compact* at the drop-down gallery.

> Display the paragraph and line formatting applied by a paragraph spacing option by hovering the mouse over the option at the drop-down gallery.

## In Brief

**Apply a Style**
1. Position insertion point.
2. Click style or click More Styles button and then click style.

**Apply a Style Set**
1. Click Design tab.
2. Click style set in style sets gallery.

**Apply Paragraph Spacing**
1. Click Design tab.
2. Click Paragraph Spacing button.
3. Click spacing option.

**Apply a Theme**
1. Click Design tab.
2. Click Themes button.
3. Click theme.

**Change Theme Colors**
1. Click Design tab.
2. Click Colors button.
3. Click color option.

**Change Theme Fonts**
1. Click Design tab.
2. Click Fonts button.
3. Click font option.

**7** Apply a theme by clicking the Themes button  in the Document Formatting group and then clicking the *Retrospect* option.

**8** Change the colors applied by the theme by clicking the Colors button in the Document Formatting group and then clicking the *Green* option at the drop-down gallery.

**9** Change the fonts applied by the theme by clicking the Fonts button A in the Document Formatting group and then clicking the *Corbel* option at the drop-down gallery.

**10** Select the title *Traveling in Europe by Train*, change the font size to 24 points, and then change the paragraph alignment to center.

**11** Save, print, and then close **2-FCTRailTravel**.

**Check Your Work** Compare your work to the model answer available in the online course.

# In Addition

## Applying the No Spacing Style

By default, a blank document contains line spacing of 1.08 and 8 points of spacing after paragraphs. The increase in line spacing and spacing after paragraphs creates more space between lines and is designed to make text easier to read on a computer screen. Change the line spacing to 1.0 and remove the spacing after paragraphs by clicking the *No Spacing* style in the Styles group on the Home tab.

## Collapsing and Expanding Headings

When heading styles are applied to text in a document, text below the headings can be collapsed. Collapse headings in a document to view the headings and use the headings to easily navigate to specific locations. Collapse text in a document by clicking the collapse arrow (gray, down-pointing triangle) when the mouse pointer is hovered over text with a heading style applied.

Expand collapsed text below a heading by clicking the expand arrow (white, right-pointing triangle) before a heading with a style applied.

## Applying Styles at the Styles Window

The Styles window provides additional styles. Display this window by clicking the Styles group dialog box launcher. The styles in the currently selected style set display in the window followed by a paragraph symbol (¶), indicating that the style applies paragraph formatting, or a character symbol (a), indicating that the style applies character formatting. If both characters display at the right of a style, the style applies both paragraph and character formatting. In addition to displaying styles that apply formatting, the Styles window also includes a Clear All style that clears all formatting from selected text.

# Features Summary

| Feature | Ribbon Tab, Group | Button/Option Box | Keyboard Shortcut |
|---|---|---|---|
| 1.5 line spacing | Home, Paragraph | | Ctrl + 5 |
| align left | Home, Paragraph | | Ctrl + L |
| align right | Home, Paragraph | | Ctrl + R |
| bold | Home, Font | **B** | Ctrl + B |
| borders | Home, Paragraph | | |
| bullets | Home, Paragraph | | |
| center | Home, Paragraph | | Ctrl + E |
| change case | Home, Font | Aa | Shift + F3 |
| clear all formatting | Home, Font | | |
| clear character formatting | | | Ctrl + spacebar |
| clear paragraph formatting | | | Ctrl + Q |
| decrease font size | Home, Font | A | Ctrl + Shift + < |
| decrease indent | Home, Paragraph | | Ctrl + Shift + M |
| double line spacing | Home, Paragraph | | Ctrl + 2 |
| Find and Replace dialog box with Replace tab selected | Home, Editing | | Ctrl + H |
| font | Home, Font | Calibri (Body) | Ctrl + Shift + F |
| font color | Home, Font | A | |
| Font dialog box | Home, Font | | Ctrl + D |
| font size | Home, Font | 11 | Ctrl + Shift + P |
| Format Painter | Home, Clipboard | | |
| hanging indent | Home, Paragraph | | Ctrl + T |
| highlight | Home, Font | | |
| increase font size | Home, Font | A | Ctrl + Shift + > |
| increase indent | Home, Paragraph | | Ctrl + M |
| insert symbol | Insert, Symbols | Ω | |
| italics | Home, Font | *I* | Ctrl + I |
| justify | Home, Paragraph | | Ctrl + J |

| Feature | Ribbon Tab, Group | Button/Option Box | Keyboard Shortcut |
|---|---|---|---|
| line and paragraph spacing | Home, Paragraph | | |
| multilevel list | Home, Paragraph | | |
| numbering | Home, Paragraph | | |
| page borders | Design, Page Background | | |
| Paragraph dialog box | Home, Paragraph | | |
| repeat a command | | | F4 |
| remove hanging indent | Home, Paragraph | | Ctrl + Shift + T |
| select | Home/Editing | | |
| shading | Home, Paragraph | | |
| single line spacing | Home, Paragraph | | Ctrl + 1 |
| spacing after | Layout, Paragraph | | |
| spacing before | Layout, Paragraph | | |
| styles | Home, Styles | | |
| style sets | Design, Document Formatting | | |
| subscript | Home, Font | $x_2$ | Ctrl + = |
| superscript | Home, Font | $x^2$ | Ctrl + Shift + + |
| Tabs dialog box | Home, Paragraph | , Tabs | |
| text effects and typography | Home, Font | A | |
| theme colors | Design, Document Formatting | | |
| theme fonts | Design, Document Formatting | A | |
| themes | Design, Document Formatting | Aa | |
| underline | Home, Font | U | Ctrl + U |

# Word

# Formatting and Enhancing a Document

 Data Files

Before beginning section work, copy the WordS3 folder to your storage medium and then make WordS3 the active folder.

## Skills

- Cut, copy, and paste text
- Use the Clipboard task pane to copy and paste items
- Change page margins, orientation, and size
- Insert a watermark, page color, and page border
- Insert a cover page, blank page, and page break
- Insert page numbering
- Insert a header and footer

- Format a document in MLA style
- Insert sources and citations
- Create a works cited page
- Edit a source
- Use the Click and Type feature
- Vertically align text
- Insert, size, and move images
- Prepare an envelope and mailing labels

## Projects Overview

Edit and format documents on Thailand and Juneau, Alaska; prepare an announcement about a workshop on traveling on a budget; format a report on the Middleton Valley in MLA style; prepare envelopes and labels for mailing fact sheets and announcements.

Format reports in MLA style; format a costume rental agreement.

Prepare an announcement about a workshop on employment opportunities in the movie industry; add a picture watermark.

Create an announcement for weekend work; prepare labels.

Prepare an announcement about internship positions available at Marquee Productions; prepare labels for the college.

 The online course includes additional training and assessment resources.

# Cutting, Copying, and Pasting Text; Using Paste Options

Use the Cut, Copy, and Paste buttons in the Clipboard group on the Home tab to move and/or copy words, sentences, or entire sections of text to other locations in a document or to another document. Text can be cut and pasted or copied and pasted within the same document or between documents. Specify the formatting of pasted text with the Paste Options button or options at the Paste Special dialog box.

**What You Will Do**   You are working on a First Choice Travel document containing information on Thailand. You decide that some of the text in the document should be reorganized, and you also decide to add additional information to the document.

Cutting, Copying, and Pasting Text

Copying and Pasting Text and Formatting

Using Paste Special

**1** Open **FCTThailand** and then save it with the name **3-FCTThailand**.

**2** Move the *Attractions* section below the *Traveling in Thailand* section. Begin by selecting the heading *Attractions* and the paragraph of text that follows it.

**3** Click the Cut button ✂ in the Clipboard group on the Home tab.

> Clicking the Cut button places the text in a special location within Word called the Clipboard.

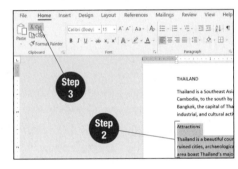

**4** Move the insertion point to the beginning of the heading *Accommodations* and then click the Paste button 📋 in the Clipboard group on the Home tab.

**5** Open **FCTThaiStats**.

> You will copy text from this document and paste it in the Thailand information document.

**6** Select the heading *Points of Interest* and the four lines of text below it and then click the Copy button 📋 in the Clipboard group.

**7** Click the Word button on the taskbar and then click the **3-FCTThailand** thumbnail.

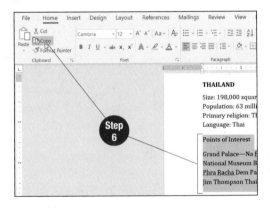

**8** Position the insertion point at the beginning of the heading *Passports/Visas* and then click the Paste button in the Clipboard group.

> A Paste Options button 📋 (Ctrl) ▼ displays below the pasted text. Click this button and a drop-down gallery of buttons displays. Use these buttons to specify the formatting of the pasted text. By default, the Keep Source Formatting button (first button from the left) is selected. With this button selected, text is pasted with the formatting from the source document. You can also click the Merge Formatting button (second button) to merge formatting with the destination formatting, click the Picture button (third button) to insert the text as an image, or click the Keep Text Only button (fourth button) to paste only the text and not the formatting.

**9** Click the Paste Options button and then click the Merge Formatting button (second button) at the Paste Options button drop-down list.

**10** Click the Word button on the taskbar and then click the **FCTThaiStats** thumbnail.

**11** Select the text *Resources:* and the three lines below it and then click the Copy button.

**12** Click the Word button on the taskbar and then click the **3-FCTThailand** thumbnail.

**13** Move the insertion point to the end of the document and then press the Enter key.

**14** Paste the copied text into the document without the formatting by clicking the Paste button arrow and then clicking *Paste Special* at the drop-down list.

**15** At the Paste Special dialog box, click *Unformatted Text* in the *As* list box and then click OK.

**16** Select the four lines of text you just pasted in the document and then remove the spacing after the paragraphs by clicking the Layout tab and then clicking the *After* measurement box down arrow two times.

> Clicking the measurement down arrow two times will change the spacing after the selected paragraphs from 10 points to 0 points.

**17** Save **3-FCTThailand**.

**18** Click the Word button on the taskbar, click the **FCTThaiStats** thumbnail, and then close the document.

> Closing the **FCTThaiStats** document displays the **3-FCTThailand** document.

**Check Your Work** Compare your work to the model answer available in the online course.

## In Addition

### Moving and Copying Text with the Mouse

Selected text can be moved using the mouse. To do this, select the text with the mouse and then move the I-beam pointer inside the selected text until the I-beam pointer turns into a mouse pointer. Click and hold down the left mouse button, drag the mouse pointer (displays with a gray box attached) to the location where the selected text is to be inserted, and then release the button. Copy and move selected text by following similar steps, but press and hold down the Ctrl key while dragging with the mouse. When pressing and holding down the Ctrl key, a box containing a plus symbol displays near the gray box by the mouse pointer.

Using the Clipboard task pane, up to 24 different items can be cut or copied and then pasted in various locations in a document. Display the Clipboard task pane by clicking the Clipboard group task pane launcher. Cut or copy an item and the item displays in the Clipboard task pane. If the item is text, the first 50 characters display. Paste an item by positioning the insertion point at the location where the item it to be pasted and then clicking the item in the Clipboard task pane. Once all items have been inserted, click the Clear All button near the top of the task pane.

**What You Will Do**   You will open another document with information on Thailand, copy items in the document, and then paste the items into the Thailand document.

Using the Clipboard
Task Pane

**1**   Make sure **3-FCTThailand** is open and then open **FCTThaiInfo**.

**2**   In **FCTThaiInfo**, display the Clipboard task pane by clicking the Clipboard group task pane launcher. If any items display in the Clipboard task pane, click the Clear All button near the top of the task pane.

Step 2

**3**   Select the heading *Food and Beverages* and the paragraph of text below it.

**4**   Click the Copy button in the Clipboard group.

> Notice how the copied item is represented in the Clipboard task pane.

**5**   Select the heading *Shopping* and the paragraph of text below it.

**6**   Click the Copy button in the Clipboard group.

**7**   Select the heading *Entertainment* and the paragraph of text below it.

**8**   Click the Copy button in the Clipboard group.

**9**   Click the Word button on the taskbar and then click the **3-FCTThailand** thumbnail.

**10**   Display the Clipboard task pane by clicking the Home tab and then clicking the Clipboard group task pane launcher.

**11**   Move the insertion point to the beginning of the heading *Accommodations*.

**12**   Click the item representing *Entertainment* in the Clipboard task pane.

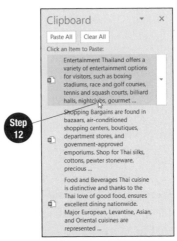

Step 12

### In Brief

#### Use Clipboard Task Pane
1. Click Clipboard group task pane launcher.
2. Select text.
3. Click Copy button.
4. Select and copy any additional items.
5. Position insertion point.
6. Click item in Clipboard task pane.
7. Paste any other items from Clipboard task pane.
8. Click Clear All button.

**13** Move the insertion point to the beginning of the heading *Points of Interest*.

**14** Click the item representing *Shopping* in the Clipboard task pane.

**15** Click the Clear All button in the upper right corner of the Clipboard task pane.

**16** Close the Clipboard task pane by clicking the Close button ☒ in the upper right corner of the task pane.

**17** Click the Word button on the taskbar, click the *FCTThaiInfo* thumbnail, and then close the document.

> The **3-FCTThailand** file displays when you close **FCTThaiInfo**.

**18** Press Ctrl + Home to move the insertion point to the beginning of the document.

**19** Click in the title *THAILAND* and then click the *Title* style in the styles gallery on the Home tab.

**20** Apply the Heading 1 style to the headings in the document (*Transportation*, *Traveling in Thailand*, *Attractions*, *Entertainment*, *Accommodations*, *Shopping*, *Points of Interest*, and *Passports/Visas*).

**21** Click the Design tab and then click the *Casual* style set in the Document Formatting group.

**22** Press Ctrl + Home to move the insertion point to the beginning of the document.

**23** Center the title *THAILAND*.

**24** Save **3-FCTThailand**.

**Check Your Work** Compare your work to the model answer available in the online course.

Step 14

Step 15

Step 16

## In Addition

### Using Clipboard Task Pane Options

Click the Options button at the bottom of the Clipboard task pane and a pop-up list displays with five options as shown at the right. Make an option active by inserting a check mark before the option. For example, the Clipboard task pane can be displayed automatically when text is cut or copied, the Clipboard can be displayed by pressing Ctrl + C two times, text can be cut or copied without displaying the Clipboard task pane, the Office Clipboard icon can be displayed on the taskbar when the Clipboard is active, or a status message can display when copying items to the Clipboard.

# Activity 3.3 Customizing the Page Setup

In Word, a page contains default formatting such as a paper size of 8.5 inches by 11 inches; top, bottom, left, and right margins of one inch; portrait page orientation; and a page break after approximately 9 inches of content on a page. These defaults can be changed with buttons in the Page Setup group on the Layout tab. Change the default margins in a document with the Margins button. Use the Orientation button to change the orientation from the default of portrait to landscape. Use the Size button in the Page Setup group to specify a paper size.

FIRST CHOICE
**TRAVEL**

**What You Will Do**   To customize the Thailand document, you will change the document margins, orientation, and paper size and apply a theme.

Tutorial

Changing Margins

Tutorial

Changing Page
Orientation

Tutorial

Changing Paper Size

**1** With **3-FCTThailand** open, change the margins by clicking the Layout tab, clicking the Margins button 🔲 in the Page Setup group, and then clicking the *Wide* option at the drop-down list.

> The *Wide* option changes the left and right margins to 2 inches each.

**2** Change the page orientation by clicking the Orientation button 🔲 in the Page Setup group on the Layout tab and then clicking *Landscape* at the drop-down list.

> Word considers a page in portrait orientation to be 8.5 inches wide and 11 inches tall. Word considers a page in landscape orientation to be 11 inches wide and 8.5 inches tall. You can also change page orientation at the Page Setup dialog box with the Margins tab selected.

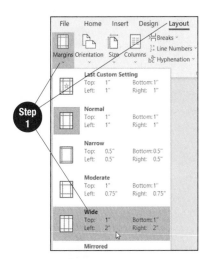

**3** Change the margins again by clicking the Margins button in the Page Setup group on the Layout tab and then clicking the *Custom Margins* option at the bottom of the drop-down list. (Make sure you click the *Custom Margins* option at the very bottom of the drop-down list.)

**4** At the Page Setup dialog box with the Margins tab selected, type 0.8 in the *Top* measurement box.

**5** Click the *Bottom* measurement box down arrow until *0.8"* displays.

**6** Click OK to close the Page Setup dialog box.

**In Brief**

**Change Margins**
1. Click Layout tab.
2. Click Margins button.
3. Click margins option.

**Change Orientation**
1. Click Layout tab.
2. Click Orientation button.
3. Click orientation option.

**Change Paper Size**
1. Click Layout tab.
2. Click Size button.
3. Click size option.

**7** Change the paper size by clicking the Size button in the Page Setup group and then clicking the *Legal* option at the drop-down list.

**8** Scroll through the document to view the pages in legal paper size.

**9** Change back to letter paper size by clicking the Size button and then clicking the *Letter* option at the drop-down list.

**10** Save **3-FCTThailand**. *Optional: Your instructor may want you to print the document at this point*.

**11** Change the page orientation by clicking the Orientation button in the Page Setup group and then clicking *Portrait* at the drop-down list.

**12** Change the margins by clicking the Margins button in the Page Setup group and then clicking *Normal* at the drop-down list.

**13** Apply a theme to the document by clicking the Design tab, clicking the Themes button in the Document Formatting group, and then clicking *Integral* at the drop-down gallery.

**14** Change the theme colors by clicking the Colors button in the Document Formatting group and then clicking *Red Orange* at the drop-down gallery.

**15** Save **3-FCTThailand**.

Check Your Work Compare your work to the model answer available in the online course.

## In Addition

### Applying Landscape Orientation

Imagine some instances in which a document might be formatted in landscape orientation. For example, a company's annual report might include a couple of tables that have several columns of text. In the default portrait orientation, the columns will need to be quite narrow, possibly so narrow that reading becomes difficult. Changing the orientation to landscape results in three more inches of usable space. Portrait and landscape orientation can be used in the same document. To do this, select the text, display the Page Setup dialog box, click the orientation, and then change the *Apply to* option to *Selected text*.

The Page Background group on the Design tab contains buttons for inserting a watermark, changing the page background color, and inserting a page border. A watermark is lightened text or an image that displays behind text. Word provides a number of predesigned watermark images that can be inserted in a document. Apply a page background color using the Page Color button. Page background color appears on the screen but does not print. The Page Borders button in the Page Background group provides another method for displaying the Borders and Shading dialog box with the Page Border tab selected.

**What You Will Do**   To make sure others know that the Thailand document is still in progress, you will insert a watermark. To add visual interest to the document, you will apply a page background color and a page border.

Inserting and
Removing a
Watermark

Applying Page
Background Color

**1** With **3-FCTThailand** open, press Ctrl + Home.

**2** Insert a watermark by clicking the Design tab and then clicking the Watermark button in the Page Background group.

**3** Scroll down the Watermark button drop-down list and then click the *DRAFT 1* option.

**4** Apply a page background color to the document by clicking the Page Color button in the Page Background group.

**5** Click the *Gold, Accent 5, Lighter 80%* option (ninth column, second row in the *Theme Colors* section).

> Page background color is designed for viewing a document on the screen and does not print.

**6** Click the Page Borders button in the Page Background group.

**7** At the Borders and Shading dialog box with the Page Border tab selected, click the *Art* option box arrow.

**8** Scroll down the list of page borders and then click the art border option shown below.

**In Brief**

**Apply Watermark**
1. Click Design tab.
2. Click Watermark button.
3. Click watermark option.

**Apply Page Background Color**
1. Click Design tab.
2. Click Page Color button.
3. Click color option.

**Apply Page Border**
1. Click Design tab.
2. Click Page Borders button.
3. Click options at Borders and Shading dialog box.
4. Click OK.

**9** Click OK to close the dialog box.

**10** Save **3-FCTThailand**.

**11** Print **3-FCTThailand**.

**12** Remove the page border by clicking the Design tab and then clicking the Page Borders button.

**13** At the Borders and Shading dialog box, click *None* in the *Setting* section.

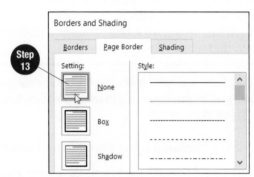

**14** Click OK to close the dialog box.

**15** Remove page background color by clicking the Page Color button in the Page Background group and then clicking *No Color*.

**16** Save **3-FCTThailand**.

**Check Your Work**  Compare your work to the model answer available in the online course.

---

## In Addition

### Changing Page Border Options

By default, a page border displays and prints 24 points from the top, left, right, and bottom edges of the page. Some printers, particularly inkjet printers, have a non-printing area around the outside edges of the page that can interfere with the printing of a border. If part of a page border does not print, consider changing measurements at the Border and Shading Options dialog box. Display this dialog box by clicking the Design tab and then clicking the Page Borders button. At the Borders and Shading dialog box with the Page Border tab selected, click the Options button. At the dialog box, increase the margin measurements to move the page border away from the edges of the page and decrease the measurements to move the page border closer to the edges of the page.

# Inserting a Cover Page, Blank Page, and Page Break

The Pages group on the Insert tab contains buttons for adding a cover page, a blank page, and a page break. Click the Cover Page button and a drop-down list displays with prede-signed cover pages. A cover page might include placeholders, which are locations where specific text is inserted. Insert a page break in a document with the keyboard shortcut Ctrl + Enter or with the Page Break button on the Insert tab. Use the Blank Page button to insert a blank page, which might be useful in a document where a blank page is needed for an illustration, graphic, or figure.

**What You Will Do**   You will insert the Motion cover page in the Thailand document and insert specific text in the cover page placeholders. You will also insert a page break and a blank page in the document.

Inserting and Removing a Cover Page

Inserting and Removing a Blank Page

Inserting and Removing a Page Break

**1** With **3-FCTThailand** open, press Ctrl + Home.

**2** Click the Insert tab and then click the Cover Page button 📄 in the Pages group.

**3** Insert a predesigned cover page by scrolling down the drop-down list and then clicking the *Motion* option.

**4** Click the *[Year]* placeholder text and then type the current year.

**5** Click the *[Document title]* placeholder text and then type Discover Thailand.

**6** Click the *[Company name]* placeholder text and then type First Choice Travel. (If a company name already displays above the date in the bottom right corner, click the company name, click the Company tab, and then type First Choice Travel).

**7** Select the name above *First Choice Travel* and then type your first and last names.

**8** Insert the current date below *First Choice Travel* by clicking the date, clicking the arrow at the right of the placeholder, and then clicking *Today*.

**9** You need a blank page at the end of the document for information that will be added later. Press Ctrl + End to move the insertion point to the end of the document.

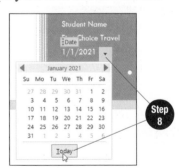

**10** Click the Blank Page button  in the Pages group.

**11** Move the insertion point to the beginning of the heading *Entertainment*.

**12** Insert a page break by clicking the Page Break button in the Pages group.

> You can also insert a hard page break with the keyboard shortcut Ctrl + Enter.

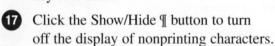

**13** Save **3-FCTThailand** and then print only pages 1 and 2.

**14** Delete the page break you inserted in Step 12 by positioning the insertion point at the end of the paragraph of text below the heading *Attractions* and then pressing the Delete key two times.

**15** Remove the blank page. Begin by clicking the Home tab and then clicking the Show/Hide ¶ button ¶ in the Paragraph group.

> Clicking the Show/Hide ¶ button on the Home tab turns on nonprinting characters such as a paragraph symbol to indicate the press of the Enter key and a small dot to indicate the press of the spacebar.

**16** Position the insertion point at the beginning of the page break on the third page and then press the Delete key two times.

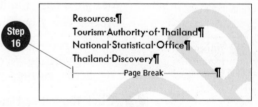

**17** Click the Show/Hide ¶ button to turn off the display of nonprinting characters.

**18** Save **3-FCTThailand**.

**Check Your Work** Compare your work to the model answer available in the online course.

## In Addition

### Inserting Page Breaks

By default, a Word document is 8.5 inches wide and 11 inches long, which is the standard letter size. With default top and bottom margins of 1 inch, a Word document can contain approximately 9 inches of content per page. At approximately the 10-inch mark, Word automatically inserts a page break. A page break inserted by Word is considered a *soft page break* and a page break inserted by the user with the Page Break button or the keyboard shortcut, Ctrl + Enter, is considered a *hard page break*. A soft page break adjusts automatically as text is added or deleted from a document. A hard page break does not adjust and therefore will remain in the place it was originally inserted.

Insert page numbers in a document with the Page Number button. Click the Page Number button in the Header & Footer group on the Insert tab and a drop-down list displays with options for inserting page numbers at the top or bottom of the page or in the page margins, removing page numbers, and formatting page numbers. Text that appears at the top of every page is called a *header* and text that appears at the bottom of every page is referred to as a *footer*. Headers and footers are common in manuscripts, textbooks, reports, and other publications. Insert a predesigned header in a document with the Header button in the Header & Footer group on the Insert tab. Insert a predesigned footer in the same manner as a header. Predesigned headers and footers contain formatting that can be customized.

**What You Will Do** You will insert identifying information in the Thailand document using a header and footer and insert page numbers.

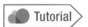

Inserting and Removing Page Numbers

Inserting and Removing a Predesigned Header and Footer

Creating a Custom Header and Footer

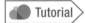

Editing a Header and Footer

**1** With **3-FCTThailand** open, move the insertion point to the beginning of the title *THAILAND* (on the second page).

**2** Click the Insert tab.

**3** Insert page numbers at the bottom of each page by clicking the Page Number button in the Header & Footer group and then pointing to *Bottom of Page*.

**4** At the drop-down list of pre-designed page numbers, click the *Accent Bar 1* option.

> The page number is inserted in the Footer pane. With the Footer pane active, the document is dimmed.

**5** Click the Close Header and Footer button to close the Footer pane and make the document active.

**6** Scroll through the document and notice how the page numbers display at the bottom of every page except the cover page.

**7** Remove page numbering by clicking the Insert tab, clicking the Page Number button in the Header & Footer group, and then clicking *Remove Page Numbers* at the drop-down list.

**8** Insert a header in the document by clicking the Header button in the Header & Footer group, scrolling down the drop-down list, and then clicking the *Facet (Odd Page)* header.

**Insert Page Numbers**
1. Click Insert tab.
2. Click Page Number button.
3. Point to location.
4. Click option at drop-down list.

**Insert Header**
1. Click Insert tab.
2. Click Header button.
3. Click option at drop-down list.

**Insert Footer**
1. Click Insert tab.
2. Click Footer button.
3. Click option at drop-down list.

**9** Click the Close Header and Footer button to close the Header pane and make the document active.

**10** Click the Insert tab.

**11** Insert a footer by clicking the Footer button in the Header & Footer group.

**12** Scroll down the Footer button drop-down list and then click the *Ion (Dark)* footer.

> Notice how the document title you entered in the cover page is inserted in the footer, as is the author's name.

**13** Click the Close Header and Footer button to close the Footer pane and make the document active.

**14** Scroll through the document and notice how the header and footer appear on each page except the cover page.

**15** Remove the header by clicking in the second page of the document (not the cover page), clicking the Insert tab, clicking the Header button in the Header & Footer group, and then clicking *Remove Header* at the drop-down list.

**16** Insert a new header by clicking the Header button in the Header & Footer group, scrolling down the drop-down list, and then clicking the *Ion (Dark)* header.

**17** Double-click in the body of the document.

> Close a Header or Footer pane by clicking the Close Header and Footer button or by double-clicking in the document.

**18** Edit the footer by clicking the Insert tab, clicking the Footer button in the Header & Footer group, and then clicking *Edit Footer* at the drop-down list.

**19** Press Ctrl + A to select the footer.

**20** Change the font size by clicking the Home tab, clicking the *Font Size* option box arrow, and then clicking *10* at the drop-down list.

**21** Click the Bold button to apply bold formatting.

**22** Double-click in the document to close the Footer pane and make the document active.

**23** Save, print, and then close **3-FCTThailand**.

**Check Your Work** Compare your work to the model answer available in the online course.

## In Addition

### Creating a Custom Header or Footer

Create a custom header or footer using the *Edit Header* or *Edit Footer* options from the corresponding button drop-down list. For example, to create a header, click the Insert tab, click the Header button, and then click *Edit Header* at the drop-down list. This opens the Header pane and also displays the Header & Footer Tools Design tab with buttons and options for editing the header. Make edits to the Header with options on the tab and then close the Header pane by clicking the Close Header and Footer button in the Close group on the Header & Footer Tools Design tab. Complete similar steps to create a custom footer.

# Formatting a Document in MLA Style; Inserting Sources and Citations

When preparing a research paper or report, consider inserting sources, citations, and a bibliography or works cited page to give credit to the sources of words, ideas, and any material summarized or quoted. Word includes some common reference styles for citing and referencing research papers and reports, including the Modern Language Association (MLA) style, which is generally used in the humanities. To create a source, display the Create Source dialog box by clicking the References tab, clicking the Insert Citation button in the Citations & Bibliography group, and then clicking *Add New Source*. At the dialog box, insert bibliography information in the required fields. Once source information is inserted in the Create Source dialog box, Word will automatically save the source information. To insert a citation in a document from a source that is already saved, click the Insert Citation button in the Citations & Bibliography group and then click the reference at the drop-down list. If a direct quote from a source in included, the page number will need to be included. To do this, click the citation in the document to select the citation placeholder, click the Citation Options arrow, and then click *Edit Citation* at the drop-down list. At the Edit Citation dialog box, type in the page or page numbers of the quote's source.

**What You Will Do**   You are responsible for preparing and formatting a report on Middleton Valley for First Choice Travel. You have been asked to format the report in the MLA style.

Tutorial

Formatting a Report in MLA Style

Tutorial

Inserting Sources and Citations

1. Open **FCTMiddletonRpt** and then save it with the name **3-FCTMiddletonRpt**.

2. Click the References tab, click the *Style* option box arrow in the Citations & Bibliography group, and then click *MLA* at the drop-down list.

   Refer to Table 3.1 for general guidelines on formatting a research paper or report in MLA style.

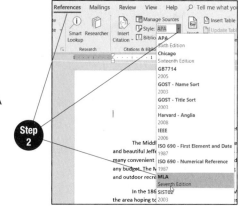

**Step 2**

3. Press Ctrl + A to select the entire document.

4. Click the Home tab, click the Font group dialog box launcher and then, at the Font dialog box, change the font to Cambria and the font size to 12.

5. With the Font dialog box still open, make 12-point Cambria the default font for the current document by clicking the Set As Default button at the bottom of the dialog box. At the message box with *This document only?* selected, click OK.

   You will be adding a header to the document and, since the default for the document is changed to 12-point Cambria, the header text will be formatted with 12-point Cambria.

**Step 5**

**Table 3.1** MLA Style General Guidelines

| |
|---|
| Use standard-sized paper (8.5 × 11 inches). |
| Set 1-inch top, bottom, left, and right margins. |
| Set text in a 12-point serif typeface (such as Cambria or Times New Roman). |
| Double-space text. |
| Indent the first line of each paragraph one-half inch. |
| Insert a header in the upper right corner of each page that prints the last name of the person writing the report followed by the page number. |

**6** With the text still selected, change the line spacing to double line spacing by clicking the Line and Paragraph Spacing button in the Paragraph group on the Home tab and then clicking *2.0* at the drop-down list.

**7** With the text still selected, remove spacing after paragraphs by clicking the Layout tab, clicking in the *After* measurement box in the *Spacing* section, typing 0, and then pressing the Enter key.

**8** Press Ctrl + Home to position the insertion point at the beginning of the document.

**9** Type your name and then press the Enter key.

**10** Type your instructor's name and then press the Enter key.

**11** Type the title of your course and then press the Enter key.

**12** Type the current date.

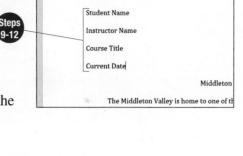

**13** Insert a header in the document by clicking the Insert tab, clicking the Header button in the Header & Footer group, and then clicking *Edit Header* at the drop-down list.

**14** Press the Tab key two times to move the insertion point to the right margin in the Header pane, type your last name, and then press the spacebar.

**15** Insert page numbers by clicking the Page Number button in the Header & Footer group on the Header & Footer Tools Design tab, pointing to *Current Position*, and then clicking the *Plain Number* option.

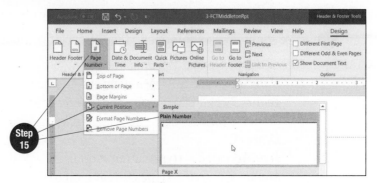

**16** Click the Close Header and Footer button.

**17** Insert a new source in the document. Begin by positioning the insertion point immediately right of the word *constructed* (but before the period) that ends the fifth sentence in the second paragraph.

**18** Click the References tab.

**19** Click the Insert Citation button ⬚ in the Citations & Bibliography group and then click *Add New Source* at the drop-down list.

**20** At the Create Source dialog box, click the *Type of Source* option box arrow and then click *Journal Article* at the drop-down list.

**21** Click in the *Author* text box, type Joanne Henderson, and then press the Tab key three times.

**22** Type Natural Resources of Middleton Valley in the *Title* text box and then press the Tab key.

**23** Type Planet Earth's Resources in the *Journal Name* text box and then press the Tab key.

**24** Type 2021 in the *Year* text box and then press the Tab key.

**25** Type 7-9 in the *Pages* text box.

**26** Click OK to close the Create Source dialog box.

**27** Position the insertion point immediately right of the word *century* (but before the period) that ends the third sentence in the third paragraph, click the Insert Citation button, and then click *Add New Source* at the drop-down list.

**28** At the Create Source dialog box, click the *Type of Source* option box arrow and then click *Web site* at the drop-down list.

**29** Click the *Show All Bibliography Fields* check box to insert a check mark.

**30** Type the following information in the specified fields:

    *Author* = Daniel Marcello
    *Name of Web Page* = Middleton Regional Planning Department
    *Year* = 2021
    *Month* = January
    *Day* = 5
    *Year Accessed* = (type current year)
    *Month Accessed* = (type current month)
    *Day Accessed* = (type current day)
    *URL* = https://ppi-edu.net/middleton

**31** After entering the information, click OK.

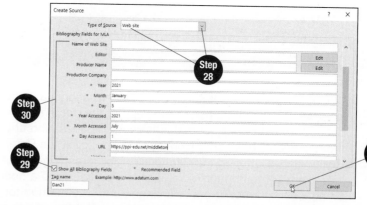

## In Brief

**Choose Reference Style**
1. Click References tab.
2. Click *Style* option box arrow.
3. Click reference style.

**Insert New Source**
1. Click References tab.
2. Click Insert Citation button.
3. Click *Add New Source* option.
4. At Create Source dialog box, specify type of source.
5. Enter information in appropriate text boxes.
6. Click OK.

**Insert Citation**
1. Position insertion point in document.
2. Click References tab.
3. Click Insert Citation button.
4. Click reference.

**Edit Citation**
1. Click in citation.
2. Click Citation Options arrow.
3. Click *Edit Citation* option.
4. Make changes at Edit Citation dialog box.
5. Click OK.

**32** Insert a citation from an existing source. Begin by positioning the insertion point between the quotation mark after the word *erosion* and the period in the second sentence in the fourth paragraph.

**33** Click the Insert Citation button in the Citations & Bibliography group and then click the *Henderson, Joanne* reference at the drop-down list.

**34** Because you are citing a direct quote, you need to include the page number of the journal article where you found the quote. Begin by clicking in the Henderson citation you just inserted.

This displays the citation placeholder.

**35** Click the Citation Options arrow at the right side of the citation placeholder and then click *Edit Citation* at the drop-down list.

**36** At the Edit Citation dialog box, type 8 in the *Pages* text box.

**37** Click OK to close the Edit Citation dialog box.

**38** Save **3-FCTMiddletonRpt**.

**Check Your Work** Compare your work to the model answer available in the online course.

## In Addition

### Formatting the First Page of an MLA-Formatted Report

Your instructor may require you to omit the header on the first page of the document. To remove the header from the first page of a document, press Ctrl + Home to move the insertion point to the beginning of the document, click the Header button in the Header & Footer group on the Insert tab, and then click *Edit Header* at the drop-down list. Click the *Different First Page* check box in the Options group on the Header & Footer Tools Design tab. This inserts a new Header pane named *First Page Header*. Since you do not want a header on the first page, leave this header blank. Click the Next button in the Navigation group on the Header & Footer Tools Design tab and, if you previously created a header in the document, it displays in the Header pane. If the document did not include a header, type or insert the header text in the Header pane.

When a report or research paper includes citations, a works cited page needs to be inserted on a separate page at the end of the document. A works cited page is an alphabetic list of the books, journal articles, web pages, and any other sources referenced in the document. To insert a works cited page, click the References tab and then click the Bibliography button in the Citations & Bibliography group. At the Bibliography drop-down list, click a format option. After inserting sources into a document, a citation may need to be edited to correct errors or change data. One method for editing a source is to click the citation in the document, click the Citation Options arrow, and then click *Edit Source* at the drop-down list. This displays the Edit Source dialog box with the original information. Make any needed changes and then click OK to close the dialog box. If a source is edited, Word will not automatically update the works cited. To update the works cited, click in the works cited page and then click the Update Citations and Bibliography tab.

**What You Will Do**  To finish the Middleton Valley report, you need to add a works cited page, edit one of the sources, and apply MLA style formatting to the works cited page.

Inserting a Works Cited Page

Editing a Citation and Source

1. With **3-FCTMiddletonRpt** open, insert a works cited page at the end of the document. Begin by pressing Ctrl + End to move the insertion point to the end of the document and then pressing Ctrl + Enter to insert a hard page break.

2. Click the References tab and then click the Bibliography button in the Citations & Bibliography group.

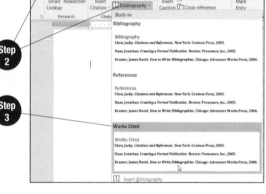

3. Click the *Works Cited* option in the *Built-In* section of the drop-down list.

4. You realize that part of the web page title is missing and you need to edit the source. Begin by clicking in the *Marcello* citation, in the first paragraph on the second page.

   This selects the citation placeholder.

5. Click the Citation Options arrow at the right side of the citation placeholder and then click *Edit Source* at the drop-down list.

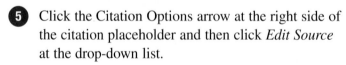

   This displays the Edit Source dialog box, which contains the same options as the Create Source dialog box.

6. At the Edit Source dialog box, click in the *Name of Web Page* text box, edit the text so it displays as *Middleton Valley Regional Planning Department*, and then click OK to close the dialog box.

7. At the message stating that the source exists in your master list and the current document and asking you if you want to update both, click the Yes button.

**In Brief**

**Insert Works
Cited Page**
1. Move insertion point to
   end of document.
2. Press Ctrl + Enter.
3. Click References tab.
4. Click Bibliography
   button.
5. Click *Works Cited*
   option.

**Edit Source**
1. Click citation in
   document.
2. Click Citation Options
   arrow.
3. Click *Edit Source*.
4. At Edit Source dialog
   box, make desired
   changes.
5. Click OK.

**Update Works
Cited Page**
1. Click in works cited
   text.
2. Click Update Citations
   and Bibliography
   placeholder tab.

**8** Update the works cited to include the edited source. Begin by pressing Ctrl + End to move the insertion point to the end of the document and then click in the works cited text.

**9** Click the Update Citations and Bibliography placeholder tab.

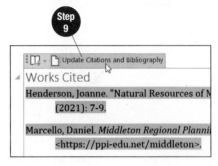

> The placeholder tab displays above the *Works Cited* title. Notice that the updated works cited page includes the edited web page name.

**10** Format the works cited page to MLA standards, which are listed in Table 3.2. Begin by selecting the *Works Cited* heading and the entries below it and then click the *No Spacing* style in the Styles group on the Home tab.

**11** With the text still selected, change the line spacing to double line spacing.

**12** Click in the title *Works Cited* and then click the Center button in the Paragraph group.

**13** Hang-indent the works cited entries. Do this by selecting only the entries and then pressing Ctrl + T.

> You can also hang-indent the entries by clicking the Paragraph group dialog box launcher, clicking the *Special* list box arrow in the *Indentation* section, clicking *Hanging* at the drop-down list, and then clicking OK to close the Paragraph dialog box.

**14** Press Ctrl + Home to move the insertion point to the beginning of the document.

**15** Save, print, and then close **3-FCTMiddletonRpt**.

**Table 3.2** MLA Style Works Cited Page Formatting Guidelines

| |
|---|
| Begin works cited on a separate page at the end of the document. |
| Include the title *Works Cited* centered at the top of the page. |
| Double-space between and within entries. |
| Begin each entry at the left margin and hang-indent the second and subsequent lines in each entry. |
| Alphabetize the entries. |

 **Check Your Work** Compare your work to the model answer available in the online course.

## In Addition

### Modifying Sources at the Source Manager Dialog Box

Copy, delete, edit, and create new sources at the Source Manager dialog box. Display this dialog box by clicking the References tab and then clicking the Manage Sources button in the Citations & Bibliography group. The *Master List* section of the dialog box displays all of the citations created in Word, and the *Current List* section displays all of the citations included in the currently open document.

One method for changing paragraph alignment is to use the Click and Type feature. To use Click and Type, position the mouse pointer at the left margin, in the center of the page, or at the right margin until the pointer displays with the desired alignment symbol and then double-click the mouse button. By default, text is aligned at the top of the page. Change this vertical alignment to center, justified, or bottom with the *Vertical alignment* option at the Page Setup dialog box with the Layout tab selected. Display the Page Setup dialog box by clicking the Layout tab and then clicking the Page Setup group dialog box launcher. Insert an image in a document from a location on the computer with the Pictures button on the Insert tab. Use the Online Pictures button on the Insert tab to search for images on the internet. Format an inserted image with buttons and options on the Picture Tools Format tab. This tab is active when an image is selected.

**What You Will Do**   First Choice Travel is planning a workshop for people interested in traveling on a budget. You will create an announcement that contains center- and right-aligned text, vertically center the text on the page, and then add visual interest by inserting an image and the company logo.

Using Click and Type

Changing Vertical Alignment

Inserting, Sizing, and Positioning an Image

Formatting an Image

**①** Press Ctrl + N to display a blank document and then press the Enter key.

**②** Position the I-beam pointer in the document between the left and right margins at about the 3.25-inch mark on the horizontal ruler and approximately one inch from the top of the page. When the center alignment lines display below the I-beam pointer, double-click the left mouse button.

**③** Type the centered text shown in Figure 3.1, pressing the Enter key between each line of text and two times after the last line of centered text.

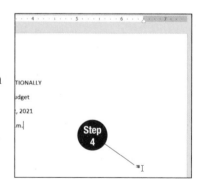

**④** Change to right alignment by positioning the I-beam pointer near the right margin at approximately the 6.5-inch mark on the horizontal ruler and the 2-inch mark on the vertical ruler. When the right alignment lines display at the left of the I-beam pointer, double-click the left mouse button.

**Figure 3.1** Step 3 and Step 5

TRAVELING INTERNATIONALLY

Traveling on a Budget

Thursday, April 22, 2021

7:00 to 8:30 p.m.

Sponsored by
First Choice Travel

**5** Type the right-aligned text shown in Figure 3.1. After typing the first line of right-aligned text, press Shift + Enter to move the insertion point to the next line.

**6** Select the centered text and then change the font to 14-point Candara bold. Select the right-aligned text, change the font to 10-point Candara bold, and then deselect the text.

**7** Vertically center the text on the page. To do this, click the Layout tab and then click the Page Setup group dialog box launcher.

**8** At the Page Setup dialog box, click the Layout tab, click the *Vertical alignment* option box arrow, and then click *Center* at the drop-down list.

**9** Click OK to close the Page Setup dialog box.

**10** Save the document and name it **3-FCTTravelIntl**.

**11** Print **3-FCTTravelIntl**.

**12** Return the vertical alignment to top alignment. To do this, click the Page Setup group dialog box launcher. At the Page Setup dialog box, click the Layout tab, click the *Vertical alignment* option box arrow, and then click *Top* at the drop-down list. Click OK to close the dialog box.

**13** Click the Insert tab and then click the Pictures button in the Illustrations group.

> This displays the Insert Picture dialog box. Online images are also available for downloading by clicking the Insert tab and then clicking the Online Pictures button. At the Online Pictures window, type a keyword in the search text box, press the Enter key, and images related to the keyword display. Click an image and then click the Insert button and the image is inserted in the document.

**14** At the Insert Picture dialog box, navigate to your WordS3 folder and then double-click the **Suitcases** image file.

> The image is inserted in the document, it is selected (sizing handles display around the image), and the Picture Tools Format tab displays as shown in Figure 3.2. A Layout Options button displays at the right of the image. Click this button to display a list of options for positioning the image and wrapping text around the image.

**15** With the image selected, click the Position button in the Arrange group and then click the *Position in Top Left with Square Text Wrapping* option (first column, first row in the *With Text Wrapping* section).

> Apply a text wrapping style to an image to specify how you want text or other items to flow around the image. Apply text wrapping with options from the Position button or with the Wrap Text button.

**Figure 3.2** Picture Tools Format Tab

**16** Add a shadow effect to the image by clicking the *Drop Shadow Rectangle* option in the Picture Styles group (fourth option).

**17** Click the Corrections button ☼ in the Adjust group and then click the *Brightness: 0% (Normal) Contrast: +40%* option (third column, bottom row in the *Brightness/Contrast* section).

**18** Click the Picture Effects button ▱ in the Pictures Styles group, point to *Glow*, and then click the *Glow: 5 point; Blue, Accent color 1* option (first column, first row in the *Glow Variations* section).

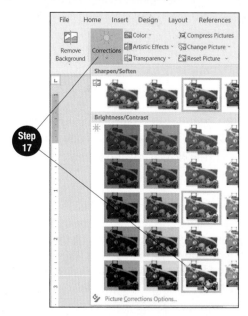

**19** Click in the *Shape Height* measurement box in the Size group, type 1.7, and then press the Enter key.

> When you change the height measurement, the width measurement is automatically changed to maintain the proportions of the image.

**20** Select and then delete the text *First Choice Travel* that displays in small font size at the right of the document.

**21** Insert the First Choice Travel logo image below *Sponsored by.* To begin, click the Insert tab and then click the Pictures button in the Illustrations group.

**22** At the Insert Picture dialog box, navigate to your WordS3 folder and then double-click *FCTLogo*.

**23** With the logo image selected in the document, click the Layout Options button ⛶ outside the upper right corner of the image and then click *Tight* (second column, first row in the *With Text Wrapping* section).

**24** Click the Layout Options button to remove the side menu.

**25** With the logo image still selected, press and hold down the Shift key, click one of the corner sizing handles (white squares) and click and hold down the left mouse button; drag to reduce the size of the image so it displays as shown in Figure 3.3; and then release the mouse button.

> Pressing and holding down the Shift key while increasing or decreasing the size of an image maintains the proportions of the image.

**26** Drag the logo image so it is positioned as shown in Figure 3.3. To drag the image, position the insertion point inside the selected image until the mouse pointer displays with a four-headed arrow attached. Click and hold down the left mouse button, drag the selected image to the desired location, and then release the mouse button.

> As you move an image near the top, left, right, or bottom margins of the document, green guidelines appear to help you position the image.

**27** Click outside the logo to deselect it.

**28** Save, print, and then close **3-FCTTravelIntl**.

**Figure 3.3** Activity 3.9

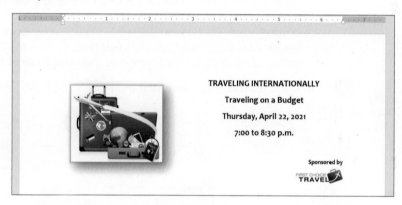

**Check Your Work** Compare your work to the model answer available in the online course.

## In Addition

### Formatting an Image with Buttons on the Picture Tools Format Tab

Images inserted in a document can be formatted in a variety of ways, which might include adding fill color and border lines, increasing or decreasing the brightness or contrast of the image, choosing a wrapping style, and cropping the image. Format an image with buttons on the Picture Tools Format tab as shown in Figure 3.2. Use buttons in the Adjust group to correct the brightness and contrast of the image; change the image color; change to a different image; reset the image to its original size, position, and color; and compress the picture. Compress a picture to reduce resolution or discard extra information to save room on the hard drive or reduce download time. Use buttons in the Picture Styles group to apply a predesigned style, insert a picture border, or apply a picture effect. The Arrange group contains buttons for positioning the image, wrapping text around the image, and aligning and rotating the image. Use options in the Size group to crop the image and specify the height and width of the image.

Word automates the creation of envelopes with options at the Envelopes and Labels dialog box with the Envelopes tab selected. At this dialog box, type a delivery address and a return address. If the Envelopes and Labels dialog box is opened in a document containing a name and address, the name and address are inserted automatically as the delivery address. If a return address is entered, Word will ask before printing if the new return address should be saved as the default return address. Click the Yes button to use the return address for future envelopes, or click the No button if a different return address will be used for future envelopes.

**What You Will Do**   You need to create an envelope for sending the information about Thailand to Camille Matsui at Marquee Productions.

Preparing an Envelope

**1** Press Ctrl + N to display a blank document.

You can also display a blank document by clicking the File tab and then clicking the *Blank document* template; or, clicking the File tab, clicking the *New* option, and then clicking the *Blank document* template. Another method is to insert a New button on the Quick Access Toolbar and then click the button to display a blank document. To insert the New button on the Quick Access Toolbar, click the Customize Quick Access Toolbar button at the right of the toolbar and then click *New* at the drop-down list.

**2** Click the Mailings tab and then click the Envelopes button ✉ in the Create group.

**3** At the Envelopes and Labels dialog box with the Envelopes tab selected, type the following name and address in the *Delivery address* text box. Press the Enter key at the end of each line, except the last line containing the city, state, and zip code.

> Camille Matsui
> Marquee Productions
> 955 South Alameda Street
> Los Angeles, CA 90037

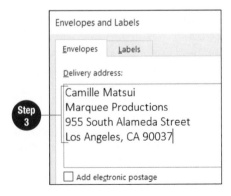

**4** If any text displays in the *Return address* text box, delete it and then type the following name and address. Type your name where you see *Student Name*.

> First Choice Travel
> Student Name
> 3588 Ventura Boulevard
> Los Angeles, CA 90102

**5** Click the Add to Document button.

Clicking the Add to Document button inserts the envelope in the document. You can also send the envelope directly to the printer by clicking the Print button.

**6** At the message asking if you want to save the new return address as the default address, click No.

**7** Save the document with the name **3-FCTEnvtoMP**.

**8** Print and then close **3-FCTEnvtoMP**. *Note: Manual feed of the envelope may be required. Please check with your instructor before printing the envelope.*

**Check Your Work** Compare your work to the model answer available in the online course.

## In Addition

### Customizing Envelopes

Use options at the Envelope Options dialog box shown at the right to customize an envelope. Display this dialog box by clicking the Options button at the Envelopes and Labels dialog box. At the Envelope Options dialog box, change the envelope size, change the font for the delivery and return addresses, and specify the positioning of the addresses in relation to the left and top edges of the envelope.

# Activity 3.11 Preparing Mailing Labels

Use Word's Labels feature to print text on mailing labels, file labels, disc labels, or other types of labels. Labels can be created for printing on a variety of predefined labels, which can be purchased at an office supply store. Use the Labels feature to create a sheet of mailing labels with the same name and address or image or enter a different name and address on each label. Create a label with options at the Envelopes and Labels dialog box with the Labels tab selected.

**What You Will Do** You will create a sheet of mailing labels containing the First Choice Travel name and address. You will also create mailing labels for sending the Thailand document to several First Choice Travel customers and create labels for the First Choice Travel office in Toronto.

**Tutorial**

Creating Mailing Labels with the Same Name and Address and an Image

**Tutorial**

Creating Mailing Labels with Different Names and Addresses

1. Press Ctrl + N to display a blank document.

2. Click the Mailings tab and then click the Labels button 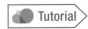 in the Create group.

3. At the Envelopes and Labels dialog box with the Labels tab selected, type the following information in the *Address* text box. Type your name where you see *Student Name*. (Press the Enter key at the end of each line except the last line.)

> First Choice Travel
> Student Name
> 3588 Ventura Boulevard
> Los Angeles, CA 90102

4. Click the Options button.

5. At the Label Options dialog box, click the *Label vendors* option box arrow and then click *Avery US Letter* at the drop-down list.

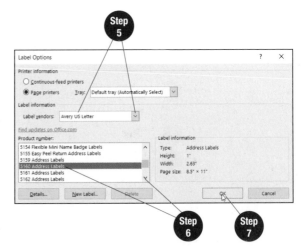

6. Scroll down the *Product number* list box and then click *5160 Address Labels*.

7. Click OK to close the dialog box.

8. Click the New Document button at the Envelopes and Labels dialog box.

9. Save the document and name it **3-FCTLALabels**.

10. Print and then close **3-FCTLALabels**.

11. Click the Mailings tab and then click the Labels button in the Create group.

12. At the Envelopes and Labels dialog box, click the New Document button.

13. At the document, type the first name and address shown in Figure 3.4 in the first label. Press the Tab key two times to move the insertion point to the next label and then type the second name and address shown in Figure 3.4. Press the Tab key two times and then type the third name and address. Press the Tab key one time and then type the fourth name and address. Continue in this manner until you have typed all of the names and addresses in Figure 3.4.

**In Brief**

**Create Mailing Labels with Same Name and Address**
1. Click Mailings tab.
2. Click Labels button.
3. Type name and address in *Address* text box.
4. Click either New Document button or Print button.

**Create Mailing Labels with Different Names and Addresses**
1. Click Mailings tab.
2. Click Labels button.
3. Click New Document button.
4. At document screen, type names and addresses.

**Create Mailing Labels with Image**
1. Click Insert tab.
2. Click Pictures button.
3. Navigate to folder.
4. Double-click image.
5. Click Mailings tab.
6. Click Labels button.
7. Click New Document button.

**14** Save the document and name it **3-FCTCustLabels**.

**15** Print and then close **3-FCTCustLabels**.

**16** At the blank document, create mailing labels for the Toronto office of First Choice Travel using an image. Begin by clicking the Insert tab and then clicking the Pictures button in the Illustrations group.

**17** At the Insert Picture dialog box, navigate to your WordS3 folder and then double-click the *FCTTorontoLabel* image file.

**18** With the label image selected, click the Position button in the Arrange group on the Picture Tools Format tab and then click the *Position in Top Center with Square Text Wrapping* option (second column, first row in the *With Text Wrapping* section).

**19** With the image still selected, click the Mailings tab and then click the Labels button.

**20** At the Envelopes and Labels dialog box, make sure the Avery US Letter label number 5160 is selected and then click the New Document button.

> When you click the New Document button, the label image is inserted in each label on the page and inserted in a new document.

**21** Save the document and name it **3-FCTTorontoLabels**.

**22** Print and then close **3-FCTTorontoLabels**.

**23** Close the document containing the label image without saving it.

**Figure 3.4** Step 13

| | | |
|---|---|---|
| Moreno Products<br>350 Mission Boulevard<br>Pomona, CA 91767 | Mr. Miguel Santos<br>12120 Barranca Parkway<br>Irvine, CA 92612 | Mr. and Mrs. Jack Lipinski<br>5534 Eagle Ridge Drive<br>Los Angeles, CA 90092 |
| Dr. Esther Riggins<br>9077 Walnut Street<br>Los Angeles, CA 90097 | Automated Services, Inc.<br>4394 Seventh Street<br>Long Beach, CA 92602 | Ms. Samantha Schwartz<br>103-B Pacific Palms<br>Los Angeles, CA 90068 |

 **Check Your Work** Compare your work to the model answer available in the online course.

## In Addition

### Customizing Labels

Click the Options button at the Envelopes and Labels dialog box with the Labels tab selected and the Label Options dialog box displays as shown at the right. At this dialog box, choose the type of printer, the label vendor, and the product number. This dialog box also displays information about the selected label, such as type, height, width, and paper size. When a label is selected, Word automatically determines label margins. These default settings can be customized by clicking the Details button at the Label Options dialog box.

# Features Summary

| Feature | Ribbon Tab, Group | Button, Option | Keyboard Shortcut |
|---|---|---|---|
| blank page | Insert, Pages | | |
| Clipboard task pane | Home, Clipboard | | |
| copy selected text | Home, Clipboard | | Ctrl + C |
| cover page | Insert, Pages | | |
| Create Source dialog box | References, Citations & Bibliography | , *Add New Source* | |
| cut selected text | Home, Clipboard | | Ctrl + X |
| Envelopes and Labels dialog box with Envelopes tab selected | Mailings, Create | | |
| Envelopes and Labels dialog box with Labels tab selected | Mailings, Create | | |
| footer | Insert, Header & Footer | | |
| hanging indent | | | Ctrl + T |
| header | Insert, Header & Footer | | |
| Insert Picture dialog box | Insert, Illustrations | | |
| page background color | Design, Page Background | | |
| page borders | Design, Page Background | | |
| page break | Insert, Pages | | Ctrl + Enter |
| page margins | Layout, Page Setup | | |
| page number | Insert, Header & Footer | | |
| page orientation | Layout, Page Setup | | |
| Page Setup dialog box | Layout, Page Setup | | |
| paper size | Layout, Page Setup | | |
| paste selected text | Home, Clipboard | | Ctrl + V |
| Paste Special dialog box | Home, Clipboard | , *Paste Special* | |
| Show/Hide | Home, Paragraph | | Ctrl + Shift + * |
| watermark | Design, Page Background | | |
| works cited page | References, Citations & Bibliography | | |

# Microsoft® Excel®

## 365

### 2019 Brief Edition

Nita Rutkosky

Audrey Roggenkamp
Pierce College Puyallup
Puyallup, Washington

Ian Rutkosky
Pierce College Puyallup
Puyallup, Washington

PARADIGM
EDUCATION SOLUTIONS

St. Paul

**Vice President, Content and Digital Solutions:** Christine Hurney
**Director of Content Development:** Carley Fruzzetti
**Testers:** Desiree Carvel; Ann E. Mills, Ivy Tech Community College of Indiana, Evansville, IN
**Director of Production:** Timothy W. Larson
**Production Editor/Project Manager:** Jen Weaverling
**Cover and Text Design:** Valerie King
**Senior Design and Production Specialist:** Julie Johnston
**Copy Editor:** Deborah Brandt
**Indexer:** Terry Casey
**Vice President, Director of Digital Products:** Chuck Bratton
**Digital Projects Manager:** Tom Modl
**Digital Solutions Manager:** Gerry Yumul
**Senior Director of Digital Products and Onboarding:** Christopher Johnson
**Supervisor of Digital Products and Onboarding:** Ryan Isdahl
**Vice President of Marketing:** Lara Weber McLellan
**Marketing and Communications Manager**: Selena Hicks

# Contents

# Excel® 365

Microsoft Excel is a popular choice among individuals and companies to organize, analyze, and present data in columns and rows in a file called a *worksheet*. More than one worksheet can be created and saved in a file called a *workbook*. Worksheets can be created to track, analyze, and chart any type of data that can be set up in a column and row format. Expenses, sales, assets, liabilities, grades, statistics, research study data, machine production records, weather records, and gas usage are just a few examples of the type of information that can be stored in an Excel workbook. While working in Excel, you will create and edit worksheets for the following six companies.

First Choice Travel is a travel center offering a full range of traveling services from booking flights, hotel reservations, and rental cars to offering travel seminars.

The Waterfront Bistro offers fine dining for lunch and dinner and also offers banquet facilities, a wine cellar, and catering services.

Worldwide Enterprises is a national and international distributor of products for a variety of companies and is the exclusive movie distribution agent for Marquee Productions.

Marquee Productions is involved in all aspects of creating movies from script writing and development to filming. The company produces documentaries, biographies, as well as historical and action movies.

Performance Threads maintains an inventory of rental costumes and also researches, designs, and sews special-order and custom-made costumes.

The mission of the Niagara Peninsula College Theatre Arts Division is to offer a curriculum designed to provide students with a thorough exposure to all aspects of the theatre arts.

# *In Section 1 you will learn how to*

## Create Worksheets to Analyze Data

Begin work in Excel by entering labels in columns or rows to create the worksheet layout. Next, add the values that correspond to the labels. Finally, create formulas to add, subtract, multiply, or divide to calculate the desired results. Once a worksheet has been created, the power and versatility of Excel is put to use by performing what-if analyses. What happens to net profit if sales increase by 4 percent? What happens to monthly cash flow if the wages of all employees are raised 3 percent? To answer these types of questions, edit a value and then watch Excel automatically update all other values dependent on the number changed.

Start a new worksheet by entering labels to create the worksheet layout.

|   | A | B | C | D | E | F | G | H | I | J | K | L |
|---|---|---|---|---|---|---|---|---|---|---|---|---|
| 1 | Payroll | | | | | | | | | | | |
| 2 | Week Ended: September 24, 2021 | | | | | | | | | | | |
| 3 | | | Sun | Mon | Tue | Wed | Thu | Fri | Sat | Total Hours | Pay Rate | Gross Pay |
| 4 | Dayna | McGuire | | | | | | | | | | |
| 5 | Heather | Kiley | | | | | | | | | | |
| 6 | Pat | Soulliere | | | | | | | | | | |
| 7 | Jasmine | Hill | | | | | | | | | | |
| 8 | Moira | Su-Lin | | | | | | | | | | |
| 9 | Carla | Modano | | | | | | | | | | |
| 10 | Toni | Williams | | | | | | | | | | |
| 11 | Tyler | Santini | | | | | | | | | | |
| 12 | Lou | Cortez | | | | | | | | | | |
| 13 | Total | | | | | | | | | | | |

Next, add the values to record quantities, rates, or other numeric entries.

|   | A | B | C | D | E | F | G | H | I | J | K | L |
|---|---|---|---|---|---|---|---|---|---|---|---|---|
| 1 | Payroll | | | | | | | | | | | |
| 2 | Week Ended: September 24, 2021 | | | | | | | | | | | |
| 3 | | | Sun | Mon | Tue | Wed | Thu | Fri | Sat | Total Hours | Pay Rate | Gross Pay |
| 4 | Dayna | McGuire | 6 | 5 | 8 | 8 | 7 | 0 | 6 | 40 | 12.5 | 500 |
| 5 | Heather | Kiley | 0 | 8 | 6 | 8 | 5 | 5 | 8 | 40 | 10.25 | 410 |
| 6 | Pat | Souliere | 8 | 8 | 0 | 8 | 7 | 7 | 0 | 38 | 10.25 | 389.5 |
| 7 | Jasmine | Hill | 8 | 0 | 8 | 8 | 0 | 8 | 6 | 38 | 11.75 | 446.5 |
| 8 | Moira | Su-Lin | 0 | 8 | 0 | 8 | 7 | 7 | 8 | 38 | 11.75 | 446.5 |
| 9 | Carla | Cumberbatch | 0 | 0 | 8 | 8 | 7 | 7 | 8 | 38 | 11.75 | 446.5 |
| 10 | Toni | Williams | 8 | 0 | 5 | 8 | 8 | 7 | 4 | 40 | 10.25 | 410 |
| 11 | Tyler | Santini | 7 | 0 | 8 | 8 | 6 | 7 | 4 | 40 | 10.25 | 410 |
| 12 | Lou | Cortez | 8 | 0 | 6 | 8 | 0 | 8 | 8 | 38 | 10.25 | 389.5 |
| 13 | Total | | 45 | 29 | 49 | 72 | 47 | 56 | 52 | 350 | | 3848.5 |

|   | A | B | C | D | E | F | G | H | I | J | K | L |
|---|---|---|---|---|---|---|---|---|---|---|---|---|
| 1 | | | | | | Payroll | | | | | | |
| 2 | | | | | | Week Ended: September 24, 2021 | | | | | | |
| 3 | | | Sun | Mon | Tue | Wed | Thu | Fri | Sat | Total Hours | Pay Rate | Gross Pay |
| 4 | Dayna | McGuire | 6 | 5 | 8 | 8 | 7 | 0 | 6 | =SUM(C4:I4) | 12.5 | =J4*K4 |
| 5 | Heather | Kiley | 0 | 8 | 6 | 8 | 5 | 5 | 8 | =SUM(C5:I5) | 10.25 | =J5*K5 |
| 6 | Pat | Souliere | 8 | 8 | 0 | 8 | 7 | 7 | 0 | =SUM(C6:I6) | 10.25 | =J6*K6 |
| 7 | Jasmine | Hill | 8 | 0 | 8 | 8 | 0 | 8 | 6 | =SUM(C7:I7) | 11.75 | =J7*K7 |
| 8 | Moira | Su-Lin | 0 | 8 | 0 | 8 | 7 | 7 | 8 | =SUM(C8:I8) | 11.75 | =J8*K8 |
| 9 | Carla | Cumberbatch | 0 | 0 | 8 | 8 | 7 | 7 | 8 | =SUM(C9:I9) | 11.75 | =J9*K9 |
| 10 | Toni | Williams | 8 | 0 | 5 | 8 | 8 | 7 | 4 | =SUM(C10:I10) | 10.25 | =J10*K10 |
| 11 | Tyler | Santini | 7 | 0 | 8 | 8 | 6 | 7 | 4 | =SUM(C11:I11) | 10.25 | =J11*K11 |
| 12 | Lou | Cortez | 8 | 0 | 6 | 8 | 0 | 8 | 8 | =SUM(C12:I12) | 10.25 | =J12*K12 |
| 13 | Total | | =SUM(C4:C12) | =SUM(D4:D12) | =SUM(E4:E12) | =SUM(F4:F12) | =SUM(G4:G12) | =SUM(H4:H12) | =SUM(I4:I12) | =SUM(J4:J12) | | =SUM(L4:L12) |

Create the formulas to add, subtract, multiply, or divide.

The desired results are shown in the finished worksheet.

|   | A | B | C | D | E | F | G | H | I | J | K | L |
|---|---|---|---|---|---|---|---|---|---|---|---|---|
| 1 | | | | | | Payroll | | | | | | |
| 2 | | | | | | Week Ended: September 24, 2021 | | | | | | |
| 3 | | | Sun | Mon | Tue | Wed | Thu | Fri | Sat | Total Hours | Pay Rate | Gross Pay |
| 4 | Dayna | McGuire | 6 | 5 | 8 | 8 | 7 | 0 | 6 | 40 | $ 12.50 | $ 500.00 |
| 5 | Heather | Kiley | 0 | 8 | 6 | 8 | 5 | 5 | 8 | 40 | $ 10.25 | $ 410.00 |
| 6 | Pat | Souliere | 8 | 8 | 0 | 8 | 7 | 7 | 0 | 38 | $ 10.25 | $ 389.50 |
| 7 | Jasmine | Hill | 8 | 0 | 8 | 8 | 0 | 8 | 6 | 38 | $ 11.75 | $ 446.50 |
| 8 | Moira | Su-Lin | 0 | 8 | 0 | 8 | 7 | 7 | 8 | 38 | $ 11.75 | $ 446.50 |
| 9 | Carla | Cumberbatch | 0 | 0 | 8 | 8 | 7 | 7 | 8 | 38 | $ 11.75 | $ 446.50 |
| 10 | Toni | Williams | 8 | 0 | 5 | 8 | 8 | 7 | 4 | 40 | $ 10.25 | $ 410.00 |
| 11 | Tyler | Santini | 7 | 0 | 8 | 8 | 6 | 7 | 4 | 40 | $ 10.25 | $ 410.00 |
| 12 | Lou | Cortez | 8 | 0 | 6 | 8 | 0 | 8 | 8 | 38 | $ 10.25 | $ 389.50 |
| 13 | Total | | 45 | 29 | 49 | 72 | 47 | 56 | 52 | 350 | | $3,848.50 |

# *In Section 2 you will learn how to*

## Edit and Format Worksheets

Excel provides formatting attributes that enhance the appearance of a worksheet and draws a reader's attention to important titles, totals, or other results. Apply a theme which coordinates colors, fonts, and effects to create a worksheet with a professional appearance in just a few mouse clicks. A variety of formats, grouped into categories, are available for numbers, dates, and times. Insert an object such as an image or a logo to enhance a worksheet or add a corporate identity.

Apply formatting enhancements including:

- adding borders
- adding fill color
- adjusting row height
- adjusting column width
- applying a cell style
- applying a theme
- changing text alignment within cells
- changing font, font size, font color
- changing font attributes to bold and/or italic
- indenting text within a cell
- formatting numbers

The Waterfront Bistro

The Waterfront Bistro

2021 Special Event Bookings

| Contact Name | Contact Phone | Event | Date | Room | Guests | Special Menu | Price per Person |
|---|---|---|---|---|---|---|---|
| Cecily Hillmore | 716 555 6598 | Business Meeting | 1/15/2021 | Starlake | 42 | No | 23.95 |
| Frances Corriveau | 716 555 3256 | Birthday Party | 1/21/2021 | Westview | 82 | Yes | 29.95 |
| Orlando Fagan | 716 555 3694 | 25th Wedding Anniversary | 3/13/2021 | Westview | 95 | Yes | 29.95 |
| Kim Pockovic | 905 555 3698 | Birthday Party | 3/20/2021 | Westview | 65 | Yes | 36.95 |
| Lane Gill | 416 555 3264 | Business Meeting | 3/25/2021 | Starlake | 55 | No | 22.95 |
| Percy Bresque | 716 555 1248 | 50th Wedding Anniversary | 4/10/2021 | Westview | 102 | Yes | 35.95 |
| Max Santore | 905 555 3264 | Wedding | 4/24/2021 | Sunset | 188 | Yes | 27.95 |
| Omar Hamid | 716 555 8796 | Engagement Party | 5/8/2021 | Sunset | 67 | Yes | 29.95 |
| Jack Torrance | 716 555 1469 | Business Meeting | 5/13/2021 | Westview | 34 | No | 24.95 |
| Dana Russell | 716 555 4965 | Birthday Party | 5/29/2021 | Starlake | 54 | No | 28.95 |
| Walter Szucs | 905 555 6998 | Birthday Party | 6/6/2021 | Starlake | 84 | No | 34.95 |
| Nicole Griffin | 905 555 4166 | 25th Wedding Anniversary | 6/12/2021 | Starlake | 78 | Yes | 34.95 |
| Zack Doucet | 716 555 3488 | Wedding | 6/26/2021 | Sunset | 215 | Yes | 29.95 |
| Jesse Golinsky | 716 555 4218 | Business Meeting | 6/30/2021 | Westview | 60 | No | 25.95 |
| Cora Jin Ping | 716 555 7774 | Baby Shower | 7/11/2021 | Sunset | 75 | Yes | 22.95 |
| Elizabeth McMaster | 716 555 9442 | Engagement Party | 7/24/2021 | Sunset | 94 | Yes | 28.95 |
| Reed Pavelich | 716 555 2286 | Wedding | 7/25/2021 | Starlake | 145 | Yes | 34.95 |
| Alfredo Juanitez | 716 555 4668 | Business Meeting | 7/28/2021 | Westview | 37 | No | 24.95 |
| Yanfang Guo | 716 555 4856 | 50th Wedding Anniversary | 8/1/2021 | Starlake | 62 | No | 34.95 |
| Jelena Boskovic | 716 555 3456 | Business Meeting | 8/9/2021 | Westview | 27 | Yes | 29.95 |
| Priscilla Melo | 716 555 3145 | Business Meeting | 8/18/2021 | Westview | 34 | Yes | 25.95 |
| Tracie McIntyre | 716 555 3496 | Birthday Party | 9/4/2021 | Sunset | 26 | No | 22.95 |
| Krista Pressey | 716 555 7469 | 50th Wedding Anniversary | 9/12/2021 | Sunset | 95 | No | 28.95 |
| Langford Hill | 716 555 8798 | Wedding | 9/18/2021 | Starlake | 185 | No | 34.95 |
| Naomi Sayers | 905 555 3486 | Wedding | 10/9/2021 | Starlake | 245 | Yes | 34.95 |
| Lesley Reedman | 716 555 4123 | Wedding | 10/16/2021 | Westview | 110 | Yes | 34.95 |
| Mitchell Langley | 905 555 4637 | Wedding | 11/14/2021 | Sunset | 85 | Yes | 29.95 |
| Sally Ramirez | 716 555 9648 | Engagement Party | 12/5/2021 | Starlake | 34 | No | 25.95 |

Insert images, display gridlines, and apply shading to enhance the appearance of a worksheet.

# *In Section 3 you will learn how to*

## Use Function Formulas and Add Visual Elements

Excel's functions make the task of writing formulas easier. Functions are grouped into categories such as statistical, financial, date, and logical. Excel provides over 300 prebuilt formulas to perform calculations. The Insert Function dialog box is available to assist with locating and creating a function. Create charts from data to emphasize trends or compare data sets. Add emphasis to worksheets or charts by drawing arrows and adding text boxes.

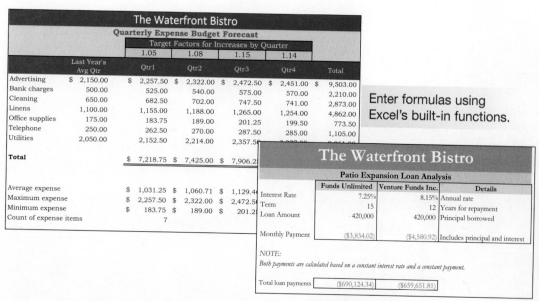

**The Waterfront Bistro**

Quarterly Expense Budget Forecast

| | Last Year's Avg Qtr | Target Factors for Increases by Quarter | | | | |
| | | 1.05 | 1.08 | 1.15 | 1.14 | |
| | | Qtr1 | Qtr2 | Qtr3 | Qtr4 | Total |
| Advertising | $ 2,150.00 | $ 2,257.50 | $ 2,322.00 | $ 2,472.50 | $ 2,451.00 | $ 9,503.00 |
| Bank charges | 500.00 | 525.00 | 540.00 | 575.00 | 570.00 | 2,210.00 |
| Cleaning | 650.00 | 682.50 | 702.00 | 747.50 | 741.00 | 2,873.00 |
| Linens | 1,100.00 | 1,155.00 | 1,188.00 | 1,265.00 | 1,254.00 | 4,862.00 |
| Office supplies | 175.00 | 183.75 | 189.00 | 201.25 | 199.50 | 773.50 |
| Telephone | 250.00 | 262.50 | 270.00 | 287.50 | 285.00 | 1,105.00 |
| Utilities | 2,050.00 | 2,152.50 | 2,214.00 | 2,357.50 | | |
| | | | | | | |
| Total | | $ 7,218.75 | $ 7,425.00 | $ 7,906.25 | | |
| | | | | | | |
| Average expense | | $ 1,031.25 | $ 1,060.71 | $ 1,129.46 | | |
| Maximum expense | | $ 2,257.50 | $ 2,322.00 | $ 2,472.50 | | |
| Minimum expense | | $ 183.75 | $ 189.00 | $ 201.25 | | |
| Count of expense items | | 7 | | | | |

Enter formulas using Excel's built-in functions.

**The Waterfront Bistro**

Patio Expansion Loan Analysis

| | Funds Unlimited | Venture Funds Inc. | Details |
| --- | --- | --- | --- |
| Interest Rate | 7.25% | 8.15% | Annual rate |
| Term | 15 | 12 | Years for repayment |
| Loan Amount | 420,000 | 420,000 | Principal borrowed |
| Monthly Payment | ($3,834.02) | ($4,580.92) | Includes principal and interest |

NOTE:
Both payments are calculated based on a constant interest rate and a constant payment.

| Total loan payments | ($690,124.34) | ($659,651.81) |

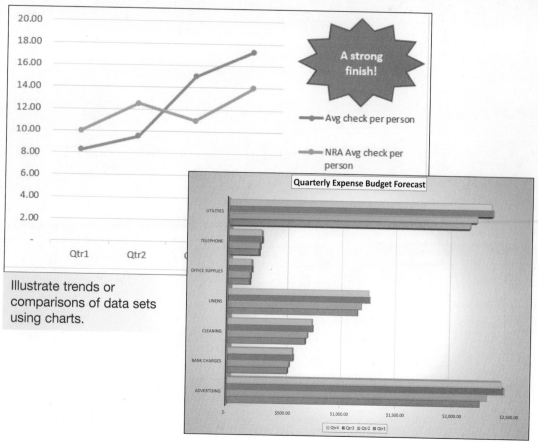

Illustrate trends or comparisons of data sets using charts.

# Excel

# Analyzing Data Using Excel

**Data Files**

Before beginning section work, copy the ExcelS1 folder to your storage medium and then make ExcelS1 the active folder.

## Skills

- Create, save, print, and close a workbook
- Select cells
- Enter data
- Navigate in a worksheet
- Scroll in a worksheet
- Use the fill handle to enter data
- Enter formulas
- Create a formula using SUM
- Copy a formula

- Editing data
- Use Undo and Redo
- Apply basic formatting to a worksheet
- Display formulas in a worksheet
- Use the Tell Me feature
- Use the Help feature
- Change the page orientation to landscape
- Preview and print a worksheet

## Projects Overview

Create a payroll worksheet, create a condensed quarterly income statement.

Complete an estimated travel costs worksheet.

Create a quarterly sales report and a bookings-by-city report.

Create a projected distribution revenue schedule for a new movie release.

NIAGARA PENINSULA COLLEGE

Create an international student registration report and a target enrollment report.

The online course includes additional training and assessment resources.

# Activity 1.1 — Creating, Saving, Printing, and Closing a Workbook

Excel is a spreadsheet application that is used to organize numerical and financial data and to analyze and evaluate information. Information is created in Excel in a worksheet and is saved in a file called a *workbook*. A workbook can contain several worksheets. Imagine a worksheet as a page with horizontal and vertical lines drawn in a grid representing columns and rows. Data is entered into a cell, which is the intersection of a column with a row. Columns are lettered A to Z, AA to AZ, BA to BZ, and so on. The last column in the worksheet is labeled *XFD*. Rows are numbered 1, 2, 3, and so on. A column letter and a row number identify each cell. For example, A1 is the cell address for the intersection of column A with row 1. By default, an Excel workbook contains one worksheet labeled Sheet1. Additional sheets can be inserted as needed.

**What You Will Do**  You have been asked to begin creating a weekly payroll report for The Waterfront Bistro by opening a blank workbook, entering data, printing the worksheet, and then closing the workbook and Excel.

 Tutorial

Opening a Blank Workbook

Tutorial

Exploring the Excel Screen

Tutorial

Saving with a New Name

Tutorial

Closing a Workbook and Closing Excel

**1** At the Windows desktop, click the Start button.

**2** At the Start menu, click the Excel tile.

> Depending on your system configuration, this step may vary.

**3** At the Excel opening screen, click the *Blank workbook* template.

**4** At the Excel screen, identify the various features by comparing your screen with the one shown in Figure 1.1. If necessary, maximize the Excel window. Depending on your screen resolution, your screen may vary slightly. Refer to Table 1.1 for a description of the screen features.

**Figure 1.1** The Excel Screen

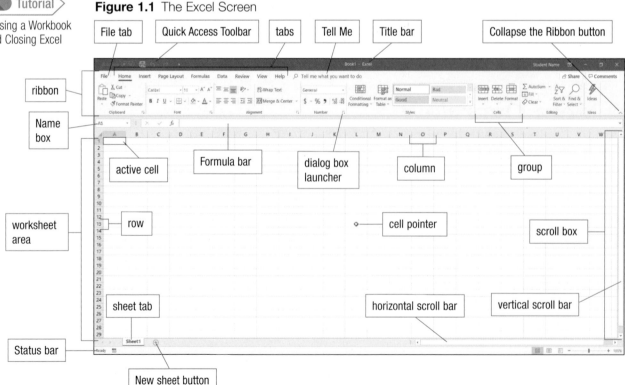

**Table 1.1** Excel Screen Features

| Feature | Description |
| --- | --- |
| active cell | location in the worksheet that will display typed data or that will be affected by a command |
| cell pointer | select cells when mouse pointer displays this icon by clicking or dragging the mouse |
| Collapse the Ribbon button | click to remove the ribbon; double-click a tab to redisplay the ribbon |
| column | an array of cells stacked on top of each other addressed with a letter |
| dialog box or task pane launcher | click the downward-pointing diagonal arrow at the bottom right in a group to open a dialog box or task pane with more options for that group |
| File tab | when clicked, displays the backstage area that contains options for working with and managing files |
| Formula bar | displays the contents stored in the active cell |
| group | area on the ribbon defined by separators that contains similar buttons or features |
| Name box | displays the active cell address or name assigned to active cell |
| New sheet button | click the button to insert a new worksheet in the workbook |
| Quick Access Toolbar | contains buttons for commonly used commands that can be executed with a single mouse click |
| ribbon | area containing the tabs with commands and buttons divided into groups |
| row | an array of cells next to each each other addressed with a number |
| scroll box | a rectangular object in the scroll bar used to scroll in a worksheet |
| sheet tab | identifies the worksheet in the workbook |
| Status bar | displays current mode, action messages, view buttons, and Zoom slider bar |
| tabs | contain commands and buttons organized into groups |
| Tell Me | used to look up a feature and provide options for using the feature |
| Title bar | displays workbook name followed by *Excel* |
| vertical and horizontal scroll bars | used to scroll horizontally or vertically to view various parts of the worksheet beyond the current screen |
| worksheet area | contains cells used to create the worksheet |

**5** With cell A1 the active cell, type Payroll as the title for the new worksheet.

> When you type a new entry in a cell, the entry appears in the Formula bar as well as within the active cell in the worksheet area. To end a cell entry, press the Tab key or Enter key to move to another cell in the worksheet.

**6** Press the Enter key.

**7** With cell A2 the active cell, type Week Ended: September 18, 2021 and then press the Enter key.

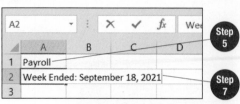

> The entry in cell A2 is overflowing into columns B, C, and D. You can allow a label to spill over into adjacent columns as long as you do not plan to enter other data in the overflow cells.

**8** Click the File tab.

**9** Click the *Print* option.

The Print backstage area contains options, galleries, and buttons for printing the active worksheet.

**10** Click the Print button.

**11** Click the File tab and then click the *Save As* option.

To save a workbook with a different name (other than Book1), use the *Save As* option. Saving a workbook with a different name is useful when you want to preserve the original file.

**12** At the Save As backstage area, click the *Browse* option.

**13** In the Navigation pane at the Save As dialog box, click the removable disk that contains the ExcelS1 folder.

If you are not saving files to a removable disk, check with your instructor to determine the steps you need to follow to access the location of your data files.

**14** Double-click the *ExcelS1* folder in the Content pane.

**15** Click in the *File name* text box.

**16** Type the file name 1-Payroll and then click the Save button or press the Enter key.

Press the F12 function key at the worksheet to display the Save As dialog box without having to click the File tab, the *Save As* option, and then the *Browse* option.

## In Brief

**Open Excel**
1. Click Start button.
2. Click Excel file.

**Enter Data**
1. Make cell active.
2. Type data.

**Print Workbook**
1. Click File tab.
2. Click *Print* option.
3. Click Print button.

**Save Workbook with New Name**
1. Click File tab.
2. Click *Save As* option.
3. Click *Browse* option.
4. Navigate to folder.
5. Click in the *File name* text box.
6. Type workbook name.
7. Click Save or press Enter key.

**Close Workbook**
1. Click File tab.
2. Click *Close* option.

**Close Excel**
Click Close button.

**17** Click the File tab and then click the *Close* option to close the workbook.

When no workbooks are open, Excel displays a blank gray screen.

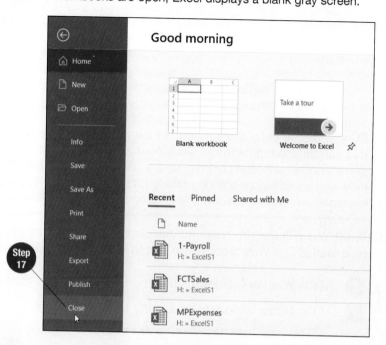

**18** Click the Close button in the upper right corner of the Excel window to close Excel and return to the Windows desktop.

**Check Your Work** Compare your work to the model answer available in the online course.

## In Addition

### Using AutoComplete

The AutoComplete feature in Excel will complete text entries as a new entry is being typed. If the first few letters typed match another entry in the column, Excel automatically fills in the remaining text. Press the Tab key, the Enter key, or one of the arrow keys to accept the text Excel suggests, or continue typing the correct text. AutoComplete can be turned off by clicking the File tab and then clicking *Options*. Click *Advanced* in the left panel of the Excel Options dialog box, click the *Enable AutoComplete for cell values* check box to remove the check mark, and then click OK.

While working in Excel, selecting cells in a worksheet may be necessary. Use the mouse or keyboard to select a specific cell or a range of cells. A range of cells is a collection of two or more adjacent cells. A label is an entry in a cell that helps the reader relate to the values in the corresponding column or row. Labels are generally entered first when creating a new worksheet since they define the layout of the data in the columns and rows. By default, Excel aligns labels at the left edge of the column. A value is a number, formula, or function that can be used to perform calculations in the worksheet. By default, Excel aligns values at the right edge of the column. Take a few moments to plan or sketch out the layout of a new worksheet before entering labels and values. Consider calculations that need to be executed and how to display the data so that it will be easily understood and interpreted.

**What You Will Do**   You need to calculate gross pay in the payroll worksheet for the hourly paid staff at The Waterfront Bistro. Begin by entering labels and values.

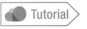

Tutorial

Opening a Workbook

Tutorial

Selecting Cells

Tutorial

Entering Data

Tutorial

Saving with the Same Name

1   At the Windows desktop, click the Start button and then click the Excel tile.

2   At the Home backstage area, click the *Open* option.

> The Open backstage area contains options, buttons, and lists for opening workbooks saved on the computer, OneDrive, and other locations.

3   Click the *Browse* option.

4   At the Open dialog box, navigate to the folder in which you saved the *1-Payroll* workbook.

5   Click *1-Payroll* in the Open dialog box and then click the Open button.

6   With cell A3 the active cell, press the Down Arrow key to make cell A4 active (surrounded by a green border).

> The arrow keys, along with other keys, are used to make a different cell active. Refer to Table 1.2 for information on how to make a specific cell active using the keyboard.

**Table 1.2** Keyboard Movement Commands

| Press | To move to |
|---|---|
| Alt + Page Down | one screen to the right |
| Alt + Page Up | one screen to the left |
| Arrow keys | one cell up, down, left, or right |
| Ctrl + Home | first cell in worksheet (cell A1) |
| Ctrl + End | last cell in worksheet containing data |
| Home | beginning of row |
| Page Down | down one screen |
| Page Up | up one screen |

**7** Type Dayna, press the Tab key, and then type McGuire.

Pressing the Tab key makes the cell to the right of the current cell active.

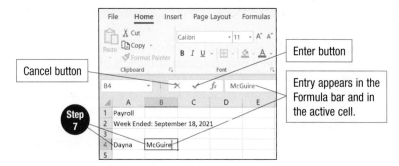

**8** Click in cell J3 to make it active.

Use the mouse to select a specific cell by clicking in the cell when the mouse pointer displays as a white cross.

**9** Type Total, press Alt + Enter, and then type Hours.

Pressing Alt + Enter inserts a line break in the cell, which places whatever is typed next on the following line. The row height will automatically adjust to accomodate the two lines of text.

**10** Enter the remaining labels as shown below by making the appropriate cell active, typing the label, and then using the mouse or keyboard to make the next cell active. (Do not complete the labels for the days of the week beyond *Sun*, as this will be completed in the next activity.)

| | A | B | C | D | E | F | G | H | I | J | K | L |
|---|---|---|---|---|---|---|---|---|---|---|---|---|
| 1 | Payroll | | | | | | | | | | | |
| 2 | Week Ended: September 18, 2021 | | | | | | | | | | | |
| 3 | | | Sun | | | | | | | Total Hours | Pay Rate | Gross Pay |
| 4 | Dayna | McGuire | | | | | | | | | | |
| 5 | Heather | Kiley | | | | | | | | | | |
| 6 | Pat | Soulliere | | | | | | | | | | |
| 7 | Jasmine | Hill | | | | | | | | | | |
| 8 | Moira | Su-Lin | | | | | | | | | | |
| 9 | Carla | Modano | | | | | | | | | | |
| 10 | Toni | Williams | | | | | | | | | | |
| 11 | Tyler | Santini | | | | | | | | | | |
| 12 | Lou | Cortez | | | | | | | | | | |
| 13 | Total | | | | | | | | | | | |
| 14 | | | | | | | | | | | | |

Step 10

**11** Click the Save button 🖫 on the Quick Access Toolbar.

Clicking the Save button on the Quick Access Toolbar saves the workbook with the same name, which overwrites the original file with the changes made in this activity.

**Check Your Work** Compare your work to the model answer available in the online course.

## In Addition

### Selecting Multiple Cells

A range of adjacent or nonadjacent cells is selected using the keyboard and/or mouse. Select a range of adjacent cells with the mouse by clicking in the first cell and holding down the left mouse button, dragging into the last cell, and then releasing the mouse button. Adjacent cells are selected using the keyboard by mak-ing the first cell in the range active, pressing and hold-ing down the Shift key, pressing the arrow key in the specific direction until the last cell is selected, and then releasing the mouse button. To select nonadjacent cells, press and hold down the Ctrl key, click in the specific cells, and then release the Ctrl key.

Excel provides a variety of methods to navigate a worksheet as data is entered and edited. The Name box (displays at the left of the Formula bar) and the Go To dialog box are used to navigate to a specific cell or range. A worksheet can also be navigated using keyboard shortcuts, such as Ctrl + Home. Worksheets can contain data that may not all fit in the worksheet area. Change what cells are visible by scrolling horizontally or vertically in the worksheet. To scroll, use the horizontal and vertical scroll bars, which display on the bottom right and right edge of the window. The scroll bars contain scroll buttons that are used to move the view by one column or row. The scroll bars also contain scroll boxes that can be clicked and dragged to change which cells are visible. The mouse wheel will also vertically scroll in a worksheet, making it more efficient to move up and down.

The Waterfront BISTRO

**What You Will Do**  You need to demonstrate that you can navigate the payroll worksheet using keyboard shortcuts, the Go To dialog box, and the Name box. You also need to demonstrate that you can scroll in the payroll worksheet.

> Tutorial
>
> Navigating and Scrolling

**1** With **1-Payroll** open, press Ctrl + Home.

Pressing Ctrl + Home makes cell A1 the active cell.

**2** Press the Page Down key.

Each time you press the Page Down key, you move the active cell down one screen.

**3** Press the Page Up key.

Each time you press the Page Up key, you move the active cell up one screen.

**4** Click the Find & Select button in the Editing group on the Home tab and then click *Go To* at the drop-down list.

**5** At the Go To dialog box, type L13 in the *Reference* text box and then click OK or press the Enter key.

Using Go To moved the position of the active cell to cell L13.

**6** Use the Up, Down, Left, and Right Arrow keys on the keyboard to practice moving the active cell around the worksheet.

Pressing and holding down a directional arrow key causes the screen to scroll very quickly. Table 1.2 (on page 6) illustrates more keyboard movement commands.

### In Brief

**Navigate to Cell with Go To**
1. Click Find & Select button.
2. Click *Go To.*
3. Type cell reference.
4. Click OK.

**Navigate to Cell with Name Box**
1. Click in Name box.
2. Type cell reference.
3. Press Enter key.

**7** Click in the Name box, to the left of the Formula bar, above cell A1.

> Clicking in the Name box will highlight the current cell reference.

**8** Type K3 and then press the Enter key.

> Make sure you press the Enter key after typing a cell reference in the Name box, otherwise no action will occur.

**9** Position the mouse pointer on the right scroll arrow at the right edge of the horizontal scroll bar and then click the left mouse button a few times to scroll to the right edge of the worksheet.

**10** Position the mouse pointer on the horizontal scroll box, click and hold down the left mouse button, drag the scroll box to the left edge of the horizontal scroll bar, and then release the mouse button.

> The width or height of the scroll box indicates the proportional number of the used cells in the worksheet that are visible in the current window. The position of the scroll box within the scroll bar indicates the relative location of the visible cells within the remainder of the worksheet.

**11** If possible, use the mouse wheel to scroll down in the worksheet area. Otherwise, click the down scroll arrow at the bottom of the vertical scroll bar to scroll in the worksheet area.

**12** Press Ctrl + Home to make cell A1 active.

**13** Click the Save button on the Quick Access Toolbar.

## In Addition

### Entering Scroll Lock Mode

Historically, computers generally only had a keyboard as an input device. The mouse wasn't popular in the infancy of personal computing, so all commands and actions were accomplished on the keyboard. For example, scrolling in an application would require the user to turn on scroll lock and then use other keys such as the arrow keys to scroll in the application. This functionality still exists in Excel, which may be a more efficient way for some users to scroll in a worksheet. Turn on scroll lock mode by pressing the Scroll Lock key (certain keyboards might not have a dedicated Scroll Lock key, and may be accessed using a Function [Fn] key). The Status bar will display the words *Scroll Lock* when the feature is turned on. Once scroll lock mode is on, use the following commands to scroll in the worksheet.

| Keys | Scroll Lock Action |
|------|-------------------|
| Arrow keys | Scrolls one column or row in the direction of the arrow keys used. |
| Page keys | Scrolls one screen up or down. |
| Home key | Makes the top left cell in the screen active. |
| End key | Makes the bottom right cell in the screen active. |

When a cell is active, a green border surrounds it and a small, green square displays in the bottom right corner of the border. This green square is called the *fill handle*. The fill handle is an AutoFill feature in Excel that enters repetitive, series, or patterned data. For example, type the first day of a week in a cell and then use the fill handle to populate the adjacent cells with the remaining days of the week. The entries that are automatically inserted in the adjacent cells are dependent on the contents of the active cell, which is called the source cell. Use the fill handle by making the source cell active, clicking the fill handle and holding down the left mouse button, dragging the pointer into the desired cell, and then releasing the mouse button.

The Waterfront BISTRO

**What You Will Do**   Finish entering the data in the payroll worksheet using the fill handle to enter repetitive and series data.

Tutorial

Entering Data Using the Fill Handle

**1** With **1-Payroll** open, click in cell C3 to make it the active cell.

> You will use the fill handle in cell C3 to automatically enter the remaining days of the week in cells D3 through I3.

**2** Point at the fill handle in cell C3. The cell pointer changes from the large white cross ✛ to a thin black cross ✚.

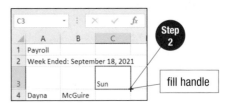

**3** Click and hold down the left mouse button, drag the pointer into cell I3, and then release the mouse button.

> The entries *Mon* through *Sat* appear in cells D3 to I3. As you drag the pointer to the right, a green border surrounds the selected cells and a ScreenTip appears below the pointer indicating the label or value that will be inserted. When you release the left mouse button, the cells remain selected and the Auto Fill Options button appears.

**4** Click in cell F4 to make it the active cell.

**5** Type 8 and then click the Enter button ✓ on the Formula bar.

**6** Click the fill handle in cell F4 and hold down the left mouse button, drag the pointer into cell F12, and then release the mouse button.

> This time the active cell contained a value. The value 8 is copied to the adjacent cells.

## In Brief

**Use Fill Handle**
1. Enter data in cell.
2. Drag fill handle into adjacent cell(s).

**Use Fill Button**
1. Select range including source cell.
2. Click Fill button.
3. Click option.

**7** Enter the remaining values for employee hours as shown below. Use the fill handle where duplicate values appear in adjacent cells to enter the data as efficiently as possible.

| | A | B | C | D | E | F | G | H | I | J |
|---|---|---|---|---|---|---|---|---|---|---|
| 1 | Payroll | | | | | | | | | |
| 2 | Week Ended: September 18, 2021 | | | | | | | | | |
| 3 | | | Sun | Mon | Tue | Wed | Thu | Fri | Sat | Total Hours |
| 4 | Dayna | McGuire | 6 | 5 | 8 | 8 | 7 | 0 | 6 | |
| 5 | Heather | Kiley | 0 | 8 | 6 | 8 | 5 | 5 | 8 | |
| 6 | Pat | Soulliere | 8 | 8 | 0 | 8 | 7 | 7 | 0 | |
| 7 | Jasmine | Hill | 8 | 0 | 8 | 8 | 0 | 8 | 6 | |
| 8 | Moira | Su-Lin | 0 | 8 | 0 | 8 | 7 | 7 | 8 | |
| 9 | Carla | Modano | 0 | 0 | 8 | 8 | 7 | 7 | 8 | |
| 10 | Toni | Williams | 8 | 0 | 0 | 8 | 8 | 7 | 4 | |
| 11 | Tyler | Santini | 8 | 0 | 8 | 8 | 6 | 7 | 0 | |
| 12 | Lou | Cortez | 8 | 0 | 6 | 8 | 0 | 8 | 8 | |
| 13 | Total | | | | | | | | | |
| 14 | | | | | | | | | | |

**Step 7**

**8** Make cell K4 the active cell, type 10.25, and then press the Enter key.

**9** Position the cell pointer over cell K4 (the mouse pointer should display as a white cross), click and hold down the left mouse button, drag into cell K12, and then release the mouse button.

**10** With the Home tab active, click the Fill button in the Editing group and then click *Down* at the drop-down list.

**11** Click the Save button on the Quick Access Toolbar.

**Step 10**

**Check Your Work** Compare your work to the model answer available in the online course.

---

# In Addition

## Using the Fill Handle

The fill handle is versatile and can be used to enter a series of values, dates, times, or other labels as a pattern. The pattern is established based on the cells selected before dragging the fill handle. In the worksheet shown below, the cells in columns C through J were all populated using the fill handle. In each row, the first two cells in columns A and B were selected and then the fill handle was dragged right into column J. Notice the variety of patterns used to extend a series.

## Using the Auto Fill Options Button

Use the Auto Fill Options button drop-down list to control how the series is entered. After dragging the fill handle, the Auto Fill Options button displays at the end of the series. Pointing at the button causes it to expand and display an arrow. Click the arrow and then select the fill action from the options in the drop-down list. By default, *Fill Series* is selected. Click the *Copy Cells* option to repeat the value in the first cell.

| | A | B | C | D | E | F | G | H | I | J | K | L | M |
|---|---|---|---|---|---|---|---|---|---|---|---|---|---|
| 1 | Examples using the fill handle to create a series or pattern in adjacent cells | | | | | | | | | | | | |
| 2 | In each row below, the first two cells were selected and then the fill handle dragged right. | | | | | | | | | | | | |
| 3 | 1 | 2 | 3 | 4 | 5 | 6 | 7 | 8 | 9 | 10 | | | |
| 4 | 10 | 20 | 30 | 40 | 50 | 60 | 70 | 80 | 90 | 100 | Copy Cells | | |
| 5 | 9:00 | 10:00 | 11:00 | 12:00 | 13:00 | 14:00 | 15:00 | 16:00 | 17:00 | 18:00 | Fill Series | | |
| 6 | 2017 | 2019 | 2021 | 2023 | 2025 | 2027 | 2029 | 2031 | 2033 | 2035 | Fill Formatting Only | | |
| 7 | Quarter 1 | Quarter 2 | Quarter 3 | Quarter 4 | Quarter 1 | Quarter 2 | Quarter 3 | Quarter 4 | Quarter 1 | Quarter 2 | Fill Without Formatting | | |
| 8 | Period 1 | Period 4 | Period 7 | Period 10 | Period 13 | Period 16 | Period 19 | Period 22 | Period 25 | Period 28 | | | |
| 9 | Year 1 | Year 6 | Year 11 | Year 16 | Year 21 | Year 26 | Year 31 | Year 36 | Year 41 | Year 46 | | | |
| 10 | | | | | | | | | | | | | |

A formula is entered into a cell to perform mathematical calculations in a worksheet. All formulas in Excel begin with the equals sign (=) as the first character. After the equals sign, the cell addresses that contain the values to be calculated are entered between mathematical operators. The mathematical operators are + (addition), - (subtraction), * (multiplication), / (division), and ^ (exponentiation). An example of a valid formula is =A3*B3. In this formula, the value in cell A3 is multiplied by the value in cell B3 and the result is placed in the formula cell. By including the cell address in the formula rather than typing the actual value, the powerful recalculation feature in Excel can be utilized. If a cell's content is changed, the worksheet is automatically recalculated so that all values are current.

The
Waterfront
BISTRO

**What You Will Do**   You will use two methods to enter formulas to calculate total hours and gross pay for the first two employees listed in the payroll worksheet for The Waterfront Bistro.

Tutorial

Entering Formulas
Using the Keyboard

Tutorial

Entering Formulas
Using the Mouse

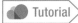
Tutorial

Determining the Order
of Operations

**1**   With **1-Payroll** open, make cell J4 the active cell.

> Begin a formula by making the cell active in which you want the result to appear.

**2**   Type =c4+d4+e4+f4+g4+h4+i4 and then press the Enter key.

> The values in cells C4 through I4 are added and the result, *40*, is displayed in cell J4. You can type cell column letters in a formula in uppercase or lowercase letters. If you type lowercase column letters in a formula, Excel will convert the letters to uppercase when you press the Enter key or click the Enter button on the Formula bar.

| | A | B | C | D | E | F | G | H | I | J | K | L |
|---|---|---|---|---|---|---|---|---|---|---|---|---|
| 1 | Payroll | | | | | | | | | | | |
| 2 | Week Ended: September 18, 2021 | | | | | | | | | | | |
| 3 | | | Sun | Mon | Tue | Wed | Thu | Fri | Sat | Total Hours | Pay Rate | Gross Pay |
| 4 | Dayna | McGuire | 6 | 5 | 8 | 8 | 7 | 0 | 6 | =c4+d4+e4+f4+g4+h4+i4 | | |
| 5 | Heather | Kiley | 0 | 8 | 6 | 8 | 5 | 5 | 8 | | 10.25 | |

Step 2

Cell references are color-coded to the originating cell for quick reference and error checking.

**3**   Press the Up Arrow key to make cell J4 the active cell.

> Notice that the result of the formula displays in the worksheet area and the formula used to calculate the result displays in the Formula bar.

**4**   Make cell J5 the active cell, type the formula =c5+d5+e5+f5+g5+h5+i5, and then press the Enter key.

> Seem like too much typing? A more efficient way to add a series of cells is available. This method will be introduced in the next activity after you learn the pointing method for entering formulas.

**5**   Make cell L4 the active cell.

> To calculate gross pay, you need to multiply the total hours by the pay rate. In Steps 6 through 10, you will enter this formula using the pointing method.

**In Brief**

**Enter a Formula Using Keyboard**
1. Make formula cell active.
2. Type =.
3. Type first cell address.
4. Type operator symbol.
5. Type second cell address.
6. Continue Steps 3–5 until finished.
7. Press Enter key or click Enter button.

**Enter a Formula Using Pointing Method**
1. Make formula cell active.
2. Type =.
3. Click first cell.
4. Type operator symbol.
5. Click second cell.
6. Repeat Steps 3–5 until finished.
7. Press Enter key or click Enter button.

**6** Type the equals sign (=).

**7** Click in cell J4.

A moving dashed border (called a *marquee*) displays around cell J4, indicating it is the cell included in the formula, and the cell address is added to the formula cell (J4) with a blinking insertion point after the reference. The word *Point* displays at the left side of the Status bar.

**8** Type an asterisk (*), which is the multiplication operator.

The marquee surrounding cell J4 disappears and cell J4 is color-coded with the cell reference *J4* within the formula cell.

**9** Click in cell K4.

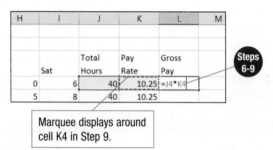

Marquee displays around cell K4 in Step 9.

**10** Click the Enter button on the Formula bar.

The result, *410*, is displayed in cell L4. In Activity 1.9, you will learn how to display two decimal places for cells containing dollar values.

**11** Click in cell K4, type 12.50, and then press the Enter key.

When the value in cell K4 was changed, the result of the formula in cell L4 changed as well.

**12** Click the Save button on the Quick Access Toolbar.

**Check Your Work** Compare your work to the model answer available in the online course.

---

# In Addition

## Determining the Order of Operations

If several operators are included in a formula, Excel calculates the result using the order of operations as follows: negations (e.g., -1) first, then percents (%), then exponentiations (^), then multiplication and division (* and /), and finally addition and subtraction (+ and -). If a formula contains more than one operator at the same level of precedence—for example, both an addition and a subtraction operation—Excel calculates the equation from left to right. To change the order of operations, put parentheses around the part of the formula to be calculated first.

| Formula | Calculation |
|---|---|
| =B5*C5/D5 | Both operators are at the same level of precedence—Excel will multiply the value in B5 times the value in C5 and then divide the result by the value in D5. |
| =B5+B6+B7*C10 | Multiplication takes precedence over addition, so Excel will first multiply the value in B7 by the value in C10. Excel will then take the value in B5 and add to it the value in B6 and then add the result of the multiplication operation. |
| =(B5+B6+B7)*C10 | Because of the parentheses, Excel will first add the values in B5 through B7 and then multiply this sum by the value in C10. |

The formulas to calculate the hours worked by the first two employees were lengthy. A more efficient way to calculate the total hours for Dayna McGuire in cell J4 would be to enter the formula =SUM(C4:I4). This formula includes one of Excel's built-in functions called SUM. A function is a preprogrammed formula. The structure of a formula utilizing a function begins with the equals sign (=), followed by the name of the function, and then the argument. *Argument* is the term given to the values identified within parentheses. In the example provided, the argument C4:I4 contains the starting cell and the ending cell separated by a colon (:). The colon is used to indicate the range to be summed; a range is a rectangular-shaped block of adjacent cells. Since the SUM function is used frequently, an AutoSum button is available on the Home tab.

The Waterfront
B STRO

Tutorial

Entering Formulas
Using the AutoSum
Button

**What You Will Do**   You decide to use a more efficient method of payroll calculation, so you will use the SUM function to complete the hours worked for the payroll worksheet.

**1** With **1-Payroll** open, make cell J4 the active cell and then press the Delete key.

This deletes the cell contents. There was nothing wrong with the formula already entered in cell J4. You are deleting it so that the formulas in the completed worksheet will be consistent.

**2** Click the AutoSum button ∑ in the Editing group on the Home tab. (Do not click the AutoSum button arrow.)

A moving marquee surrounds cells C4 through I4 and a ScreenTip appears below the formula cell indicating the correct format for the SUM function. Excel enters the formula =SUM(C4:I4) in cell J4. The suggested range C4:I4 is selected within the formula so that you can highlight a different range with the mouse if the suggested range is not correct.

Excel enters formula
with suggested range.

ScreenTip displays correct
format for SUM function.

**3** Press the Enter key.

Since the range Excel suggests is the correct range, you can finish the formula by pressing the Enter key or by clicking the Enter button on the Formula bar.

**4** With cell J5 the active cell, press the Delete key to delete the existing formula.

**5** Click the AutoSum button and, when Excel displays the formula =SUM(C5:I5), click the Enter button on the Formula bar.

**6** Make cell J6 the active cell and then click the AutoSum button.

This time the range of cells Excel is suggesting to add (J4:J5) is the wrong range. When you click the AutoSum button, Excel looks for multiple values in the cells immediately above the active cell. In this case, multiple values appear above cell J6, so Excel inserts J4:J5 as the range in the SUM formula.

**7** Position the cell pointer over cell C6, click and hold down the left mouse button, drag the pointer into cell I6, and then release the mouse button.

Steps 6-7

**8** Press the Enter key.

Now that you have seen how the AutoSum button operates, you already know that the suggested range for the next employee's total hours will be incorrect.

**9** Position the cell pointer over cell C7, click and hold down the left mouse button, drag the pointer into cell J7, and then release the mouse button.

Notice you are including cell J7, the cell that will display the result, in the range of cells.

**10** Click the AutoSum button.

The result, *38*, appears in cell J7.

Step 9

Step 10

**11** Click in cell J7 and then look at the formula the SUM function created in the Formula bar: *=SUM(C7:I7)*.

Since Excel created the correct SUM formula from a range of selected cells, you decide to try calculating total hours for more than one employee in one step using the method employed in Steps 9 and 10 but with an expanded range.

**12** Position the cell pointer over cell C8, click and hold down the left mouse button, drag the pointer into cell J12, and then release the mouse button.

**13** Click the AutoSum button.

Steps 12-13

**14** Click in cells J8, J9, J10, J11, and J12 to confirm that the correct formulas appear in the Formula bar.

**15** Click the Save button on the Quick Access Toolbar.

**Check Your Work** Compare your work to the model answer available in the online course.

A worksheet may contain several formulas that are basically the same. For example, in the payroll worksheet, the formula to total the hours for Dayna McGuire is =SUM(C4:I4), the formula for Heather Kiley is =SUM(C5:I5), and so on. The only difference between the two formulas is the row number. Whenever formulas are this similar, use the Copy and Paste feature or the fill handle to copy the formula from one cell to another. The cell containing the original formula is called the *source*, and the cell(s) to which the formula is copied is called the *destination*. When the formula is pasted, Excel automatically changes column letters or row numbers to reflect the destination location. By default, Excel assumes relative addressing, which means that cell addresses update relative to the destination.

**What You Will Do** To simplify your completion of the payroll worksheet, you will copy formulas using two methods: Copy and Paste and the fill handle.

**Tutorial**
Copying Formulas

**1** With **1-Payroll** open, make cell L4 the active cell.

> This cell contains the formula =J4*K4 to calculate the gross pay for Dayna McGuire. You will copy this formula to the remaining cells in column L to finish the *Gross Pay* column.

**2** Click the Copy button in the Clipboard group on the Home tab. (Do not click the Copy button arrow.)

> A moving marquee surrounds the active cell indicating that the source contents have been copied to the Clipboard, which is a temporary storage location. The source being copied is the formula =J4*K4, not the result value, *500*.

**3** Select the range L5:L12. To do this, position the cell pointer over cell L5, click and hold down the left mouse button, drag the pointer to cell L12, and then release the mouse button.

marquee indicating source range

**4** Click the Paste button in the Clipboard group. (Do not click the button arrow.)

> Excel copies the formula to the selected cells and displays the results. The Paste Options button (Ctrl) also appears. Clicking the Paste Options button will display a drop-down list with various alternatives for pasting the data. The moving marquee remains around the source cell and the destination cells remain highlighted. The moving marquee disappears as soon as you start another activity or press the Esc key.

**5** Press the Esc key to remove the marquee and the Paste Options button, click in cell L5, and then look at the entry in the Formula bar: =J5*K5.

> The row number in the source formula was increased by one to reflect the destination. The actions you completed in Steps 1 through 4 are called *relative copying*.

Paste Options button

**6** Use the Down Arrow key to check the remaining formulas in column L.

**7** Make cell C13 the active cell.

**In Brief**

**Copy Formula**
1. Make source cell active.
2. Click Copy button.
3. Select destination cell(s).
4. Click Paste button.

**Copy Formula with Fill Handle**
1. Make source cell active.
2. Click and hold down fill handle.
3. Drag to last cell.
4. Release mouse button.

**8** Click the AutoSum button and then click the Enter button on the Formula bar.

The SUM function inserts the formula =*SUM(C4:C12)*.

**9** Drag the fill handle in cell C13 into cell L13.

When the active cell contains a formula, dragging the fill handle causes Excel to copy the formula and change cell references relative to each destination location.

| C13 | | fx | =SUM(C4:C12) | | | | | | | | | |
|---|---|---|---|---|---|---|---|---|---|---|---|---|
| | A | B | C | D | E | F | G | H | I | J | K | L | M |
| 1 | Payroll | | | | | | | | | | | | |
| 2 | Week Ended: September 18, 2021 | | | | | | | | | | | | |
| 3 | | | Sun | Mon | Tue | Wed | Thu | Fri | Sat | Total Hours | Pay Rate | Gross Pay | |
| 4 | Dayna | McGuire | 6 | 5 | 8 | 8 | 7 | 0 | 6 | 40 | 12.5 | 500 | |
| 5 | Heather | Kiley | 0 | 8 | 6 | 8 | 5 | 5 | 8 | 40 | 10.25 | 410 | |
| 6 | Pat | Soulliere | 8 | 8 | 0 | 8 | 7 | 7 | 0 | 38 | 10.25 | 389.5 | |
| 7 | Jasmine | Hill | 8 | 0 | 8 | 8 | 0 | 8 | 6 | 38 | 10.25 | 389.5 | |
| 8 | Moira | Su-Lin | 0 | 8 | 0 | 8 | 7 | 7 | 8 | 38 | 10.25 | 389.5 | |
| 9 | Carla | Modano | 0 | 0 | 8 | 8 | 7 | 7 | 8 | 38 | 10.25 | 389.5 | |
| 10 | Toni | Williams | 8 | 0 | 0 | 8 | 8 | 7 | 4 | 35 | 10.25 | 358.75 | |
| 11 | Tyler | Santini | 8 | 0 | 8 | 8 | 6 | 7 | 0 | 37 | 10.25 | 379.25 | |
| 12 | Lou | Cortez | 8 | 0 | 6 | 8 | 0 | 8 | 8 | 38 | 10.25 | 389.5 | |
| 13 | Total | | 46 | 29 | 44 | 72 | 47 | 56 | 48 | 342 | 94.5 | 3595.5 | |
| 14 | | | | | | | | | | | | | |
| 15 | | | | | | | | | | | | | |

Step 9

**10** Make cell K13 the active cell and then press the Delete key.

The sum of the *Pay Rate* column is not useful information.

**11** Make cell D13 the active cell and look at the entry in the Formula bar: =*SUM(D4:D12)*.

The column letter in the source formula was changed to reflect the destination.

**12** Use the Right Arrow key to check the formulas in the remaining columns.

**13** Click the Save button on the Quick Access Toolbar.

**Check Your Work** Compare your work to the model answer available in the online course.

## In Addition

### Understanding Copy and Paste versus Fill

What is the difference between copying and pasting and using the fill handle? When the Copy button is used, the contents of the source cell(s) are placed in the Clipboard. The data will remain in the Clipboard and can be pasted several times in the current worksheet, into any other worksheet that is open, or into an open file in another application. Use the Copy and Paste buttons when the formula is to be inserted more than once or into nonadjacent cells. Use the fill handle when the formula is only being copied to adjacent cells.

Data in Excel can be edited after it is entered. Once data is edited in a cell, any formulas that use the data in the edited cell will update according to the new data. This feature is useful to forecast, estimate, or otherwise test how certain key variables affect the overall worksheet. Edit a cell by double-clicking in the cell and then using the keyboard to make changes. Another method is to click in a cell to make it active and then edit its contents in the Formula bar. Although it's not technically considered editing, replace a cell's contents by clicking in the cell to make it active and then typing the new data. When editing the contents of a cell is finished, press the Enter key or click the Enter button on the Formula bar.

Use the Undo button on the Quick Access Toolbar to reverse the last action. Use the Redo button to restore an action that was reversed using the Undo button. Excel stores up to 100 actions that can be undone or redone, and actions can be repeated as many times as needed. Some actions (such as Save) cannot be reversed with Undo.

**What You Will Do** You have been provided updated information on the employee hours and pay rates. Edit the workbook so that it contains the new information.

Tutorial
Editing Data

Tutorial
Using Undo and Redo

**1** With **1-Payroll** open, double-click in cell B6.

Double-clicking in a cell places the insertion point in the cell in the approximate location where you double-clicked.

**2** Press the Right Arrow key or Left Arrow key until the insertion point is between the two *l*s in the text *Soulliere*.

| 4 | Dayna | McGuire |
| 5 | Heather | Kiley |
| 6 | Pat | Soulliere |
| 7 | Jasmine | Hill |
| 8 | Moira | Su-Lin |

**3** Press the Backspace or Delete key to remove one of the *l*s so that the text displays as *Souliere* and then press the Enter key.

**4** Make cell A2 the active cell.

**5** Click in the Formula bar to position the insertion point in it and then press the Right Arrow key or Left Arrow key until the insertion point is between the numbers *1* and *8* in the date.

**6** Press the Delete key to remove the 8, type 1, and then click the Enter button on the Formula bar.

The text in cell A2 should now display as *Week Ended: September 11, 2021*.

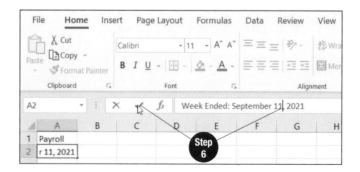

**7** Click in cell B9 to make it active, type Cumberbatch, and then press the Enter key.

The last name *Modano*, previously in cell B9, is replaced with the new last name *Cumberbatch*. Replacing data in a cell instead of editing it manually is sometimes more efficient.

**8** Click in cell E10 to make it active, type 5, and then press the Enter key.

**9** Make cell I11 the active cell, type 4, and then press the Enter key.

> The total hours for Tyler Santini, displayed in cell J11, are one hour over 40 hours total for the week, which is a mistake in the payroll.

**10** Click the Undo button  on the Quick Access Toolbar.

> Clicking the Undo button reverses the replacement of the *0* by *4* in the previous step.

Step 10

**11** Click the Redo button ↻ ˅ on the Quick Access Toolbar.

> You realize that you still need to adjust some of the other data for Tyler Santini and that he in fact did work four hours on Saturday.

**12** Make cell C11 the active cell, type 7, and then press the Enter key.

**13** Make cell K7 the active cell, edit the cell contents in the Formula bar so that the value is *11.75*, and then click the Enter button on the Formula bar.

**14** Click the fill handle in cell K7 and hold down the left mouse button, drag to cell K10, and then release the mouse button.

> Using the fill handle to enter data will also replace data in cells.

Step 14

| J | K | L |
|---|---|---|
| Total Hours | Pay Rate | Gross Pay |
| 40 | 12.5 | 500 |
| 40 | 10.25 | 410 |
| 38 | 10.25 | 389.5 |
| 38 | 11.75 | 446.5 |
| 38 | 11.75 | 446.5 |
| 38 | 11.75 | 446.5 |
| 40 | 11.75 | 470 |
| 40 | 10.25 | 410 |
| 38 | 10.25 | 389.5 |

**15** Click the Undo button on the Quick Access Toolbar.

> You accidently replaced the pay rate for Toni Williams.

**16** Click the fill handle in cell K7 and hold down the left mouse button, drag to cell K9, and then release the mouse button.

**17** Click the Save button on the Quick Access Toolbar.

**Check Your Work** Compare your work to the model answer available in the online course.

## In Addition

### Undoing and Redoing Multiple Actions

In addition to undoing or redoing the previous action, the Undo and Redo buttons on the Quick Access Toolbar can be used to undo or redo multiple actions. Click the button arrow to display a list of previous actions. Click an action on the Undo button drop-down list and that action, along with any preceding actions, will be undone. The same applies for redoing multiple actions. Excel will store up to 100 actions that can be undone or redone. Once a workbook is closed, the actions stored in the Undo and Redo buttons are removed.

Basic formatting should be applied to even the simplest worksheets to ensure that the information they contain is easy to understand. Some of the most basic formatting options in Excel are number, alignment, and font formatting, all of which are on the Home tab. Apply formatting to a cell by first making it active and then using the buttons and options on the Home tab to format the cell. Formatting can also be applied to ranges of cells, which saves the time spent to individually format each cell.

When finished building a worksheet, verifying the accuracy of the formulas entered in the worksheet is a good idea. The worksheet could contain formulas that are correct in structure but not mathematically correct for the situation. For example, the wrong range may be included in a SUM formula, or parentheses missing from a multioperator formula may cause an incorrect result. One method of reviewing formulas for accuracy is to display formulas in the cells of the worksheet. To display formulas in cells, click the Formulas tab and then click the Show Formulas button in the Formula Auditing group. Formulas can also be displayed with the keyboard shortcut Ctrl + `. The display formulas feature is a toggle, so clicking the Show Formulas button or pressing the keyboard shortcut again will display the results of the formulas.

**What You Will Do**   To improve the appearance of the payroll worksheet, you will apply basic formatting. You will also confirm the accuracy of your calculations in the payroll worksheet by displaying the formulas in the worksheet and visually checking the formulas for errors.

Tutorial
Displaying Formulas

Tutorial
Merging and Centering Cells

**1** With **1-Payroll** open, select the range K4:L13.

> In columns K and L, the amount of digits displayed after the decimal point is inconsistent. Since the *Pay Rate and Gross Pay* columns represent money, you will format these cells to display a dollar symbol and show two digits past the decimal point.

**2** Click the Accounting Number Format button $ in the Number group on the Home tab. (Do not click the button arrow.)

> The Accounting format adds a dollar symbol, a comma in the thousands place, and displays two digits after the decimal point for each value in the selection.

Step 2

**3** AutoFit column B so the last name in cell B9 is completely visible by double-clicking the border between the column B and column C headings.

Step 3

**4** Select the range A1:L1.

**5** Click the Merge & Center button in the Alignment group on the Home tab.

Step 5

**6** Select the range A2:L2 and then click the Merge & Center button.

**7** Select the range C3:L3.

**In Brief**

**Display Formulas**
1. Click Formulas tab.
2. Click Show Formulas button.

OR

Press Ctrl + `.

**8** Click the Align Right button ≡ in the Alignment group.

Step 8

The data labels are now aligned above the data below them, making identifying values in the worksheet easier.

**9** Select the range A13:L13.

**10** Click the Bold button **B** in the Font group.

Step 10

The Total row is now bolded, making identifying the totals for each column easier.

**11** If the value in cell L13 displays as pound symbols (########), AutoFit column L so the number value is completely visible by double-clicking the border between column L and column M.

If text entered in a cell does not fit into the cell, it overlaps into the next cell. If a number entered in a cell does not fit, Excel changes the number to number symbols (###). This change is made because Excel does not want to mislead users by a number when only a portion of it displays in the cell.

**12** Click the Formulas tab.

**13** Click the Show Formulas button 🖽 in the Formula Auditing group.

The cells in the worksheet are automatically expanded and cells that contain formulas now display the formula in the worksheet area.

Step 12

Step 13

**14** Click the File tab and then click the *Print* option.

**15** At the Print backstage area, click the Print button.

The worksheet will print on two pages with cell formulas visible.

**16** Press Ctrl + ` to turn off the display of formulas.

The ` symbol is the grave symbol. On the keyboard, it is usually on the key immediately to the left of the number 1 key.

**17** Click the Save button on the Quick Access Toolbar.

**Check Your Work** Compare your work to the model answer available in the online course.

## In Addition

### Rotating Text in Cells

The Alignment group on the Home tab contains an Orientation button 📐, which can be used to rotate text within cells. Text can be rotated counterclockwise, clockwise, changed to a vertical alignment, rotated up vertically, or rotated down vertically. Often, text set in narrow columns is angled to improve the label appearance. In the screen shown at the right, the cells containing the days of the week in the payroll worksheet are angled counterclockwise.

Excel includes the Tell Me feature, which provides information and guidance on how to complete a command. To use Tell Me, click in the *Tell Me* text box on the ribbon to the right of the Help tab and then type a command. As text is typed in the *Tell Me* text box, a drop-down list displays with options for completing the command and information on the command from sources on the Web. At the drop-down list, position the mouse pointer over the *Get Help on* option to display Help articles on the entered command. Click an article at the side menu to display the article in the Help task pane. The Help task pane can also be displayed by clicking the Help tab and then clicking the Help button or by pressing the F1 function key. Help is also available for some buttons, dialog boxes, and backstage areas.

The Waterfront BISTRO

**What You Will Do** After reviewing the payroll worksheet, you think the first two title rows would look better if the text was enlarged. You will use the Tell Me feature to do this.

**1** With **1-Payroll** open, make the range A1:A2 active.

> To increase the font size of the title rows above the columns in the worksheet, you decide to use the Tell Me feature.

Tutorial

Using the Tell Me Feature

**2** Click in the *Tell Me* text box.

Tutorial

Using the Help Feature

**3** Type font in the *Tell Me* text box.

> A drop-down list appears with options such as *Font, Font Size, Theme Fonts,* and *Font Color*.

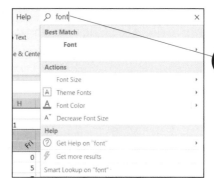

Step 3

**4** Position the mouse pointer on the *Font Size* option in the drop-down list.

> When you position the mouse pointer on an option with an arrow at the side, a side menu displays.

**5** At the side menu, click *14*.

> The size of the text in cells A1 and A2 is increased to 14 points.

Step 4

Step 5

**6** Make the Home tab active and then position the mouse pointer on the Font Color button ⓐ in the Font group.

> A ScreenTip displays with basic information on changing the font color, along with a Tell me more hyperlink.

**7** Click the Tell me more hyperlink and then read the information in the Help task pane.

> You can also access the Help task pane by clicking the Help tab and then clicking the Help button or by pressing the F1 function key.

Step 7

**8** Close the Help task pane by clicking the Close button in the upper right corner of the task pane.

**9** Click in the *Tell Me* text box, type preview worksheet, and then click *Get Help on "preview worksheet"* near the bottom of the *Tell Me* drop-down list.

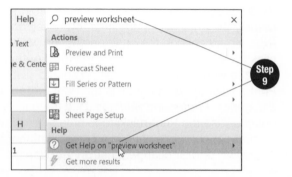

**10** Click the *Preview worksheet pages before you print* option at the side menu.

Clicking the option in the side menu displays the Help task pane with an article on previewing worksheet pages before printing.

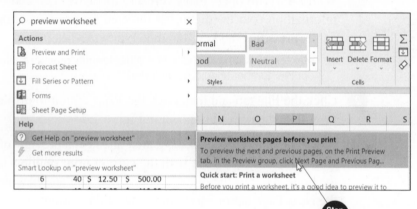

**11** Read the information about previewing a worksheet in the Help task pane and then close the task pane.

**12** Click the Save button on the Quick Access Toolbar.

**Check Your Work** Compare your work to the model answer available in the online course.

## In Addition

### Using the Help Tab

Click the Help tab on the ribbon and buttons display in the Help group with options for getting help. Click the Help button to display the Help task pane. Click the Contact Support button and the Help task pane displays with options for contacting Microsoft and for getting help on a specific issue. Provide feedback to Microsoft on a specific feature by clicking the Feedback button. This displays the Feedback backstage area with buttons for indicating something positive, something negative, and for providing a suggestion. Microsoft provides training videos on some Office features. Click the Show Training button to display the Help task pane with some training videos. Click a video and then the video will play in the Help task pane.

Print a worksheet to have a paper copy, also called a *hard copy*, to file or to attach to a report. Large, complex worksheets are often easier to proofread and check on a hard copy. Display the Print backstage area to preview the worksheet and modify print options. For example, to change the page orientation while previewing how the worksheet will print, click the File tab and then click the *Print* option. At the Print backstage area, a preview of how the worksheet will look when printed displays at the right. The second panel of the Print backstage area contains the Print button, the *Copies* measurement box, and two categories: *Printer* and *Settings*. Use the galleries available in each category to modify print options. Use the Print backstage area to preview the worksheet before printing to avoid wasted paper by checking in advance whether the entire worksheet will fit on one page, or to preview and/or change other print options.

**What You Will Do**   The payroll worksheet is finished. You want to preview the worksheet and then print a copy for the office manager.

Printing a Worksheet

**1** With **1-Payroll** open, make cell A15 the active cell and then type the student information your instructor has directed for printouts. For example, type your first name, press the Tab key, and then type your last name.

Make sure you have checked if other identifying information such as your program or course number should be included.

**2** Click the File tab and then click the *Print* option to display the worksheet in the Print backstage area as shown in Figure 1.2.

**3** The right side of the backstage area displays a preview of the first page of the worksheet as it will print with the current print options. Notice the pages indicator at the bottom left of the preview shows that you are viewing page 1 of 2 pages. Click the Next Page button ▶ to the right of the current page number to display page 2.

**Figure 1.2** Print Backstage Area

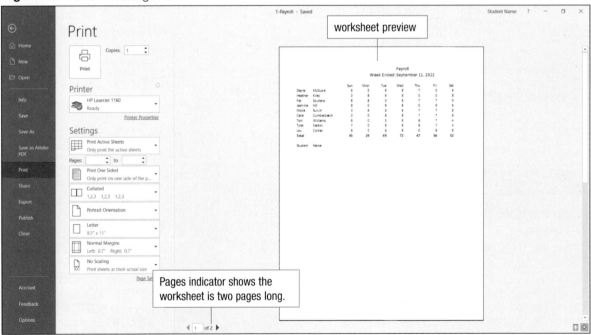

**4** The second page of the printout appears showing the columns that could not fit on page 1.

**5** Click the orientation gallery (currently displays *Portrait Orientation*) in the *Settings* category in the Print backstage area.

> One method to reduce the printout to one page is to change the orientation of the paper from portrait to landscape. In portrait orientation, the page is printed on paper taller than it is wide. In landscape orientation, the data is rotated to print on paper that is wider than it is tall.

**6** Click *Landscape Orientation* at the drop-down list.

> The preview updates to show the worksheet in landscape orientation. Notice that all of the columns now fit on one page.

**7** Click the Print button.

> The Print backstage area closes and the worksheet prints on the default printer. The default settings in the Print backstage area are to print one copy of all pages in the active worksheet. You will learn how to adjust page layout and print settings in a later section.

**8** At the worksheet, scroll right if necessary until you see the vertical dashed line at the right of the *Gross Pay* column.

> The dashed vertical line is a page break. Page breaks appear after you have previewed or printed a worksheet. A worksheet that spans many rows will display a horizontal dashed line below the last row that can fit on the page. The dashed lines do not print.

**9** Save and then close **1-Payroll**.

 **Check Your Work** Compare your work to the model answer available in the online course.

# Features Summary

| Feature | Ribbon Tab, Group | Button | File Tab Option | Keyboard Shortcut |
|---|---|---|---|---|
| Accounting format | Home, Number | $ ˅ | | |
| align right | Home, Alignment | ≡ | | |
| close a workbook | | | *Close* | Ctrl + F4 |
| copy | Home, Clipboard | | | Ctrl + C |
| fill | Home, Editing | | | Ctrl + D |
| Go To dialog box | Home, Editing | , *Go To* | | Ctrl + G |
| Help task pane | Help, Help | ? | | F1 |
| insert line break | | | | Alt + Enter |
| merge and center | Home, Alignment | | | |
| new workbook | | | *New* | Ctrl + N |
| Open backstage area | | | *Open* | Ctrl + O |
| Open dialog box | | | *Open, Browse* | Ctrl + F12 |
| paste | Home, Clipboard | | | Ctrl + V |
| Print backstage area | | | *Print* | Ctrl + P or Ctrl + F2 |
| Redo | | ↷ ˅ | | Ctrl + Y |
| save | | 💾 | *Save* | Ctrl + S |
| save with a new name | | | *Save As, Browse* | F12 |
| show formulas | Formulas, Formula Auditing | | | Ctrl + ` |
| SUM function | Home, Editing OR Formulas, Function Library | Σ | | Alt + = |
| Undo | | ↶ ˅ | | Ctrl + Z |

# Excel

# Editing and Formatting Worksheets

> **Data Files**
>
> Before beginning section work, copy the
> ExcelS2 folder to your storage medium
> and then make ExcelS2 the active folder.

## Skills

- Clear cells and cell formats
- Use spell check and thesaurus
- Insert and delete columns and rows
- Move and copy cells
- Use Paste Options to link cells
- Adjust column width and row height
- Change the font type, size, color, and style
- Apply numeric formats and adjust the number of digits displayed after the decimal point
- Change cell alignment
- Change indentation

- Add borders
- Add fill color
- Use Repeat
- Copy formats using Format Painter
- Apply cell styles
- Apply and modify a theme
- Find and replace cell entries and formats
- Freeze and unfreeze panes
- Change the zoom percentage
- Insert, move, and size images

## Projects Overview

Edit and format a quotation and invoice for catering services. View and edit a special events booking worksheet.

Create a direct wages budget for a remote film shoot.

Complete and format a costume cost report and an invoice for costume production.

Create a room timetable.

Edit and format a revenue summary report for movie distribution.

 The online course includes additional training and assessment resources.

# Clearing Cells; Checking Spelling and Using the Thesaurus

The contents of a cell can be edited directly within the cell or in the Formula bar. Clearing a cell can involve removing the cell contents, format, or both. The Spelling feature is a useful tool to assist with correcting typing errors within a worksheet. After completing a spelling check, the worksheet will still need to be proofread since the spelling checker will not highlight all errors and cannot check the accuracy of the formulas or values. Other proofing tools include a Thesaurus, which will find words with similar meanings.

**What You Will Do** Dana Hirsch, manager of The Waterfront Bistro, has begun a catering services quotation for Marquee Productions. Dana has asked you to finish the quotation by correcting spelling, following up on costs, and improving the appearance of the document. You will be working on this quotation through most of this section.

Clearing Cell Contents and Formatting

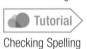

Checking Spelling

**1** Open **WBQuoteToMP**. *Note: This worksheet contains intentional spelling errors that will be corrected in this activity.*

**2** Save the workbook with the name **2-WBQuoteToMP**.

**3** Make cell A7 the active cell and then press the Delete key.

The Delete key or Backspace clears only the contents of the cell; formats applied to the cell remain in effect.

**4** Make cell A1 the active cell and then press the Delete key.

The text is deleted from the cell but the color in the background of the cell remains.

**5** Select the range A1:C1. Click the Clear button in the Editing group on the Home tab and then click *Clear All* at the drop-down list.

Clear All removes everything from a cell, including formats or comments.

**6** Click in cell A1, click the Review tab, and then click the Spelling button in the Proofing group.

Spell check begins at the active cell. Words within the worksheet that are not found in the dictionary are highlighted as potential errors. Use buttons in the Spelling dialog box to skip the word (Ignore Once or Ignore All), replace the word with the highlighted word in the *Suggestions* list box (Change or Change All), or add the word to the dictionary (Add to Dictionary) if spelled correctly.

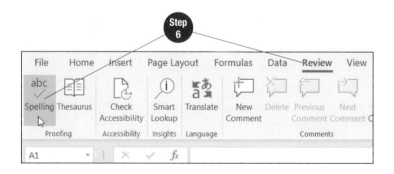

## In Brief

**Clear Cell**
1. Click Clear button.
2. Click *Clear All, Clear Formats, Clear Contents, Clear Comments,* or *Clear Hyperlinks.*

**Spell Check**
1. Click Review tab.
2. Click Spelling button.
3. Click Ignore Once, Ignore All, Change, Change All, or Add to Dictionary button as required.
4. Click OK when spelling check is complete.

**Use Thesaurus**
1. Make cell active.
2. Click Review tab.
3. Click Thesaurus button.
4. Point to replacement word.
5. Click arrow on replacement word.
6. Click *Insert.*

**7** Click the Ignore All button in the Spelling dialog box to skip all occurrences of *Rivermist* in the worksheet since the street name is spelled correctly.

**8** Click the Change button in the Spelling dialog box to replace *Remoat* with *Remote.*

**9** Click the Change button in the Spelling dialog box to replace *Persns* with *Persons.*

Step 7

**10** Complete the spell check, changing words as required. Click OK at the message that the spelling check is complete.

> Double-click the correct spelling in the *Suggestions* list box if it is not initially selected. Click in the *Not in Dictionary* text box if the correct spelling is not in the list, edit as required, and then click the Change button. You can drag the Spelling dialog box out of the way if you need to see the selected word within the worksheet.

**11** Make cell A36 the active cell.

**12** Click the Thesaurus button 📖 in the Proofing group on the Review tab.

> When you click the Thesaurus button, the Thesaurus task pane displays at the right side of the screen. Use the Thesaurus task pane to replace a word in the worksheet with another word with a similar meaning.

Step 12

**13** Point to the word *Transport* in the Thesaurus task pane word list, click the arrow that appears, and then click *Insert* at the drop-down list.

> The word *Delivery* is replaced with *Transport* in cell A36.

**14** Click the Close button in the upper right corner of the Thesaurus task pane.

**15** Save **2-WBQuoteToMP**.

Step 14

Step 13

🔵 **Check Your Work** Compare your work to the model answer available in the online course.

---

## In Addition

### Using the Smart Lookup Task Pane

Use the Smart Lookup task pane to search for information online without leaving the worksheet. For example, an internet search can be conducted to look up information in online encyclopedias or business reference sites. Display the Smart Lookup task pane by making a cell active and then clicking the Smart Lookup button in the Insights group on the Review tab. The Smart Lookup task pane, with the *Explore* option selected, displays information about the selected text from online sources. Click the *Define* option to display a definition of the selected text from the Oxford Dictionary.

Insert rows or columns in a worksheet using options from the Insert button in the Cells group on the Home tab or from the context-sensitive shortcut menu that displays when right-clicking a selected area. Inserted rows are placed above the active cell or selected rows and existing rows are shifted down. Columns are inserted left of the active cell or selected columns and existing columns are shifted right. Delete rows or columns using options from the Delete button in the Cells group or from the context-sensitive shortcut menu that displays when right-clicking a selected area. When rows or columns are deleted, data is automatically shifted up or left to fill in space, and relative references in formulas are updated.

**What You Will Do** You will add items to and delete items from the catering services quotation by inserting and deleting rows and columns.

Tutorial

Inserting Columns and Rows

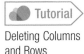

Tutorial

Deleting Columns and Rows

**1** With **2-WBQuoteToMP** open, position the cell pointer (displays as a right-pointing black arrow ➡) over row indicator 21, click and hold down the left mouse button, drag the mouse down over row indicator 22, and then release the mouse.

> This selects rows 21 and 22. Inserted rows are placed *above* the selected rows and columns are inserted to the left.

**2** Click the Home tab, click the Insert button arrow in the Cells group, and then click *Insert Sheet Rows* at the drop-down list.

> Two blank rows are inserted. The amount of rows inserted into the worksheet depends on the number of rows selected. All rows below the inserted rows are shifted down.

**3** Click in cell A21, type Vegetable tray with dip, and then press the Enter key.

**4** Type Seafood hors d'oeuvres and then press the Enter key.

**5** Make active any cell in row 29.

**6** Click the Delete button arrow in the Cells group and then click *Delete Sheet Rows* at the drop-down list.

> The data in row 29 is removed from the worksheet. All rows below the deleted row shift up to fill in the space and Excel automatically adjusts the row catering services numbers to remain sequential.

## In Brief

**Insert Rows or Columns**
1. Select required number of rows or columns.
2. Click Insert button arrow.
3. Click *Insert Sheet Rows* or *Insert Sheet Columns*.

**Delete Rows or Columns**
1. Select rows or columns to be deleted.
2. Click Delete button arrow.
3. Click *Delete Sheet Rows* or *Delete Sheet Columns*.

**7** Right-click the row 19 indicator to display the shortcut menu and Mini toolbar and then click *Delete*.

**8** Right-click the row 26 indicator to display the shortcut menu and Mini toolbar and then click *Delete*.

**9** Delete row 30 from the worksheet.

**10** Position the cell pointer over column indicator letter *F* (displays as a down-pointing black arrow ↓), right-click the mouse, and then click *Delete* at the shortcut menu.

    Data in columns to the right of the deleted column are shifted left to fill in the space.

**11** Click in any cell to deselect the column.

**12** Make cell F8 the active cell, type November 5, 2021, and then press the Enter key.

    By default, Excel displays dates in the format d-mmm-yy (5-Nov-21).

**13** Save **2-WBQuoteToMP**.

**Check Your Work** Compare your work to the model answer available in the online course.

---

## In Addition

### Inserting and Deleting Cells

In this activity, entire rows and columns were selected before inserting or deleting. This practice is the more common method when data is added or deleted from a worksheet. Another method, used less frequently, is to insert new blank cells or delete a range of cells within the worksheet area. To insert new blank cells, select the number of cells needed to add near the location the cells will be added and then click the Insert button in the Cells group on the Home tab, or click the Insert button arrow and then click *Insert Cells* at the drop-down

list to display the dialog box shown below. Use options in the dialog box to shift existing cells right or down. Click the Delete button in the Cells group to delete a

selected range of cells and shift up the cells below the deleted range. Click the Delete button arrow and then click *Delete Cells* to open the Delete dialog box with options similar to those for Insert.

# Activity 2.3   Moving, Copying, and Linking Cells

In a previous activity, formulas were copied and pasted in the payroll worksheet for The Waterfront Bistro. Contents of a cell or range of cells can also be cut and pasted to another location in the worksheet. The selected cells being cut or copied are called the *source* and the cell or range of cells that is receiving the source data is called the *destination*. If data already exists in the destination cells, Excel replaces the contents. Cells cut or copied to the Clipboard can be pasted more than once in the active workbook, in another workbook, or in another Microsoft Office application. Link data between cells using the Paste Link button at the Paste button drop-down gallery or by inserting a simple formula.

**What You Will Do**   Continue to work on the catering services quotation by moving text in the quotation, duplicating a price, linking cells containing prices, and by copying a food item description.

Tutorial
Moving Cells

Tutorial
Copying and Pasting Cells

Tutorial
Linking Data

**1** With **2-WBQuoteToMP** open, make cell A38 the active cell.

**2** Click the Cut button in the Clipboard group on the Home tab.

> A moving marquee surrounds the source after you use Cut or Copy, indicating the cell contents have been placed in the Clipboard.

**3** Make cell E15 the active cell and then click the Paste button in the Clipboard group. (Do not click the Paste button arrow because this displays a drop-down gallery of *Paste* options.)

**4** Select the range of cells A14:B15.

**5** Point at any one of the four borders surrounding the selected range.

> When you point at a border, the pointer changes from the thick white cross to a white arrow with the move icon attached to it (four-headed arrow).

**6** Click and hold down the left mouse button, drag the top left corner of the range into cell E12, and then release the mouse button.

> A green border will appear as you drag, indicating the placement of the range when you release the mouse. The destination range displays in a ScreenTip below the green border.

| 10 | | Los Angeles, CA 90037 | | | |
| 11 | | | | | |
| 12 | ATT: | Camille Matsui | | | |
| 13 | | | | | |
| 14 | RE: | Remote Location Filmin | E12:F13 | | |
| 15 | | July 11 to August 31 | | | Note: All prices include |
| 16 | | | | | |
| 17 | Item | | No of Pers | Price per P | No of Day: Total |
| 18 | Buffet Lunch | | 56 | 8.74 | 52  25450.88 |

**Move or Copy Cells**
1. Select source cells.
2. Click Cut button or Copy button.
3. Select starting destination cell.
4. Click Paste button.

**Copy and Link Cells**
1. Select source cells.
2. Click Copy button.
3. Select destination cell.
4. Click Paste button arrow.
5. Click Paste Link button.

**7** Make cell D25 the active cell.

**8** Click the Copy button 🗐 in the Clipboard group.

**9** Make cell D29 the active cell, click the Paste button arrow in the Clipboard group, and then click the Paste Link button in the *Other Paste Options* section of the drop-down gallery.

The existing data in cell D29 is replaced with the value copied from cell D25, and the source and destination cells are now linked. Linking the cells means that any change made to the source cell (D25) will automatically be applied to the destination cell (D29).

**10** Press Esc to remove the moving marquee from cell D25.

**11** Make cell D25 the active cell, change the value to *3.91*, and then press the Enter key

The value in cell D29 is also changed automatically to 3.91.

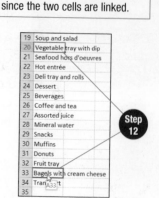

Cell D29 changes automatically since the two cells are linked.

**12** Make cell A20 the active cell. Point at any one of the four borders surrounding cell A20 until the pointer displays as a white arrow with the move icon attached to it, press and hold down the Ctrl key, click and hold down the left mouse button, and then drag to cell A33.

**13** Release the mouse button first and then release the Ctrl key.

A plus sign attached to the pointer indicates the source contents are being copied when you drag and drop using the Ctrl key.

**14** If necessary, click the OK button at the message box.

**15** Save **2-WBQuoteToMP**.

**Check Your Work** Compare your work to the model answer available in the online course.

## In Addition

### Using the Paste Gallery

The Paste gallery (shown at the right) appears in three places: click the Paste button arrow in the Clipboard group, click the Paste Options (Ctrl) button that appears after an entry has been pasted into a cell, or right-click in a cell to display the shortcut menu. The gallery is divided into three sections: *Paste, Paste Values,* and *Other Paste Options*. Within each section, buttons are included for various paste options. Hover the mouse over a button in the gallery to view a ScreenTip that describes the button's purpose as well as to see a preview of the *Paste* option applied to the cell in the worksheet. The Paste gallery is context sensitive, meaning the buttons that appear are dependent on the type of content that has been copied and the location in which the content is being pasted.

By default, columns are the same width and rows are the same height with columns set by default to a width of 8.43 characters and rows to a height of 15.00 points. (Your default column width and row height numbers may vary.) Column width and row height can be adjusted both manually or automatically. Multiple methods are available to manually adjust the column width or row height, such as using the Format button in the Cells group on the Home tab, or click-dragging column or row heading boundaries. As learned in Section 1, AutoFit a column or row by double-clicking a heading boundary. Excel automatically adjusts the height of rows to accommodate the size of the text within the cells. Manually increasing the row height adds more space between rows, which can be used to improve readability or as a design technique to draw attention to a series of cells.

**What You Will Do** You will widen the columns in which labels are shortened to make sure each entry is entirely visible to readers and increase the height of the row containing the column headings to make them stand out from the text below.

Adjusting Column
Width and Row Height

**1** With **2-WBQuoteToMP** open, make any cell active in column A.

**2** Click the Format button ⊞ in the Cells group on the Home tab and then click *Column Width* at the drop-down list.

**3** At the Column Width dialog box, type 14 and then click OK or press the Enter key.

**4** Position the mouse pointer on the boundary line in the column indicator row between columns D and E until the pointer changes to a vertical line with a left-and-right-pointing arrow ✛.

**5** Click and hold down the left mouse button, drag the boundary line to the right until *Width: 15.00* displays in the ScreenTip, and then release the mouse button. ***Note: The pixel amount in parentheses will vary depending on your monitor's settings. Use the 15.00 character measurement in this activity.***

As you drag the boundary line to the right or left, a line appears in the column in the worksheet area, indicating the new width. If, after decreasing a column's width, cells that previously had values in them display as a series of pound symbols (######), the column is now too narrow. Widen the column to redisplay the values.

**6** Position the mouse pointer on the boundary line in the column indicator row between columns C and D until the pointer changes to a vertical line with a left-and-right-pointing arrow and then double-click the left mouse button.

Double-clicking the boundary line sets the width to fit the length of the longest entry within the column. This feature is referred to as the Autofit feature.

**In Brief**

**Increase or Decrease Column Width**
1. Select column(s).
2. Click Format button in Cells group.
3. Click *Column Width*.
4. Type width.
5. Click OK.

**Increase or Decrease Row Height**
1. Select row(s).
2. Click Format button in Cells group.
3. Click *Row Height*.
4. Type height.
5. Click OK.

**Adjust Width or Height Using Mouse**
Drag boundary to right of column or below row, or double-click boundary to AutoFit.

**7** Make cell E17 the active cell, click the Format button in the Cells group, and then click *AutoFit Column Width* at the drop-down list.

> *AutoFit Column Width* adjusts the width of the column to accommodate the amount of text in the active cell. After reviewing the worksheet, you decide all of the columns with numeric values should be the same width.

**8** Position the mouse pointer on column indicator letter C, click and hold down the left mouse button, drag the mouse right over column F, and then release the mouse button.

> This selects columns C through F.

**9** Position the mouse pointer on the right boundary line for column E within the selected range of columns until the pointer changes to a vertical line with a left-and-right-pointing arrow.

> Any changes made to the width of one column boundary will affect all of the selected columns.

**10** Drag the boundary line right until *Width: 15.00* displays in the ScreenTip and then release the mouse button.

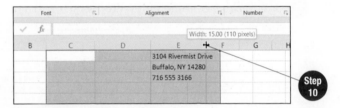

**11** Click in any cell to deselect the columns.

> Do not be concerned that the columns are now too wide after this step—you have many formatting tasks to complete that will improve the layout as you work through the next few activities.

**12** Move E12:F13 to A14:B15 and then click in any cell to deselect the range.

> Refer to Activity 2.3 if you need assistance with this step.

**13** Position the mouse pointer on the boundary line below row 17 until the pointer changes to a horizontal line with an up and down arrow .

**14** Drag the boundary line down until *Height: 21.00* displays in the ScreenTip and then release the mouse button.

**15** Save **2-WBQuoteToMP**.

>  **Check Your Work** Compare your work to the model answer available in the online course.

## In Addition

### Using the Row Height Dialog Box

A sequence of steps similar to those used to adjust column width at the Column Width dialog box can be used to increase or decrease the height of a row with the Row Height dialog box, shown at the right. Click in any cell within the row, click the Format button in the Cells group on the Home tab, and then click *Row Height* at the drop-down list. Type the height and then press the Enter key or click OK.

The font is the typeface used to display and print data. The default font in Excel is Calibri, but many other fonts are available. The size of the font is measured in units called *points*. A point is approximately 1/72 of an inch measured vertically. The default font size in Excel is 11 points. The larger the point size, the larger the type. Each font's style can be enhanced to **bold**, *italic*, or ***bold italic***. Change the color of text to improve worksheet appearance or give emphasis to certain figures, such as changing the font color of negative numbers to red.

**Tutorial**

Applying Font Formatting

**What You Will Do**   To add to the visual appeal of the quotation, you will change the font and font size and apply attributes such as font color to the title *Quotation*.

**1**   With **2-WBQuoteToMP** open, make cell A5 the active cell.

**2**   Click the *Font* option box arrow in the Font group on the Home tab, scroll down the drop-down gallery of fonts, and then point to *Book Antiqua* at the drop-down gallery.

Excel applies the font you are pointing at to the active cell so that you can preview the result, which is the live preview feature.

**3**   Click *Book Antiqua* at the drop-down gallery.

Live preview shows you how the cell will look before you choose the font so you can try different font options before making your selection.

Your list of fonts may vary.

Steps 2-3

**4**   Click the *Font Size* option box arrow in the Font group and then click *18* at the drop-down gallery.

The row height is automatically increased to accommodate the larger font size.

Step 4

**In Brief**

**Change Font Type**
1. Select cells.
2. Click *Font* option box arrow.
3. Click font.

**Change Font Size**
1. Select cells.
2. Click *Font Size* option box arrow.
3. Click font size.

**Change Font Color**
1. Select cells.
2. Click Font Color button arrow.
3. Click color option.

**Change Font Style**
1. Select cells.
2. Click attribute button.

**5** With cell A5 still active, click the Font Color button arrow A ⋎ in the Font group and then click the *Blue* color option (eighth option in the *Standard Colors* section).

**6** Select the range A5:F5 and then click the Merge & Center button in the Alignment group.

**7** Make cell F36 the active cell.

**8** Click the Bold button **B** and then click the Italic button *I* in the Font group.

**9** Save **2-WBQuoteToMP**.

**Check Your Work** Compare your work to the model answer available in the online course.

## In Addition

### Using the Format Cells Dialog Box

Select the cells to be formatted and then click the Font group dialog box launcher ⌐ to open the Format Cells dialog box with the Font tab active. Use the Format Cells dialog box with the Font tab selected (shown at the right) to change the font, font size, font style, and color of text. Additional Underline style options such as *Single, Double, Single Accounting,* and *Double Accounting* are available, as well as the *Effects* options: *Strikethrough, Superscript,* and *Subscript.*

Excel provides specialized formatting options for numeric values. The Accounting format adds a dollar symbol ($), a comma in the thousands place, two digits that display after the decimal point, and displays negative values in brackets. Other numeric formats include Comma, Percentage, and Currency. By default, cells are initially set to the General format, which has no specific numeric style. The number of digits that display after the decimal point in a selected range of cells can be increased or decreased using the Increase Decimal and Decrease Decimal buttons in the Number group on the Home tab. Accountants follow a formatting standard where the top and bottom row containing monetary values display with the dollar symbol and the rest of the values do not include the dollar symbol.

**What You Will Do** To display a consistent number of characters for the numeric values, you will apply the Accounting and Comma formats to selected ranges within the quotation.

**1** With **2-WBQuoteToMP** open, make cell F18 the active cell.

**2** Press and hold down the Ctrl key and then click in cell F36.

**3** Click the Accounting Number Format button in the Number group on the Home tab.

**4** Click in any cell to deselect the cells.

**5** Select the range F25:F34.

**6** Click the Comma Style button [,] in the Number group.

> The Comma Style button formats cells the same as the Accounting Number Format button with the exception of the dollar or alternative currency symbol.

**7** Click in any cell to deselect the range and review the numeric values in the worksheet.

> Column D could be improved by applying a format option to the cell that is not showing the same number of digits past the decimal point as other values in the column.

**8** Make cell D34 the active cell.

**9** Click the Increase Decimal button 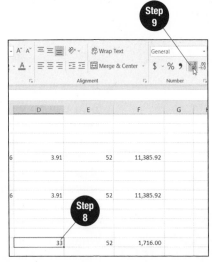 in the Number group.

> One digit past the decimal point is added to or removed from the cells in the selected range each time you click the Increase Decimal or Decrease Decimal button.

**10** With cell D34 still selected, click the Increase Decimal button again.

> The value now displays as *33.00*, which is consistent with the number of digits past the decimal point for the other values in column D.

**11** Select the range F18:F36 and then click the Decrease Decimal button  two times.

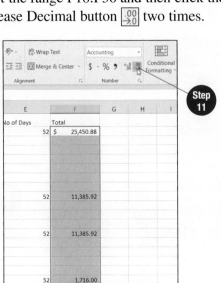

**12** Save **2-WBQuoteToMP**.

💧 **Check Your Work** Compare your work to the model answer available in the online course.

---

## In Addition

### Accessing Additional Number Format Options

Click the *Number Format* option box arrow in the Number group on the Home tab to display a drop-down list (shown at the right) with additional numeric format options including date, time, fraction, and scientific options. Click the *More Number Formats* option at the bottom of the list to open the Format Cells dialog box with the Number tab selected. Use options in this dialog box to further customize formatting such as displaying negative values in red or creating a custom format code.

Data in a cell can be left-aligned, right-aligned, or centered within the column. Cells that have had Merge & Center applied can be formatted to align the text in the merged cell at the left or right. Use the Increase Indent and Decrease Indent buttons in the Alignment group on the Home tab to indent text from the left edge of the cell approximately one character width each time the button is clicked. Use buttons along the top row in the Alignment group to change vertical alignment, rotate text, or wrap text. Use the keyboard shortcut Ctrl + Y or F4 to repeat the last action on another cell. This is useful when performing the same action several times in a row.

**The Waterfront BISTRO**

Tutorial

Applying Alignment Formatting

**What You Will Do** To improve the appearance of the quotation, you will change the alignment of column headings and values and indent labels from the left edge of column A.

**1** With **2-WBQuoteToMP** open, edit the column headings in cells C17 and E17 to include a period (.) after the abbreviation for number. For example, the edited column heading in cell C17 will be *No. of Persons*.

**2** Select the range C17:F17.

**3** Click the Center button ☰ in the Alignment group on the Home tab to horizontally center the data in the cells.

**4** Select the range C18:C29 and then horizontally center the data in the cells.

**5** Select the range E18:E34 and then horizontally center the data in the cells.

**6** Select the range A19:A24.

**7** Click the Increase Indent button ⇥☰ in the Alignment group.

> Each time you click the Increase Indent button, the contents of the selected cells are indented by approximately one character width. If you click Increase Indent too many times, click the Decrease Indent button ☰⇤ to return the text to the previous indent position.

**8** Select the range A26:A28 and then click the Increase Indent button.

**9** Select the range A30:A33 and then click the Increase Indent button.

**10** Select the range A17:F17 and then apply bold formatting.

**11** Make cell F8 the active cell and then click the Align Left button ☰ in the Alignment group.

> By default, Excel aligns date entries at the right edge of a column.

**In Brief**

**Change Horizontal or Vertical Alignment**
1. Select cells.
2. Click alignment button.
3. Deselect cells.

**Indent Text within Cells**
1. Select cells.
2. Click Increase Indent button.
3. Deselect cells.

**Decrease Text Indent within Cells**
1. Select cells.
2. Click Decrease Indent button.
3. Deselect cells.

**12** Select the range A17:F17.

In Activity 2.4, you increased the height of row 17 to 21.00 points. The Alignment group contains buttons that allow you to control the alignment of the text between the top and bottom of the cell boundaries.

**13** Click the Middle Align button ☰ in the Alignment group.

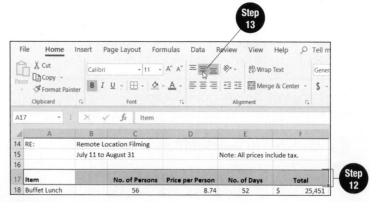

**14** Deselect the range.

**15** Select the range E1:F1 and then click the Merge & Center button in the Alignment group.

**16** Select the range E2:F2 and then press Ctrl + Y (the Repeat command).

You can also press the F4 function key to repeat an action or you can add a Repeat button to the Quick Access Toolbar.

**17** Select the range E3:F3 and then press Ctrl + Y.

You can merge and center in only one row at a time in this situation because data already exists in all three rows.

**18** Select the range E1:E3 and then click the Align Right button in the Alignment group.

**19** Deselect the range.

**20** Save **2-WBQuoteToMP**.

☁ **Check Your Work** Compare your work to the model answer available in the online course.

## In Addition

### Wrapping Text within a Cell

A Wrap Text button 🔲 is available in the Alignment group on the Home tab. Use the Wrap Text button to wrap text within a cell if the column should not be widened. Text too wide for the column is displayed on multiple lines and the height of the row is automatically increased. In the example shown at the right, the original cells are shown on the left and the wrapped cells in column A are displayed on the right.

# Adding Borders and Fill Color; Using Format Painter

Borders in various styles and colors can be applied to display and print in selected cells within the worksheet. Borders can be added to the top, left, bottom, or right edge of a cell. Use borders to underscore headings or totals or to emphasize other cells. Fill color adds color and/or pattern to the background of a cell. Format Painter copies formatting from a selected cell to another cell. Use this feature to apply multiple format options from one cell to another cell.

The Waterfront BISTRO

**What You Will Do**   As you near completion of the catering services quotation, you will spend time improving the presentation of the worksheet by adding borders and shading.

**1** With **2-WBQuoteToMP** open, select the range A17:F17.

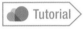
Tutorial
Adding Borders to Cells

Tutorial
Adding Fill Color to Cells

Tutorial
Using Format Painter and the Repeat Command

Tutorial
Applying Formatting Using the Format Cells Dialog Box

**2** Click the Borders button arrow ⊞ ▾ in the Font group on the Home tab. (When Excel is first opened, the button name is Bottom Border. The name changes as border options are selected at the button drop-down list.)

A drop-down list of border style options displays. The *More Borders* option at the bottom of the list opens the Format Cells dialog box with the Border tab selected, where you can create a custom border.

**3** Click *Top and Bottom Border* at the drop-down list.

**4** Click in any cell to deselect the range and view the border.

**5** Select the range A18:B18, click the Borders button arrow (now referred to as the Top and Bottom Border button), and then click *Outside Borders* at the drop-down list.

As mentioned earlier, the name of the button updates to reflect the most recently selected border style.

**6** Select the range A25:B25 and then click the Borders button. (Do not click the arrow.)

Since the Borders button updates to the most recently selected border style, you can apply the *Outside Borders* option to the active cell without displaying the drop-down list.

**7** Select the range A29:B29 and then click the Borders button.

**8** Deselect the range.

**9** Make cell F36 the active cell, click the Borders button arrow, and then click *Top and Double Bottom Border* at the drop-down list.

**10** Make cell A8 the active cell, apply bold formatting, and right-align the cell.

**11** With cell A8 still the active cell, double-click the Format Painter button 🖌 in the Clipboard group.

A moving marquee surrounds the source cell and a paintbrush displays attached to the cell pointer.

**Add Borders**
1. Select cells.
2. Click Borders button arrow.
3. Click border style.
4. Deselect cells.

**Add Fill Color**
1. Select cells.
2. Click Fill Color button arrow.
3. Click fill color option.

**Copy Formats**
1. Make active cell containing source formats.
2. Single-click (copy once) or double-click (copy more than once) Format Painter button.
3. Click destination cell(s).
4. If necessary, click Format Painter button to turn off feature.

**12** Click in cell A12.

**13** Click in cell E12.

**14** Click in cell E8.

Moving marquee in cell A8 indicates cell formats are being copied from this cell.

**Step 12**

**Step 13**

**Step 14**

**15** Click the Format Painter button to turn off the feature.

**16** Click in cell A5.

**17** Click the Fill Color button arrow  and then click the *Blue, Accent 1, Lighter 80%* color option (fifth column, second row in the *Theme Colors* section).

**18** Save **2-WBQuoteToMP**.

**Step 17**

**Check Your Work** Compare your work to the model answer available in the online course.

# In Addition

## Creating a Custom Border

If the borders available in the drop-down list do not provide the needed formatting, a custom border can be created. Click the *More Borders* option at the bottom of the Borders button drop-down list to open the Format Cells dialog box with the Border tab selected, as shown below. Use options in this dialog box to change to a different line style by clicking another line option in the *Style* list box, and/or change the line color by clicking

the *Color* option box arrow and then choosing the new color at the color palette. Next, specify the outside and/or inside border by clicking one of the buttons in the *Presets* section, clicking one or more of the Border buttons along the perimeter of the preview box, or by clicking inside the preview box at the edge of the cell along which the border is to appear. When finished creating the border, click OK.

Choose the border line style here.

Change the border line color here.

Specify the border by clicking a button in the *Presets* section, a border button, or by clicking inside the preview box along the edge where the border is to appear.

Cell styles contain a group of predefined formatting options. Styles are an efficient method for consistently applying formats and creating a professional, consistent worksheet appearance. Excel includes several predefined styles that can be applied or modified or a custom cell style can be created. A *theme* is a set of formatting choices that include a set of colors, a set of heading and body text fonts, and a set of lines and fill effects. Excel provides a variety of themes for formatting text and cells in a worksheet.

**What You Will Do**   Your final steps in improving the presentation of the worksheet will involve applying cell styles and a theme.

**1**  With **2-WBQuoteToMP** open, make cell A5 the active cell.

> You decide to change the formatting of the *Quotation* title to a predefined cell style.

Tutorial

Applying Cell Styles

**2**  Click the Cell Styles button 🗒 in the Styles group on the Home tab.

> A drop-down gallery appears with the predefined cell styles grouped into five sections: *Good, Bad and Neutral*; *Data and Model*; *Titles and Headings*; *Themed Cell Styles*; and *Number Format*.

Tutorial

Applying and Modifying Themes

**3**  Move the mouse pointer over several of the cell style options in the drop-down gallery and watch live preview show the style applied to the title in cell A5.

**4**  Click the *Title* style in the *Titles and Headings* section of the gallery.

Live preview shows how the cell will look when the Title style is applied to cell A5.

**5** Select the range A17:F17, click the Cell Styles button in the Styles group, and then click the *Accent2* style in the *Themed Cell Styles* section.

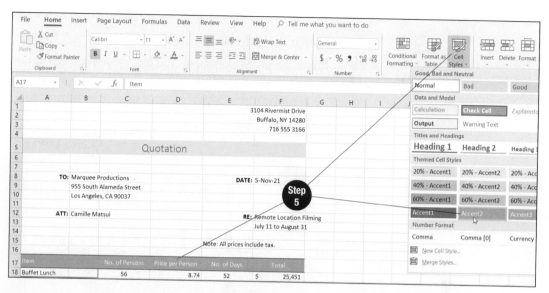

**6** Select the range A18:B18, press and hold down the Ctrl key, select the ranges A25:B25 and A29:B29, and then release the Ctrl key.

**7** Click the Cell Styles button and then click the *Accent1* style in the *Themed Cell Styles* section of the drop-down gallery.

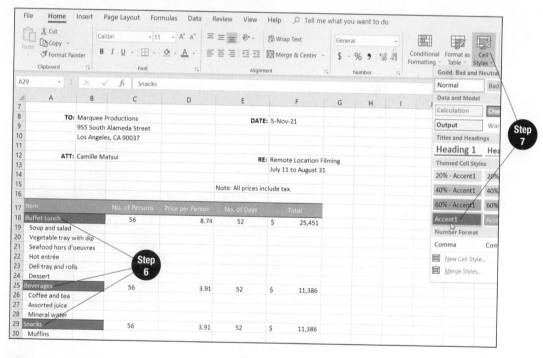

**8** Deselect the cells.

**9** Click the Page Layout tab.

**10** Click the Themes button  in the Themes group.

**11** Move the mouse pointer over several of the themes in the drop-down gallery and watch live preview show the changes that will take place in the worksheet.

**12** Click *Retrospect* at the drop-down gallery.

> A theme affects the entire worksheet. You did not select a cell or range of cells before you applied a theme.

**13** Click the Colors button 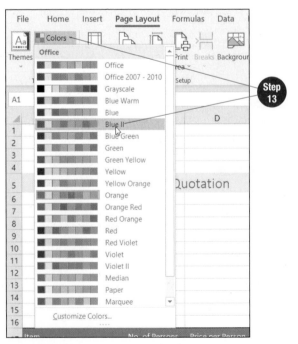 in the Themes group and then click *Blue II* at the drop-down gallery.

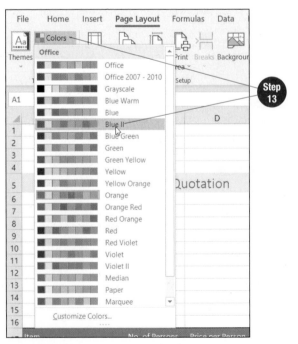

**In Brief**

**Apply Cell Styles**
1. Select cells.
2. Click Cell Styles button.
3. Click style.

**Apply Theme**
1. Click Page Layout tab.
2. Click Themes button.
3. Click theme.

**14** Click the Fonts button [A] in the Themes group, scroll down the drop-down gallery, and then click *Garamond*.

**15** Make cell A1 the active cell, type The Waterfront Bistro, and then press the Enter key.

**16** Select the range A1:D3 and then click the Home tab.

**17** Click the Merge & Center button in the Alignment group and then click the Middle Align button.

**18** With cell A1 still the active cell, click the Cell Styles button and then click *Accent2* in the *Themed Cell Styles* section of the drop-down gallery.

**19** With cell A1 still the active cell, change the font size to 28 points.

**20** Select the range E1:E3 and then apply the Accent2 cell style.

**21** Click in any cell to deselect the range.

**22** Click the File tab, click the *Print* option, and then click the Print button to print the finished quotation.

**23** Save and then close **2-WBQuoteToMP**.

**Check Your Work** Compare your work to the model answer available in the online course.

## In Addition

### Creating a New Style

Create a custom style using the *New Cell Style* option at the bottom of the Cell Styles button drop-down gallery. First, select a cell in the current worksheet and apply all of the formatting to the cell to be saved in the style. Second, with the cell active to which the formats have been applied, click the Cell Styles button and then click *New Cell Style* at the drop-down gallery. At the Style dialog box, shown at the right, type a name for the style in the *Style name* text box and then click OK. The new style will appear at the top of the Cell Styles gallery in a new section titled *Custom*. Custom styles are saved in the workbook in which they are created. The new style will not be available in a new workbook; however, styles can be copied from one workbook to another.

Use the Find feature to search for specific labels or values to be verified or edited. The Find feature will move to each cell containing the specified text. The Replace feature will search for a label, value, or format and replace it with another label, value, or format. Use Find and Replace to ensure that all occurrences of the specified label or value are verified or edited.

**What You Will Do**   Dana Hirsch wants to know how many weddings are booked in 2021. You will use the Find feature to review the wedding bookings in the special events workbook. Dana has also advised you that the prices that were input at $32.95 should be $34.95. You will use the Replace feature to correct these errors.

 Tutorial

Finding Data

 Tutorial

Replacing Data

 Tutorial

Replacing Formatting

**1** Open **WBSpecEvents** and then save it with the name **2-WBSpecEvents**.

**2** Press Ctrl + Home to make cell A1 the active cell.

**3** Click the Find & Select button 🔍 in the Editing group on the Home tab and then click *Find* at the drop-down list.

**4** Type wedding in the *Find what* text box and then click the Find Next button.

> Excel moved to cell C6, which has the entry *25th Wedding Anniversary*. This cell contains the search text *wedding*, but you do not want to review wedding anniversary events.

**5** Click the Options button in the Find and Replace dialog box, click the *Match entire cell contents* check box to insert a check mark, and then click the Find Next button.

> When you clicked the Options button, the dialog box expanded to reveal find and replace options. When you clicked the Find Next button, Excel skipped the entry *50th Wedding Anniversary* in cell C9 and moved directly to cell C10, which contains only the text *Wedding*.

**6** Click the Find Next button.

**7** Click the Find Next button.

**8** Continue clicking the Find Next button until the active cell returns to cell C10 near the top of the worksheet.

> Your review has determined that seven weddings are booked in 2021. In this small worksheet, you could

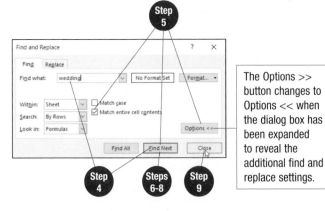

The Options >> button changes to Options << when the dialog box has been expanded to reveal the additional find and replace settings.

easily have completed this calculation by quickly scanning the contents of column C. In a large worksheet with many rows and columns, the Find feature is an efficient method of moving to a specific cell. Typing a specific value into the *Find what* text box could move to a section title or label very quickly.

**9** Click the Close button to close the Find and Replace dialog box.

**In Brief**

**Find Label or Value**
1. Click Find & Select button.
2. Click *Find.*
3. Type label or value in *Find what* text box.
4. Click Find Next button.

**Replace Label or Value**
1. Click Find & Select button.
2. Click *Replace.*
3. Type label or value in *Find what* text box.
4. Type replacement label or value in *Replace with* text box.
5. Click Find Next or Replace All button.

**10** Click the Find & Select button in the Editing group and then click *Replace* at the drop-down list.

**11** With *Match entire cell contents* still selected in the Find and Replace dialog box with the Replace tab selected, double-click the text *wedding* in the *Find what* text box and then type 32.95.

**12** Press the Tab key to move the insertion point to the *Replace with* text box and then type 34.95.

**13** Click the Replace All button.

> Excel searches through the entire worksheet and automatically changes all occurrences of *32.95* to *34.95.*

**14** Click OK at the message that Excel has completed the search and has made four replacements.

**15** Click the *Match entire cell contents* check box to remove the check mark, click the Options button to remove the expanded find and replace options, and then click the Close button to close the Find and Replace dialog box.

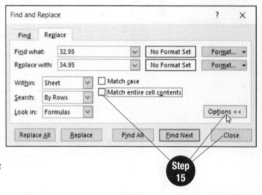

**16** Review the entries in column H and note that no prices exist at $32.95.

**17** Save **2-WBSpecEvents**.

**Check Your Work**  Compare your work to the model answer available in the online course.

---

## In Addition

### Replacing Formats

The Replace feature can be used to find formatting and replace it with other formatting or no formatting. For example, use the Replace feature to find all occurrences of bold and blue font color applied to a cell and replace them with italic and green font color. At the Find and Replace dialog box with the Replace tab selected, click the Options button to expand the dialog box and display Format buttons to the right of the *Find what* and *Replace with* text boxes (shown at the right). Use these buttons to specify the formatting options. The Preview boxes to the left (which initially display *No Format Set*) display the formatting Excel will find and replace.

click to specify formatting options

# Activity 2.11   Freezing Panes; Changing the Zoom

When scrolling horizontally or vertically in a worksheet to view parts of the worksheet that do not fit in the current window, some column or row headings may scroll off the screen, making relating to text or values difficult. Freezing panes causes rows and columns to remain fixed when scrolling. Magnify or reduce the worksheet display by dragging the Zoom slider bar button, clicking the Zoom In or Zoom Out buttons, or by specifying a percentage to zoom to at the Zoom dialog box. Changing the magnification does not affect printing since worksheets automatically print at 100% unless scaling options are changed.

**What You Will Do**   You will freeze column and row headings in the special events worksheet to facilitate scrolling and practice with various Zoom settings to view more cells within the current window.

Tutorial

Freezing and Unfreezing Panes

Tutorial

Changing the Zoom

**1** With **2-WBSpecEvents** open, make cell A4 the active cell.

**2** Click the View tab.

**3** Click the Freeze Panes button in the Window group.

**4** Click *Freeze Panes* at the drop-down list.

> The position of the active cell before you freeze panes is important since all rows above and all columns left of the active cell will be frozen. Notice you made cell A4 the active cell, so rows 1–3 are now frozen. A horizontal black line appears, indicating which rows remain fixed when scrolling.

**5** Press the Page Down key a few times to scroll down the worksheet.

> Look at Figure 2.1 and notice rows 1 through 3 do not scroll off the screen.

**Figure 2.1** Step 5

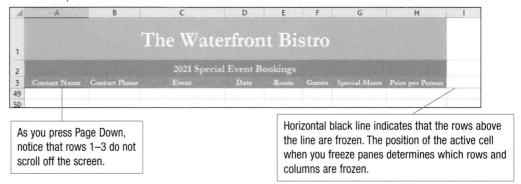

As you press Page Down, notice that rows 1–3 do not scroll off the screen.

Horizontal black line indicates that the rows above the line are frozen. The position of the active cell when you freeze panes determines which rows and columns are frozen.

**6** Press Ctrl + Home. Excel returns to cell A4 instead of cell A1, since cell A1 is frozen.

**7** Click the Freeze Panes button in the Window group and then click *Unfreeze Panes*.

The *Freeze Panes* option changes to *Unfreeze Panes* when rows or columns have been frozen.

**8** Practice dragging the button on the Zoom slider bar (near the right side of the Status bar above the system time) and watch the cells enlarge and shrink as you drag right and left.

**9** Drag the button to the halfway mark on the Zoom slider bar to redisplay the worksheet at 100%.

**10** Click *100%* at the right of the Zoom slider bar to open the Zoom dialog box.

**11** At the Zoom dialog box, click *75%* and then click OK.

**12** Click the Zoom In button at the right of the Zoom slider bar (displays as a plus sign [+]).

**13** Continue to click the Zoom In button until the zoom percentage returns to 100%.

When the worksheet is set to 100% magnification, clicking the Zoom In or Zoom Out buttons at either side of the Zoom slider bar magnifies or shrinks the display of the worksheet by 10% each time the button is clicked.

**14** Save **2-WBSpecEvents**.

**Check Your Work**  Compare your work to the model answer available in the online course.

## In Addition

### Using Buttons in the Zoom Group

The View tab contains a Zoom group with three buttons to change zoom settings. Click the Zoom button in the Zoom group to open the Zoom dialog box. This is the same dialog box that displayed in Step 10. Click the 100% button to return the view to 100%. Select a range of cells and then click the Zoom to Selection button to cause Excel to scale the zoom setting so that the selected range fills the worksheet area.

# Inserting, Moving, and Sizing Images

Microsoft Office includes a gallery of media images that can be inserted in a worksheet, such as clip art, photographs, and illustrations. A company logo or other digital image can be inserted in a worksheet using the Pictures button in the Illustrations group on the Insert tab. Click the Pictures button and the Insert Picture dialog box displays. At this dialog box navigate to the location where the image file is and then double-click the image. Use the Online Pictures button on the Insert tab to search for and insert images from online sources. Once an image has been inserted, it can be moved, sized, or deleted. Format an image with options at the Picture Tools Format tab.

**What You Will Do**   Before printing the special events worksheet, you decide to add an image to the top right and the bistro's logo to the top left of the worksheet. After inserting the images, you will size and move them.

Tutorial

Inserting an Image

Tutorial

Modifying Images

1. With **2-WBSpecEvents** open, make cell A1 the active cell.

2. Click the Insert tab and then click the Pictures button in the Illustrations group.

   This displays the Insert Picture dialog box with a navigation pane at the left.

3. Navigate to your ExcelS2 folder, click **lobster** to select it, and then click the Insert button.

   The image is inserted in the worksheet starting at cell A1.

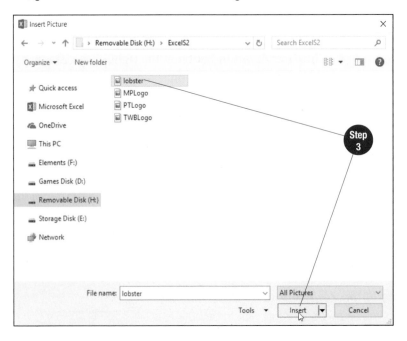

4. Position the mouse pointer on the white sizing handle in the bottom right corner of the image, click and hold down the left mouse button, drag the pointer up and left until the image fits within the first two rows and columns as shown at the right, and then release the mouse button.

**5** Move the mouse pointer over the image until the four-headed arrow move icon appears attached to the pointer, click and hold down the left mouse button, and then drag the image until the right edge of the image is aligned at the right edge of the worksheet, and then release the mouse button.

**6** Click in cell A1, click the Insert tab, and then click the Pictures button in the Illustrations group.

**7** At the Insert Picture dialog box with your ExcelS2 folder contents displayed, double-click the **TWBLogo** image file.

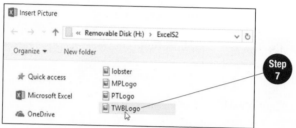

**8** Click in the *Height* measurement box in the Size group on the Picture Tools Format tab, type 1.1, and then press the Enter key.

**9** Using the mouse, drag the logo image so it is positioned as shown below.

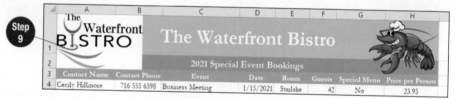

**10** Click in any cell to deselect the logo image.

**11** Select the range A1:A2 and add outside borders.

**12** Select the range A3:H36 and add borders to all of the sides of the cells.

**13** Change to landscape orientation in the Print backstage area and then print the worksheet.

**14** Save and then close **2-WBSpecEvents**.

**Check Your Work** Compare your work to the model answer available in the online course.

## In Addition

### Using the Picture Tools Format Tab

When an image inserted from a file is selected, the Picture Tools Format tab becomes available. Customize the image using picture tools or picture styles. For example, use the Crop button to cut an unwanted area from the image, or set a specific height or width measurement for the image. Use buttons in the Arrange group to group multiple images together, as well as control the alignment, rotation, and order of the image(s) within the worksheet. Use buttons in the Adjust group to control the brightness, contrast, and color of the image(s).

# Features Summary

| Feature | Ribbon Tab, Group | Button | Keyboard Shortcut |
|---|---|---|---|
| align left | Home, Alignment | | |
| borders | Home, Font | | Ctrl + Shift + & |
| cell styles | Home, Styles | | |
| center | Home, Alignment | | |
| clear cell | Home, Editing | | |
| cut | Home, Clipboard | | Ctrl + X |
| decrease decimal places | Home, Number | | |
| decrease indent | Home, Alignment | | |
| delete cell, column, sheet, or row | Home, Cells | | |
| fill color | Home, Font | | |
| find | Home, Editing | | Ctrl + F |
| font | Home, Font | | |
| font color | Home, Font | | |
| font size | Home, Font | | |
| Format Painter | Home, Clipboard | | |
| freeze panes | View, Window | | |
| image from file | Insert, Illustrations | | |
| increase decimal places | Home, Number | | |
| increase indent | Home, Alignment | | |
| insert cell, column, sheet or row | Home, Cells | | |
| middle-align | Home, Alignment | | |
| replace | Home, Editing | | Ctrl + H |
| Spelling | Review, Proofing | | F7 |
| theme | Page Layout, Themes | | |
| theme colors | Page Layout, Themes | | |
| theme fonts | Page Layout, Themes | | |
| Thesaurus | Review, Proofing | | Shift + F7 |

# Excel

# Using Functions, Setting Print Options, and Adding Visual Elements

**Data Files**

Before beginning section work, copy the ExcelS3 folder to your storage medium and then make ExcelS3 the active folder.

## Skills

- Create formulas with absolute addresses
- Create AVERAGE, COUNT, MAX, and MIN formulas to perform statistical analysis
- Create NOW and TODAY formulas
- Use PMT functions to calculate loan payments
- Create and use range names
- Use an IF function to return a result based on a logical test
- Create, edit, and format a column, pie, hierarchy, and line chart

- Insert and format shapes
- Modify and format charts
- Adjust page scaling
- Change page margins
- Change horizontal and vertical centering
- Manipulate a worksheet in Page Layout view
- Insert headers and footers

## Projects Overview

Add functions, create charts, and change page layout options for a quarterly expense and revenue budget forecast; finish an overdue accounts worksheet by entering dates and changing page layout options; calculate loan payment amounts for a patio expansion loan; calculate year-end bonuses; create charts for performance benchmarks.

Calculate and analyze sales commissions; create charts, apply formatting enhancements, and change page layout options in a European Destinations report.

Calculate payments for an office expansion loan for two finance companies.

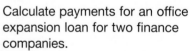 **NIAGARA PENINSULA COLLEGE**

Create and format charts for a grades analysis report; create a chart and apply formatting enhancements to an international student registration report.

Create two charts that depict movie attendance statistics for a staff development workshop.

The online course includes additional training and assessment resources.

55

In the previous two sections, when formulas were copied and pasted in worksheets, the cell addresses in the destination cells changed automatically relative to the destination row or column. The formulas in these worksheets used relative addressing. Sometimes a cell address needs to remain fixed when it is copied to another location in the worksheet. To do this, the formulas must include absolute addressing for those cell addresses that should not change. Make a cell address absolute by typing a dollar symbol ($) in front of the column letter or row number that cannot be changed. The F4 function key can also be used to toggle through variations of the address as relative, absolute, or mixed, in which either the row is absolute and the column is relative or vice versa.

**What You Will Do**   Dana Hirsch has started a worksheet to forecast next year's expenses by quarter. Dana uses a model wherein next year's expenses are estimated based on last year's average quarter values multiplied by a factor that represents the expected increase for this year. For example, a factor of 1.05 means Dana is expecting the expense to increase by 5%. You will calculate each quarter's expense using the factors in the model Dana has started.

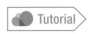

**Absolute Addressing**

**1**   Open **WBQtrExpBudg** and then save it with the name **3-WBQtrExpBudg**.

**2**   Review the layout of the worksheet. The values in the range D4:G4 are factors that represent the increases by quarter for next year's expenses. For example, advertising in quarter 1 is expected to increase by a factor of 1.05 (an increase of five percent).

**3**   Make cell D6 active. All of the values in column D will be created by multiplying last year's average quarter amount by the factor in cell D4. The formula will include an address that should not change when the formula is copied (D4). To create a formula with an absolute address, type =b6*d4 and then press the F4 function key.

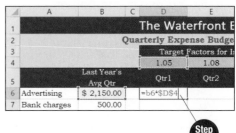

Step 3

Pressing F4 causes Excel to insert dollar symbols in front of the row number and column letter immediately left of the insertion point — *d4* becomes *$D$4*, an absolute address. You can enter column letters in formulas in either uppercase or lowercase. Excel will convert lowercase letters to uppercase automatically when you press the Enter key after typing the formula or when you press F4 to specify an absolute reference.

**4**   Press the Enter key.

The result *$2,257.50* is entered in cell D6. In the cell D6 formula, the first cell reference (B6) is relative and the second cell reference (D4) is absolute. When the formula is copied in a later step, only cell D4 will remain the same.

**5**   With cell D7 active, type =b7*$d$4 and then press the Enter key.

You can also type the dollar symbol in front of the column letter or row number to make an address absolute.

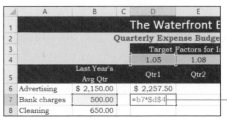

Step 5

**6**   Make cell D7 active and then drag the fill handle into cell D12.

**In Brief**

**Make Cell Address Absolute**
With insertion point positioned just after cell address or with cell address selected in Formula bar, press F4.
OR
Type dollar symbol immediately preceding column letter and/or row number.

**7** Click in cell D8 and look at the formula in the Formula bar. The first cell address (B8) has changed relative to the current row number but the second cell address ($D$4) has remained the same as it was when the formula was copied.

**8** Make cell E6 active, type =b6*e4, press F4, and then press the Enter key.

**9** Make cell F6 active and then create the formula =B6*$F$4 by either typing =b6*f4 and then pressing F4 or by typing dollar symbols before *f* and *4*.

**10** Make cell G6 active and then create the formula =B6*$G$4 by either typing =b6*g4 and then pressing F4 or by typing dollar symbols before *g* and *4*.

**11** Select the range E6:G6 and then drag the fill handle into row 12.

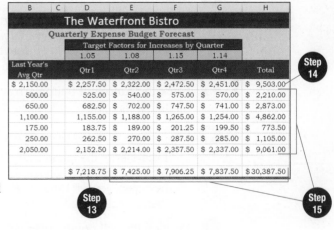

**Steps 8-11**

**12** Click a few cells in the copied range and verify that in each case, the cell reference with the dollar symbols remained the same when the formula was copied.

**13** Make cell D14 active and then click the AutoSum button to calculate the total for column D. Click the AutoSum button a second time to accept the suggested formula =SUM(D6:D13).

**14** Make cell H6 active, click the AutoSum button, and then press the Enter key to accept the suggested formula =SUM(D6:G6).

**15** Complete the formulas in the ranges H7:H12 and E14:H14 by copying the appropriate SUM functions.

**16** Select the range E7:H12 and then apply the Comma format (using the Comma Style button).

**17** Save **3-WBQtrExpBudg**.

Check Your Work  Compare your work to the model answer available in the online course.

## In Addition

### Learning More about Mixed Addressing

Excel can be instructed to fix only the row number or the column letter of a cell that is copied and pasted to another location. This table shows more ways that a cell address can use absolute, mixed, or relative referencing. Pressing F4 repeatedly causes Excel to scroll through each of these variations for the selected cell address.

| Example | Action |
|---|---|
| =$A$12*.01 | Neither the column nor the row will change. |
| =$A12*.01 | The column will remain fixed at column A, but the row will change. |
| =A$12*.01 | The column will change, but the row remains fixed at row 12. |
| =A12*.01 | Both the column and row will change. |

Until now, only the SUM function has been used when clicking the AutoSum button in the Editing group on the Home tab. Excel includes numerous other built-in formulas that are grouped into function categories. The *Statistical* category contains several functions that can be used to perform statistical analysis on data, such as calculating medians, variances, frequencies, and so on. The structure of a function formula begins with the equals sign (=) followed by the name of the function and then the argument within parentheses. *Argument* is the term given to the values to be included in the calculation. The structure of the argument is dependent on the function being used and can include a single range of cells, multiple ranges, single cell references, or a combination thereof.

The Waterfront BISTRO

**What You Will Do**   Dana Hirsch has asked you to add statistics below the quarterly expenses budget forecast. Specifically, you will calculate the average, maximum, and minimum expenses, as well as the total number of expense items.

Tutorial

Using Statistical Functions

**1** With **3-WBQtrExpBudg** open, type the following labels in the cells indicated.

A17:   Average expense
A18:   Maximum expense
A19:   Minimum expense
A20:   Count of expense items

**2** Make cell D17 active.

In the next steps, you will insert the AVERAGE function to determine the arithmetic mean of the expenses in column D. If an empty cell or a cell containing text is included in the argument, Excel ignores the cell when determining the result. If, however, the cell contains a zero value, it is included in the average calculation.

**3** Click the AutoSum button arrow in the Editing group on the Home tab.

**4** Click *Average* at the drop-down list.

Excel inserts the formula *=AVERAGE(D14:D16)* in the active cell with the suggested range highlighted. In the next step, you will drag to select the correct range and then complete the formula.

Step 3
Step 4

**5** Position the cell pointer over cell D6, click and hold down the left mouse button, drag to cell D12, and then release the left mouse button.

Excel inserts the range D6:D12 in the formula and the moving marquee expands to include the selected cells.

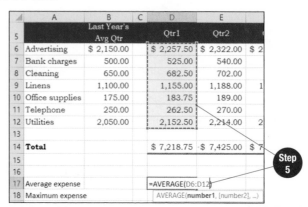

| | A | B | C | D | E | |
|---|---|---|---|---|---|---|
| 5 | | Last Year's Avg Qtr | | Qtr1 | Qtr2 | |
| 6 | Advertising | $ 2,150.00 | | $ 2,257.50 | $ 2,322.00 | $ 2 |
| 7 | Bank charges | 500.00 | | 525.00 | 540.00 | |
| 8 | Cleaning | 650.00 | | 682.50 | 702.00 | |
| 9 | Linens | 1,100.00 | | 1,155.00 | 1,188.00 | 1 |
| 10 | Office supplies | 175.00 | | 183.75 | 189.00 | |
| 11 | Telephone | 250.00 | | 262.50 | 270.00 | |
| 12 | Utilities | 2,050.00 | | 2,152.50 | 2,214.00 | 2 |
| 13 | | | | | | |
| 14 | **Total** | | | $ 7,218.75 | $ 7,425.00 | $ 7 |
| 15 | | | | | | |
| 16 | | | | | | |
| 17 | Average expense | | | =AVERAGE(D6:D12) | | |
| 18 | Maximum expense | | | AVERAGE(**number1**, [number2], ...) | | |

Step 5

In Brief

Use AVERAGE, MAX,
MIN, COUNT Functions
1. Make cell active.
2. Click AutoSum button
   arrow.
3. Click function.
4. Type or select
   argument range.
5. Press Enter key or
   click Enter button.

**6** Press the Enter key or click the Enter button on the Formula bar.

**7** Make cell D18 active, click the AutoSum button arrow, and then click *Max* at the drop-down list.

The MAX function returns the largest value in the argument.

| | A | B | C | D | E |
|---|---|---|---|---|---|
| 5 | | Last Year's Avg Qtr | | Qtr1 | Qtr2 |
| 6 | Advertising | $ 2,150.00 | | $ 2,257.50 | $ 2,322.00 |
| 7 | Bank charges | 500.00 | | 525.00 | 540.00 |
| 8 | Cleaning | 650.00 | | 682.50 | 702.00 |
| 9 | Linens | 1,100.00 | | 1,155.00 | 1,188.00 |
| 10 | Office supplies | 175.00 | | 183.75 | 189.00 |
| 11 | Telephone | 250.00 | | 262.50 | 270.00 |
| 12 | Utilities | 2,050.00 | | 2,152.50 | 2,214.00 |
| 13 | | | | | |
| 14 | **Total** | | | $ 7,218.75 | $ 7,425.00 |
| 15 | | | | | |
| 16 | | | | | |
| 17 | Average expense | | | $  1,031.25 | |
| 18 | Maximum expense | | | =MAX(d6:d12) | |
| 19 | Minimum expense | | | MAX(**number1**, [number2], ...) | |

Step 8

**8** Type d6:d12 and then press the Enter key.

Excel returns the result $2,257.50 in cell D18. Typing the range into the formula is sometimes faster if you are sure of the starting and ending cell references.

**9** With cell D19 active, type the function =min(d6:d12) and then press the Enter key.

MIN returns the smallest value in the argument. As soon as you type the letter *m* after the equals sign, the Formula AutoComplete feature displays a drop-down list of functions that begin with the letter typed. Formula AutoComplete helps you to write formulas by displaying function names, descriptions, and argument syntax. You can scroll the list and point to a function name to display in a ScreenTip the function's purpose. Double-click a function name to enter the function into the cell.

**10** With cell D20 active, type the function =count(d6:d12) and then press the Enter key.

COUNT returns the number of cells that contain numbers or numbers that have been formatted as text and dates. Empty cells, text labels, or error values in the range are ignored.

**11** Select the range D17:D19 and then drag the fill handle into column H. (You are not including the COUNT formula in cell D20 since the count value [7] does not change.)

This copies the AVERAGE, MAX, and MIN formulas to columns E through H.

| | A | B | C | D | E | F | G | H |
|---|---|---|---|---|---|---|---|---|
| 5 | | Last Year's Avg Qtr | | Qtr1 | Qtr2 | Qtr3 | Qtr4 | Total |
| 6 | Advertising | $ 2,150.00 | | $ 2,257.50 | $ 2,322.00 | $ 2,472.50 | $ 2,451.00 | $ 9,503.00 |
| 7 | Bank charges | 500.00 | | 525.00 | 540.00 | 575.00 | 570.00 | 2,210.00 |
| 8 | Cleaning | 650.00 | | 682.50 | 702.00 | 747.50 | 741.00 | 2,873.00 |
| 9 | Linens | 1,100.00 | | 1,155.00 | 1,188.00 | 1,265.00 | 1,254.00 | 4,862.00 |
| 10 | Office supplies | 175.00 | | 183.75 | 189.00 | 201.25 | 199.50 | 773.50 |
| 11 | Telephone | 250.00 | | 262.50 | 270.00 | 287.50 | 285.00 | 1,105.00 |
| 12 | Utilities | 2,050.00 | | 2,152.50 | 2,214.00 | 2,357.50 | 2,337.00 | 9,061.00 |
| 13 | | | | | | | | |
| 14 | **Total** | | | $ 7,218.75 | $ 7,425.00 | $ 7,906.25 | $ 7,837.50 | $30,387.50 |
| 15 | | | | | | | | |
| 16 | | | | | | | | |
| 17 | Average expense | | | $  1,031.25 | $  1,060.71 | $  1,129.46 | $  1,119.64 | $  4,341.07 |
| 18 | Maximum expense | | | $  2,257.50 | $  2,322.00 | $  2,472.50 | $  2,451.00 | $  9,503.00 |
| 19 | Minimum expense | | | $  183.75 | $  189.00 | $  201.25 | $  199.50 | $  773.50 |
| 20 | Count of expense items | | | 7 | | | | |

Step 11

**12** Click in any cell to deselect the range D17:H19.

**13** Save, print, and then close **3-WBQtrExpBudg**.

 **Check Your Work** Compare your work to the model answer available in the online course.

Excel provides the TODAY and NOW date and time functions that insert the current date or date and time in a worksheet. The advantage to using the functions rather than just typing the date and time is that the date and time are automatically updated when the worksheet is opened. When a date is typed in a cell, Excel stores the date as a serial number. Serial numbers in Excel begin with the number 1 (which represents January 1, 1900) and increase sequentially. Because dates are stored as numbers, they can be used in formulas. A date will appear in a cell based on how it is entered. Specify the appearance of dates in a worksheet with options at the Format Cells dialog box with the Number tab selected.

**What You Will Do** An overdue accounts worksheet needs to be completed by entering the current date, formatting the dates, and calculating the account due dates. You will open the overdue accounts worksheet and experiment with the TODAY and NOW functions, change the formatting of the dates, and write a formula that determines the due date.

Using Date and Time Functions

1. Open **WBOverdueAccts** and then save it with the name **3-WBOverdueAccts**.

2. Make cell B4 active, type =now(), and then press the Enter key.

   The current date and time are inserted in cell B4. In the next steps, you will delete the date and time and then use the TODAY function to see the difference between the two date functions. Instead of typing a function (as you did in Step 2), you can insert a date and time function with the Date & Time button on the Formulas tab.

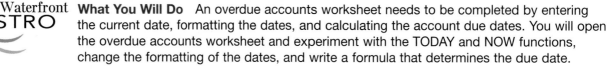

3. Make cell B4 active and then press the Delete key to delete the date and time.

4. Click the Formulas tab, click the Date & Time button  in the Function Library group, and then click *TODAY* at the drop-down list.

5. At the Function Arguments dialog box, click OK.

   The current date is inserted in the cell with the time displayed as *0:00*. Normally, the time does not display with the TODAY function; however, since the NOW function was used first, Excel retained the time format for the cell. In the next steps, you will change the formatting of the date.

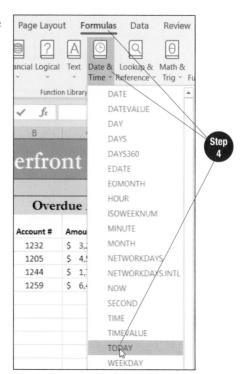

## In Brief

**Use a Date Function**
1. Make cell active.
2. Click Formulas tab.
3. Click Date & Time button.
4. Click function.
5. If necessary, enter references in Function Arguments dialog box.
6. Click OK.

**6** With cell B4 the active cell, click the Home tab, click the *Number Format* option box arrow in the Number group, and then click the *More Number Formats* option at the bottom of the drop-down list.

**7** At the Format Cells dialog box, click *Date* in the *Category* list box and then double-click the fifth option in the *Type* list box (the option that displays the date as *#/##/##*).

**8** Select the range D7:D10 and then apply the same date formatting you applied to cell B4.

**9** Display formulas by clicking the Formulas tab and then clicking the Show Formulas button in the Formula Auditing group.

With the display of formulas turned on, the dates in the range D7:D10 display as serial numbers.

**10** Press Ctrl + ` to turn off the display of formulas.

The grave symbol (`) is to the left of the number 1 key on most keyboards.

**11** Make cell F7 active and then insert a formula that calculates the date plus the days in the *Terms* column by typing =d7+e7 and then pressing the Enter key.

Excel used the date serial number in cell D7, added the number of days in the *Terms* column, and then inserted the due date in the date format.

**12** Copy the formula in cell F7 down to the range F8:F10.

**13** Save, print, and then close **3-WBOverdueAccts**.

**Check Your Work** Compare your work to the model answer available in the online course.

## In Addition

### Using the TIME Function

Time values are stored as decimal numbers that represent the portion of a day starting at 0 (12:00:00 AM) and continuing up to 0.999988426 (23:59:59 PM). The format of the TIME function using the 24-hour clock is *=TIME(hour,minute,second)*. In the worksheet shown at the right, cell D2 contains the formula *=(C2-B2)\*24*, which calculates how many hours an employee worked.

Use Excel's financial functions to calculate depreciation, interest rates, payments, terms, present values, future values, and so on. The PMT function is used to calculate a payment for a loan based on constant payments, a constant interest rate, and a set period of time. When borrowing money, this function is useful for estimating payment based on a specific interest rate and length of time for paying back the loan. To use the PMT function correctly, the time periods for the interest rate and the term have to be consistent. For example, to calculate the monthly payment on a loan, make sure the interest rate and the number of periods are expressed in months, or convert the interest rate and time period to months within the formula. The PMT function requires three arguments: the interest rate for the loan (*Rate*), the number of payments to be made (*Nper*), and the amount of money that is borrowed (*Pv*).

**What You Will Do**   The Waterfront Bistro is planning a patio expansion next year. Dana Hirsch has received preapproval from two finance companies and wants you to estimate monthly loan payments for each to help decide from which company to borrow funds.

**Tutorial**

Using Financial Functions

1. Open **WBPatioLoan** and then save it with the name **3-WBPatioLoan**.

2. Make cell B10 active.

3. Click the Formulas tab and then click the Financial button in the Function Library group.

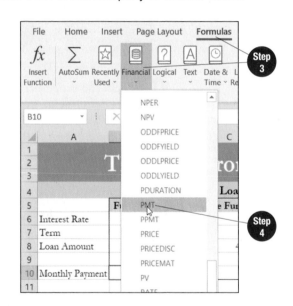

4. Scroll down the Financial button drop-down list and then click *PMT*.

5. If necessary, drag the Function Arguments dialog box Title bar to the right of column B.

6. With the insertion point positioned in the *Rate* text box, click in cell B6 and then type /12.

> The interest rate in cell B6 is 7.25%, which is the annual interest rate. Typing /12 divides the annual interest rate by 12 to obtain a monthly interest rate. Since you want to calculate a payment per month, you need to ensure the time periods for all input values are the same.

7. Click in the *Nper* text box, click in cell B7, and then type *12.

> The term in cell B7 represents the number of years that loan payments will be made. Multiplying this value by 12 represents the total number of loan payments to be made for the year. Note that you have converted both the interest rate and the number of payments within the function arguments to months.

8. Click in the *Pv* text box, click in cell B8, and then click OK.

> Pv stands for *present value* and represents the principal amount that is being borrowed. Excel returns the payment amount *$3,834.02* for the Funds Unlimited loan in cell B10. Payments are displayed as negative values; in this worksheet, negative values are displayed in red and within parentheses. Consider loan payments as money that is subtracted from your cash balance, which helps you relate to the negative value returned in the formula cell. If you prefer, you can enter a negative value in cell B8 (-420,000) and the calculated payment will display as a positive number.

Use a Financial Function
1. Make cell active.
2. Click Formulas tab.
3. Click Financial button.
4. Click function.
5. Enter references in Function Arguments dialog box.
6. Click OK.

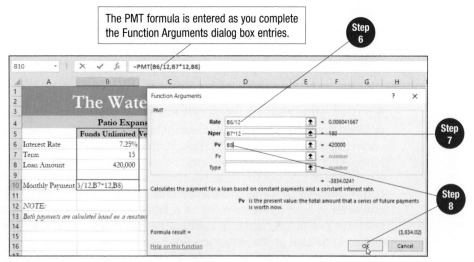

The PMT formula is entered as you complete the Function Arguments dialog box entries.

**9** Make cell C10 active.

**10** Click the Insert Function button $fx$ on the Formula bar.

> The Insert Function dialog box can be used to find an Excel function. This is useful if you do not know the category with which a function is associated. You can locate a function by typing a description of the formula and then clicking the Go button.

**11** At the Insert Function dialog box, type loan payments in the *Search for a function* text box and then click the Go button.

**12** With *PMT* already selected in the *Select a function* list box, click OK.

**13** At the Function Arguments dialog box, enter the parameters below and then click OK.

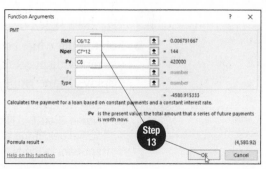

| Rate | C6/12 |
| Nper | C7*12 |
| Pv | C8 |

**14** Make cell A15 active, type Total loan payments, and then press the Enter key.

**15** Make cell B15 active, type =b10*12*b7, and then press the Enter key.

> This calculates the total amount that will have to be paid back for the loan from Funds Unlimited.

**16** Use the fill handle in cell B15 to copy the formula to cell C15.

**17** Use Format Painter to copy the formats from cell B10 to the range B15:C15 and then apply the *All Borders* option to the range B15:C15.

> The loan from Venture Funds Inc. is a better choice for The Waterfront Bistro, provided that they can afford the higher monthly payments. Although the interest rate is higher than Funds Unlimited's loan rate, the shorter term means the loan is repaid faster with a lower total cost.

**18** Save, print, and then close **3-WBPatioLoan**.

 Check Your Work  Compare your work to the model answer available in the online course.

Assigning a name to a cell or a range of cells allows cell(s) to be referenced with a descriptive label rather than the cell address or range address when creating formulas, printing, or when navigating in a large worksheet. Referencing by name makes a formula easier to understand. For example, a formula such as =*Sales-Expenses* is readily understood. A formula such as =*D3-D13* requires the reader to look at the labels next to the values in the formula cells in order to grasp the formula's purpose. A range name can be a combination of letters, numbers, underscore characters, and periods up to 255 characters. The first character in a range name must be a letter, an underscore, or a backslash (\). Spaces are not valid in a range name. To create a range name, select the cells and then type the name in the Name box at the left of the Formula bar.

**What You Will Do**  The profit-sharing bonus for the employees needs to be calculated. Dana Hirsch has started the worksheet and asked you to finish it. Since the bonus amount varies depending on the employee's years of service, you decide to begin by naming cells so that you can use names in the function to help you build the correct formula.

Tutorial

Naming and Using a Range

**1** Open **WBEmpBonus** and then save it with the name **3-WBEmpBonus**.

To begin, you want to name the cells in column B *Years*. The first step in naming a range is to select the cell or group of cells to which the name will be associated.

**2** Select the range B7:B15.

**3** Point at the white box at the left of the Formula bar (currently displays *B7*) and notice that the ScreenTip displays Name Box.

The white box at the left of the Formula bar is called the Name Box. The Name Box displays the address of the active cell. If the active cell has been named, the name appears in the Name box instead. To assign a new name to a cell or selected range, click in the Name box and then type the name.

**4** Click in the Name box, type Years, and then press the Enter key.

Notice that the range name now appears in the Name box. You want to assign a name to each cell that will be referenced when you create the profit-sharing formula in the next activity. In the next steps, you will assign a range name to the individual cells that will be needed to calculate the profit-sharing bonus.

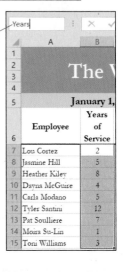

**5** Make cell E7 active.

**6** Click in the Name box, type Profit, and then press the Enter key.

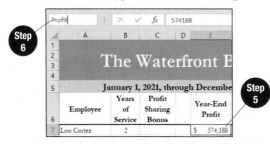

**In Brief**

**Name a Range**
1. Select cell(s).
2. Click in Name box.
3. Type range name.
4. Press Enter key.

**7** Make cell F7 active, click in the Name box, type *FiveAndOver*, and then press the Enter key.

**8** Make cell G7 active, click in the Name box, type *LessThanFive*, and then press the Enter key.

**9** Make cell A1 active and then click the arrow at the right of the Name box.

A drop-down list of range names in the current workbook appears. To move the active cell to a named cell or range, click the range name at the drop-down list.

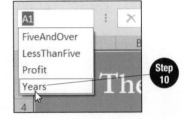

Step 10

**10** Click *Years* at the drop-down list.

The range B7:B15 is selected since this is the group of cells associated with the name *Years*.

**11** Make cell A19 active, type *Average service*, and then press the Enter key.

**12** Make cell B19 active, type *=average(years)*, and then press the Enter key.

Range names are not case sensitive when you use them in a formula. When you type the range name *years* in the formula, notice that Excel color-codes the range B7:B15 to show you the cells that are being referenced in the formula.

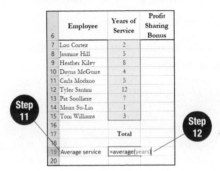

Step 11 / Step 12

**13** Format cell B19 to display only one digit past the decimal point.

**14** Save **3-WBEmpBonus**.

**Check Your Work** Compare your work to the model answer available in the online course.

---

## In Addition

### Managing Range Names

To edit or delete a range name, display the Name Manager dialog box shown at the right. To do this, click the Formulas tab and then click the Name Manager button in the Defined Names group. The Name Manager dialog box displays the range names in the active workbook and provides buttons to edit or delete them.

The IF function, also called a logical test, returns one of two values in a cell based on a true-or-false answer to a question. The format of an IF function is *=IF(logical_test,value_if_true,value_if_false)*. For example, assume a salesperson earns a 3% commission if his or her sales are greater than or equal to $100,000, or a 2% commission for sales less than $100,000. Assume the sales value resides in cell B4. The logical test in this example would be *B4>=100000*. Excel can only return a true-or-false answer when this test is performed. The commission will be calculated with either *B4\*3% (value_if_true)* or *B4\*2% (value_if_false)*. In this example, the IF function formula would be *=IF(B4>=100000,B4\*3%,B4\*2%)*.

**What You Will Do** The catering staff participate in a profit-sharing bonus at the end of each year. The bonus amount is based on the year-end profit and the employee's years of service—2.5% for those with 5 or more years and 1.25% for those employees with less than 5 years. Since the percentage bonus can be either one of two values, you need an IF function to calculate the bonus.

Using Logical IF Functions

**1** With **3-WBEmpBonus** open, make cell C7 the active cell.

**2** Click the Formulas tab.

**3** Click the Logical button [?] in the Function Library group.

**4** Click *IF* at the drop-down list.

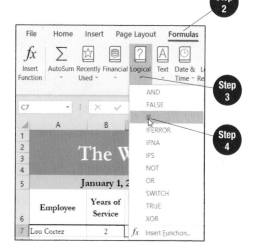

> The Function Arguments dialog box for the IF statement opens. Notice the three arguments: *Logical_test, Value_if_true*, and *Value_if_false*. To begin, you want Excel to test whether the value in the Years of Service column (column B) is less than 5. This test determines whether Excel calculates the bonus using the lower percent paid to employees with fewer than five years of service or the higher percent paid to employees with five or more years of service. Recall that in the last project you created range names. In the next steps, you will see how using range names will make the IF statement much easier to create and understand.

**5** With the insertion point positioned in the *Logical_test* text box, type years<5 and then press the Tab key.

> Watch the entries that appear at the right of each argument text box as you build the formula. Excel updates these entries to show you how the formula is working as you build each argument. Notice that next to the *Logical_test* text box you now see the TRUE and FALSE results Excel is calculating for each entry in the Years range.

**6** With the insertion point positioned in the *Value_if_true* text box, type profit\*lessthanfive and then press the Tab key.

> If the value in cell B7 is less than 5, Excel calculates the bonus as the profit (cell E7) multiplied by 1.25% (cell G7). Another advantage to using range names is that by default, range names refer to the named cell using absolute references. Since the formula will be copied to rows 8 through 15, absolute references are required for those cells that reference the profit and the percents.

**In Brief**

**Use an IF Function**
1. Make cell active.
2. Click Formulas tab.
3. Click Logical button.
4. Click *IF*.
5. Type formula in *Logical_test* text box.
6. Type value or formula in *Value_if_true* text box.
7. Type value or formula in *Value_if_false* text box.
8. Click OK.

**7** With the insertion point positioned in the *Value_if_false* text box, type profit*fiveandover.

If the value in cell B7 is greater than or equal to 5, the formula calculates the profit (cell E7) multiplied by 2.5% (cell F7). Notice that below the text boxes, Excel shows the result that will be placed in the active cell: *= 7177.35*. Looking at cell B7, you will note that Lou Cortez has 2 years of service, so Excel calculates Lou's bonus as $574,188 times 1.25%.

**8** Click OK.

**9** Drag the fill handle in cell C7 into row 15 and then click in any cell to deselect the range.

**10** Make cell C17 active, click the AutoSum button in the Function Library group, and then press the Enter key to calculate the total bonuses to be paid.

**11** Apply the Comma format to the values in column C. If necessary, increase the width of column C to display the entire amounts in the column.

**12** Click in cell C7 and review in the Formula bar the formula that was created using the IF Function Arguments dialog box: *=IF(Years<5,Profit*LessThanFive,Profit*FiveAndOver)*.

The formula may be easier to comprehend if you include the range names.

**13** Save and then close **3-WBEmpBonus**.

**Check Your Work** Compare your work to the model answer available in the online course.

---

## In Addition

### Learning More about IF Function Arguments

One advantage to creating an IF function using the Function Arguments dialog box is that the correct syntax is automatically applied to the formula. For example, in this project, typing commas between arguments or the opening and closing parentheses was not necessary. These elements are automatically added to the formula. Notice also that the range names in the completed formula are displayed in the case used when the range name is created. For example, *profit*lessthanfive* was typed, but the formula reviewed in Step 12 displayed this entry as *Profit*LessThanFive*. When creating range names, consider the readability of the formula and use upper- and lowercase letters to facilitate comprehension. Another alternative is to use underscores between words in a range name.

Numerical values are often more easily understood when presented visually in a chart. Excel includes several chart types such as column, line, pie, bar, area, scatter, and others that can be used to graphically portray data. The chart can be placed in the same worksheet as the data or it can be inserted into its own worksheet. To create a chart, first select the cells containing the data to be graphed and then choose the chart type. Excel graphs the data in a separate object that can be moved, sized, and formatted.

The Waterfront BISTRO

**Tutorial**

Creating Charts

**Tutorial**

Changing Chart Design

**What You Will Do**   Dana Hirsch has asked you to create a chart to compare the quarterly expenses in the budget forecast you completed earlier in this section.

**1**  Open **3-WBQtrExpBudg**, select the range A5:A12, press and hold down the Ctrl key, and then select the range D5:G12.

> The first step in creating a chart is to select the range of cells containing the data you want to graph. The range that you are using includes the row labels in column A. Labels are included to provide the frame of reference for each bar, column, or other chart series. If you select multiple ranges, ensure that the data in each range includes a consistent number of cells.

**2**  Click the Insert tab.

**3**  Click the Insert Column or Bar Chart button in the Charts group.

**4**  Click *3-D Clustered Column* at the drop-down gallery (first option in the *3-D Column* section).

> Excel graphs the data in a 3-D column chart and places the chart inside an object box in the center of the worksheet.

Step 3

Step 4

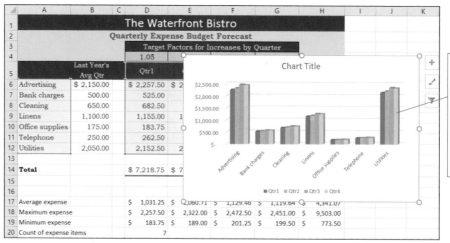

3-D column chart created in Step 4 is placed in an object box, which can be moved, sized, and formatted as needed.

**5**  Click the Move Chart button in the Location group on the Chart Tools Design tab.

Step 5

**6** At the Move Chart dialog box, click the *New sheet* option.

**7** With *Chart1* selected in the *New sheet* text box, type ColumnChart and then click OK.

The chart object is moved to a new sheet in the workbook with a tab labeled ColumnChart. The chart is automatically scaled to fill the entire page in landscape orientation.

**8** Click the Quick Layout button 📊 in the Chart Layouts group and then click *Layout 3* at the drop-down gallery.

**9** Click *Chart Title* to select the title object, click at the beginning of the text to place the insertion point inside the chart title box, delete *Chart Title*, and then type Quarterly Expense Budget Forecast.

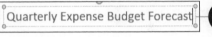

Quarterly Expense Budget Forecast

**10** Click in the chart area to deselect the title text.

**11** Click the *Style 3* chart style in the Chart Styles group on the Chart Tools Design tab.

**12** Save, print, and then close **3-WBQtrExpBudg**.

☁ **Check Your Work** Compare your work to the model answer available in the online course.

## In Addition

### Creating a Recommended Chart

When determining what type of chart will best illustrate data, consider letting Excel recommend a chart. To do this, select the data, click the Insert tab, and then click the Recommended Charts button 📊 in the Charts group. This displays the data in a chart in the Insert Chart dialog box. Customize the recommended chart with options in the left panel of the dialog box. Click OK to insert the recommended chart in the worksheet. A recommended chart can also be inserted in the worksheet with the keyboard shortcut Alt + F1.

Hierarchy charts illustrate each data point's size in proportion to the total of all items in the parent hierarchical level and may include additional levels of hierarchy. A hierarchy chart should include at least a base hierarchical level and one sublevel. For example, a data set could have the base hierarchical level of *Quarterly Sales* and a subcategory of *Monthly Sales*. The addition of hierarchical levels gives users a further breakdown of the general base level data. Choose to display the actual values used to generate the chart using the chart buttons that display outside the top right corner of the chart and/or the Format Data Labels task pane. Other chart elements can be modified and a chart style can be applied using the chart buttons.

FIRST CHOICE
**TRAVEL**

**What You Will Do**   Terry Blessing has requested a second chart from the quarterly expense budget forecast worksheet that displays each expense as a proportion of the total expenses.

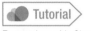
Tutorial

Formatting with Chart
Buttons

**1** Open **FCTSalesGraphic** and then save it with the name **3-FCTSalesGraphic**.

**2** Select the range A3:C19.

**3** Click the Insert tab.

**4** Click the Insert Hierarchy Chart button ▣˅ in the Charts group.

**5** Click the *Treemap* option at the drop-down gallery.

**6** Point to the border of the chart object until the pointer displays with the four-headed-arrow move icon, click and hold down the left mouse button, and then drag the chart, positioning its top left corner in the upper left corner of cell D3.

**7** Size the chart by clicking the bottom right sizing handle and holding down the left mouse button, dragging the bottom right corner of cell J19, and then releasing the mouse button.

**8** With the chart selected, click the Chart Elements button at the right of the chart.

> When a chart is selected, two or three buttons display outside upper right corner of the chart. With the these buttons, you can insert or remove chart elements, apply chart styles, and edit what data points and names display in the chart.

**9** Point to the *Data Labels* option at the drop-down list and then click the expand triangle at the right of the option.

**10** Click *More Data Label Options* at the side menu.

> This displays the Format Data Labels task pane at the right side of the screen.

**11** At the Format Data Labels task pane, click the Label Options icon and then click the *Label Options* heading to expand the *Label Options* section.

**12** Click in the *Value* check box to insert a check mark and display the values in the chart.

**In Brief**

**Create Pie Chart**
1. Select cells.
2. Click Insert tab.
3. Click Insert Pie or Doughnut Chart button.
4. Click desired pie type.
5. Move and/or size chart as required.
6. Apply design options.

**Create Hierarchy Chart**
1. Select cells.
2. Click Insert tab.
3. Click Insert Hierarchy Chart button.
4. Click desired hierarchy type.
5. Move and/or size chart as required.
6. Apply design options.

**13** Close the Format Data Labels task pane.

**14** Click the Chart Styles button at the right of the chart.

**15** Click the fourth style option at the side menu.

**16** Click the Chart Elements button at the right of the chart and then click the *Legend* check box to remove the check mark and the legend from the chart.

**17** Change the chart title to *Quarterly Sales Performance*.

Refer to Activity 3.7, Steps 9–10, if you need assistance with this step.

**18** Click in the chart area to select the entire chart.

**19** If necessary, click the Chart Tools Design tab and then click the Change Colors button in the Chart Styles group.

**20** Click the *Monochromatic Palette 5* option (fifth row in the *Monochromatic* section) at the drop-down gallery.

**21** Click in the worksheet area to deselect the chart.

If the chart remains selected, the chart will be the only thing that is printed in the next step.

**22** Change to landscape orientation.

**23** Save, print, and then close **3-FCTSalesGraphic**.

Check Your Work  Compare your work to the model answer available in the online course.

# In Addition

## Adding Sparklines

The Insert tab contains a Sparklines group. Sparklines are miniature charts that can be added to a cell. These miniature charts illustrate changes from a specified row or column of data. For example, in the worksheet shown below, the sparkline chart was created in cell F4 based on the values in the range B4:E4. Click the Insert tab and then click the Line, Column, or Win/Loss buttons in the Sparklines group. At the Create Sparklines dialog box, select the data range that contains the values on which to base the chart (B4:E4), select the cell in which to draw the chart (F4), and then click OK.

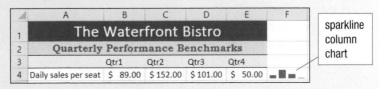

sparkline column chart

# Creating a Line Chart;
## Inserting and Formatting Shapes

A line chart shows trends and change over time at even intervals. Line charts emphasize the rate of change over time rather than the magnitude of the change. Use a line chart to spot trends, look for unusual points in a data series, or even predict future values based on a line chart's shape and direction. The Shapes button on the Insert tab includes buttons for drawing lines, rectangles, basic shapes, block arrows, equation shapes, flowchart symbols, stars and banners, and callouts. Enclosed shapes can also contain text. Draw shapes to add emphasis or to insert explanatory notes in a worksheet.

The Waterfront BISTRO

**What You Will Do** Dana Hirsch has created a worksheet with the bistro's performance statistics by quarter, along with the National Restaurant Association's statistics. Dana would like you to create charts in order to compare the data visually.

Tutorial
Inserting a Shape

Tutorial
Formatting a Shape

**1** Open **WBPerfStats** and then save it with the name **3-WBPerfStats**.

**2** Select the range A3:E4, press and hold down the Ctrl key, and then select the range A8:E8.

**3** Click the Insert tab, click the Insert Line or Area Chart button in the Charts group, and then click *Line with Markers* at the drop-down gallery (fourth column, first row in the *2-D Line* section).

> The line chart clearly shows that the bistro performed below the association's average check per person for the first half of the year but finished the year well above it.

**4** With the Chart Tools Design tab active, click the Quick Layout button and then click the *Layout 12* option at the drop-down gallery (third column, fourth row).

**5** Point to the border of the chart object until the pointer displays with a four-headed-arrow attached, click and hold down the left mouse button, and then drag the chart below the worksheet data approximately centered below columns A through E and with the top edge in row 11.

**6** Select the ranges A3:E3, A5:E5, and A9:E9 and then create a line chart similar to the one created in Steps 3 and 4.

**7** Move the new line chart below the first one, leaving one blank row between the two charts.

> In the next steps, you will draw shapes and add text to the shapes to emphasize the two line charts.

**In Brief**

**Create Line Chart**
1. Select cells.
2. Click Insert tab.
3. Click Insert Line or Area Chart button.
4. Click desired line type.
5. Move and/or size chart as required.
6. Apply design options.

**Insert Shape**
1. Click Insert tab.
2. Click Shapes button.
3. Click desired shape.
4. Click in worksheet or drag to create shape.
5. Move, size, or format shape as required.

**8** Click the Insert tab and then click the Shapes button 🔲 in the Illustrations group.

> The Shapes button drop-down list contains shape buttons grouped by category.

Step 8

**9** Click *Star: 12 Points* in the *Stars and Banners* section (ninth column, first row).

> When a shape object tool has been selected, the pointer changes to crosshairs.

**10** Click in the white space above the legend in the first line chart.

> This inserts a star shape in the worksheet with default measurements of 1 inch for the height and width. The shape contains eight white sizing handles around the perimeter as well as a white rotation handle and an orange circle center point. The Drawing Tools Format tab becomes active with options to customize the shape.

Step 9

**11** With the shape selected, click in the *Width* measurement box, type 1.5, and then press the Enter key.

**12** With the shape still selected, type A strong finish!

> You can type text in a selected shape. You can also right-click the shape and then click *Edit Text* at the shortcut menu.

↕ Height: 1"

⊟ Width: 1.5|

Size

Step 11

**13** Select the text you just typed and then press Ctrl + E to center it horizontally in the shape. Click the Home tab, click the Middle Align button, change the font size to 10 points, and then apply bold formatting.

**14** Position the shape inside the first line chart as shown at the right.

Steps 10-14

Steps 16-20

**15** Click the Insert tab, click the Shapes button, and then click *Wave* in the *Stars and Banners* section (seventh column, second row).

**16** Click in the white space above the legend in the second line chart.

**17** With the shape selected, click in the *Width* measurement box, type 1.5, and then press the Enter key.

**18** Type Qtr 4 30% above NRA! in the shape.

**19** Select the text you just typed and then press Ctrl + E to center it horizontally. Click the Home tab, click the Middle Align button, change the font size to 10 points, and then apply bold formatting.

**20** Position the shape inside the second line chart as shown above.

**21** Save, print, and and then close **3-WBPerfStats**.

To make changes to an existing chart, click in the chart or chart element to display a border around the chart object. Click the border to move the chart or click one of the eight sizing handles to size it. When the chart is selected, the Chart Tools Design and Chart Tools Format tabs become available. Use these tabs to add, delete, or modify the chart or chart elements as needed.

**What You Will Do**   You will modify the charts created for the quarterly expense budget forecast worksheet by formatting the legend, changing the font in the chart title, and changing the chart type.

Tutorial

Changing Chart
Formatting

**1** Open **3-WBQtrExpBudg** and then click in the column chart to select the chart object.

> Once a chart is selected, two additional tabs become available—the Chart Tools Design tab and the Chart Tools Format tab.

**2** Click in the column chart legend.

> Eight sizing handles appear around the legend, indicating that the object is selected. You can drag the legend to another location or size it using one of the handles.

**3** Click the Chart Tools Format tab.

**4** Click the Shape Outline button arrow in the Shape Styles group and then click the *Light Blue* color option (seventh option in the *Standard Colors* section).

> This adds a thin, light-blue border around the legend.

**5** Click the chart title to select it and then click the *Colored Outline - Blue, Accent 1* option in the *Theme Styles* section in the Shape Styles gallery (second column, first row).

**6** Click inside the chart area to deselect the chart title.

**7** Click any of the gray columns in the chart area.

> This selects all seven gray columns.

**8** Click the Shape Fill button arrow in the Shape Styles group and then click the *Green* color option (sixth option in the *Standard Colors* section).

**In Brief**

**Modify Chart**
1. Click to select chart or chart element.
2. Use buttons and options on the Chart Tools Design tab or the Chart Tools Format tab to modify the chart.

**9** Click in the chart area outside the columns.

**10** Click the Chart Tools Design tab and then click the Change Chart Type button in the Type group.

**11** At the Change Chart Type dialog box, click *Bar* in the left panel and then click the *3-D Clustered Bar* option (fourth option near the top of the middle panel).

**12** Click OK.

**13** Print the chart.

**14** Click the Sheet1 sheet tab.

**15** Click the File tab and then click the *Print* option.

**16** Click the scaling gallery in the *Settings* category (gallery that displays *No Scaling*) and then click *Fit Sheet on One Page* at the drop-down list.

> The worksheet is scaled so that all of the columns will print on one page.

**17** Click the Print button.

**18** Save and then close **3-WBQtrExpBudg**.

**Check Your Work** Compare your work to the model answer available in the online course.

## In Addition

### Editing Chart Elements

Another method to edit a chart is to right-click a chart element to display the shortcut menu. For example, right-clicking the axis labels in the bar chart displays the shortcut menu shown at the right. The bottom section of the shortcut menu changes depending on the element clicked.

The Page Layout tab contains buttons to modify the page setup and scaling options for printing purposes. Print options can also be changed while previewing the worksheet in the Print backstage area. The margins on a worksheet are the blank spaces at the top, bottom, left, and right edges of the page and the beginning of the printed text. The default margins are 0.75-inch top and bottom and 0.7-inch left and right. Smaller worksheets can be centered horizontally and/or vertically to improve the printed appearance. For larger worksheets, consider shrinking text by scaling the size of printed text to force the printout to a maximum number of pages. For example, in the previous activity the quarterly expense budget forecast was scaled to print on one page.

**What You Will Do**   You need to print the overdue accounts worksheet completed in Activity 3.3. Prior to printing, you will adjust the margins to improve the worksheet's appearance using the Print backstage area. Dana Hirsch would also like the worksheet printed with the loan analysis for the patio expansion. You will center the worksheet horizontally before printing.

Changing Page Layout Options

1 Open **3-WBOverdueAccts**.

2 Click the File tab and then click the *Print* option to display the Print backstage area.

> The overdue accounts worksheet is not balanced on the page. In the next steps, you will change the margins to improve the page layout.

3 Click the margins gallery in the *Settings* category (currently displays *Normal Margins*).

4 Click *Custom Margins* at the drop-down list.

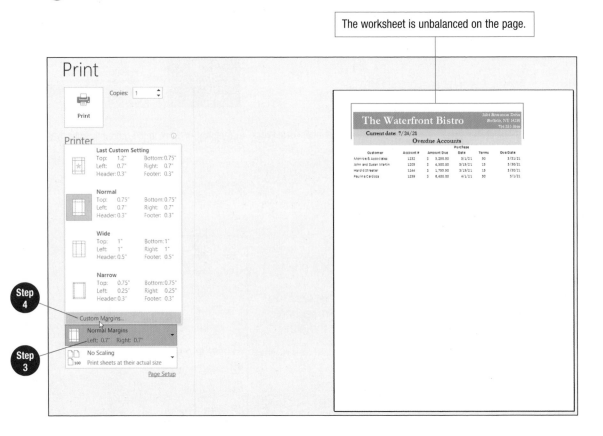

The worksheet is unbalanced on the page.

**5** Select the number in the *Top* measurement box and then type 1.25. Select the number in the *Left* measurement box, type 1.25, and then click OK.

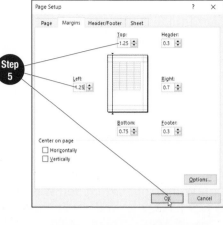

The preview pane in the Print backstage area shows the worksheet with the new margins applied. The page layout is improved for printing.

**6** Click the Print button.

**7** Save and then close **3-WBOverdueAccts**.

**8** Open **3-WBPatioLoan**.

**9** Click the Page Layout tab, click the Orientation button in the Page Setup group, and then click *Landscape*.

**10** Click the Margins button in the Page Setup group and then click *Custom Margins* at the drop-down list.

The Page Setup dialog box opens with the Margins tab active. This is another way to open the same Page Setup dialog box you accessed using the margins gallery in the Print backstage area.

**11** Change the top margin to 1.25 inches.

**12** Click the *Horizontally* check box in the *Center on page* section and then click OK.

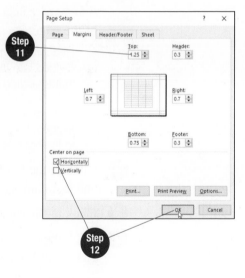

Centering the worksheet horizontally is another method you can use to ensure the worksheet prints balanced between the left and right edges of the page. You can choose both the *Horizontally* and *Vertically* check boxes to print a worksheet that is centered between both the left and right edges (horizontally), and the top and bottom edges (vertically) of the page.

**13** Print the worksheet.

**14** Save and then close **3-WBPatioLoan**.

 **Check Your Work** Compare your work to the model answer available in the online course.

---

## In Addition

### Printing Column or Row Headings on Multiple Pages

Use the Print Titles button in the Page Setup group on the Page Layout tab to define column or row headings to repeat at the top or left edge of each page. Printing column and/or row headings makes the data in rows and columns in a multipage printout easier to identify.

Display a worksheet in Page Layout to view the worksheet along with print settings. Page Layout view also displays horizontal and vertical rulers to assist with measurements. A *header* is text that prints at the top of each worksheet and a *footer* is text that prints at the bottom of each worksheet. Excel includes predefined headers and footers that can be selected from a drop-down list or custom headers or footers can be created.

**What You Will Do**   Before printing the profit-sharing bonus worksheet completed earlier, you want to add identifying information in a custom header and footer and check other print options using Page Layout view.

Inserting Headers and Footers

**1** Open **3-WBEmpBonus**.

**2** Click the Page Layout button 🔲 at the right side of the Status bar near the Zoom slider bar.

**3** If necessary, use the horizontal and vertical scroll bars to adjust the window so that the worksheet, including the white space for the top, left, and right margins, is entirely visible.

**4** Hover your mouse over the text *Add header* near the top center of the page.

Headers and footers are divided into three boxes. Click in the desired box and then type text or insert header and footer elements. By default, text in the left box is left aligned, text in the center box is centered, and text in the right box is right aligned.

**5** Click in the left header box and then type your first and last names.

**6** Click in the right header box, type Date Printed:, and then press the spacebar.

**7** Click the Current Date button 🗓️ in the Header & Footer Elements group on the Header & Footer Tools Design tab.

Excel inserts the code *&[Date]*, which causes the current date to be inserted at the location of the code when the worksheet is printed.

**In Brief**

**Insert Header or Footer**
1. Switch to Page Layout view.
2. Click over *Click to add header* or *Click to add footer*.
3. Insert header and footer elements and/or type text in left, center, or right box.
4. Click in the worksheet area to end header or footer editing.

**8** Click the Go to Footer button  in the Navigation group on the Header & Footer Tools Design tab.

> The right footer box at the bottom of the page opens for editing.

**9** Click in the center footer box to open the box for editing.

**10** Click the File Name button 🖺 in the Header & Footer Elements group.

> Excel inserts the code *&[File]*, which causes the workbook file name to be inserted at the location of the code when the worksheet is printed.

**11** Click in the worksheet area outside the footer.

**12** Scroll to the top of the worksheet to view the header. Excel now displays the current date in place of the *&[Date]* code.

**13** Look at the bottom of the worksheet and notice that the workbook file name now displays in place of the *&[File]* code.

**14** Click the Page Layout tab.

> By default, the header and footer margin is 0.3 inch. In the next step, you will adjust the header and footer margins to provide more white space at the top and bottom of the page.

**15** Click the Margins button in the Page Setup group and then click *Custom Margins* at the drop-down list. Change the margin settings as indicated below at the Page Setup dialog box with the Margins tab active:

| | | | |
|---|---|---|---|
| *Top:* | 1 | *Header:* | 0.5 |
| *Bottom:* | 1 | *Footer:* | 0.5 |
| *Left:* | 1 | | |

**16** Click OK to close the Page Setup dialog box.

**17** Review the new margin settings in Page Layout view.

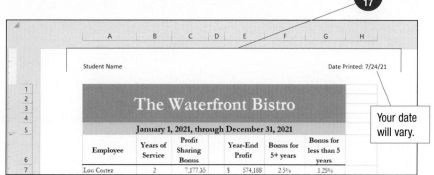

Your date will vary.

**18** Print the worksheet.

**19** Click the Normal button ⊞ at the right side of the Status bar near the Zoom slider bar (immediately left of the Page Layout button).

**20** Save and then close **3-WBEmpBonus**.

> **Check Your Work** Compare your work to the model answer available in the online course.

# Features Summary

| Feature | Ribbon Tab, Group | Button |
|---------|-------------------|--------|
| change margins | Page Layout, Page Setup OR File, *Print* | |
| create a column or bar chart | Insert, Charts | |
| create a hierarchy chart | Insert, Charts | |
| create a line or area chart | Insert, Charts | |
| Date & Time functions | Formulas, Function Library | |
| Financial functions | Formulas, Function Library | |
| insert a shape | Insert, Illustrations | |
| insert function | Formulas, Function Library | *fx* |
| insert header or footer | Insert, Text OR Page Layout view | |
| Logical functions | Formulas, Function Library | |
| Page Layout view | View, Workbook Views | OR |
| scale page width and/or height | Page Layout, Scale to Fit OR File, *Print* | |
| Statistical functions | Formulas, Function Library | |

MARQUEE SERIES

# Microsoft®
# Access®
# 365
## 2019 Brief Edition

Nita Rutkosky

Audrey Roggenkamp
Pierce College Puyallup
Puyallup, Washington

Ian Rutkosky
Pierce College Puyallup
Puyallup, Washington

PARADIGM
EDUCATION SOLUTIONS

St. Paul

**Vice President, Content and Digital Solutions:** Christine Hurney
**Director of Content Development:** Carley Fruzzetti
**Testers:** Desiree Carvel; Ann E. Mills, Ivy Tech Community College of Indiana, Evansville, IN
**Director of Production:** Timothy W. Larson
**Production Editor/Project Manager:** Jen Weaverling
**Cover and Text Design:** Valerie King
**Senior Design and Production Specialist:** Julie Johnston
**Copy Editor:** Deborah Brandt
**Indexer:** Terry Casey
**Vice President, Director of Digital Products:** Chuck Bratton
**Digital Projects Manager:** Tom Modl
**Digital Solutions Manager:** Gerry Yumul
**Senior Director of Digital Products and Onboarding:** Christopher Johnson
**Supervisor of Digital Products and Onboarding:** Ryan Isdahl
**Vice President of Marketing:** Lara Weber McLellan
**Marketing and Communications Manager**: Selena Hicks

© 2020 by Paradigm Publishing, LLC
875 Montreal Way
St. Paul, MN 55102
Email: CustomerService@ParadigmEducation.com
Website: ParadigmEducation.com

Printed in the United States of America

28 27 26 25 24 23 22 21 20 19    1 2 3 4 5 6 7 8 9 10 11 12

# Contents

# Access®

Microsoft Access is a *database management system (DBMS)* included with the Microsoft Office suite. Interacting with a DBMS occurs often as one performs daily routines such as withdrawing cash from the ATM, purchasing gas using a credit card, or looking up a telephone number in an online directory. In each of these activities a DBMS is accessed to retrieve information, and data is viewed, updated, and/or printed. Any application that involves storing and maintaining a large amount of data in an organized manner can be set up as an Access database. Examples include customers and invoices, suppliers and purchases, inventory and orders. While working in Access, you will create and maintain databases for the following six companies.

First Choice Travel is a travel center offering a full range of traveling services from booking flights, hotel reservations, and rental cars to offering travel seminars.

The Waterfront Bistro offers fine dining for lunch and dinner and also offers banquet facilities, a wine cellar, and catering services.

Worldwide Enterprises is a national and international distributor of products for a variety of companies and is the exclusive movie distribution agent for Marquee Productions.

Marquee Productions is involved in all aspects of creating movies from script writing and development to filming. The company produces documentaries, biographies, as well as historical and action movies.

Performance Threads maintains an inventory of rental costumes and also researches, designs, and sews special-order and custom-made costumes.

The mission of the Niagara Peninsula College Theatre Arts Division is to offer a curriculum designed to provide students with a thorough exposure to all aspects of the theatre arts.

# *In Section 1 you will learn how to*

## Maintain Data in Tables

Access databases are comprised of a series of objects. A table is the first object that is created in a new Access database. Information in the database is organized by topic, and a table stores data for one topic. For example, one table in a customer database might store customer names and addresses while another table stores the customer invoices and yet another table stores the customer payments. Table datasheets are organized like a spreadsheet, with columns and rows. Each column in the table represents one *field*, which is a single unit of information about a person, place, item, or object. Each row in the table represents one *record*, which includes all of the related fields for one person, place, item, or object. Working in tables involves adding or deleting records; editing fields; and sorting, filtering, or formatting datasheets. Access provides the Navigation pane for managing database objects.

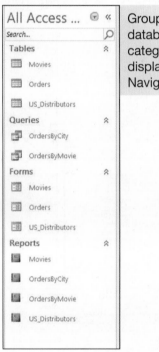

Group objects in the database by various categories and display them in the Navigation pane.

Data in tables display in a datasheet comprised of columns and rows similar to an Excel worksheet. Each column in a table datasheet represents one field. Each row in a table datasheet represents one record.

record ——

| | |
|---|---|
| field | |

# *In Section 2 you will learn how to*

## Create New Tables and Establish Relationships

New tables can be created starting with a blank datasheet or by creating the table structure by defining fields in a view called *Design view*. Each field in a table has a set of *field properties*, which are characteristics that control how the field interacts with data in objects such as tables, forms, queries, or reports. The ability to create a relationship between two tables allows one to maintain or extract data in multiple tables as if they were one large table.

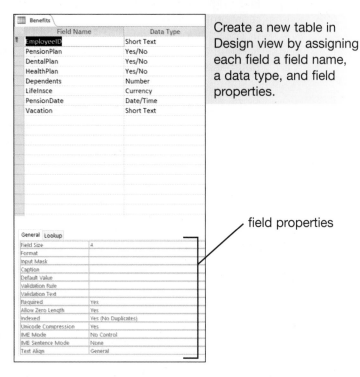

Create a new table in Design view by assigning each field a field name, a data type, and field properties.

field properties

Designate one field in a table as a primary key—a field that will contain unique data for each record.

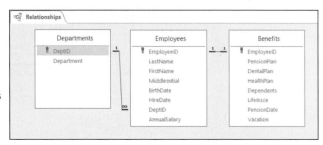

Create relationships between tables by joining one table to another using a common field. These relationships are displayed in the Relationships window using black join lines between table field list boxes.

# *In Section 3 you will learn how to*

## Create Queries, Forms, and Reports

Queries and forms are objects based on tables and are created to extract, view, and maintain data. Queries can be used to view specific fields from tables that meet a particular criterion. For example, create a query to view customers from a specific state or zip code. Forms provide a more user-friendly interface for entering, editing, deleting, and viewing records in tables. Create a report to generate professionally designed printouts of information from tables or queries.

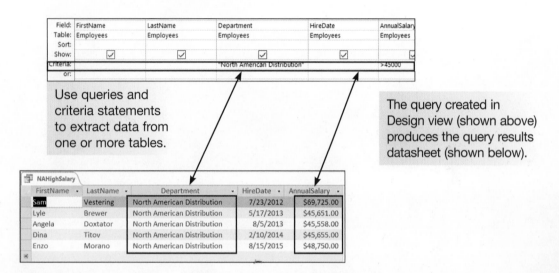

Use queries and criteria statements to extract data from one or more tables.

The query created in Design view (shown above) produces the query results datasheet (shown below).

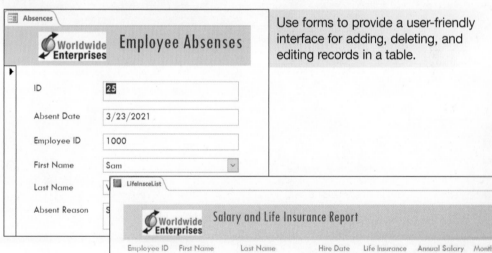

Use forms to provide a user-friendly interface for adding, deleting, and editing records in a table.

Create professional-quality printed reports using the Report tool. Report columns can be easily moved, resized, and formatted in Layout view.

# Access

# Maintaining Data in Access Tables

**Data Files**

Before beginning section work, copy the AccessS1 folder to your storage medium and then make AccessS1 the active folder.

## Skills

- Open and close Access
- Open and close an existing database
- Open and close tables, queries, forms, and reports
- Explore and navigate in tables
- Adjust field column widths
- Find and replace data
- Add and delete records in a table and form

- Sort and filter records
- Preview and print a table
- Change margins
- Change the page orientation
- Use the Help and Tell Me features
- Change the font size for records in a table
- Hide columns in a table

## Projects Overview

Add, delete, find, sort, and filter records; change page orientation and margins; format and hide columns in a table in two databases.

Find student records and enter grades into the Grades database.

Maintain the Inventory database by adding and deleting records. Add, delete, and modify records; sort, filter, and set print options for a Catering Event database.

Delete records and sort and print a report from the Costume Inventory database. Create field names and table names for a new Custom Costume database.

 The online course includes additional training and assessment resources.

Note: On some computer systems, a file downloaded from the internet, or copied from a storage medium retains the source file's read-only attribute. If this occurs, you will not be able to make changes to the database file. Complete the following steps to check and then remove a file's read-only status:

1. Open a File Explorer window.
2. Navigate to the drive representing your storage medium.
3. Navigate to the AccessS1 folder.
4. Right-click a database file and then click *Properties* at the shortcut menu.
5. At the Properties dialog box with the General tab selected, look at the *Read-only* check box in the *Attributes* section. If it contains a check mark, click the check box to remove it; if the check box is empty, the read-only attribute is not turned on (no action is required).
6. Click OK.

If the read-only attribute is not active for one file in the copied folder, then you can assume all files copied without an active read-only attribute. If you cleared the *Read-only* check box for one file, you will need to clear the attribute for all files after downloading from Cirrus. You can select multiple files and remove the read-only attribute in one operation.

# Opening and Closing a Database and Database Objects

Organizations use databases to keep track of customers, suppliers, employees, inventory, sales, orders, purchases, and much more. A database can be defined as a collection of data that has been organized so that the data can be easily stored, sorted, extracted, and reported. A key concept for understanding databases is that the data has to be organized. Data is organized first into a series of tables within the database, where one table contains all of the data that describe a person, place, object, event, or other subject. Within a database, a series of objects exist for entering, managing, and viewing data. The first objects created are *tables*. Once a table exists, other objects can be created that use the table structure as a means to enter and view the data. Some other database objects include queries, forms, and reports.

**Worldwide Enterprises**

**What You Will Do**   You will open a database used by Worldwide Enterprises to keep track of distributors, orders, and movies and open and close the objects in the database to gain an understanding of important Access concepts and terminology.

*Note: Make sure you have downloaded the files from Cirrus to your storage medium. Please refer to the note on page 1 regarding checking and removing read-only attributes before proceeding with the activities in this section.*

Opening an Existing Database

Opening and Closing an Object

Tutorial
Closing a Database and Closing Access

**1** At the Windows desktop, click the Start button and then click the Access tile.

> Depending on your system configuration, these steps may vary.

**2** At the Access opening screen, click the <u>Open Other Files</u> hyperlink at the bottom of the Recent list.

**3** At the Open backstage area, click the *Browse* option.

**4** At the Open dialog box, click *Removable Disk (F:)* in the Navigation pane.

> If you are opening and saving files in a location other than a USB flash drive, please check with your instructor. You can bypass the Open backstage area and go directly to the Open dialog box by pressing Ctrl + F12.

**5** Double-click the *AccessS1* folder in the Content pane of the Open dialog box.

**6** Double-click *1-WEDistributors* in the Content pane.

> A security warning message bar displays if Access determines the file you are opening did not originate from a trusted location on your computer. This often occurs when you copy a file from another medium (such as a flash drive or the Web).

**7** If a security warning message bar displays, click the Enable Content button.

> Identify the various features of the Access screen by comparing your screen with the one shown in Figure 1.1.

Step 6

**Figure 1.1** The Access Screen

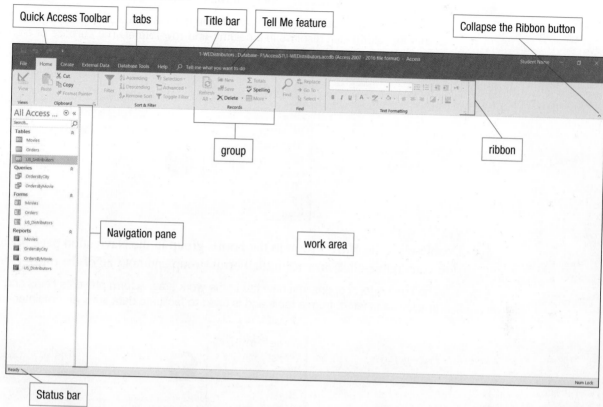

**8** Double-click the *Orders* table in the Tables group in the Navigation pane.

The Orders table opens in Datasheet view in the work area with a tab in the upper left corner identifying the table name. Each column in the table contains only one unit of information and each row represents one record. A table is an object in a database and other objects are created using data from a table or multiple tables. Refer to Table 1.1 for a description of database objects.

**Table 1.1** Database Objects

| Object | Description |
|---|---|
| table | organizes data in fields (columns) and records (rows); a database must contain at least one table. The table is the base upon which other objects are created |
| query | displays data from one or more tables that meets a conditional statement (for example, records in which the city is Toronto); performs calculations |
| form | allows fields and records to be presented in a different layout than the datasheet; used to facilitate data entry and maintenance |
| report | prints data from tables or queries |
| macro | automates repetitive tasks |
| module | advances automation through programming using Visual Basic for Applications |

**9** Double-click the *OrdersByCity* query in the Queries group in the Navigation pane.

> The OrdersByCity query opens in a new tab in the work area. A query resembles a table in that the information displays in a column-and-row format. The purpose of a query is to display data from one or more related tables that meets a conditional statement.

**10** Double-click the *Movies* form in the Forms group in the Navigation pane. (Make sure you double-click *Movies* in the Forms group and not one of the other groups.)

> The Movies form opens in a new tab in the work area. A form presents fields and records in a layout different from a table and is used to facilitate data entry and maintenance.

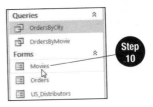

**11** Right-click the *US_Distributors* report in the Reports group in the Navigation pane. (Make sure you right-click *US_Distributors* in the Reports group and not one of the other groups.)

> Right-clicking the report displays the shortcut menu. The shortcut menu provides another method for opening an object.

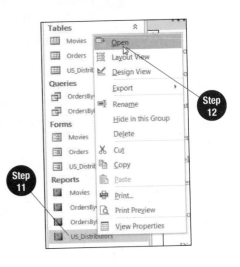

**12** Click *Open* at the shortcut menu.

> The US_Distributors report opens in a new tab in the work area. Reports are used to display or print data from one or more tables in a specific layout. In a report, data can be arranged, formatted, grouped, and sorted. Descriptive labels, a logo, or other items can be included.

**13** Click the Orders tab in the work area.

> Clicking a tab in the work area moves that object to the foreground.

**14** Close the Orders table by clicking the Close button in the upper right corner of the work area.

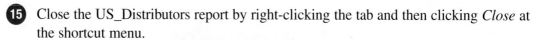

**15** Close the US_Distributors report by right-clicking the tab and then clicking *Close* at the shortcut menu.

> The shortcut menu provides another method for closing an object.

**16** Close both of the two open objects by right-clicking the Movies tab and then clicking *Close All* at the shortcut menu.

**17** Close the **1-WEDistributors** database by clicking the File tab and then clicking the *Close* option.

> Clicking the File tab displays the backstage area with options for working with and managing databases.

**18** Close Access by clicking the Close button in the upper right corner of the screen.

## In Addition

### Learning More about the Access User Interface

While several files of the same type can be opened in the other Microsoft Office applications, only one Access database can be open at a time. If a database is open and then another one is opened, the first database closes. In other Microsoft Office applications, revisions, such as editing text or values, must be saved. In a database, changes to the data are saved automatically when the insertion point is moved to the next record. For this reason, the Undo command is often unavailable. If a prompt to save changes displays when closing an object in Access, the prompt is referring to changes made to the layout and/or formatting of the object.

In a database, tables are the first objects created, since all other objects rely on tables as the source for their data. Each table in a database contains data for one subject such as customers, orders, suppliers, and so on. Within a table, the data is broken down into units of information about the subject, called *fields*. All of the data about one subject in the table is called a *record*. For example, in a table containing data on suppliers, one record contains the data for one supplier. Navigate in an open table using the mouse, keys on the keyboard, and/or the Record Navigation bar at the bottom of the work area.

**Worldwide Enterprises**

**What You Will Do**   You will open the database used by Worldwide Enterprises and examine the tables to determine how information is organized. You will also navigate to various fields and records in the tables.

Tutorial

Navigating in Objects

**1** Open Access and then open the **1-WEDistributors** database from your AccessS1 folder and enable the content, if necessary.

**2** Double-click the *US_Distributors* table in the Navigation pane.

Each column in the table in Datasheet view contains only one unit of information. Each column represents one field. Identify the fields and field names at the top of each column by comparing your screen with the one shown in Figure 1.2. The field names *DistID*, *CompanyName*, *StreetAdd1*, and so on display in the header row at the top of the table.

**3** Double-click the *Movies* table in the Navigation pane.

The Movies table opens in the work area on top of the US_Distributors table. Examine the fields and records in the table to determine how the information is organized.

**4** Double-click the *Orders* table in the Navigation pane.

The Orders table opens in the work area on top of the other two tables. Database designers often create a visual representation of the database's structure in a diagram similar to the one in Figure 1.3. Each table is represented in a box with the table name at the top of the box. Within each box, the fields that will be stored in the table are listed. The field with the asterisk is called the *primary key field*, which holds the data that uniquely identifies each record in the table (usually an identification number).

**Figure 1.2** US_Distributors Table in Datasheet View

Each object opens in a tab in the work area.

field name

| DistID | CompanyNar | StreetAdd1 | StreetAdd2 | City | State | ZIPCode | Telephone | Fax | EmailAdd | Click to Add |
|---|---|---|---|---|---|---|---|---|---|---|
| 1 | All Nite Cinema: | 2188 Third Stree | | Louisville | KY | 40201 | 502-555-4238 | 502-555-4240 | allnite@ppi-edu | |
| 2 | Century Cinema | 3687 Avenue K | | Arlington | TX | 76013 | 817-555-2116 | 817-555-2119 | centurycinemas | |
| 3 | Countryside Cin | 22 Hillside Stree | | Bennington | VT | 05201 | 802-555-1469 | 802-555-1470 | countryside@pp | |
| 4 | Danforth Cinem | PO Box 22 | 18 Pickens Stree | Columbia | SC | 29201 | 803-555-3487 | 803-555-3421 | danforth@ppi-e | |
| 5 | Eastown Movie | PO Box 722 | 1 Concourse Av | Cambridge | MA | 02142 | 413-555-0981 | 413-555-0226 | eastown@ppi-e | |
| 6 | Hillman Cinema | 55 Kemble Aven | | Baking Ridge | NJ | 07920 | 201-555-1147 | 201-555-1143 | hillman@ppi-ed | |
| 7 | LaVista Cinema | 111 Vista Road | | Phoenix | AZ | 86355-6014 | 602-555-6231 | 602-555-6233 | lavista@ppi-edu | |
| 8 | Liberty Cinemas | PO Box 998 | 12011 Ruston W | Atlanta | GA | 73125 | 404-555-8113 | 404-555-2349 | libertycinemas@ | |
| 9 | Mainstream Mo | PO Box 33 | 333 Evergreen E | Seattle | WA | 98220-2791 | 206-555-3269 | 206-555-3270 | mainstream@pp | |
| 10 | Marquee Movie | 1011 South Alar | | Los Angeles | CA | 90045 | 612-555-2398 | 612-555-2377 | marqueemovies | |
| 11 | Midtown Movie | 1033 Commerci | | Emporia | KS | 66801 | 316-555-7013 | 316-555-7022 | midtown@ppi-e | |
| 12 | Mooretown Mc | PO Box 11 | 331 Metro Plac | Dublin | OH | 43107 | 614-555-8134 | 614-555-8339 | mooretown@pp | |
| 13 | O'Shea Movies | 59 Erie | | Oak Park | IL | 60302 | 312-555-7719 | 312-555-7381 | oshea@ppi-edu | |
| 14 | Redwood Cinem | PO Box 112F | 336 Ninth Stree | Portland | OR | 97466-3359 | 503-555-8641 | 503-555-8633 | redwoodcinema | |
| 15 | Sunfest Cinema | 341 South Fourt | | Tampa | FL | 33562 | 813-555-3185 | 813-555-3177 | sunfest@ppi-ed | |
| 16 | Victory Cinema | 12119 South 23 | | San Diego | CA | 97432-1567 | 619-555-8746 | 619-555-8748 | victory@ppi-ed | |
| 17 | Waterfront Cin | PO Box 3255 | | Buffalo | NY | 14288 | 716-555-3845 | 716-555-3947 | waterfrontciner | |
| 18 | Wellington 10 | 1203 Tenth Sou | | Philadelphia | PA | 19178 | 215-555-9045 | 215-555-9048 | wellington10@p | |
| 19 | Westview Movi | 1112 Broadway | | Newark | NY | 10119 | 212-555-4875 | 212-555-4877 | westview@ppi- | |
| (New) | | | | | | | | | | |

Each row is one record in the table.

Each column represents a field in the table.

Record Navigation bar

Record: ◄ ◄ 1 of 19 ► ►► ►* No Filter   Search

**Figure 1.3** Database Diagram for 1-WEDistributors Database

**⑤** Change how objects display in the Navigation pane by clicking the menu bar at the top of the Navigation pane and then clicking *Tables and Related Views* at the drop-down list.

> Originally, the Navigation pane displayed the objects grouped by type (table, query, form, and report). Clicking *Tables and Related Views* displays each table in the Navigation pane followed by the objects related to the table.

**⑥** Show only the Orders table and related objects by clicking the Navigation pane menu bar and then clicking *Orders* in the *Filter By Group* section of the drop-down list.

**⑦** Redisplay by object type by clicking the button on the menu bar containing a down-pointing triangle in a circle and then clicking *Object Type* at the drop-down list.

> Clicking *Object Type* displays *All Access Objects* in the *Filter By Group* section of the drop-down list. Display the Navigation pane drop-down list by clicking the menu bar or by clicking the button on the menu bar. The name of the button changes depending on what is selected.

**⑧** To view more of the open objects in the work area, click the Shutter Bar Open/Close Button in the upper right corner of the Navigation pane.

> The Navigation pane collapses to a bar at the left of the screen with the text *Navigation Pane* displayed vertically.

**⑨** Redisplay the Navigation pane by clicking the Shutter Bar Open/Close Button.

> You can also collapse or redisplay the Navigation pane by pressing the F11 function key.

**10** Close the Orders table by right-clicking the Orders tab and then clicking *Close* at the shortcut menu.

**11** Close the Movies table by right-clicking the Movies tab and then clicking *Close* at the shortcut menu.

> The US_Distributors table should be the only open table.

**12** Press the Tab key to make the next field in the current record active.

> Navigate in a table using keys on the keyboard, the mouse, or the Record Navigation bar. Pressing the Tab key makes the next field in the current record active. Refer to Table 1.2 for information on keyboard commands for navigating in a table.

**13** Press Shift + Tab to make the previous field in the current record active.

**14** Press Ctrl + End to make the last field in the last record active.

**15** Press Ctrl + Home to make the first field in the first record active.

**16** Move the insertion point to a field in the *CompanyName* field column by clicking in the company name *Century Cinemas* in record 2.

**17** Make record 3 active by clicking the Next record button on the Record Navigation bar.

**18** Make the last record active by clicking the Last record button on the Record Navigation bar.

**Table 1.2** Navigating in an Access Table Using the Keyboard

| Press | To move to |
| --- | --- |
| Home | first field in the current record |
| End | last field in the current record |
| Tab | next field in the current record |
| Shift + Tab | previous field in the current record |
| Ctrl + Home | first field in the first record |
| Ctrl + End | last field in the last record |

**In Brief**

**Change Navigation Pane View**
1. Click All Access Objects button at top of Navigation pane.
2. Click view.

**19** Make the first record active by clicking the First record button on the Record Navigation bar.

Step 19

**20** Navigate to record 14 by triple-clicking the text *1 of 19* that displays in the *Current Record* text box on the Record Navigation bar, typing 14, and then pressing the Enter key.

Step 20

**21** Close the US_Distributors table by clicking the Close button in the upper right corner of the work area.

# In Addition

## Planning and Designing a Table

The table below describes the steps involved in planning and designing a new database. The design process may seem time-consuming; however, the time expended to produce a well-designed database saves time later. A database that is poorly designed will likely have logical or structural errors that require redefining of data or objects after live data has been entered.

| Step | Description |
|------|-------------|
| 1. Determine the purpose of the database. | Describe who will use the database and for what purpose. This helps to focus the efforts for the remaining steps on the mission the database is to fulfill. |
| 2. Determine all of the data that will need to be tracked in the database. | Gather all of the data elements that you will need to store in the database. You can find this information by looking at records of invoices, inventory lists, purchase orders, and so on. You can also ask individuals what information they want to get out of the database to help you determine the required data. |
| 3. Group the data elements into tables. | Divide the information into subjects (also referred to as *entities*) so that one table will be about one subject only. |
| 4. Decide the fields and field names for each table. | Break down each data element into its smallest unit. For example, a person's name could be broken down into first name, middle name, and last name. |
| 5. Make sure each table includes a field that will be used to uniquely identify each record in the table. | Access can create an *ID* field for you if you do not have an existing unique identification number such as a product number, student number, social security number, or similar field. |
| 6. Decide which tables need to be linked by a relationship and include in the table the common field upon which to join the tables if necessary. | Identifying relationships at this stage helps you determine if you need to add a field to a related table to allow you to join the table. You will learn more about relationships in Section 2. |

Access creates columns in a table with a default width of 13.1111 characters, which is the approximate number of characters that will display in a column. Column width can be increased or decreased to accommodate the data with options at the Column Width dialog box, by double-clicking the column boundary line to adjust the width to the longest entry (referred to as best fit), or by dragging a column boundary line to the desired position. The width of multiple adjacent columns can be best fit by selecting the columns and then clicking one of the column boundary line.

**Worldwide Enterprises**

**What You Will Do**   You will reopen the US_Distributors table and adjust column widths to accommodate the longest entries in each column.

Tutorial

Adjusting Field
Column Width

**1**  With the **1-WEDistributors** database open, double-click the US_Distributors table in the Navigation pane.

**2**  With the first field selected in the *DistID* field column, click the More button in the Records group on the Home tab.

**3**  Click *Field Width* at the drop-down list.

**4**  At the Column Width dialog box with the current width selected in the *Column Width* measurement box, type 8 and then click OK.

> If the data entered in a field in a column does not fill the entire field, consider decreasing the column width to save space in the work area and when the table is printed.

**5**  Click in the first field in the *CompanyName* field column (the field containing the text *All Nite Cinemas*).

> Clicking in a field in the *CompanyName* field column makes the column active and *CompanyName* in the header row displays with an orange background.

**6**  Click the More button in the Records group and then click *Field Width* at the drop-down list.

**7**  At the Column Width dialog box with the current width selected in the *Column Width* measurement box, type 20 and then click OK.

**8**  Click in the first field in the *StreetAdd1* field column (the field containing the text *2188 Third Street*).

**9**  Click the More button and then click *Field Width* at the drop-down list.

**In Brief**

**Adjust Column Width**
1. Position insertion point in column.
2. Click More button.
3. Click *Field Width*.
4. Type column width number or click Best Fit button.
OR
Drag or double-click right column boundary line in header row.

**10** At the Column Width dialog box, click the Best Fit button.

Clicking the Best Fit button causes the width of the *StreetAdd1* column to adjust to accommodate the longest entry.

**11** Use the mouse to adjust the *StreetAdd2* field column. To do this, position the mouse pointer on the column boundary line between the *StreetAdd2* and *City* field column headings until the pointer displays as a left-and-right pointing arrow with a vertical line between, click and hold down the left mouse button, drag to the right approximately one-half inch, and then release the mouse button. Make sure all of the entries in the column are visible. If not, continue to increase the width of the column.

**12** Select the remaining columns by positioning the mouse pointer in the *City* field column heading, clicking and holding down the left mouse button, dragging to the right to the *EmailAdd* field column heading, and then releasing the mouse button.

**13** With the columns selected, double-click the column boundary line between the *City* and *State* field column headings.

Double-clicking the column boundary line best fits all of the selected columns. Double-check that the *EmailAdd* field column has fully expanded to display all entries. If not, double-click the column boundary line between the *Fax* and *EmailAdd* field column headings. You may need to scroll to the right to display the entire field.

**14** Click the First record button on the Record Navigation bar.

**15** Click the Save button on the Quick Access Toolbar.

Clicking the Save button saves the changes made to the column widths.

**16** Close the US_Distributors table.

**Check Your Work** Compare your work to the model answer available in the online course.

# In Addition

## Using the Record Navigation Bar Search Text Box

Use the Record Navigation bar search text box to search for a specific entry in a field in a table. To use the search text box, click in the text box and then begin typing the search data. As text is typed, text that matches what is typed is selected in the table, which is referred to as *word-wheeling*. For example, to search for Mooretown Movies in the US_Distributors table, start by clicking at the beginning of the first field below the *CompanyName* field column heading, clicking in the search text box, and then typing *m*. This causes Access to select the letter *m* in *Cinemas* in the first entry in the *CompanyName* field column. Type the letter *o* and Access selects *Mo* in the *Eastown Movie House* entry. Type the letter *o* again and Access selects *Moo* in *Mooretown Movies*.

Use the Find and Replace dialog box with the Find tab selected to search for specific data in a table. Display this dialog box with the Find button on the Home tab. Using the Find and Replace dialog box saves time when searching for data when the table contains many records that are not all visible on the screen. Use the Find and Replace dialog box with the Replace tab selected to find specific data in a table and replace it with other data. Display this dialog box with the Replace button on the Home tab. Use options at the Find and Replace dialog box with either tab selected to specify where to search, such as the current field or the entire table, and what to search, such as any part of a field, the whole field, or the start of a field.

**Worldwide Enterprises**

**What You Will Do**  You have received a note from Sam Vestering that the city for Westview Movies was entered incorrectly and should be *New York* instead of *Newark*. He also indicated that the post office reference in the addresses should appear as *P.O.* and not *PO*. You will use the Find and Replace dialog box to locate and make the changes.

Tutorial

Finding Data

Tutorial

Finding and Replacing Data

**1**  With **1-WEDistributors** open, open the US_Distributors table and then click the first field in the *City* field column (contains the text *Louisville*).

**2**  Click the Find button 🔍 in the Find group on the Home tab.

Clicking the Find button displays the Find and Replace dialog box with the Find tab selected.

**3**  Type Newark in the *Find What* text box.

**4**  Click the Find Next button.

The city *Newark* is selected in record 19.

**5**  Click the Cancel button to close the Find and Replace dialog box.

**6**  With *Newark* selected, type New York.

As you type *New York* a pencil icon displays in the record selector bar at the left of the table, indicating that the current record is being edited and the change has not been saved. When you complete Step 7, the change is saved and the pencil icon disappears.

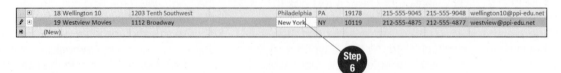

**7**  Click in the first field in the *DistID* field column (contains the number *1*).

**8** Click the Replace button  in the Find group on the Home tab.

**9** At the Find and Replace dialog box with the Replace tab selected, type PO in the *Find What* text box.

**10** Press the Tab key to move the insertion point to the *Replace With* text box and then type P.O.

**11** Click the *Look In* option box arrow and then click *Current document* at the drop-down list.

> Changing the *Look In* option to *Current document* tells Access to search all fields in the table.

**12** Click the *Match* option box arrow and then click *Any Part of Field* at the drop-down list.

> Changing the *Match* option to *Any Part of Field* tells Access to search for data that matches any part of a field—not only the entire field.

**13** Click the *Match Case* check box to insert a check mark.

> Inserting a check mark in the *Match Case* check box tells Access to search only for the uppercase letters *PO*.

**14** Click the Replace All button.

**15** At the message indicating that you cannot undo the action and asking if you want to continue, click Yes.

> Clicking the Yes button closes the message and replaces all occurrences of *PO* with *P.O.*

**16** Click the Cancel button to close the Find and Replace dialog box.

**Check Your Work** Compare your work to the model answer available in the online course.

## In Addition

### Exploring the Find and Replace Dialog Box Options

By default, the *Look In* option at the Find and Replace dialog box is set to *Current field*. At this setting, Access will search only in the field where the insertion point is positioned. Change this option to *Current document* and Access will search all fields in the table. The *Match* option has a default setting of *Whole Field*, which means Access will search for data that matches the entire entry in a field. To search for data that matches only partial field entries, change the *Match* option to *Any Part of Field* or *Start of Field* to search entries in fields that begin with the data entered in the *Find What* text box. The *Search* option has a default setting of *All*, which means Access will search all of the data in the specific field or table. This can be changed to *Up* to search from the insertion point to the beginning of the table or *Down* to search from the insertion point to the end of the table. To find data that contains specific uppercase or lowercase letters, insert a check mark in the *Match Case* check box.

Tables are the first objects created in a database and all other objects rely on a table as the source for their data. Managing the tables in a database is important for keeping the database up to date and may include adding and deleting records. Add a new record to a table in Datasheet view by clicking the New (blank) record button on the Record Navigation bar, or clicking the New button in the Records group on the Home tab. Delete a record in a table by clicking in any field in the record, clicking the Delete button arrow in the Records group on the Home tab, and then clicking *Delete Record* at the drop-down list. Another method for deleting a record is to select the record by clicking the record selector bar at the left of the record and then clicking the Delete button on the Home tab.

**What You Will Do** Worldwide Enterprises has signed two new distributors in the United States and one company has signed with another movie distributing company. You will add the new information in two records in the US_Distributors table and delete the old company.

Adding and Deleting
Records in a Table

**1** With 1-WEDistributors open and the US_Distributors table open, click the New (blank) record button ▶ᵃ in the Record Navigation bar.

> The insertion point moves to the first field in the blank row at the bottom of the table in the *DistID* field column. The *Current Record* text box in the Record Navigation bar indicates you are editing record 20 of 20 records.

**2** Press the Tab key to move past the *DistID* field (currently displays *(New)*) since Access automatically assigns the next sequential number to this field.

> You will learn more about the AutoNumber data type field in Section 2. The number will not appear in the field until you type an entry in the next field.

**3** Type Dockside Movies in the *CompanyName* field and then press the Tab key.

**4** Type P.O. Box 224 and then press the Tab key.

**5** Type 155 Central Avenue and then press the Tab key.

**6** Type Baltimore and then press the Tab key.

**7** Type MD and then press the Tab key.

**8** Type 21203 and then press the Tab key.

**9** Type 301-555-7732 and then press the Tab key.

**10** Type 301-555-9836 and then press the Tab key.

**In Brief**

**Add Records to Datasheet**
1. Open table.
2. Click New (blank) record button in Navigation bar or click New button in Records group.
3. Type data in fields.

**11** Type dockside@ppi-edu.net and then press the Tab key.

> The insertion point moves to a new row when you press the Tab key or the Enter key after the last field in a new record to allow you to continue typing the next new record in the table. The record just entered is saved automatically.

**12** Type the following information in the appropriate fields in the next row:

> Renaissance Cinemas
> 3599 Woodward Avenue
> Detroit, MI 48211
> 313-555-1693
> 313-555-1699
> rencinemas@ppi-edu.net

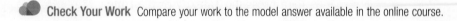

| | | | | | | | | | | |
|---|---|---|---|---|---|---|---|---|---|---|
| | 14 Redwood Cinemas | P.O. Box 112F | 336 Ninth Street | Portland | OR | 97466-3359 | 503-555-8641 | 503-555-8633 | redwoodcinemas@ppi-edu.net |
| | 15 Sunfest Cinemas | 341 South Fourth Avenue | | Tampa | FL | 33562 | 813-555-3185 | 813-555-3177 | sunfest@ppi-edu.net |
| | 16 Victory Cinemas | 12119 South 23rd | | San Diego | CA | 97432-1567 | 619-555-8746 | 619-555-8748 | victory@ppi-edu.net |
| | 17 Waterfront Cinemas | P.O. Box 3255 | | Buffalo | NY | 14288 | 716-555-3845 | 716-555-3947 | waterfrontcinemas@ppi-edu.net |
| | 18 Wellington 10 | 1203 Tenth Southwest | | Philadelphia | PA | 19178 | 215-555-9045 | 215-555-9048 | wellington10@ppi-edu.net |
| | 19 Westview Movies | 1112 Broadway | | New York | NY | 10119 | 212-555-4875 | 212-555-4877 | westview@ppi-edu.net |
| | 20 Dockside Movies | P.O. Box 224 | 155 Central Avenue | Baltimore | MD | 21203 | 301-555-7732 | 301-555-9836 | dockside@ppi-edu.net |
| | 21 Renaissance Cinemas | 3599 Woodward Avenue | | Detroit | MI | 48211 | 313-555-1693 | 313-555-1699 | rencinemas@ppi-edu.net |
| | (New) | | | | | | | | |

Step 12

**13** Position the mouse pointer in the record selector bar (empty column to the left of the *DistID* field) for record 3 (*Countryside Cinemas*) until the pointer changes to a right-pointing black arrow and then click the left mouse button.

> This action selects the entire record.

**14** Click the Delete button  in the Records group on the Home tab.

Step 14

**15** Access displays a message box indicating you are about to delete 1 record and that the undo operation is not available after this action. Click the Yes button to confirm the deletion.

> Access does not renumber the remaining records in the *DistID* field once record 3 has been deleted from the table. The *DistID* field is defined as an AutoNumber data type field. For this field data type, once a number has been used, Access does not make the number available again for another record even after the record is deleted.

**16** Close the US_Distributors table.

**Check Your Work** Compare your work to the model answer available in the online course.

# In Addition

### Understanding the Primary Key Field

In each table, one field is designated as the primary key field. A primary key field is the field by which the table is sorted whenever the table is opened. The primary key field must contain unique data for each record. When a new record is added to a table, Access checks to ensure that no record exists with the same data in the primary key field. If a record does exist with the same data in the primary key field, Access displays an error message indicating there are duplicate values and will not allow the record to be saved. The primary key field cannot be left blank when a new record is added, since it is the field that is used to sort and check for duplicates. Access includes a feature where a field named *ID* defined as the primary key field is included automatically in a new table that is created in a blank datasheet. The *ID* field uses the AutoNumber data type, which assigns the first record a field value of *1* and each new record the next sequential number.

# Activity 1.6　Adding and Deleting Records in a Form

Forms are used to enter, edit, view, and print data. Adding records in a form is easier than using a table since all of the fields in the table are presented in a different layout, which usually allows all fields to be visible at the same time. Other records in the table do not distract the user since only one record displays at a time. Add records to a form using the New (blank) record button on the Record Navigation bar or with the New button in the Records group on the Home tab. Delete a record in a form by making the record active and then clicking the Delete button in the Records group on the Home tab.

**Worldwide Enterprises**

**What You Will Do**　Worldwide Enterprises has just signed two new distributors in New York and one company has signed with another movie distributing company. You will add two new records and delete one record from the US_Distributors table using a form.

Tutorial

Adding and Deleting Records in a Form

**1** With **1-WEDistributors** open, double-click the *US_Distributors* form in the Forms group in the Navigation pane.

　The US_Distributors form opens with the first record in the US_Distributors table displayed in the form.

**2** Click the New button 📇 in the Records group on the Home tab.

　A blank form displays and the Record Navigation bar indicates you are editing record number 21. The New (blank) record and Next record buttons on the Record Navigation bar are dimmed.

**3** Press the Tab key to move to the *CompanyName* field, since Access automatically assigns the next sequential number to the *DistID* field.

　The *DistID* field does not display a field value until you begin to type data in another field in the record.

**4** Type Movie Emporium and then press the Tab key or the Enter key.

**5** Type 203 West Houston Street and then press the Tab key or the Enter key.

　Use the same navigation methods you learned in Activity 1.5 to add the record to the table.

**6** Type the remaining field values as shown at the right. Press the Tab key or the Enter key after typing the last field.

　When you press the Tab key or the Enter key after the *EmailAdd* field, a new form will appear in the work area.

Step 1

US Distributors

| | |
|---|---|
| DistID | 22 |
| CompanyName | Movie Emporium |
| StreetAdd1 | 203 West Houston Street |
| StreetAdd2 | |
| City | New York |
| State | NY |
| ZIPCode | 10014 |
| Telephone | 212-555-7278 |
| Fax | 212-555-7280 |
| EmailAdd | emporium@ppi-edu.net |

Step 4

Step 5

Step 6

**In Brief**

**Add Record in Form View**
1. Open form.
2. Click New (blank) record button in Navigation bar or click New button in Records group.
3. Type data in fields.

**7** Type the following information in the appropriate fields in a new form for record 22:

Cinema Festival
318 East 11th Street
New York, NY 10003

212-555-9715
212-555-9717
cinemafest@ppi-edu.net

**8** Click the First record button in the Record Navigation bar.

This displays the record for All Nite Cinemas.

**9** Click in the first field in the *CompanyName* field column (*All Nite Cinemas*) and then click the Find button in the Find group on the Home tab.

**10** At the Find and Replace dialog box with the Find tab selected, type Victory Cinemas and then click the Find Next button.

**11** When the record for Victory Cinemas displays, click the Cancel button to close the Find and Replace dialog box.

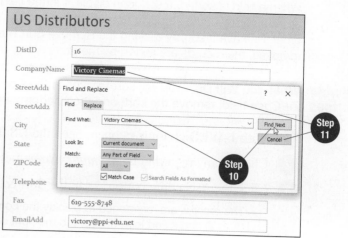

**12** Click the Delete button arrow in the Records group on the Home tab and then click *Delete Record* at the drop-down list.

**13** Click Yes to confirm the deletion.

**14** Close the US_Distributors form.

**15** Open the US_Distributors table and then view the two records added to and the one record deleted from the table using the form.

**16** Close the US_Distributors table.

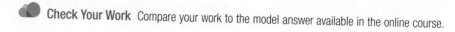

**Check Your Work** Compare your work to the model answer available in the online course.

# In Addition

## Navigating in Form View Using the Keyboard

Navigate records in a form using the following keyboard commands:
- Press Page Down to display the next record.
- Press Page Up to display the previous record.
- Press Ctrl + End to move to the last field in the last record.
- Press Ctrl + Home to move to the first field in the first record.

Records in a table are displayed alphanumerically and sorted in ascending order by the primary key field values. To rearrange the order of records in a table, click in any entry in the field to sort by and then click the Ascending button or Descending button in the Sort & Filter group on the Home tab. Text is sorted from A to Z (ascending) or Z to A (descending), numbers (values) are sorted from lowest to highest (ascending) or highest to lowest (descending), and dates are sorted from earliest to latest (ascending) or latest to earliest (descending). To sort by more than one field column, select the field columns first and then click the Ascending or Descending button. Access sorts first by the leftmost field column in the selection and then by the next field column. Select adjacent field columns by positioning the mouse pointer on the header row of the first field column to be selected, click and hold down the left mouse button, drag to the header row of the last field column, and then release the mouse button. When a field is sorted, a sort icon displays in the field's header row. The sort icon displays as an up arrow if the sort is in ascending order and a down arrow if the sort is in descending order. Remove a sort by clicking the Remove Sort button on the Home tab. When a sort is removed, the records are sorted by the primary key field.

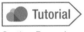
**Worldwide Enterprises**

**What You Will Do**  You will sort records in the *CompanyName* field, sort the records in the *ZIPCode* field, remove the sort, and then perform a multiple-field sort.

Tutorial

Sorting Records in a Table

**1** With **1-WEDistributors** open, open the US_Distributors table.

**2** Click in any record in the *CompanyName* field column.

**3** Click the Ascending button in the Sort & Filter group on the Home tab.

The records are rearranged to display the company names in ascending alphabetic order (A to Z) and a sort icon displays to the right of *CompanyName* in the header row.

**4** Click the Descending button in the Sort & Filter group.

The records are rearranged to display the companies in descending alphabetic order (Z to A). The sort icon changes from an up arrow to a down arrow.

**5** Click in any record in the *ZIPCode* field column.

**6** Click the Descending button in the Sort & Filter group.

**7** Click the Remove Sort button in the Sort & Filter group.

Removing the sort from the *ZIPCode* field sorts the records by the primary key field (the *DistID* field).

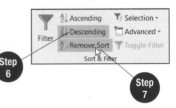

## In Brief

**Sort Datasheet by Single Field**
1. Open table.
2. Click in field in column by which to sort.
3. Click Ascending or Descending button.

**Sort Datasheet by Multiple Fields**
1. Open table.
2. Select columns from left to right in order of the sort.
3. Click Ascending or Descending button.

**8** Position the mouse pointer in the *State* header row until the pointer changes to a down-pointing black arrow, click and hold down the left mouse button, drag to the right to select the *ZIPCode* field column, and then release the mouse button.

The *State* and *ZIPCode* field columns are both selected.

Step 8

| City ▾ | State ▾ | ZIPCode ▾ | Telephone ▾ |
|--------|---------|-----------|-------------|
| Louisville | KY | 40201 | 502-555-4238 |
| Arlington | TX | 76013 | 817-555-2116 |
| Columbia | SC | 29201 | 803-555-3487 |
| Cambridge | MA | 02142 | 413-555-0981 |

**9** Click the Ascending button in the Sort & Filter group.

**10** Click in any field to deselect the two field columns.

The records are sorted first by state and then by ZIP code within each state, as shown in Figure 1.4.

**11** Close the US_Distributors table. Click Yes when prompted to save the design changes.

**Figure 1.4** Records Sorted by State and Then by ZIP Code within Each State

| DistID ▾ | CompanyName ▾ | StreetAdd1 ▾ | StreetAdd2 ▾ | City ▾ | State ↑ | ZIPCode ↑ |
|----------|---------------|--------------|--------------|--------|---------|-----------|
| 7 | LaVista Cinemas | 111 Vista Road | | Phoenix | AZ | 86355-6014 |
| 10 | Marquee Movies | 1011 South Alameda Street | | Los Angeles | CA | 90045 |
| 15 | Sunfest Cinemas | 341 South Fourth Avenue | | Tampa | FL | 33562 |
| 8 | Liberty Cinemas | P.O. Box 998 | 12011 Ruston Way | Atlanta | GA | 73125 |
| 13 | O'Shea Movies | 59 Erie | | Oak Park | IL | 60302 |
| 11 | Midtown Moviehouse | 1033 Commercial Street | | Emporia | KS | 66801 |
| 1 | All Nite Cinemas | 2188 Third Street | | Louisville | KY | 40201 |
| 5 | Eastown Movie House | P.O. Box 722 | 1 Concourse Avenue | Cambridge | MA | 02142 |
| 20 | Dockside Movies | P.O. Box 224 | 155 Central Avenue | Baltimore | MD | 21203 |
| 21 | Renaissance Cinemas | 3599 Woodward Avenue | | Detroit | MI | 48211 |
| 6 | Hillman Cinemas | 55 Kemble Avenue | | Baking Ridge | NJ | 07920 |
| 23 | Cinema Festival | 318 East 11th Street | | New York | NY | 10003 |
| 22 | Movie Emporium | 203 West Houston Street | | New York | NY | 10014 |
| 19 | Westview Movies | 1112 Broadway | | New York | NY | 10119 |
| 17 | Waterfront Cinemas | P.O. Box 3255 | | Buffalo | NY | 14288 |
| 12 | Mooretown Movies | P.O. Box 11 | 331 Metro Place | Dublin | OH | 43107 |
| 14 | Redwood Cinemas | P.O. Box 112F | 336 Ninth Street | Portland | OR | 97466-3359 |
| 18 | Wellington 10 | 1203 Tenth Southwest | | Philadelphia | PA | 19178 |
| 4 | Danforth Cinemas | P.O. Box 22 | 18 Pickens Street | Columbia | SC | 29201 |
| 2 | Century Cinemas | 3687 Avenue K | | Arlington | TX | 76013 |
| 9 | Mainstream Movies | P.O. Box 33 | 333 Evergreen Building | Seattle | WA | 98220-2791 |

The ZIP codes are sorted in ascending order within each state.

 **Check Your Work** Compare your work to the model answer available in the online course.

## In Addition

### Learning More about Sorting

When sorting records, consider the following alphanumeric rules:

- Numbers stored in fields that are not defined as numeric, such as social security numbers or telephone numbers, are sorted as characters (not numeric values). To sort them as numbers, all field values must be the same length.
- Records in which the selected field is empty are listed first.
- Numbers are sorted before letters.

### Moving a Column

When sorting on more than one column, the columns must be adjacent. If necessary, columns can be moved to accommodate a multiple-field sort. To move a column, click the field name in the header row to select the column. Position the mouse pointer on the field name of the selected column, click and hold down the left mouse button, drag the thick black line that displays to the desired location, and then release the mouse button.

A filter is used to view only those records that meet specified criteria. The records that do not meet the filter criteria are hidden from view temporarily. Use a filter to view, edit, and/or print a subset of rows within the table. For example, a filter can be used to view only those records of distributors in one state. Apply a filter using the filter arrow at the right of the column heading or click the Filter button on the Home tab. Insert or remove check marks from the field entries to be filtered. Toggle between the data in the table and the filtered data using the Toggle Filter button on the Home tab and use the *Clear All Filters* option from the Advanced button drop-down list to clear all filters from the table. Records can be sorted by specific values using the *Text Filters* option at the filter drop-down list for fields containing text, the *Number Filters* option for fields that contain number values, or the *Date Filters* option for fields containing dates.

**Worldwide Enterprises**

**What You Will Do**   You want to view a list of distributors in New York state and then further filter the list to display only those in the city of New York. In a second filter operation, you will view the distributors located in California and Georgia.

**Tutorial**

Filtering Records

**1** With **1-WEDistributors** open, open the US_Distributors table.

**2** Click in any field in the *State* field column.

**3** Click the Filter button 🔽 in the Sort & Filter group on the Home tab.

**4** Click the *(Select All)* check box to remove the check marks from all of the check boxes.

At the drop-down list, click the check boxes for those states that you do not wish to view to remove the check marks.

**5** Scroll down the filter list box, click the check box next to *NY*, and then click OK.

The filter list box closes and only four records remain, as shown below. Two icons display next to *State* indicating the field is both filtered and sorted and the message *Filtered* displays in the Record Navigation bar.

Only those records that meet the filter criterion, the *State* field, are displayed in Step 5.

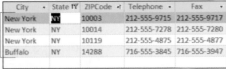

| City | State | ZIPCode | Telephone | Fax |
|------|-------|---------|-----------|-----|
| New York | NY | 10003 | 212-555-9715 | 212-555-9717 |
| New York | NY | 10014 | 212-555-7278 | 212-555-7280 |
| New York | NY | 10119 | 212-555-4875 | 212-555-4877 |
| Buffalo | NY | 14288 | 716-555-3845 | 716-555-3947 |

**6** Click the filter arrow at the right of *City* in the header row to display the filter drop-down list.

**7** Click the check box next to *Buffalo* to remove the check mark and then click OK.

The record for the company located in Buffalo is removed and only three records remain.

**8** Click the Toggle Filter button in the Sort & Filter group.

> Click the Toggle Filter button to toggle between the data in the table and the filtered data. The message in the Record Navigation bar changes to *Unfiltered*.

**9** Remove both filters from the table by clicking the Advanced button in the Sort & Filter group on the Home tab and then clicking *Clear All Filters*.

**10** Save and then close the US_Distributors table.

**11** Open the Orders table and then click in any field in the *Fee* field column.

**12** Click the filter arrow at the right of *Fee* in the header row.

**13** Point to *Number Filters* and then click *Less Than* at the side menu.

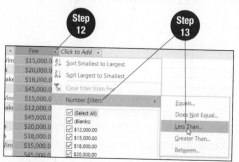

**14** At the Custom Filter dialog box, type 15000.

> Typing *15000* in the Custom Filter dialog box specifies that you want to filter and display only those records with a fee amount less than or equal to $15,000.

**15** Click OK.

> Six records display with a fee amount less than or equal to $15,000.

**16** Close the Orders table and at the message that displays asking if you want to save the changes, click the No button.

---

# In Addition

### Filtering by Selection

Another method for filtering is to select specific text in a field and then click the Selection button in the Sort & Filter group on the Home tab. A drop-down list displays with filtering options such as *Equals* and *Does Not Equal*. The options vary depending on the data selected. For example, select *NY* in the *State* field in the US_Distributors table and the drop-down list displays the options *Equals "NY"*, *Does Not Equal "NY"*, *Contains "NY"*, and *Does Not Contain "NY"*. Click one of the options to filter the data.

To print a table in Datasheet view, click the File tab, click the *Print* option in the backstage area, and then click the *Quick Print* or *Print* option. To avoid wasting paper, use the *Print Preview* option at the Print backstage area to see how the table will appear on the page before printing the table. By default, Access prints a table on letter-size paper in portrait orientation. Change the paper size, orientation, or margins using buttons in the Page Size and Page Layout groups on the Print Preview tab.

**What You Will Do**   Sam Vestering has requested a list of the US distributors. You will open the US_Distributors table, preview the printout, change the page orientation, change the left and right margins, and then print the table.

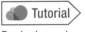

Previewing and
Printing a Table

**1** With **1-WEDistributors** open, open the US_Distributors table.

**2** Click the File tab, click the *Print* option, and then click the *Print Preview* option.

The table displays in the Print Preview window as shown in Figure 1.5.

**3** Move the mouse pointer (displays as a magnifying glass) over the top center of the table and then click the left mouse button.

Clicking the left mouse button changes the display percentage to 100%. Access prints the table name at the top center and the current date at the top right of the page. At the bottom center, Access prints the word *Page* followed by the current page number.

**4** Click the left mouse button again to display the current page in the Print Preview window.

**5** Click the Next Page button on the Navigation bar at the bottom left of the Print Preview window.

The US_Distributors table requires two pages to print with the default margins and orientation. In the next step, you will change to landscape orientation to see if all of the columns will fit on one page.

**Figure 1.5** Print Preview Window

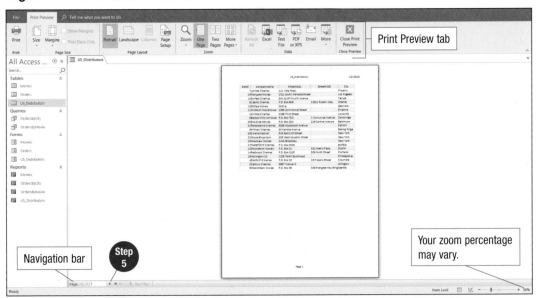

In Brief

**Display Table in Print Preview**
1. Click File tab.
2. Click *Print* option.
3. Click *Print Preview* option.

**Change to Landscape Orientation**
1. Display table in Print Preview window.
2. Click Landscape button.
3. Click Close Print Preview button.

**Change Margins**
1. Display table in Print Preview window.
2. Click Margins button.
3. Click predefined margins option.
OR
1. Display table in Print Preview window.
2. Click Page Setup button.
3. Change margins settings.
4. Click OK.

**6** Click the Landscape button  in the Page Layout group on the Print Preview tab.

Landscape orientation rotates the printout to print wider than it is tall. Changing to landscape orientation allows more columns to fit on a page, but the US_Distributors table still needs two pages to print.

**7** Click the Margins button in the Page Size group and then click the *Narrow* option at the drop-down list.

The *Narrow* option changes all margins to 0.25 inches.

**8** Click the Page Setup button in the Page Layout group.

**9** At the Page Setup dialog box with the Print Options tab active, select *0.25* in the *Top* measurement box and then type *2*.

**10** Select *0.25* in the *Left* measurement box and then type *.75*.

**11** Click OK.

**12** Click the Print button in the Print group and then click OK at the Print dialog box.

In a few seconds, the table will print on the default printer installed on your computer. Even in landscape orientation with narrow margins, the table does not fit on one page. In Section 3, you will learn how to create a report for a table. Using a report, you can control the data layout on the page and which columns are printed.

**13** Click the Close Print Preview button in the Close Preview group.

**14** Close the US_Distributors table.

Check Your Work Compare your work to the model answer available in the online course.

# In Addition

## Previewing Multiple Pages

Use buttons in the Zoom group on the Print Preview tab to view a specific number of pages in a multiple-page table. Click the Two Pages button to view the table with two pages side-by-side. Click the More Pages button and then choose *Four Pages*, *Eight Pages*, or *Twelve Pages* at the drop-down list. The US_Distributors table is shown at the right in the Two Pages view.

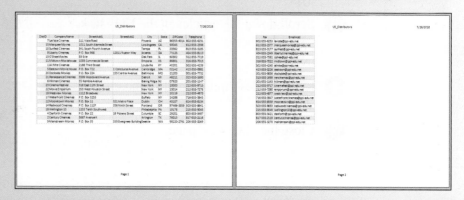

Microsoft provides help resources that contain information on Access features and commands. Press the F1 function key or click the Help tab and then click the Help button in the Help group to display the Help task pane. Or, open a dialog box, click the Help button in the upper right corner of the dialog box (displays as a question mark) and the Microsoft Office support website displays with information related to the dialog box. Click the Help button in the upper right corner of a backstage area and the Microsoft Office support website displays with information related to the specific backstage area. Access also includes the Tell Me feature, which provides information and guidance on how to complete a function. To use Tell Me, click in the *Tell Me* text box on the ribbon and then type the function. As text is typed in the *Tell Me* text box, a drop-down list displays with options that are refined as the text is typed. The drop-down list displays options for completing the function, displaying information on the function from sources on the Web, or displaying help information on the function. Hide a column in a table in Datasheet view if a field exists in the table that is not needed for data entry or editing purposes. Hiding the column provides more space in the work area, and hidden columns do not print. To hide a column, right-click the field name in the header row and then click *Hide Fields* at the shortcut menu.

**Worldwide Enterprises**

**What You Will Do**  You will explore topics in the Help feature and use the Tell Me feature to change the font size of the text in the datasheet. Finally, you will reprint the formatted datasheet with two columns hidden that you decide you do not need on the printout.

*Note: The following steps assume you are connected to the internet to access online resources.*

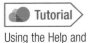
**Tutorial**

Using the Help and
Tell Me Features

**1**  With **1-WEDistributors** open, open the US_Distributors table.

**2**  Press the F1 function key to display the Help task pane.

> Find information in help resources by typing a search word or phrase and then pressing the Enter key or clicking the Search help button.

**3**  At the Help task pane, type keyboard shortcuts in the search text box and then press the Enter key.

> Keyboard shortcuts are helpful to know since they help you perform frequently used commands more quickly.

**4**  Click the Keyboard shortcuts for Access hyperlink.

**5**  Scroll down the articles in the Help task pane and then click the Edit text or data hyperlink.

**6**  Read the descriptions and keyboard shortcuts.

**7**  Close the Help task pane.

**8** At the US_Distributors table, click in the *Tell Me* text box and then type font size.

A drop-down list displays with options such as *Font Size*, *Choose Page Size*, and *Font Color*.

**9** Position the mouse pointer on the *Font Size* option at the drop-down list and then click *10* at the side menu.

The Tell Me feature guided you through the steps for changing font size of the text in the table.

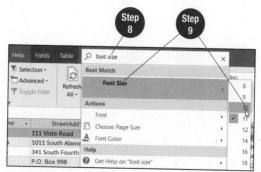

**10** Right-click the *DistID* field name in the header row and then click *Hide Fields* at the shortcut menu.

**11** Right-click the *EmailAdd* field name and then click *Hide Fields* at the shortcut menu.

**12** Click the File tab, click the *Print* option, and then click the *Print Preview* option.

**13** Change to landscape orientation.

**14** Print the table by clicking the Print button on the Print Preview tab and then clicking OK at the Print dialog box.

**15** Close the Print Preview window and then close the US_Distributors table. Click Yes when prompted to save the layout changes.

**16** Click the File tab and then click the *Close* option.

 **Check Your Work** Compare your work to the model answer available in the online course.

## In Addition

### Accessing Help Information

The following options are available for displaying help information at the Help task pane:
- Press the F1 function key.
- Click the Help tab and then click the Help button.
- Type a function in the *Tell Me* text box, click the last option, and then click a resource at the side menu.

The following options are available for displaying help information at the Microsoft Office support website:
- Click the Help button in a dialog box.
- Click the Help button at a backstage area.

# Features Summary

| Feature | Ribbon Tab, Group | Button | Keyboard Shortcut |
|---|---|---|---|
| change font size | Home, Text Formatting | | |
| change margins | Print Preview, Page Size OR Page Layout | OR to open Page Setup | |
| column width | Home, Records | | |
| delete records | Home, Records | | Delete |
| filter | Home, Sort & Filter | | |
| find | Home, Find | | Ctrl + F |
| Help | Help, Help | | F1 |
| landscape orientation | Print Preview, Page Layout | | |
| Print backstage area | File, *Print* | | |
| Print dialog box | File, *Print, Print* | | Ctrl + P |
| Print Preview | File, *Print, Print Preview* | | |
| replace | Home, Find | | Ctrl + H |
| remove sort | Home, Sort & Filter | | |
| save | | | Ctrl + S |
| sort ascending order | Home, Sort & Filter | | |
| sort descending order | Home, Sort & Filter | | |
| Tell Me feature | *Tell Me* text box | | Alt + Q |

# Access

# Creating Tables and Relationships

**Data Files**

Before beginning section work, copy the AccessS2 folder to your storage medium and then make AccessS2 the active folder.

## Skills

- Create a new database
- Create a table in Datasheet view
- Assign data types to fields
- Create captions for fields
- Limit the number of characters allowed in a field
- Create a default value for a field
- Create and modify a table in Design view
- Set the primary key field for a table
- Verify data entry using a validation rule
- Restrict data entry using an input mask

- Set the format for displaying data
- Create a lookup list in a field
- Insert, move, and delete fields
- Apply formatting to data in a table
- Add a total row to a table
- Create, edit, and delete a one-to-many relationship
- Create and print a relationship report
- Create and edit a one-to-one relationship

## Projects Overview

Create and modify tables to store distributor contract information and employee benefit and review information; create relationships between tables. Review tables in an existing database and improve the table design.

Create a table to store student grades for a course in the Theatre Arts Division.

Create a new database to store contact information.

Create a new database to store employee expense claims. Modify a database on tour bookings.

Modify and correct field properties in a costume inventory table to improve the design.

The online course includes additional training and assessment resources.

Tables form the basis for all other objects in a database and each table must be planned to adhere to database design principles. Creating a new table generally involves determining fields, assigning a data type to each field, designating the primary key field, and naming the table. This process is referred to as *defining the table structure*. As explained in Section 1, Access saves data automatically as records are entered into a datasheet. For this reason, to begin a new database, choose the Blank database template at the Access opening screen, assign the database a file name, and navigate to the storage location. Once the database has been created, a new blank table is presented in Datasheet view. Create the table and then enter records in the table.

**Worldwide Enterprises**

**What You Will Do**   Riya Singh, a paralegal at Worldwide Enterprises, has asked you to create a new database in which distributor contracts can be maintained. You will create a new database file in which to store the contracts and then create the Contracts table. After the table is created, you will look at the table in a view that allows you to make changes to the table's structure.

**Tutorial**

Opening a Blank
Database

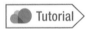
**Tutorial**

Creating a Table in
Datasheet View

① Open Access and then click the *Blank database* template at the Access opening screen.

② At the Blank database window, type 2-WEContracts in the *File Name* text box.

> One of the differences between Access and other programs is that the file name is assigned before any data is entered. Do not remove your storage medium while working in Access since the file will frequently have data written to it.

③ Click the Browse button 📁 at the right of the *File Name* text box.

④ At the File New Database dialog box, navigate to your AccessS2 folder and then click OK.

⑤ Click the Create button.

> A blank table appears in the work area with a tab labeled *Table1*. A column with the field name *ID* has been created automatically. The heading *Click to Add* appears at the top of the first blank column.

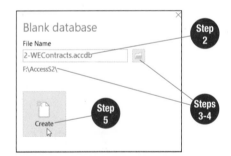

⑥ Review the table design shown in Figure 2.1. This is the table you will create in Steps 7–23. Refer to Table 2.1 for guidelines for naming fields. Note that in the Contracts table design the *ID* field that Access automatically creates will be used for the primary key field.

> Before you begin creating a table, refer to Table 2.2 on page 30 for information on field data types.

**Figure 2.1** Fields for Contracts Table

| Contracts | | |
|---|---|---|
| **Field Name** | **Data Type** | **Sample Data** |
| *ID | AutoNumber | |
| ContractNo | Short Text | 2021-034 |
| Company | Short Text | West Coast Movies |
| ContactFN | Short Text | Jordan |
| ContactLN | Short Text | Daniels |
| Phone | Short Text | 604-555-2886 |
| Renewal | Yes/No | Yes |
| StartDate | Date & Time | July 1, 2021 |
| EndDate | Date & Time | June 30, 2023 |
| ShipFee | Currency | $500 |
| Percentage | Number | 10 |
| Notes | Long Text | Jordan is an active member of the Western Film Association. |

**Table 2.1** Field Name Guidelines

A field name can be up to 64 characters and can include both letters and numbers. Some symbols are permitted, but others are excluded, so avoiding symbols is best. An exception is the underscore, which is often used as a word separator.

Do not use a space in a field name. Although a space is an accepted character, most database designers avoid using spaces in field names and object names. This practice facilitates easier management of the data with scripting or other database programming tools. Use compound words for field names or the underscore character as a word separator. For example, a field to hold a person's last name could be named *LastName*, *Last_Name*, or *LName*.

Abbreviate field names so that the names are as short as possible while still able to be readily understood. For example, a field such as *ContactLastName* could be abbreviated to *ContactLN* or a field such as *Telephone* to *Phone*. Shorter names are easier to manage and type into expressions.

**7** Click the Short Text button AB in the Add & Delete group on the Table Tools Fields tab.

> Access adds a new column to the datasheet with the Short Text data type assigned and selects the field name in the table header row for you to type the correct field name.

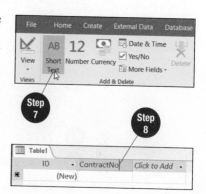

**8** Type ContractNo and then press the Enter key.

> Access moves to the *Click to Add* column and opens the data type drop-down list for the next new column.

**9** Click *Short Text* at the drop-down list.

**10** Type Company and then press the Enter key.

**11** Click *Short Text* at the drop-down list, type ContactFN, and then press the Enter key.

**12** Click *Short Text* at the drop-down list, type ContactLN, and then press the Enter key.

**13** Click *Short Text* at the drop-down list, type Phone, and then press the Enter key.

**14** Click *Yes/No* at the drop-down list.

> The *Renewal* column will contain only one of two entries: *Yes* for those records that represent renewals of existing contracts or *No* if the record is a contract for a new distributor. When you change the data type to Yes/No, a check box is inserted in the column.

**Table 2.2** Common Field Data Types in Datasheet View

| Option | Description |
|---|---|
| Short Text | Alphanumeric data up to 255 characters in length, such as a name, address, or value such as a telephone number or social security number that is used as an identifier and not for calculating. |
| Number | Positive or negative values that can be used in calculations; do not use for values that will calculate monetary amounts (see *Currency*). |
| Currency | Values that involve money; Access will not round off during calculations. |
| Date & Time | Use this type to ensure dates and times are entered and sorted properly. |
| Yes/No | Data in the field will be either Yes or No, True or False, On or Off. |
| Lookup & Relationship | Can be used to enter data in the field from another existing table or display a list of values in a drop-down list for the user to choose from. |
| Long Text | Alphanumeric data up to 64,000 characters in length. |
| AutoNumber | Access automatically numbers each record sequentially (incrementing by 1) when you begin typing a new record. |
| Calculated Field | The contents of a calculated field are generated by Access from an expression you create; for example, a total cost could be calculated by adding a price plus a sales tax column. |

15 Type Renewal and then press the Enter key.

16 Continue changing the data types and typing the field names for the remainder of the fields as shown in Figure 2.1 (on page 28).

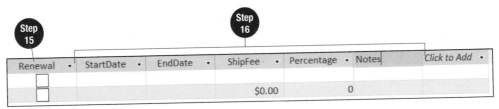

17 Press the Enter key after typing *Notes*. Click in any empty field below a column heading to remove the drop-down list and end the table.

18 If necessary, scroll to the left edge of the table. Click in the empty field below *ContractNo*, type 2021-034, and then press the Enter key or the Tab key to move to the next field.

19 Continue typing the sample data for the remainder of the fields as shown in Figure 2.1 on page 28. At the first field in the *Renewal* column, click the check box or press the spacebar to insert a check mark in the box, indicating that the field entry is *Yes*.

> Access converts dates you enter into the format *m/d/yyyy*. When entering dates, be careful to use the proper punctuation and spacing between the month, day, and year so that Access recognizes the entry as a valid date.

20 Click the Save button 🖫 on the Quick Access Toolbar.

**In Brief**

**Create New Database**
1. Start Access.
2. Click *Blank database* template.
3. Type database name.
4. Click Browse button.
5. Navigate to drive and/or folder.
6. Click OK.
7. Click Create button.

**Create Table**
1. Click data type in Add & Delete group on Table Tools Field s (Sp. Fields) tab.
2. Type field name and press Enter key.
3. Click field data type.
4. Type field name and press Enter key.
5. Repeat Steps 3–4 for remaining columns.
6. Click Save button.
7. Type table name.
8. Press Enter key or click OK.

**21** At the Save As dialog box with *Table1* selected in the *Table Name* text box, type Contracts and then press the Enter key or click OK.

**22** Click the View button in the Views group on the Home tab. (Do not click the button arrow.)

> The View button toggles between Design view and Datasheet view. In Design view, each row represents one field in the table and is used to define the field name, the field's data type, and an optional description. The *Field Properties* section in the lower half of the work area displays the properties for the active field. The properties will vary depending on the active field. A key icon displays in the field selector bar (blank column at the left of the field names) for the *ID* field, identifying it as the primary key field.

**23** Compare the entries in the *Field Name* and *Data Type* columns for each field with those shown in Figure 2.1 on page 28. If necessary, correct a typing error in a field name by positioning the insertion point over the existing field name, clicking to open the field, and then inserting or deleting text as necessary. To change a data type, click in the *Data Type* column for the field, click the down arrow, and then click the correct data type at the drop-down list.

**24** Click the View button in the Views group on the Table Tools Design tab. If you made changes while in Design view, you will be prompted to save the table when you switch views. If necessary, click the Yes button at any prompts that appear.

> Since you were in Design view, the View button changed to the Datasheet view button. Click the button to change back to Datasheet view.

**25** Adjust the width of the columns to best fit the longest entries.

**26** Print the table in landscape orientation and then close the table, saving the changes to the table layout.

**Check Your Work** Compare your work to the model answer available in the online course.

## In Addition

### Pinning/Unpinning a Database File

At the Access opening screen and the Open backstage area, Access displays the most recently opened databases. If a database is opened on a regular basis, consider pinning the database to the Recent list at the Access opening screen or to the *Recent* option list in the Open backstage area. To pin a database, hover the mouse over the database file name and then click the push pin at the right of the file name. Whether a database file is pinned at the Access opening screen or the Open backstage area, it displays in both. Unpin a database file by hovering the mouse over the database file name and then clicking the push pin at the right of the file.

Each field has characteristics associated with it, called field properties. Field properties are used to control the behavior or interactivity of the field in database objects. Use buttons and options in the Properties group on the Table Tools Fields tab to modify field properties. Click the Name & Caption button and the Enter Field Properties dialog box displays with options for creating a descriptive title for fields. This is useful for providing a descriptive name if a field name is abbreviated in the table or to show spaces between words in a compound field name. Type a description in the *Description* text box and the description displays above the Status bar when entering records in the table. Use the *Field Size* option box to limit the number of characters that are allowed in a field entry. A field size of *4* for an *ID* field would prevent ID numbers longer than four characters from being stored in a record. If most records are likely to contain the same data, create a default entry to save typing and reduce errors. Click the Default Value button in the Properties group to display the Expression Builder dialog box with options for entering a default value.

**Worldwide Enterprises**

**What You Will Do**   You will modify the field properties of some of the fields in the Contracts table by providing a caption and description, specifying a field size, and/or providing a default value.

Tutorial

Modifying Field Properties in Datasheet View

① With **2-WEContracts** open, open the Contracts table.

② Click the *ContactFN* field name in the header row.

③ Click the Table Tools Fields tab.

④ Click the Name & Caption button 📋 in the Properties group.

⑤ At the Enter Field Properties dialog box, click in the *Caption* text box and then type First Name.

⑥ Click in the *Description* text box and then type Enter contact's first name.

⑦ Click OK to close the dialog box.

> The caption *First Name* now displays in the header row instead of *ContactFN*. The field name is still *ContactFN*, but the user-friendly caption displays in the header row.

⑧ Limit the field size for the contact's first name by clicking the number *255* in the *Field Size* option box in the Properties group, typing 20, and then pressing Enter.

⑨ At the message that displays indicating that the size of the field has been changed to a shorter size and asking if you want to continue, click Yes.

⑩ Click the *ContactLN* field name in the header row.

⑪ Click the Name & Caption button in the Properties group.

**12** At the Enter Field Properties dialog box, click in the *Caption* text box and then type Last Name.

**13** Click in the *Description* text box, type Enter contact's last name, and then click OK.

**14** Click the number *255* in the *Field Size* option box, type 25, and then press the Enter key.

**15** At the message that displays indicating that the size of the field has been changed to a shorter size and that some of the data may be lost, click the Yes button.

**16** Click the *Renewal* field name in the header row.

**17** Click the Default Value button 🔲 in the Properties group.

**18** At the Expression Builder dialog box, select the current default value *No* in the text box and then type Yes.

**19** Click OK.

> With a default value of *Yes*, a check mark will automatically appear in the *Renewal* check box for new records entered in the table.

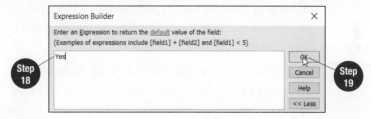

**20** Print the table in landscape orientation and then close the table, saving the changes to the table layout.

**21** Close **2-WEContracts**.

> **Check Your Work** Compare your work to the model answer available in the online course.

## In Addition

### Changing an AutoNumber Data Type Field

Access automatically applies the AutoNumber data type to the first field in a table created in Datasheet view and assigns a unique number to each record. In many cases, letting Access automatically assign a number to a record is a good idea. Some situations may arise, however, when the unique value in the first field is something other than a number. Trying to change the AutoNumber data type in the first column by clicking one of the data type buttons in the Add & Delete group on the Table Tools Fields tab causes Access to create another field. To change the AutoNumber data type for the first field, click the *Data Type* option box arrow in the Formatting group on the Table Tools Fields tab and then click data type at the drop-down list.

As an alternative to creating a table in Datasheet view, a table can be created in Design view, where field properties can be set before entering data. When using Design view, Access does not add the *ID* field to the new table automatically. As mentioned previously, a table should have a primary key field, or a field used to store a unique value for each record. Examples of fields suitable for a primary key field are those that store an identification value such as an employee number, a part number, a vendor number, or a customer number. If, when designing a table, no data is suited to a primary key field, create a field labeled *ID* and set the data type to AutoNumber. When creating a table in Datasheet view, the Properties group on the Table Tools Fields tab contains buttons and an option for modifying or adding field properties. In Design view, the *Field Properties* section contains property boxes with options for adding or modifying field properties.

**Worldwide Enterprises**

**What You Will Do**  Rhonda Trask, human resources manager, has asked you to work in the employees database. Rhonda would like you to create a new table in the file in which to store the employee benefit plan information. You decide to create this table in Design view and add and modify field properties.

**Tutorial**

Creating a Table in Design View

**Tutorial**

Setting the Primary Key Field

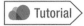
**Tutorial**

Modifying Field Properties in Design View

**1** Open **2-WEEmployees** and enable the content, if necessary.

> This database is similar to the database you worked with in the Skills Review for Section 1. This version of the database has additional records added.

**2** Click the Create tab and then click the Table Design button in the Tables group.

**3** With the insertion point positioned in the *Field Name* column in the first row, type EmployeeID and then press the Enter key or the Tab key to move to the next column.

**4** With *Short Text* already entered in the *Data Type* column, change the default field size from *255* to *4* by double-clicking the number *255* in the *Field Size* property box in the *Field Properties* section and then typing 4.

> The *EmployeeID* field will contain numbers; however, leave the data type defined as *Short Text* since no calculations will be performed with employee numbers. Notice the information that displays at the bottom right corner of the Design window. Access displays information about the field in which the insertion point is positioned.

**5** Click in the *Description* column at the right of *Short Text*, type Type the four-digit employee number, and then press the Enter key to move to the second row.

**6** Type PensionPlan in the *Field Name* column in the second row and then press the Enter key.

**7** Click the arrow at the right of the *Data Type* column and then click *Yes/No* at the drop-down list.

> In this field, the data is only one of two entries: *Yes* if the employee is enrolled in the pension plan or *No* if the employee is not.

**8** Change the default value from *No* to *Yes* by double-clicking *No* in the *Default Value* property box in the *Field Properties* section and then typing Yes.

Step 8

**9** Click in the *Description* column at the right of *Yes/No*, type Click or press spacebar for Yes; leave empty for No, and then press the Enter key.

**10** Enter the remaining field names, data types, and descriptions as shown in Figure 2.2 by completing steps similar to those in Steps 3–9. Change the default value for the *HealthPlan* field to *Yes*.

**11** Click in the *EmployeeID* field name.

**12** Click the Primary Key button 🔑 in the Tools group on the Table Tools Design tab.

> A key icon appears in the field selector bar at the left of *EmployeeID*, indicating the field is the primary key field.

Step 12

Step 11

**13** Click the Save button on the Quick Access Toolbar.

**14** At the Save As dialog box, type Benefits in the *Table Name* text box and then press the Enter key or click OK.

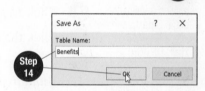

Step 14

**15** Close the Benefits table.

**Figure 2.2** Design View Table Entries

| Field Name | Data Type | |
| --- | --- | --- |
| EmployeeID | Short Text | Type the four-digit employee number |
| PensionPlan | Yes/No | Click or press spacebar for Yes; leave empty for No |
| DentalPlan | Yes/No | Click or press spacebar for Yes; leave empty for No |
| HealthPlan | Yes/No | Click or press spacebar for Yes; leave empty for No |
| Dependents | Number | Type the number of dependents related to this employee |
| LifeInsce | Currency | Type the amount of life insurance subscribed by this employee |

**Check Your Work** Compare your work to the model answer available in the online course.

# In Addition

## Using the More Button on the Table Tools Fields tab in Datasheet View

Click the More Fields button to choose from a list of other field data types and fields that have predefined field properties. Scroll down the More Fields button drop-down list to the Quick Start category. Use options in this category to add a group of related fields in one step. For example, click *Address* to add five new fields with the captions: *Address*, *City*, *State Province*, *ZIP Postal*, and *Country Region*.

The accuracy of data in a table is extremely important. To control the data entered in a field and improve the accuracy of the data, apply a validation rule. For example, a validation rule can be applied that specifies amounts entered in a field must be less than a certain number. Apply a validation rule to a field in Datasheet view with the Validation button in the Field Validation group on the Table Tools Fields tab or with the *Validation Rule* property box in Design view. A validation message can be included that displays if the data entered in a field violates the validation rule. Use the Validation button in Datasheet view or the *Validation Text* property box in Design view to create a validation message.

**Worldwide Enterprises**

**What You Will Do**   Worldwide Enterprises offers health benefits to a maximum of five dependents. You will use the Validation button on the Table Tools Fields tab to add a validation rule and message indicating that the number in the *Dependents* field must be less than six. The company offers life insurance in amounts up to a maximum of $200,000 per employee. You will use field properties in Design view to ensure that no amounts greater than $200,000 are entered in the *LifeIns* field.

**Tutorial**
Applying a Validation
Rule in Datasheet View

**Tutorial**
Applying a Validation
Rule in Design View

**1**   With **2-WEmployees** open, open the Benefits table in Datasheet view.

**2**   Click *Dependents* in the header row.

**3**   Click the Table Tools Fields tab.

**4**   Click the Validation button 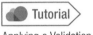 in the Field Validation group and then click the *Field Validation Rule* option.

**5**   At the Expression Builder dialog box, type <6 in the text box and then click OK.

**6**   Click the Validation button and then click the *Field Validation Message* option.

**7**   Type Enter a number less than 6 in the text box in the Enter Validation Message dialog box and then click OK.

**8**   Click the View button in the Views group to switch to Design view.

**9**   Click *LifeInsce* in the *Field Name* column to display the associated field properties.

**10** Click in the *Validation Rule* property box, type <=200000, and then press the Enter key.

Pressing the Enter key after typing the validation rule moves the insertion point to the *Validation Text* property box. If an invalid syntax error displays, check your typing. Do not type a dollar symbol or comma in the validation rule statement. Also, make sure you have the correct less-than symbol (<) and equals sign (=) and that the order is <=.

**11** Type Enter a value that is less than or equal to $200,000 and then press the Enter key.

**12** Click the Save button.

**13** Click the View button in the Views group to switch to Datasheet view.

**14** Add the following record to the table (press the Enter key after typing *210000*):

| | |
|---|---|
| *EmployeeID* | 1003 |
| *PensionPlan* | Yes |
| *DentalPlan* | Yes |
| *HealthPlan* | Yes |
| *Dependents* | 2 |
| *LifeInsce* | 210000 |

When you enter *210000* into the *LifeInsce* field and then press the Enter key or the Tab key, Access displays an error message. The text in the error message is the text you entered in the *Validation Text* property box.

**15** Click OK at the Microsoft Access error message.

**16** Delete *210000*, type *200000*, and then press the Enter key.

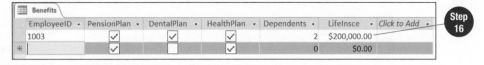

**17** Close the Benefits table.

**Check Your Work** Compare your work to the model answer available in the online course.

## In Addition

### Understanding Other Types of Validation Rules

Validation rules should be created whenever possible to avoid data entry errors. The examples at the right illustrate various ways to use a validation rule to verify data.

| Field Name | Validation Rule | Data Check |
|---|---|---|
| *CustomerNo* | >1000 And <1100 | Limits customer numbers to 1001 through 1099. |
| *CreditLimit* | <=5000 | Restricts credit limits to values of 5000 or less. |
| *State* | "CA" | Only the state of California is accepted. |
| *Country* | "CA" Or "US" | Only the United States or Canada is accepted. |
| *OrderQty* | >=25 | Quantity ordered must be a minimum of 25. |

An input mask provides a pattern in a table or form indicating how data is to be entered into a field. For example, an input mask in a telephone number field that displays (___)___-____ indicates to the user that a three-digit area code is to be entered in front of all telephone numbers. Input masks ensure that data is entered consistently in tables. In addition to specifying the position and number of characters in a field, a mask can be created that restricts the data entered to digits, letters, or characters, and specifies whether or not each digit, letter, or character is required or optional. Create an input mask in Design view with the *Input Mask* property box. Use the *Format* property box to control how the data is displayed in the field after it has been entered.

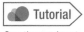
**Worldwide Enterprises**

**What You Will Do**   You will create a new field in the Benefits table for pension plan eligibility dates and include an input mask and format property in the field.

Tutorial

Creating an Input Mask

**1**  With **2-WEEmployees** open, open the Benefits table in Design view.

**2**  Click in the *Field Name* column in the blank row below *LifeInsce*, type PensionDate, and then press the Enter key.

**3**  Change the data type to Date/Time and then press the Enter key.

**4**  Type Type date employee is eligible for pension plan in the format dd-mmm-yy (example: 31-Dec-21).

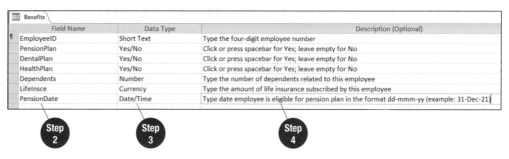

| Field Name | Data Type | Description (Optional) |
| --- | --- | --- |
| EmployeeID | Short Text | Type the four-digit employee number |
| PensionPlan | Yes/No | Click or press spacebar for Yes; leave empty for No |
| DentalPlan | Yes/No | Click or press spacebar for Yes; leave empty for No |
| HealthPlan | Yes/No | Click or press spacebar for Yes; leave empty for No |
| Dependents | Number | Type the number of dependents related to this employee |
| LifeInsce | Currency | Type the amount of life insurance subscribed by this employee |
| PensionDate | Date/Time | Type date employee is eligible for pension plan in the format dd-mmm-yy (example: 31-Dec-21) |

Step 2    Step 3    Step 4

**5**  Click the Save button.

**6**  With the *PensionDate* field active, click in the *Input Mask* property box in the *Field Properties* section and then click the Build button ⟨...⟩ at the right side of the box.

**7**  Click *Medium Date* at the first Input Mask Wizard dialog box and then click the Next button.

> The input masks that display in the list in the first dialog box are dependent on the data type for the field for which you are creating an input mask.

**8**  Click the Next button at the second Input Mask Wizard dialog box.

> This dialog box shows the input mask code in the *Input Mask* text box and sets the placeholder character that displays in the field. The default placeholder is the underscore character.

Step 7

**In Brief**

**Use Input Mask Wizard**
1. Open table in Design view.
2. Click in field row.
3. Click in *Input Mask* property box.
4. Click Build button.
5. Click input mask you want to create.
6. Click Next.
7. Select placeholder character.
8. Click Next.
9. Click Finish at the last wizard dialog box.
10. Click Save button.

**9** Click the Finish button at the last Input Mask Wizard dialog box to complete the entry in the *Input Mask* property box and then press the Enter key.

**10** Click in the *Format* property box.

The input mask controls how a date is entered into the field; however, by default, Access displays dates in the format *m/d/yyyy*. To avoid confusion, you will format the field to display the date in the same format that the input mask accepts the data.

**11** Click the arrow at the right side of the property box and then click *Medium Date* at the drop-down list.

**12** Click in the *Caption* property box and then type Pension Date.

**13** Click the Save button and then switch to Datasheet view.

**14** Click in the first field in the *Pension Date* column in the datasheet.

The input mask __-___-__ appears in the field.

**15** Type 080721.

A beep sounds as you type every character after *08*. The only characters allowed after the first hyphen are letters. Notice the insertion point remains in the month section of the field.

**16** With the insertion point positioned in the month section of the field, type jul21 and then press the Enter key.

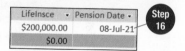

Notice that you did not have to type the hyphens or capitalize the first letter of the month. The greater than symbol (>) preceding *L* in the mask causes Access to convert the first character to uppercase.

**17** Adjust the width of the *Pension Date* column to best fit the longest entry.

**18** Close the Benefits table. Click Yes when prompted to save changes to the layout.

**Check Your Work** Compare your work to the model answer available in the online course.

---

# In Addition

## Input Mask Codes

The Input Mask Wizard is only available for fields with the Short Text or Date/Time data types. For fields with data types such as Number or Currency or for an input mask for which the wizard does not provide an option, create an input mask by entering the codes directly into the property box. At the right is a list of commonly used input mask codes.

| Use | To restrict data entry to |
|---|---|
| 0 | digit, zero through nine, entry is required |
| 9 | digit or space, entry is not required |
| L | letter, A through Z, entry is required |
| ? | letter, A through Z, entry is not required |
| > | all characters following are converted to uppercase |
| < | all characters following are converted to lowercase |

Create a lookup field to restrict the data entered into the field to a specific list of items. The Lookup tab in the *Field Properties* section in Design view contains the options used to create a lookup field. Access includes the Lookup Wizard to facilitate entering the lookup settings.

**Worldwide Enterprises**

**What You Will Do**   You will create a new field in the Benefits table to store vacation entitlement for each employee. You want the field to display a drop-down list of vacation periods and restrict the field to accept only those entries that match items in the list.

**Tutorial**

Creating a Lookup Field

**1**   With **2-WEEmployees** open, open the Benefits table in Design view.

**2**   Click in the *Field Name* column in the blank row below *PensionDate*, type Vacation, and then press the Enter key.

**3**   Click the arrow at the right of the *Data Type* column and then click *Lookup Wizard* at the drop-down list.

**4**   At the first Lookup Wizard dialog box, click the *I will type in the values that I want* option and then click the Next button.

> If you press the Enter key by mistake and find yourself at the next step in the Lookup Wizard, click the Back button to return to the previous dialog box.

**5**   Click in the blank row below *Col1*, type 1 week, and then press the Tab key.

**6**   Type 2 weeks and then press the Tab key.

**7**   Type 3 weeks and then press the Tab key.

**8**   Type 4 weeks and then click the Next button.

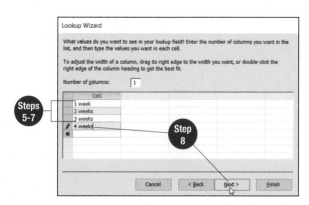

**9**   Click the Finish button in the last Lookup Wizard dialog box to accept the default label *Vacation*. No entry is required in the *Description* column.

**In Brief**

**Create List of Values Using Lookup Wizard**
1. Open table in Design view.
2. Type field name and press Enter key.
3. Change data type to *Lookup Wizard*.
4. Click *I will type in the values that I want.*
5. Click Next.
6. Type field values in *Col1* column.
7. Click Next.
8. Click Finish.
9. Click Save.

**10** Click the Lookup tab in the *Field Properties* section and then view the entries made to each property by the Lookup Wizard.

**11** Click in the *Limit To List* property box, click the arrow that appears, and then click *Yes*.

By changing the Limit To List property to *Yes*, you are further restricting the field to only those items in the drop-down list. If someone attempts to type an entry other than *1 week*, *2 weeks*, *3 weeks*, or *4 weeks*, Access will display an error message and will not store the data.

**12** Click in the *Allow Value List Edits* property box, click the arrow that appears, and then click *No*.

You want to make sure that changes to the list that you created are not allowed by someone using the table or a form.

**13** Click the Save button and then click the View button to switch to Datasheet view.

**14** Click in the first field in the *Vacation* column, type 6 weeks, and then press the Enter key.

**15** Click OK at the message informing you that the text entered isn't an item in the list.

**16** Click *3 weeks* at the drop-down list and then press the Enter key.

**17** Display the table in Print Preview. Change to landscape orientation and then print the table.

**18** Close the Benefits table.

**Check Your Work** Compare your work to the model answer available in the online course.

# In Addition

## Looking Up Data from Another Table

Items in a drop-down list can also be generated by specifying an existing field in another table or query. To do this, click the Next button at the first Lookup Wizard dialog box to accept the default setting *I want the lookup field to get the values from another table or query*. In the remaining wizard dialog boxes, choose the table or query and the field to be used, choose the sort order for displaying the field values, adjust the column width for the lookup list, select the value to store, and assign a label to the column. Creating field entries using this method ensures that data is consistent between tables and eliminates duplicate typing of information that can lead to data errors. For example, in a database used to store employee information, one table could be used to enter employee numbers and then the remaining tables look up the employee number by scrolling a list of employee names.

Fields in Datasheet view can be inserted, moved, deleted, hidden, or frozen. Perform most field management tasks with buttons in the Records group on the Home tab. In Design view, fields can be inserted, moved, and deleted. Apply formatting to data in a table in Datasheet view with buttons and options in the Text Formatting group on the Home tab. Use the Totals button in the Records group on the Home tab to add a total row to a data-sheet and then choose from a list of functions to find the sum, average, maximum, mini-mum, count, standard deviation, or variance result in a numeric column.

**Worldwide Enterprises**

**What You Will Do**  You will make changes to the structure of the Employees table in Datasheet view and Design view, apply formatting to the data in the table, and then add a total row and sum the amounts in the *AnnualSalary* column.

Tutorial

Managing Fields in Datasheet View

Tutorial

Managing Fields in Design View

Tutorial

Formatting Table Data

Tutorial

Inserting a Total Row

① With **2-WEEmployees** open, open the Employees table in Datasheet view.

② Click the *MiddleInitial* field column heading.

③ Click the Delete button ⊠ in the Records group on the Home tab.

④ At the message asking you to confirm the deletion, click Yes.

⑤ Select the *Department* field column by clicking the *Department* column heading.

⑥ Position the mouse pointer in the *Department* column heading (make sure the mouse pointer displays as a white arrow); click and hold down the left mouse button, drag the thick, black, vertical line to the left so it is positioned between the *EmployeeID* and *LastName* field columns; and then release the mouse button.

When you release the mouse button, the *Department* field column is moved between the *EmployeeID* and *LastName* field columns.

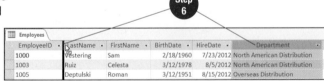

⑦ Click the View button to switch to Design view.

Even though the *Department* field column was moved in Datasheet view, the field remains in its original location in Design view.

⑧ Select the *AnnualSalary* field row by positioning the mouse pointer on the field selector bar at the left of *AnnualSalary* field row and then clicking the left mouse button.

⑨ Position the mouse pointer (white arrow) in the field selector bar for *AnnualSalary* field row; drag the black, horizontal line up so it displays between the *BirthDate* and *HireDate* field row; and then release the left mouse button.

The field moved in Design view remains in the original location in Datasheet view.

⑩ Click in a field in the *Department* row.

⑪ Click the Insert Rows button ⧉ in the Tools group on the Table Tools Design tab.

A new blank row is inserted above the *Department* field row.

**In Brief**

**Delete Field in Datasheet View**
1. Click field name in header row.
2. Click Delete button.
3. Click Yes.

**Delete Field in Design View**
1. Select field row.
2. Click Delete Rows button.
3. Click Yes.

**Insert Field in Design View**
1. Make field active that will display after new field.
2. Click Insert Rows button.

**Move Field in Datasheet View**
1. Click field name in header row.
2. Drag vertical line to new position and then release button.

**Move Field in Design View**
1. Select field using field selector bar.
2. Drag horizontal line to new position and then release mouse button.

**Insert Total Row**
1. Display table in Datasheet view.
2. Click Totals button.

**12** With the insertion point positioned in the *Field Name* column for the new row, type Supervisor and then press the Enter key. (Access will automatically assign the Short Text data type.)

**13** Click the Save button and then click the View button to switch to Datasheet view.

**14** Click the *Font* option box arrow in the Text Formatting group on the Home tab, scroll down the drop-down list, and then click *Candara*.

**15** Click the *Font Size* option box arrow in the Text Formatting group and then click *12* at the drop-down list.

**16** Click the Alternate Row Color button arrow in the Text Formatting group and then click the *Tan, Background 2* color option (third column, first row in the *Theme Colors* section).

**17** Click the Gridlines button in the Text Formatting group and then click *Gridlines: None* at the drop-down list.

**18** Select the *EmployeeID* field by clicking the *EmployeeID* column heading.

**19** Click the Center button in the Text Formatting group.

**20** Click the Totals button ∑ in the Records group on the Home tab.

Access adds a row to the bottom of the table with the label *Total* at the left.

**21** Click in the field in the *Total* row in the *AnnualSalary* column.

**22** Click the arrow that appears at the left, click *Sum* at the drop-down list, and then click in any field in the table to deselect the total amount.

The sum *$1,163,808.00* appears at the bottom of the *AnnualSalary* field column.

**23** Automatically adjust the width of the *Department* column to best fit the longest entry.

**24** Display the table in Print Preview, change to landscape orientation, and then print the table.

**25** Close the Print Preview window and then close the Employees table. Click Yes when prompted to save changes.

**26** Click the File tab and then click the *Close* option.

**Check Your Work** Compare your work to the model answer available in the online course.

## In Addition

### Working with Wide Tables

When working in a table with many columns, scrolling right can make relating to the record in which changes need to be made difficult, since descriptor field columns such as *EmployeeID* or *LastName* may have scrolled off the screen. To alleviate this problem, freeze columns so they do not disappear when the datasheet is scrolled right. To do this, select the columns to freeze, click the More button in the Records group on the Home tab, and then click *Freeze Fields*.

# Activity 2.8 Creating a One-to-Many Relationship

Access is referred to as a *relational database management system*. A *relational database* is one in which tables have been joined. When two or more tables are joined to create a relationship, data can be looked up or reports can be created from multiple tables as if they were one table. Relationships help avoid data duplication. For example, in an employee database, the employee's first and last names would only need to appear in one table. In the remaining tables, only the employee identification number is needed. In most cases, tables are joined by a common field that exists in both tables. When two tables are joined in a relationship, one table is called the *primary table* and the other table is called the *related table*. One type of relationship is a *one-to-many relationship*, where one table in the relationship contains one unique record in the field used to join the tables while the other table can have several records with a matching field value in the joined field. In this type of relationship, the common field is the primary key field in the primary table and the field in the related table is the foreign key field. The referential integrity in a relationship can be enforced, which means that a value for the primary key field must first be entered in the primary table before it can be entered in the related table. Once referential integrity is enforced, other options become available for specifying that any change to the primary key field in the primary table is automatically updated in the related table and any record deleted in the primary table is automatically deleted in the related table. Establish a relationship between tables at the Relationships window. Display this window by clicking the Relationships button on the Database Tools tab.

**Worldwide Enterprises**

**What You Will Do**  You have been given a new employee database file that has additional records in the Benefits table and a new table that is used to store absence reports. You will create a one-to-many relationship between the Employees table and the Absences table using the common *EmployeeID* field. You will enforce referential integrity and cascade updated and deleted fields.

Tutorial

Creating a One-to-Many Relationship

**1** Open **2-WEEmpRelationships** and enable the content, if necessary.

**2** Open the Absences table and review the entries.

> This table is used to record employee absence reports. Notice that some employees have more than one record in the table.

**3** Open the Benefits table and review the entries.

**4** Open the Employees table and review the entries.

> Notice that the Employees table includes fields for the employees' names.

**5** Click the Absences table tab at the top of the work area and notice that the names are not duplicated in the table. However, all three tables contain an *EmployeeID* field.

Step 5

**6** Close all three tables.

**7** Click the Database Tools tab.

**8** Click the Relationships button in the Relationships group.

> The Relationships window opens in the work area.

Step 8    Step 7

**9** If necessary, click the Show Table button [icon] in the Relationships group. (Skip this step if the Show Table dialog box displays in the Relationships window.)

**10** At the Show Table dialog box with the Tables tab selected and *Absences* selected in the list box, click the Add button.

> A table field list box for the Absences table is added to the Relationships window. The Show Table dialog box remains open for you to add the next table.

**11** Click *Benefits* in the list box and then click the Add button.

> Depending on the position of the Show Table dialog box in the Relationships window, the Benefits table field list box may be hidden behind the dialog box. If necessary, drag the Show Table dialog box title bar to move the dialog box out of the way.

**12** Double-click *Employees* in the list box.

> Double-clicking a table name is another way to add a table field list box to the Relationships window.

**13** Click the Close button in the Show Table dialog box.

> The three table field list boxes are side by side in the window. The *EmployeeID* field is the primary key field in the Employees table, but it is not the primary key field in the Absences table. This is because an employee can be absent many times; therefore, the *EmployeeID* field could not be a primary key field in the Absences table.

**14** Position the mouse pointer on the bottom border of the Benefits table field list box until the pointer changes to an up-and-down arrow and then drag the bottom border down until the vertical scroll bar disappears.

> This action expands the height of the table field list box so you can see all of the field names in the box.

**15** Expand the height of the Employees table field list box to see all of the field names by completing a step similar to Step 14.

**16** Position the mouse pointer on the Employees table field list box title bar and then drag the table field list box below the Benefits table field list box.

**17** Move the Benefits table field list box to the right and then move the Employees table field list box up to fill in the space as shown below by dragging the table field list box title bars.

> You have been arranging the table field list boxes in the Relationships window to position the Employees table in the middle of the other two tables that will be joined. This layout will make it easier to create the relationship and understand the join lines that will appear.

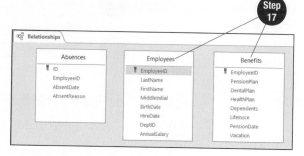

**18** Position the mouse pointer on the *EmployeeID* field in the Employees table field list box, click and hold down the left mouse button, drag the pointer left to the *EmployeeID* field in the Absences table field list box, and then release the mouse button.

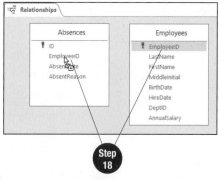

Step 18

> A relationship is created by dragging the common field name from the primary table field list box to the related table field list box.

**19** At the Edit Relationships dialog box, notice that *One-To-Many* displays in the *Relationship Type* section of the dialog box.

> Access determined the relationship type based on the common field that was used to join the tables. In the primary table (Employees), *EmployeeID* is the primary key field while in the related table (Absences), the *EmployeeID* field is not the primary key field. In the Absences table, the *EmployeeID* field is referred to as the *foreign key*.

**20** Click the *Enforce Referential Integrity* check box to insert a check mark.

> *Referential integrity* means that Access will ensure that a record with the same employee number already exists in the primary table when a new record is added to the related table. This prevents what are known as *orphan records*—records in a related table for which no matching records are found in the primary table.

**21** Click the *Cascade Update Related Fields* check box to insert a check mark.

> With a check mark in the *Cascade Update Related Fields* check box, make a change to a primary key field value and Access will automatically update the matching value in the related table.

**22** Click the *Cascade Delete Related Records* check box to insert a check mark.

> With a check mark in the *Cascade Delete Related Records* check box, delete a record in the primary table and Access will delete any related records in the related table.

**23** Click the Create button.

> A black line, called the *join line*, displays connecting the *EmployeeID* field in the Employees table field list box to the *EmployeeID* field in the Absences table field list box. Because you enforced referential integrity in the relationship, the join line displays with a *1* at the Employees table field list box and an infinity symbol at the Absences table field list box.

Join line illustrating the relationship that links the tables at the common field in each table.

**24** Click the Show Table button in the Relationships group.

**25** At the Show Table dialog box, double-click *Departments* in the list box.

**26** Click the Close button to close the Show Table dialog box.

### In Brief

**Create One-to-Many Relationship**
1. Open Relationships window.
2. If necessary, add tables to window.
3. Close Show Table dialog box.
4. Drag common field name from primary table field list box to related table field list box.
5. Specify relationship options.
6. Click Create.
7. Click Save.

**27** Position the mouse pointer on the *DeptID* field in the Departments table field list box, click and hold down the left mouse button, drag the pointer to the *DeptID* field in the Employees table field list box, and then release the mouse button.

**28** Click the Create button.

Since referential integrity was not enforced in this relationship, the black join line does not display with a 1 at one end and the infinity symbol at the other.

**29** Click the Save button.

**30** Click the Close button ⊠ on the Relationship Tools Design tab to close the Relationships window.

**31** Open the Absences table.

**32** Click in the blank row at the bottom of the datasheet in the *EmployeeID* field column, type 1099, and then press the Enter key.

**33** Type March 3, 2021 in the *Absent Date* field column and then press the Enter key.

**34** With *Sick Day* the default value in the *Absent Reason* field column, press the Enter key to accept the entry.

Access displays an error message indicating you cannot add or change a record because a related record is required in the Employees table.

**35** Click OK at the Microsoft Access message box.

Microsoft Access ×

⚠ You cannot add or change a record because a related record is required in table 'Employees'.

OK    Help

Step 35

**36** Close the Absences table. Click OK at the Microsoft Access error message that appears for the second time.

**37** Click Yes at the second error message box to close the table and confirm that the data changes will be lost.

**Check Your Work** Compare your work to the model answer available in the online course.

## In Addition

### Clearing the Relationships Window Layout

To clear the layout of the table field list boxes in the Relationships window and to remove relationships created between tables, click the Clear Layout button in the Tools group on the Relationship Tools Design tab. At the message indicating the the layout will be cleared and asking if you want to continue, click the Yes button.

A relationship between tables can be edited with options at the Edit Relationships dialog box. Display this dialog box at the Relationships window by clicking the Edit Relationships button on the Relationship Tools tab. Relationships can be deleted if the database is redesigned and the existing relationship no longer applies. A relationship also may need to be deleted in order to make a structural change to a table. In this case, the relationship can be deleted, the change made, and then the relationship re-created. Once all relationships have been created in a database, printing a hard copy of the relationship report to file away for future reference is a good idea. This documentation is a quick reference of all the table names, fields within each table, and relationships between the tables. Should a relationship need to be re-created, this documentation will be of assistance.

**Worldwide Enterprises**

**What You Will Do**  You will edit the relationship between the Departments table and Employees table, delete a relationship, and then create and then print a relationship report.

Tutorial

Editing and Deleting a Relationship

Tutorial

Creating a Relationship Report

1. With **2-WEEmpRelationships** open, open the Relationships window by clicking the Database Tools tab and then clicking the Relationships button in the Relationships group.

2. Click the Edit Relationships button in the Tools group.

3. At the Edit Relationships dialog box, click the *Table/Query* option box arrow and then click *Departments* at the dropdown list.

> Since the Departments table contains only one relationship, *Employees* automatically displays in the *Related Table/Query* option box and *DeptID* displays below each table name.

4. Click the *Enforce Referential Integrity* check box, the *Cascade Update Related Fields* check box, and the *Cascade Delete Related Records* check box to insert check marks.

5. Click OK.

6. Right-click the black join line between the Absences table field list box and the Employees table field list box.

7. Click *Delete* at the shortcut menu.

Right-click the join line to display the shortcut menu.

## In Brief

**Delete a Relationship**
1. Open Relationships window.
2. Right-click join line between tables.
3. Click *Delete*.
4. Click Yes.

**Print a Relationship Report**
1. Open Relationships window.
2. Click Relationship Report button.
3. Click Print.
4. Click OK.
5. Click Close Print Preview.
6. Close report in work area.
7. Click Yes to save report, or No to close without saving.
8. Type report name.
9. Click OK.
10. Close Relationships window.

**8** Click Yes at the Microsoft Access message box asking if you are sure you want to permanently delete the relationship.

**9** Click the Relationship Report button  in the Tools group on the Relationship Tools Design tab.

Access generates the report and displays it in Print Preview in a new tab in the work area.

**10** Click the Print button  in the Print group.

**11** At the Print dialog box, click OK.

**12** Click the Close button at the top right of the work area to close the report.

**13** Click Yes at the Microsoft Access message box asking if you want to save the report.

**14** At the Save As dialog box with the existing report name already selected in the *Report Name* text box, type Relationships and then click OK or press the Enter key.

**15** Close the Relationships window.

**Check Your Work** Compare your work to the model answer available in the online course.

# In Addition

## Displaying Records in a Subdatasheet

When two tables are joined, related records within a subdatasheet can be viewed. A subdatasheet is a datasheet within a datasheet. When the primary table is opened in Datasheet view, a column of plus symbols (referred to as *expand indicators*) displays between the record selector bar and the first column. To view related records, click the expand indicator next to the specific record. A subdatasheet opens, similar to the one shown below. The plus symbol changes to a minus symbol when a record has been expanded. Click the minus symbol (referred to as a *collapse indicator*) to close the subdatasheet.

Click to collapse the record and remove the subdatasheet.

subdatasheet

# Activity 2.10  Creating a One-to-One Relationship

A one-to-one relationship exists when both the primary table and the related table contain only one record with a matching field value in the common field. In this relationship, the common field used to join the tables is the primary key field in each table. For example, the Employees table would contain only one record for each employee. The Benefits table would also contain only one record for each employee. If these tables are joined on the common *EmployeeID* field, a one-to-one relationship would be created. In this type of relationship, consider the primary table to be the table with the fields (such as the employee names) that describe the identity of each employee number (the person for whom the employee number was created).

**What You Will Do**   You will create a one-to-one relationship between the Employees and the Benefits tables and then edit the relationship after it has been created.

Creating a One-to-One Relationship

**1** With **2-WEEmpRelationships** open, open the Relationships window.

**2** Notice the *EmployeeID* field is the primary key field in both the Employees table field list box and the Benefits table field list box.

**3** Position the mouse pointer on the *EmployeeID* field in the Employees table field list box, click and hold down the left mouse button, drag the pointer to the *EmployeeID* field in the Benefits table field list box, and then release the mouse button.

> Access determined the relationship type as one-to-one since the common field that was used to join the two table field list boxes is the primary key field in each table. In both tables, only one record can exist for each unique employee number.

**4** Click the Create button.

> The black join line connecting the two *EmployeeID* fields appears between the two table field list boxes in the Relationships window. The join line does not show a *1* at each end because referential integrity was not enforced.

**5** Click the Save button.

**6** Click the Close button on the Relationship Tools Design tab to close the Relationships window.

> In the next steps, you will add a record to the Benefits table to illustrate why referential integrity is a good idea to ensure primary tables are updated first.

**7** Open the Benefits table and then add the following record to the table:

| | |
|---|---|
| *EmployeeID* | 1100 |
| *Pension Plan* | Yes |
| *Dental Plan* | Yes |
| *Health Plan* | Yes |
| *Dependents* | 5 |
| *Life Insurance* | 200000 |
| *Pension Date* | 31-Dec-21 |
| *Vacation* | 1 week |

**In Brief**

**Create a One-to-One Relationship**
1. Open Relationships window.
2. If necessary, add tables to window.
3. Close Show Table dialog box.
4. Drag common field name from primary table field list box to related table field list box.
5. Specify relationship options.
6. Click Create.
7. Click Save.

**8** Open the Employees table. If necessary, scroll down to view the last record in the table. No employee record exists in the table with an employee ID of 1100.

Since referential integrity was not turned on when the relationship was created between the Employees and the Benefits tables, you were able to add a record to the related table for which no matching record is found in the primary table. Although you could easily add the matching record to the Employees table afterwards, establishing the employee's record in the first primary table is considered good practice.

**9** Close the Employees table.

**10** Delete the record you added at Step 7, the record with *1100* in the *EmployeeID* field in the Benefits table, and then close the table.

**11** Open the Relationships window.

**12** Right-click the black join line between the Employees table field list box and the Benefits table field list box and then click *Edit Relationship* at the shortcut menu.

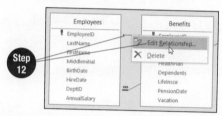

**13** Click the *Enforce Referential Integrity* check box at the Edit Relationships dialog box and then click OK.

With referential integrity turned on, the join line displays a *1* at each end.

Join line displays 1 at each end now that referential integrity is turned on.

**14** Close the Relationships window.

**15** Close **2-WEEmpRelationships**.

**Check Your Work** Compare your work to the model answer available in the online course.

# Features Summary

| Feature | Ribbon Tab, Group | Button |
|---|---|---|
| alternate row color | Home, Text Formatting | |
| create table | Create, Tables | |
| create table in Design view | Create, Tables | |
| Datasheet view | Home, Views | |
| delete fields | Table Tools Design, Tools | |
| edit relationships | Relationship Tools Design, Tools | |
| font | Home, Text Formatting | |
| font size | Home, Text Formatting | |
| gridlines | Home, Text Formatting | |
| insert fields | Table Tools Design, Tools | |
| insert totals | Home, Records | |
| primary key field | Table Tools Design, Tools | |
| relationship report | Relationship Tools Design, Tools | |
| relationships | Database Tools, Relationships | |

# Access

# Creating Queries, Forms, and Reports

**Data Files**

Before beginning section work, copy the AccessS3 folder to your storage medium and then make AccessS3 the active folder.

## Skills

- Create a query using the Simple Query Wizard
- Create a query in Design view using one table
- Create a query in Design view using multiple tables
- Add criteria statements to a query
- Sort and hide columns in a query results datasheet
- Design a query with an *And* criteria statement and design a query with an *Or* criteria statement

- Perform calculations in a query
- Create and format a form
- Add an existing field to a form
- Manage control objects in a form
- Create and format a report
- Manage control objects in a report

## Projects Overview

Create queries to produce custom employee lists, add criteria, and calculate pension contributions and monthly salaries; create and modify forms to facilitate data entry and viewing of records; create and modify reports to produce custom printouts of data.

Create a query, and create and print a report that lists all costumes rented in a particular month; create and modify a form for browsing the costume inventory and entering new records; continue design work on a new database for custom costume activities by creating a form and a report.

Create and print a query to extract records of students who achieved A+ in all of their courses.

Create queries and design a report for the catering events database to extract event information for a banquet room, extract all events booked in a particular month, and calculate the estimated revenue from the catering events.

The online course includes additional training and assessment resources.

A *query* is an Access object designed to extract data from one or more tables. Usually a query is created to select records that answer a question. For example, a question such as *Which employees are enrolled in the Pension Plan?* could be answered with a query. The query would be designed to select records for those employees with a *Yes* in the *PensionPlan* field. Query results display in a datasheet that pulls the data from existing tables. A query can be created to serve a variety of purposes, from very simple field selections to complex conditional statements or calculations. In its simplest form, a query may be used to display or print selected fields from two tables. Access includes the Simple Query Wizard to facilitate creating a query.

**Worldwide Enterprises**

**What You Will Do** Using the Simple Query Wizard, you will generate a list of each employee's first and last names and benefit selections. This will allow you to print a list by selecting fields from two tables.

**Tutorial**

Creating a Query Using the Simple Query Wizard

1. Open **3-WEEmployees** and enable the content, if necessary.

2. Click *Employees* in the Tables group in the Navigation pane and then click the Create tab.

3. Click the Query Wizard button ⬚ in the Queries group.

4. At the New Query dialog box, with *Simple Query Wizard* already selected in the list box, click OK.

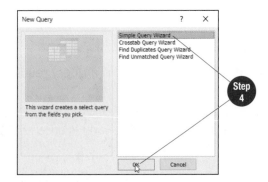

5. At the first Simple Query Wizard dialog box, with *Table: Employees* selected in the *Tables/Queries* option box and *EmployeeID* selected in the *Available Fields* list box, click the One Field button > to move *EmployeeID* to the *Selected Fields* list box.

6. With *LastName* now selected in the *Available Fields* list box, click the One Field button to move *LastName* to the *Selected Fields* list box.

7. Click the One Field button to move *FirstName* to the *Selected Fields* list box.

8. Click the the *Tables/Queries* option box arrow and then click *Table: Benefits* at the drop-down list.

   The list of fields in the *Available Fields* list box changes to display the field names from the Benefits table.

9. Double-click *PensionPlan* in the *Available Fields* list box.

   Double-clicking a field name is another way to move a field to the *Selected Fields* list box.

**In Brief**

**Create Query Using Simple Query Wizard**
1. Click Create tab.
2. Click Query Wizard button.
3. Click OK.
4. Choose table(s) and field(s) to include in query.
5. Click Next.
6. Choose *Detail* or *Summary* query.
7. Click Next.
8. Type title for query.
9. Click Finish.

**10** Double-click the following fields in the *Available Fields* list box to move them to the *Selected Fields* list box:

> DentalPlan
> HealthPlan
> Vacation

**11** Click the Next button.

**12** Click the Next button at the second Simple Query Wizard dialog box to accept *Detail (shows every field of every record)* in the *Would you like a detail or summary query?* section.

**13** At the third Simple Query Wizard dialog box, select the current text in the *What title do you want for your query?* text box, type BenefitPlans, and then click the Finish button.

> View the query results datasheet shown in Figure 3.1. A query results datasheet can be sorted, edited, or formatted in a manner similar to a table. Data displayed in query results is not stored as a separate entity—the query is simply another

interface for viewing and editing data in the associated table(s). Each time a saved query is opened, Access dynamically updates the query results by running the query.

**14** Display the query in Print Preview, change to landscape orientation, and then print the query.

**15** Close the Print Preview window and then close the BenefitPlans query.

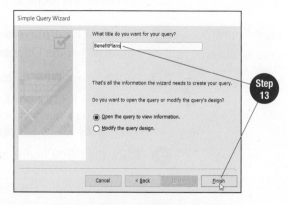

**Figure 3.1** BenefitPlans Query Results Datasheet

| EmployeeID | LastName | FirstName | Pension Plan | Dental Plan | Health Plan | Vacation |
|---|---|---|---|---|---|---|
| 1000 | Vestering | Sam | ☑ | ☑ | ☑ | 4 weeks |
| 1003 | Ruiz | Celesta | ☑ | ☑ | ☑ | 3 weeks |
| 1005 | Deptulski | Roman | ☑ | ☑ | ☐ | 3 weeks |
| 1013 | Chippewa | Gregg | ☑ | ☑ | ☑ | 3 weeks |
| 1015 | Brewer | Lyle | ☐ | ☑ | ☑ | 4 weeks |
| 1020 | Doxtator | Angela | ☑ | ☑ | ☐ | 3 weeks |
| 1023 | Bulinkski | Aleksy | ☐ | ☐ | ☐ | 3 weeks |
| 1025 | Biliski | Jorge | ☑ | ☑ | ☑ | 4 weeks |
| 1030 | Hicks | Thom | ☐ | ☐ | ☐ | 2 weeks |
| 1033 | Titov | Dina | ☑ | ☑ | ☑ | 3 weeks |
| 1040 | Lafreniere | Guy | ☑ | ☑ | ☑ | 3 weeks |
| 1043 | Morano | Enzo | ☑ | ☑ | ☑ | 3 weeks |
| 1045 | Yiu | Terry | ☐ | ☐ | ☐ | 2 weeks |
| 1050 | Zakowski | Carl | ☑ | ☐ | ☑ | 2 weeks |
| 1053 | O'Connor | Shauna | ☑ | ☑ | ☑ | 3 weeks |
| 1060 | McKnight | Donald | ☑ | ☑ | ☑ | 3 weeks |
| 1063 | McPhee | Charlotte | ☑ | ☐ | ☑ | 2 weeks |
| 1065 | Liszniewski | Norm | ☑ | ☑ | ☑ | 2 weeks |
| 1073 | Judd | Marsha | ☑ | ☑ | ☑ | 2 weeks |
| 1080 | Couture | Leo | ☑ | ☑ | ☐ | 1 week |
| 1083 | Arnold | Drew | ☑ | ☐ | ☑ | 1 week |
| 1085 | Armine | Yousef | ☐ | ☑ | ☑ | 1 week |
| 1090 | Quinte | Maria | ☑ | ☐ | ☑ | 1 week |
| 1093 | Vaquez | Luis | ☑ | ☑ | ☐ | 1 week |
| 1095 | Kilarney | Patrick | ☐ | ☐ | ☐ | 1 week |

**Check Your Work** Compare your work to the model answer available in the online course.

Section 2 provided information on working with tables in Design view to define or modify the table structure. Similarly, Design view can be used to create a query. Designing a query consists of identifying the table or tables containing the data to be extracted, the field or fields from which the data will be drawn, and the critera for selecting the data. After designing the query, display the records matching the criteria by switching to Datasheet view or by clicking the Run button.

**Worldwide Enterprises**

**What You Will Do** Rhonda Trask, human resources manager, has asked for a list of employees with their annual salaries and hire dates. You will produce the list by creating a query to obtain the required fields from the Employees table.

Tutorial

Creating a Query in Design View

**1** With **3-WEEmployees** open and the Create tab active, click the Query Design button ![icon] in the Queries group.

**2** At the Show Table dialog box with the Tables tab selected, double-click *Employees*.

> A table field list box for the Employees table is added to the query. The first step in building a query in Design view is to add a table field list box for each table from which records will be selected.

**3** Click the Close button to close the Show Table dialog box.

**4** Double-click the *EmployeeID* field in the Employees table field list box.

> The blank columns at the bottom represent the columns in the query results datasheet and are referred to as the *query design grid*. You place the field names in the columns in the order in which you want the fields displayed in the query results datasheet. Double-clicking a field name adds the field to the next available column. In Steps 5 and 6, you will practice two other methods of adding fields to the query design grid.

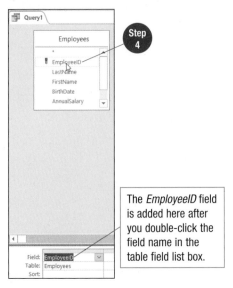

The *EmployeeID* field is added here after you double-click the field name in the table field list box.

**Create Query in Design View with Single Table**
1. Click Create tab.
2. Click Query Design button.
3. Double-click table in Show Table dialog box.
4. Close Show Table dialog box.
5. Add field names from table field list box to columns in query design grid.
6. Click Save button.
7. Type query name and click OK.
8. Click Run button.

**5** Position the mouse pointer on the *FirstName* field in the Employees table field list box, click and hold down the left mouse button, drag to the second field in the *Field* row of the query design grid, and then release the mouse button.

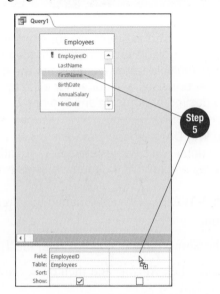

**6** Click in the third field in the *Field* row of the query design grid, click the arrow that appears, and then click *LastName* at the drop-down list.

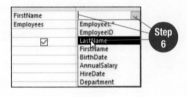

**7** Using any of the three methods in Steps 4–6, add the *AnnualSalary* and *HireDate* fields from the Employees table field list box to the query design grid.

**8** Click the Save button 🖫 on the Quick Access Toolbar.

**9** At the Save As dialog box, type SalaryList in the *Query Name* text box and then press the Enter key or click OK.

**10** Click the Run button ❗ in the Results group on the Query Tools Design tab.

> A query stores instructions on how to select data. The Run command instructs Access to carry out the instructions and display the results.

**11** Print the query.

**12** Close the SalaryList query.

Check Your Work  Compare your work to the model answer available in the online course.

## In Addition

### Understanding Action Queries

In the last activity and in this activity, select queries were created that displayed selected fields from tables. Another type of query, called an *action query*, makes changes to a group of records. Four types of action queries are available in Access: delete, update, append, and make-table. A delete query deletes records. An update query makes global changes to a field. An append query adds a group of records from one table to the end of another table. A make-table query creates a new table from all or part of the data in existing tables.

Often a query is used to select records from more than one table. In Activity 3.1, a query results datasheet displayed records from the Employees table and the Benefits table. In Design view, multiple tables are added to the query at the Show Table dialog box. Once a table field list box has been added for each table, the fields are added to the query design grid in the desired order using any one of the three methods learned in the last activity.

**Worldwide Enterprises**

**What You Will Do**   Rhonda Trask has asked for a list of employees, along with their hire and review dates. This data is stored in two different tables. You will produce the list by creating a query to obtain the required fields from each table to generate the list.

**Tutorial**

Creating a Query in Design View Using Multiple Tables

**1** With **3-WEEmployees** open and the Create tab active, click the Query Design button.

**2** At the Show Table dialog box with the Tables tab selected, double-click *Employees*.

**3** Double-click *Review* and then click the Close button to close the Show Table dialog box.

> A black join line with *1* at each end of the line between the Employees table field list box and the Review table field list box illustrates the one-to-one relationship that has been defined between the two tables.

join line showing relationship

Step 3

**4** Double-click the *EmployeeID* field in the Employees table field list box.

**5** Double-click the *FirstName* field in the Employees table field list box.

**6** Double-click the *LastName* field in the Employees table field list box.

**7** Double-click the *SupervisorFName* field and then double-click the *SupervisorLName* field in the Review table field list box to add the fields from the second table to the query design grid.

**8** Double-click the *HireDate* field in the Employees table field list box.

> You can add fields in any order from either table to the query design grid.

Step 8

Steps 4-7

## In Brief

**Create Query in Design View with Multiple Tables**
1. Click Create tab.
2. Click Query Design button.
3. Double-click tables in Show Table dialog box.
4. Close Show Table dialog box.
5. Add field names from table field list boxes to columns in query design grid.
6. Click Save button.
7. Type query name and click OK.
8. Click Run button.

**9** Double-click the *AnnualRevDate* field in the Review table field list box.

**10** Look at the table names in the *Table* row in the query design grid. The table with which each field is associated is displayed.

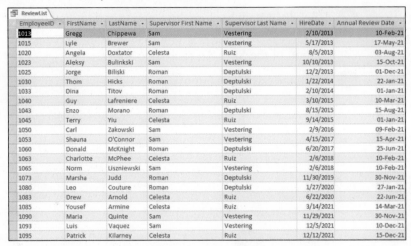

Step 10

**11** Click the Save button on the Quick Access Toolbar.

**12** At the Save As dialog box, type ReviewList in the *Query Name* text box and then press the Enter key or click OK.

Step 12

**13** Click the Run button in the Results group on the Query Tools Design tab.

View the query results in Figure 3.2.

**14** Display the datasheet in Print Preview, change to landscape orientation, and then print the datasheet.

**15** Close the Print Preview window and then close the ReviewList query.

**Figure 3.2** ReviewList Query Results Datasheet

| EmployeeID | FirstName | LastName | Supervisor First Name | Supervisor Last Name | HireDate | Annual Review Date |
|---|---|---|---|---|---|---|
| 1013 | Gregg | Chippewa | Sam | Vestering | 2/10/2013 | 10-Feb-21 |
| 1015 | Lyle | Brewer | Sam | Vestering | 5/17/2013 | 17-May-21 |
| 1020 | Angela | Doxtator | Celesta | Ruiz | 8/5/2013 | 03-Aug-21 |
| 1023 | Aleksy | Bulinski | Sam | Vestering | 10/10/2013 | 15-Oct-21 |
| 1025 | Jorge | Biliski | Roman | Deptulski | 12/2/2013 | 01-Dec-21 |
| 1030 | Thom | Hicks | Roman | Deptulski | 1/22/2014 | 22-Jan-21 |
| 1033 | Dina | Titov | Roman | Deptulski | 2/10/2014 | 01-Jan-21 |
| 1040 | Guy | Lafreniere | Celesta | Ruiz | 3/10/2015 | 10-Mar-21 |
| 1043 | Enzo | Morano | Roman | Deptulski | 8/15/2015 | 15-Aug-21 |
| 1045 | Terry | Yiu | Celesta | Ruiz | 9/14/2015 | 01-Jan-21 |
| 1050 | Carl | Zakowski | Sam | Vestering | 2/9/2016 | 09-Feb-21 |
| 1053 | Shauna | O'Connor | Sam | Vestering | 4/15/2017 | 15-Apr-21 |
| 1060 | Donald | McKnight | Roman | Deptulski | 6/20/2017 | 25-Jun-21 |
| 1063 | Charlotte | McPhee | Celesta | Ruiz | 2/6/2018 | 10-Feb-21 |
| 1065 | Norm | Liszniewski | Sam | Vestering | 2/6/2018 | 10-Feb-21 |
| 1073 | Marsha | Judd | Roman | Deptulski | 11/30/2019 | 30-Nov-21 |
| 1080 | Leo | Couture | Roman | Deptulski | 1/27/2020 | 27-Jan-21 |
| 1083 | Drew | Arnold | Celesta | Ruiz | 6/22/2020 | 22-Jun-21 |
| 1085 | Yousef | Armine | Celesta | Ruiz | 3/14/2021 | 14-Mar-21 |
| 1090 | Maria | Quinte | Sam | Vestering | 11/29/2021 | 30-Nov-21 |
| 1093 | Luis | Vaquez | Sam | Vestering | 12/5/2021 | 10-Dec-21 |
| 1095 | Patrick | Kilarney | Celesta | Ruiz | 12/12/2021 | 15-Dec-21 |

**Check Your Work** Compare your work to the model answer available in the online course.

## In Addition

### Learning More about Adding Tables to the Query Design Grid

If, after closing the Show Table dialog box, another table field list box needs to be added to the query design grid, click the Show Table button in the Query Setup group on the Query Tools Design tab to redisplay the dialog box.

Click the Show Table button to add a table field list box to the query design grid.

# Activity 3.4 — Adding a Criteria Statement to a Query; Sorting and Hiding Columns

In the previous queries, all records from the tables were displayed. Adding a criterion statement to the query design grid will cause Access to display only those records that meet the criterion. For example, a list of employees who are entitled to four weeks of vacation can be generated. Extracting specific records from tables is where the true power in creating queries is found. Use the *Sort* row in the design grid to specify the field by which records should be sorted. By default, each check box in the *Show* row in the query design grid contains a check mark, meaning the column will be displayed in the query results datasheet. Clear the check mark from a field's *Show* row to hide the column in the query results datasheet.

**Worldwide Enterprises**

**What You Will Do** Rhonda Trask has requested a list of employees who receive four weeks of vacation. Since you already have the employee names and vacation fields set up in an existing query, you decide to modify the query by adding the vacation criteria and then save the query using a new name.

 Tutorial
Adding a Criteria Statement to a Query

Tutorial
Sorting Data and Hiding Fields in Query Results

1. With **3-WEEmployees** open, right-click *BenefitPlans* in the Queries group in the Navigation pane and then click *Design View* at the shortcut menu.

2. Click the File tab, click the *Save As* option, and then click the *Save Object As* option in the *File Types* section of the Save As backstage area.

3. Click the Save As button.

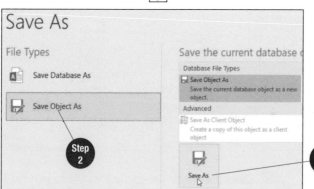

4. Type 4WksVac in the *Save 'BenefitPlans' to* text box at the Save As dialog box and then click OK.

5. With the Query Tools Design tab active, click in the field in the *Criteria* row in the *Vacation* column in the query design grid (the blank field below the check box).

   Before you type a criteria statement, make sure you have placed the insertion point in the *Criteria* row for the field by which you will be selecting records.

6. Type 4 weeks and then press the Enter key.

   The insertion point moves to the field in the *Criteria* row in the next column and Access inserts quotation marks around *4 weeks* in the field in the *Vacation* column. Since quotation marks are required in criteria statements for text fields, Access automatically inserts them if they are not typed into the field in the *Criteria* row.

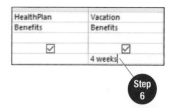

7 Click in the field in the *Sort* row in the *LastName* column, click the down arrow, and then click *Ascending* at the drop-down list.

8 Click the Run button in the Results group on the Query Tools Design tab.

9 View the query results in the datasheet (the results are sorted in alphabetic order by last name) and then click the View button in the Views group on the Home tab to switch to Design view. (Do *not* click the View button arrow.)

Since Rhonda Trask is interested only in the employee names and vacation, you will instruct Access not to display the other fields in the query results datasheet.

10 Click the check box in the *Show* row in the *PensionPlan* column to remove the check mark.

Removing the check mark instructs Access to hide the column in the query results datasheet.

11 Remove the check marks from the *Show* check box in the *DentalPlan* and *HealthPlan* columns in the query design grid.

12 Click the View button to switch to Datasheet view.

The columns for which you removed the check mark from the *Show* check box do not display in the query results. Notice that you displayed the query results datasheet by switching views. Clicking the Run button or switching views achieves the same result.

13 Print the query results datasheet.

14 Close the 4WksVac query. Click the Yes button to save changes to the design of the query.

**Check Your Work** Compare your work to the model answer available in the online course.

## In Addition

### Learning More about Criteria Statement

The following are examples of criteria statements for text, number, and date fields showing the proper syntax required by Access. Access inserts the quotation marks (") automatically for text fields and the pound symbols (#) automatically for date fields when a valid entry is typed in a field in the *Criteria* row.

| Criterion Statement | Records That Would Be Extracted |
|---|---|
| "Finance Department" | those with Finance Department in the field |
| Not "Finance Department" | all except those with Finance Department in the field |
| "Fan*" | those that begin with Fan and end with any other characters in the field |
| >15000 | those with a value greater than 15,000 in the field |
| #5/1/21# | those that contain the date May 1, 2021 in the field |
| >#5/1/21# | those that contain dates after May 1, 2021 in the field |

# Designing a Query with an *And* Criteria Statement

A query may need more than one criterion to select specific records. For example, designing a query that displays records of employees who have enrolled in multiple benefit plans would require more than one criterion. In the query design grid, more than one column can have an entry in the *Criteria* row. Multiple criteria all entered in the same *Criteria* row become an *And* statement wherein each criterion must be met for the record to be selected. For example, the word *Yes* in the *PensionPlan* column and the *DentalPlan* column in the *Criteria* row would mean a record would need to have a check mark in both check boxes in order for Access to display the record in the query results datasheet.

**Worldwide Enterprises**

**What You Will Do**   Rhonda Trask is reviewing salaries and has requested a list of employees who work in the North American Distribution Department and earn over $45,000. You will create a new query in Design view to produce the list.

**Tutorial**

Designing a Query with an *And* Criteria Statement

**1** With **3-WEEmployees** open, click the Create tab and then click the Query Design button.

**2** At the Show Table dialog box, double-click *Employees* and then click the Close button.

**3** Double-click the following fields to add them to the query design grid. *Note: You may have to scroll down the table field list box to see all of the fields*.
> FirstName
> LastName
> Department
> HireDate
> AnnualSalary

**4** Click in the field in the *Criteria* row in the *Department* column in the query design grid, type North American Distribution, and then press the Enter key.

**5** Position the mouse pointer on the right column boundary line for the *Department* field in the gray header row at the top of the query design grid until the pointer changes to a left-and-right pointing arrow with a vertical line in the middle and then double-click the left mouse button to best fit the column width.

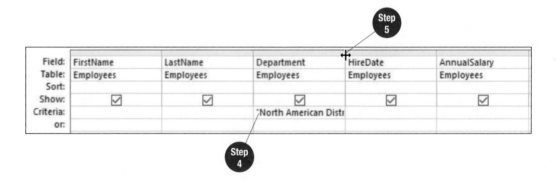

| Field: | FirstName | LastName | Department | HireDate | AnnualSalary |
|---|---|---|---|---|---|
| Table: | Employees | Employees | Employees | Employees | Employees |
| Sort: | | | | | |
| Show: | ☑ | ☑ | ☑ | ☑ | ☑ |
| Criteria: | | | "North American Distri | | |
| or: | | | | | |

**Designing a Query with an *And* Statement**
1. Start new query in Design view.
2. Add table(s) and field(s) to query design grid.
3. Click in *Criteria* row in column in which you want to write criterion statement.
4. Type criterion statement.
5. Repeat Steps 3–4 for the remaining criterion fields.
6. Save query.
7. Run query.

**6** Click in the field in the *Criteria* row in the *AnnualSalary* column, type >45000, and then press the Enter key.

> Placing multiple criterion statements on the same row in the query design grid means that each criterion must be satisfied in order for Access to select the record.

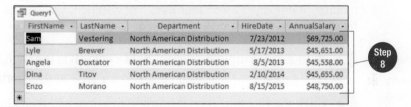

**7** Click the Run button.

**8** Review the records selected in the query results datasheet.

> The field value for each record in the *Department* column is *North American Distribution* and the field values in the *AnnualSalary* column are all greater than $45,000.

| FirstName | LastName | Department | HireDate | AnnualSalary |
|---|---|---|---|---|
| Sam | Vestering | North American Distribution | 7/23/2012 | $69,725.00 |
| Lyle | Brewer | North American Distribution | 5/17/2013 | $45,651.00 |
| Angela | Doxtator | North American Distribution | 8/5/2013 | $45,558.00 |
| Dina | Titov | North American Distribution | 2/10/2014 | $45,655.00 |
| Enzo | Morano | North American Distribution | 8/15/2015 | $48,750.00 |

**9** Click the Save button, type NAHighSalary in the *Query Name* text box, and then press the Enter key or click OK.

**10** Print the query results datasheet.

**11** Close the NAHighSalary query.

**Check Your Work** Compare your work to the model answer available in the online course.

# In Addition

## Learning More about *And* Criteria Statements

The following are additional examples of *And* criteria statements.

| Criterion Statement in *PensionPlan* Column | Criterion Statement in *HireDate* Column | Criterion Statement in *AnnualSalary* Column | Records That Would Be Extracted |
|---|---|---|---|
| | >#1/1/2021# | >40000 And <50000 | employees hired after January 1, 2021 who earn between $40,000 and $50,000 |
| Yes | >#1/1/2021# | >45000 | employees hired after January 1, 2021 who are enrolled in the pension plan and earn over $45,000 |
| No | Between #1/1/2021# And #12/31/2021# | <50000 | employees hired between January 1, 2021 and December 31, 2021 who are not enrolled in the pension plan and earn less than $50,000 |

Multiple criterion statements on different rows in the query design grid become an *Or* statement in which any of the criteria can be met in order for Access to select the record. For example, in this activity, a list of employees who are entitled to either three or four weeks of vacation will be generated. Creating select queries with *Or* statements is often used to generate mailing lists. For example, if a business wants to create mailing labels for customers who live in either Texas or Nevada, the query to select the records needs to be an *Or* statement since the *State* field in a customer table would have a value of *Texas* or *Nevada*. (Having both state names in the same record would not be possible.)

 **Worldwide Enterprises**

**What You Will Do**   Rhonda Trask has requested a list of employees who receive either three or four weeks of vacation. Since you already have a query created that selected the records of employees with four weeks of vacation, you decide to modify the existing query by adding the second vacation criteria.

 Tutorial

Designing a Query with an *Or* Criteria Statement

**1** With **3-WEEmployees** open, right-click *4WksVac* in the Queries group in the Navigation pane and then click *Design View* at the shortcut menu.

**2** Click the File tab, click the *Save As* option, and then click the *Save Object As* option in the *File Types* section of the Save As backstage area.

**3** Click the Save As button.

**4** Type 3or4WksVac in the *Save '4WksVac' to* text box at the Save As dialog box and then click OK.

**5** With the Query Tools Design tab active, click in the field in the *or* row in the *Vacation* column in the query design grid (the blank row below "4 weeks"), type 3 weeks, and then press the Enter key.

Including a second criterion below the first one instructs Access to display records that meet either of the two criteria.

| Field: | EmployeeID | LastName | FirstName | Vacation |
|---|---|---|---|---|
| Table: | Employees | Employees | Employees | Benefits |
| Sort: | | Ascending | | |
| Show: | ☑ | ☑ | ☑ | ☑ |
| Criteria: | | | | "4 weeks" |
| or: | | | | "3 weeks" |

**6** Click the Run button.

**Extract Records Using**
*Or* **Criteria**
1. Start new query in Design view.
2. Add table(s) and field(s) to query design grid.
3. Click in *Criteria* row in column in which you want to write criterion statement.
4. Type criterion statement.
5. Click in *or* row in column below the *Criteria* row in the column containing the first criterion statement.
6. Type criterion statement.
7. Repeat Steps 5–6 as necessary, moving down one field in *Criteria* row for each new criterion.
8. Save query.
9. Run query.

**7** View the query results datasheet.

The records that have been selected contain either *4 weeks* or *3 weeks* in the *Vacation* field column.

| 3or4WksVac | | | |
|---|---|---|---|
| EmployeeID ▾ | LastName ▾ | FirstName ▾ | Vacation ▾ |
| 1025 | Biliski | Jorge | 4 weeks |
| 1015 | Brewer | Lyle | 4 weeks |
| 1023 | Bulinkski | Aleksy | 3 weeks |
| 1013 | Chippewa | Gregg | 3 weeks |
| 1005 | Deptulski | Roman | 3 weeks |
| 1020 | Doxtator | Angela | 3 weeks |
| 1040 | Lafreniere | Guy | 3 weeks |
| 1060 | McKnight | Donald | 3 weeks |
| 1043 | Morano | Enzo | 3 weeks |
| 1053 | O'Connor | Shauna | 3 weeks |
| 1003 | Ruiz | Celesta | 3 weeks |
| 1033 | Titov | Dina | 3 weeks |
| 1000 | Vestering | Sam | 4 weeks |

Step 7

**8** Print the query results datasheet.

**9** Click the Save button to save the revised query.

**10** Close the 3or4WksVac query.

**Check Your Work** Compare your work to the model answer available in the online course.

# In Addition

## Combining *And* and *Or* Criteria Statements

Assume that Rhonda Trask wants to further explore the vacation entitlements for the North American Distribution employees only. Rhonda wants a list of employees who work in the North American Distribution Department *and* have four weeks of vacation *or* who work in the North American Distribution Department *and* have three weeks of vacation. To perform this query, two rows in the query design grid would be used to enter the criteria as shown below. Note that the *Department* column has been added to the query design grid.

| Field: | EmployeeID | LastName | FirstName | Vacation | Department |
|---|---|---|---|---|---|
| Table: | Employees | Employees | Employees | Benefits | Employees |
| Sort: | | Ascending | | | |
| Show: | ☑ | ☑ | ☑ | ☑ | ☑ |
| Criteria: | | | | "4 weeks" | "North American Distribution" |
| or: | | | | "3 weeks" | "North American Distribution" |

multiple *And/Or* criteria

query results datasheet

| 3or4WksVac | | | | |
|---|---|---|---|---|
| EmployeeID ▾ | LastName ▾ | FirstName ▾ | Vacation ▾ | Department ▾ |
| 1025 | Biliski | Jorge | 4 weeks | North American Distribution |
| 1015 | Brewer | Lyle | 4 weeks | North American Distribution |
| 1020 | Doxtator | Angela | 3 weeks | North American Distribution |
| 1043 | Morano | Enzo | 3 weeks | North American Distribution |
| 1053 | O'Connor | Shauna | 3 weeks | North American Distribution |
| 1003 | Ruiz | Celesta | 3 weeks | North American Distribution |
| 1033 | Titov | Dina | 3 weeks | North American Distribution |
| 1000 | Vestering | Sam | 4 weeks | North American Distribution |

Calculations involving mathematical operations such as adding or multiplying a field value can be included in a query. In a blank field in the *Field* row in Query Design view, type the text that will appear as the column heading, followed by a colon (:) and then the mathematical expression for the calculated values. Field names in the mathematical expression are encased in square brackets. For example, the entry *TotalSalary:[BaseSalary]+[Commission]* would add the value in the field named *BaseSalary* to the value in the field named *Commission*. The result of the equation would be placed in a new column in the query datasheet with the column heading *TotalSalary*. Calculated columns do not exist in the associated table; the values are calculated dynamically each time the query is run. Numeric format and the number of digits after the decimal point for calculated columns are set using the *Format* property box in the Property Sheet task pane in Design view.

**Worldwide Enterprises**

**What You Will Do**  Worldwide Enterprises contributes 3% of each employee's annual salary to a registered pension plan. You will create a new query to calculate the employer's annual pension contributions.

Tutorial

Performing
Calculations
in a Query

**1**  With **3-WEEmployees** open, click the Create tab and then click the Query Design button.

**2**  At the Show Table dialog box, double-click *Employees* and then click the Close button.

**3**  Double-click the following fields in the order shown to add them to the query design grid:

　　*EmployeeID*
　　*FirstName*
　　*LastName*
　　*AnnualSalary*

**4**  Click in the field in the *Field* row to the right of the *AnnualSalary* column in the query design grid.

Step 4

**5**  Type PensionContribution:[AnnualSalary]*.03 and then press the Enter key.

**6**  Position the mouse pointer on the right column boundary line for the *PensionContribution* field in the gray header row at the top of the query design grid until the pointer changes to a left-and-right-pointing arrow with a vertical line in the middle and then double-click the left mouse button to best fit the column width.

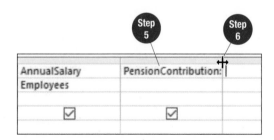

Step 5　　Step 6

**7** Click the Save button. At the Save As dialog box, type PensionCont in the *Query Name* text box and then press the Enter key or click OK.

**8** Click the Run button.

**9** In the query results datasheet, adjust the column width to best fit the entries in the *PensionContribution* column.

> The values in the calculated column need to be formatted to display a consistent number of decimal places.

**10** Switch to Design view.

**11** Click in the first field in the *PensionContribution* column in the query design grid.

**12** Click the Property Sheet button  in the Show/Hide group on the Query Tools Design tab.

> Available properties for the active field display in the Property Sheet task pane at the right side of the work area.

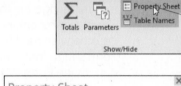

Step 12

**13** Click in the *Format* property box in the Property Sheet task pane, click the down arrow that appears, and then click *Currency* at the drop-down list.

**14** Click the Close button in the top right corner of the Property Sheet task pane.

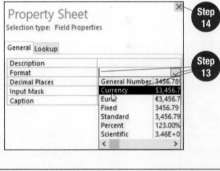

Step 14

Step 13

**15** Click the Save button and then click the Run button.

**16** Click the Totals button $\Sigma$ in the Records group to add a total row to the bottom of the datasheet and then add a Sum function to the bottom of the *AnnualSalary* and *PensionContribution* field columns. ***Note: Refer to Activity 2.7 if you need assistance with this step.***

**17** Print the query results datasheet.

**18** Close the PensionCont query. Click Yes when prompted to save changes to the query.

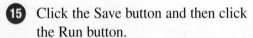

| EmployeeID | FirstName | LastName | AnnualSalary | PensionContribution |
|---|---|---|---|---|
| 1000 | Sam | Vestering | $69,725.00 | $2,091.75 |
| 1003 | Celesta | Ruiz | $41,875.00 | $1,256.25 |
| 1005 | Roman | Deptulski | $72,750.00 | $2,182.50 |
| 1013 | Gregg | Chippewa | $48,650.00 | $1,459.50 |
| 1015 | Lyle | Brewer | $45,651.00 | $1,369.53 |
| 1020 | Angela | Doxtator | $45,558.00 | $1,366.74 |
| 1023 | Aleksy | Bulinkski | $51,450.00 | $1,543.50 |
| 1025 | Jorge | Biliski | $44,892.00 | $1,346.76 |
| 1030 | Thom | Hicks | $42,824.00 | $1,284.72 |
| 1033 | Dina | Titov | $45,655.00 | $1,369.65 |
| 1040 | Guy | Lafreniere | $45,395.00 | $1,361.85 |
| 1043 | Enzo | Morano | $48,750.00 | $1,462.50 |
| 1045 | Terry | Yiu | $42,238.00 | $1,267.14 |
| 1050 | Carl | Zakowski | $44,387.00 | $1,331.61 |
| 1053 | Shauna | O'Connor | $43,695.00 | $1,310.85 |
| 1060 | Donald | McKnight | $42,126.00 | $1,263.78 |
| 1063 | Charlotte | McPhee | $43,695.00 | $1,310.85 |
| 1065 | Norm | Liszniewski | $43,695.00 | $1,310.85 |
| 1073 | Marsha | Judd | $44,771.00 | $1,343.13 |
| 1080 | Leo | Couture | $43,659.00 | $1,309.77 |
| 1083 | Drew | Arnold | $43,659.00 | $1,309.77 |
| 1085 | Yousef | Armine | $42,177.00 | $1,265.31 |
| 1090 | Maria | Quinte | $42,177.00 | $1,265.31 |
| 1093 | Luis | Vaquez | $42,177.00 | $1,265.31 |
| 1095 | Patrick | Kilarney | $42,177.00 | $1,265.31 |
| | Total | | $1,163,808.00 | $34,914.24 |

Step 16

**Check Your Work** Compare your work to the model answer available in the online course.

In Access, forms provide a user-friendly interface for viewing, adding, editing, and deleting records. The Form button creates a new form with one mouse click. All fields in the selected table are added to the form in a columnar layout. The form is comprised of a series of objects referred to as *controls*. Each field from the table has a label control and a text box control object. The label control object contains the field name or caption and the text box control object is the field placeholder where data is entered or edited. A form may also contain other controls such as a title, logo, and date and time control object. The form appears in the work area in Layout view, which is used to make changes to the form. Three tabs become active when a form has been created. Use buttons on the Form Layout Tools Design tab to change the theme or add new control objects to the form. The Form Layout Tools Arrange tab contains buttons to rearrange the fields from columnar to tabular or stacked or to otherwise modify the position of the control objects on the form. To make changes to the form's font, font attributes, or other format characteristics, use the Form Layout Tools Format tab. In the Form Wizard, the user is guided through a series of dialog boxes to generate the form, including selecting the fields to be included and the form layout.

**Worldwide Enterprises**

**What You Will Do**   You decide to create two forms for the assistant who works with you since she prefers to see only one record at a time while entering data. One form will be used to record employee absences and the other will be used to enter new employee records.

**Tutorial**
Creating a Form Using the Form Button

**Tutorial**
Formatting a Form

**Tutorial**
Creating a Form Using the Form Wizard

**1** With **3-WEEmployees** open, click *Absences* in the Tables group in the Navigation pane to select but not open the table.

> In order to create a form using the Form tool, you first select the table or query object upon which to base the new form.

**2** Click the Create tab and then click the Form button ⬚ in the Forms group.

> Access creates the form using all fields in the table in a vertical layout and displays the form in Layout view with the Form Layout Tools Design tab active.

**3** Click the View button ⬚ in the Views group on the Form Layout Tools Design tab to switch to Form view.

> When working in a form, you can use the View button to switch back and forth between Form view, where you view the data, and Layout view, where you make changes to the form's appearance and structure.

**4** Click the Next record button on the Record Navigation bar a few times to scroll through a few records in Form view.

**5** Click the View button ⬚ in the Views group on the Home tab to return to Layout view.

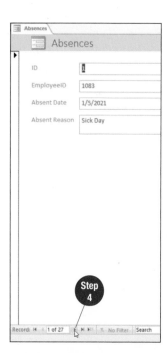

**6** Click the Themes button  in the Themes group on the Form Layout Tools Design tab and then click *Retrospect* at the drop-down gallery.

> Themes in the Microsoft Office suite are standardized across the applications. A business can apply a consistent look to documents, workbooks, presentations, and databases by using the same theme in each application.

**7** Click the Colors button in the Themes group and then click *Green* at the drop-down list.

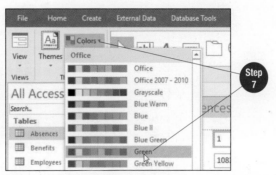

**8** Click the Fonts button and then click *Candara* at the drop-down list.

**9** Click the Title button 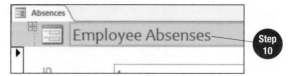 in the Header/Footer group.

Clicking the Title button selects the text *Absences* in the title control object.

**10** Type Employee Absences and then press the Enter key.

**11** Click the Form Layout Tools Format tab.

**12** Click the *Font Size* option box arrow in the Font group on the Form Layout Tools Format tab and then click *24* at the drop-down list.

**13** Press Ctrl + A to select all of the control objects in the form.

**14** Click the Font Color button arrow and then click the *Dark Blue* color option (ninth column, bottom row in the *Standard Colors* section).

**15** Close the Absences form. Click the Yes button to save the changes to the form's design and then click OK at the Save As dialog box to accept the default form name *Absences*.

**16** Click the Create tab and then click the Form Wizard button 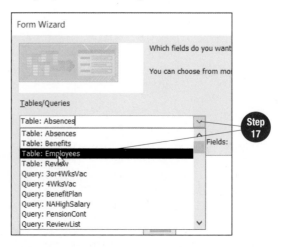 in the Forms group.

**17** At the first Form Wizard dialog box, click the *Tables/Queries* option box arrow and then click *Table: Employees* at the drop-down list.

**In Brief**

**Create Form Using Form Button**
1. Click table name in Navigation pane.
2. Click Create tab.
3. Click Form button.

**Create Form Using Form Wizard**
1. Click Create tab.
2. Click Form Wizard button.
3. Choose table or query from which to create form.
4. Select fields to include in form.
5. Click Next.
6. Choose form layout.
7. Click Next.
8. Type form title.
9. Click Finish.

**18** Click the All Fields button >> to move all of the fields in the *Available Fields* list box to the *Selected Fields* list box and then click the Next button.

**19** At the second Form Wizard dialog box with *Columnar* already selected as the form layout, click the Next button.

**20** Click the Finish button at the last Form Wizard dialog box to accept the default title of *Employees* and the option *Open the form to view or enter information*.

**21** Click the Next record button on the Record Navigation bar a few times to scroll through a few records in Form view and then close the Employees form.

**Check Your Work** Compare your work to the model answer available in the online course.

## In Addition

### Applying Conditional Formatting

Use the Conditional Formatting button to apply formatting to data that meets a specific criterion. For example, conditional formatting can be applied to sales amounts that displays amounts greater than a specified number in a different color. To apply conditional formatting, click the Conditional Formatting button in the Control Formatting group on the Form Layout Tools Format tab and the Conditional Formatting Rules Manager dialog box displays. At this dialog box, click the New Rule button and the New Formatting Rule dialog box displays. Use options in this dialog box to specify the conditional formatting that is to be applied to data in a field that matches a specific condition.

# Activity 3.9  Adding an Existing Field to a Form

When two tables have been joined by a relationship, fields from a related table can be added to a form. For example, in the Absences form created in the previous activity, the names of the employees are not on the form because the first and last name fields are not in the Absences table. Being able to see the employee's name while entering an absence report would be helpful so that the correct employee ID can be verified as a new record is being added. Add fields from another table to a form using the Field List task pane in Layout view.

**Worldwide Enterprises**

**What You Will Do**   You will edit the Absences form to add the employee's first and last names from the Employees table.

Adding an Existing Field to a Form

**1** With **3-WEEmployees** open, double-click *Absences* in the Forms group in the Navigation pane to open the form.

**2** Click the View button in the Views group on the Home tab to switch to Layout view.

**3** With the Form Layout Tools Design tab active, click the Add Existing Fields button in the Tools group.

The Field List task pane opens at the right side of the work area in one of two states: with one section titled *Fields available for this view* and with a <u>Show all tables</u> hyperlink at the top of the Field List task pane; or, with three sections titled *Fields available for this view*, *Fields available in related tables*, and *Fields available in other tables*. A Show only <u>fields in the current record source</u> hyperlink is at the top of the Field List task pane when it displays three sections.

**4** Click <u>Show all tables</u> at the top of the Field List task pane. *Note: Skip this step if the hyperlink at the top of the Field List task pane on your computer reads* **Show only fields in the current record source**.

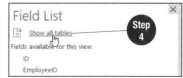

Clicking <u>Show all tables</u> in the Field List task pane displays two new sections: *Fields available in related tables* and *Fields available in other tables*. Within each section box, each table name displays with an expand button (plus symbol) you can use to display the fields in the related table.

**5** Click the expand button next to the Employees table name in the *Fields available in related tables* list box to expand the list.

**6** Click to select *FirstName* in the expanded Employees table field list.

**7** Position the mouse pointer on the selected *FirstName* field in the Field List task pane, click and hold down the left mouse button, drag the field name to the form between the *EmployeeID* and *Absent Date* fields, and then release the mouse button.

As you drag the field over the form, a pink indicator bar identifies where the field will be positioned between existing fields. When you release the mouse, the field is added to the form. The Field List task pane updates to move the Employees table to the *Fields available for this view* section. By adding a field from the related table, the Employees table is now associated with the Absences table.

## In Brief

**Add Fields to Form from Another Table**
1. Open Form.
2. Switch to Layout view.
3. Click Add Existing Fields button.
4. Click Show all tables.
5. Click expand button next to appropriate table.
6. Drag field from Field List task pane to form.
7. Repeat Step 6 for all fields to be added.
8. Close Field List task pane.
9. Save and close form.

**8** Position the mouse pointer on the *LastName* field in the *Fields available for this view* section of the Field List task pane, click and hold down the left mouse button, drag the field name to the form between the *FirstName* and *Absent Date* fields, and then release the mouse button.

**9** Click the Close button in the upper right corner of the Field List task pane.

**10** Click the Save button to save the revised form design.

**11** Switch to Form view and scroll through a few records.

**12** Click the New button in the Records group on the Home tab, press the Tab key to move past the *ID* AutoNumber data type field, type 1063 in the *EmployeeID* field, and then press the Tab key or the Enter key.

> Access automatically displays *Charlotte* in the *FirstName* field, *McPhee* in the *LastName* field, and *Sick Day* in the *Absent Reason* field. Since the Employees and Absences tables are related, Access matches the *EmployeeID* field values and displays the three field entries from the primary table.

**13** Press the Tab key two times to move to the *Absent Date* field, type 3/30/2021, press the Tab key (this selects the current text), type Personal leave day in the *Absent Reason* field, and then press the Enter key.

**14** Close the Absences form.

**Check Your Work** Compare your work to the model answer available in the online course.

# Activity 3.10 Managing Control Objects in a Form

A form is comprised of a series of objects referred to as *controls*. Each field from the table has a label control and a text box control object placed side by side, with the label control object placed first. The label control object contains the field name or the caption property text if a caption has been added to the field's properties. The text box control object is the field placeholder where data is entered or edited. The controls can be moved, sized, formatted, or deleted from the form. Use buttons on the Form Layout Tools Design tab and Form Layout Tools Arrange tab to manage control objects. The Property Sheet task pane contains options for changing the width and height of control objects in the form.

**Worldwide Enterprises**

**What You Will Do** You decide to further customize the Absences form by inserting the Worldwide Enterprises logo, resizing control objects, changing the width and height of control objects, and moving control objects.

Tutorial

Managing Control Objects in a Form

1 With **3-WEEmployees** open, right-click *Absences* in the Forms group in the Navigation pane and then click *Layout View* at the shortcut menu.

2 Click the Logo button in the Header/Footer group on the Form Layout Tools Design tab.

Step 2

3 At the Insert Picture dialog box, navigate to your AccessS3 folder (if AccessS3 is not the current folder) and then double-click the **WELogo-Small** image file.

4 Position the mouse pointer on the right edge of the selected logo control object until the pointer changes to a left-and-right pointing arrow, click and hold down the left mouse button, drag the control to the approximate width shown at the right, and then release the mouse button. Resize the object as necessary until you can see the entire logo within the control object.

Step 4

5 Click in the text box control object containing the number *25* (to the right of the *ID* label control object).

6 Click the Property Sheet button in the Tools group.

7 In the Property Sheet task pane with the Format tab active, select the current measurement in the *Width* property box, type 2.2, and then press the Enter key.

8 With the current measurement in the *Height* property box selected, type 0.3 and then press the Enter key.

9 Click in the label control object containing the text *ID*.

Step 7
Step 8

**10** In the Property Sheet task pane, select the current measurement in the *Width* property box, type 1.1, and then click the Close button to close the Property Sheet task pane.

**11** Click the *Absent Date* label control object, press and hold down the Shift key, click the text box control object containing the date *3/23/2021*, and then release the Shift key.

**12** Click the Form Layout Tools Arrange tab.

**13** Click the Move Up button  in the Move group three times to move the *Absent Date* label control and text box control objects above *EmployeeID*.

**14** Click to select the *EmployeeID* label control object and then click the object again. Move the insertion point between the *e* and the *I* in *EmployeeID*, press the spacebar to insert a space, and then press the Enter key.

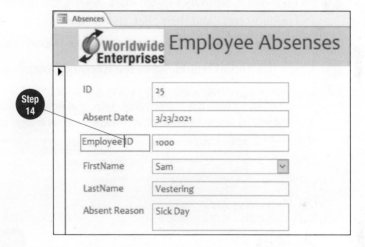

**15** Edit the *FirstName* label control to *First Name* and the *LastName* label control to *Last Name* by completing steps similar to those in Step 14.

**16** Scroll through the records in the form until you reach the absence report for employee ID 1063 (Charlotte McPhee).

**17** Display the form in Print Preview.

**18** Click the Columns button in the Page Layout group on the Print Preview tab.

**19** Select the current measurement in the *Width* measurement box, type 8, and then click OK.

**20** Close Print Preview and then press Ctrl + P to display the Print dialog box.

**21** Click *Selected Records(s)* in the *Print Range* section and then click OK.

**22** Close the Absences form. Click Yes when prompted to save changes to the form's design.

**Check Your Work** Compare your work to the model answer available in the online course.

# Activity 3.11　Creating and Formatting a Report

Information from a database can be printed while viewing tables in Datasheet view, while viewing a query results datasheet, or while browsing through forms. In these printouts, all of the fields are printed in a tabular layout for datasheets or in the designated layout for forms. Create a report to specify which fields to print and to have more control over the report layout and format. Access includes a Report button (similar to the Form button) that can be used to generate a report with one mouse click. Reports are generally created for viewing and printing purposes only.

**Worldwide Enterprises**

**What You Will Do**　Rhonda Trask has requested a hard copy of the NAHighSalary query. You decide to experiment with the Report feature to print the data.

Tutorial
Creating a Report

Tutorial
Formatting a Report

**1**　With **3-WEEmployees** open, click *NAHighSalary* in the Queries group in the Navigation pane and then click the Create tab.

> Select a table or query before clicking the Report button.

**2**　Click the Report button 📄 in the Reports group.

> Access generates the report using a tabular layout with records displayed in rows. A title, along with the current day, date, and time are placed automatically at the top of the report, as is a container for an image such as a logo at the left of the title text.

**3**　Click the Themes button in the Themes group on the Report Layout Tools Design tab and then click the *Integral* theme.

**4**　Click the Colors button in the Themes group and then click the *Yellow Orange* color option.

**5**　Click the Title button in the Header/Footer group.

**6**　Type Employees in North American Distribution, press Shift + Enter to insert a line break,

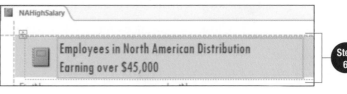

type Earning over $45,000, and then press the Enter key.

**7**　With the title control object still selected, click the Report Layout Tools Format tab, click the *Font Size* option box arrow in the Font group, and then click *16* at the drop-down list.

**In Brief**

**Create Report Using Report Tool**
1. Click object name in Navigation pane.
2. Click Create tab.
3. Click Report button.

**8** Click the Report Layout Tools Design tab and then click the Logo button in the Header/Footer group.

**9** At the Insert Picture dialog box, navigate to your AccessS3 folder (if AccessS3 is not the current folder) and then double-click **WELogo-Small**. Resize the logo object to the approximate width shown below.

**10** Click the Report Layout Tools Format tab and then click the Select All button 🔲 in the Selection group.

**11** Click the Font Color button arrow and then click the *Dark Blue* color option (ninth column, bottom row in the *Standard Colors* section).

**12** Click the total amount at the bottom of the *AnnualSalary* field column and then double-click the bottom border to display the entire amount.

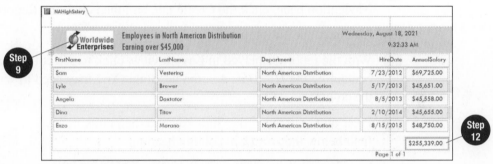

**13** Minimize the Navigation pane by clicking the Shutter Bar Open/Close Button at the top of the Navigation pane.

> A dashed line in the middle of the *HireDate* field column indicates a page break. Changing to landscape orientation will allow all of the columns to print on the same page.

**14** Click the Report Layout Tools Page Setup tab.

**15** Click the Landscape button 🔲 in the Page Layout group.

> The page break disappears, indicating all columns now fit on one page.

**16** Click the Save button. At the Save As dialog box, click OK to accept the default report name *NAHighSalary*.

**17** Print and then close the report.

**18** Redisplay the Navigation pane by clicking the Shutter Bar Open/Close Button.

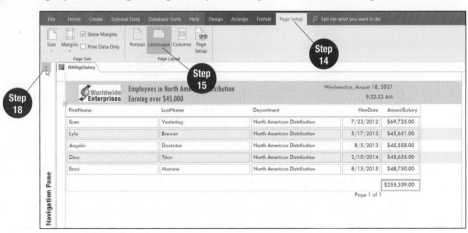

**Check Your Work** Compare your work to the model answer available in the online course.

Once a report has been created, it can be modified by opening it in Layout view. A report is similar to a form in that it is comprised of a series of controls. Control objects in a report can be resized, moved, and deleted.

**Worldwide Enterprises**

**What You Will Do** Rhonda Trask would like a hard copy of the ReviewList query. You decide to create a new report and move and resize columns to provide a better layout for the report.

Tutorial

Managing Control Objects in a Report

**1** With **3-WEEmployees** open, click *ReviewList* in the Queries group in the Navigation pane, click the Create tab, and then click the Report button.

**2** Minimize the Navigation pane.

**3** With the report displayed in Layout view, click to select the control object containing the *HireDate* column heading. (You may need to scroll to the right to see the column.)

**4** Press and hold down the Shift key and then click in any field below the *HireDate* column heading.

> This selects the entire column, as indicated by the gold borders around all of the cells in the column.

**5** Position the mouse pointer inside the selected control object containing the *HireDate* column heading until the pointer displays with the four-headed arrow attached.

Steps 3-5

**6** Drag the column to the left, between the *LastName* column and the *Supervisor First Name* column.

> A vertical pink indicator bar identifies the location where the column will be placed when you release the mouse.

| 9:41:09 AM | | | |
|---|---|---|---|
| Supervisor First Name | | Supervisor Last Name | HireDate |
| Sam | | Vestering | 2/10/2013 |
| Sam | | Vestering | 5/17/2013 |
| Celesta | | Ruiz | 8/5/2013 |
| Sam | | Vestering | 10/10/2013 |

Step 6

**7** Click the *FirstName* column heading to select the control object.

**8** Click the Property Sheet button in the Tools group.

**9** With the Format tab selected, select the current measurement in the *Width* measurement box, type 0.8, and then click the Close button to close the Property Sheet task pane.

**10** Click the *LastName* column heading to select the control object, position the mouse pointer on the right border of the selected control object until the pointer displays as a left-and-right-pointing arrow and then drag to the left until *Lines: 1 Characters: 14* displays at the left side of the Status bar.

In addition to the *Width* measurement box at the Property Sheet task pane, a column width can be changed to a specific width using the line and character numbers that display at the left side of the Status bar.

**11** Decrease the width of the *Supervisor First Name* column and the *Supervisor Last Name* column to *Lines 1: Characters 24*.

**12** Click the Report Layout Tools Page Setup tab and then change to landscape orientation.

**13** Edit the title text to *Employee Review List*.

**14** Click to select the logo control object and then press the Delete key.

**15** Click to select the control object that contains the current day and date. Position the mouse pointer on the right edge of the selected control until the pointer changes to a left-and-right-pointing arrow. Click and hold down the left mouse button, drag right until the right edge of the date aligns with the right edge of the last column, and then release the mouse button.

Access prints the current day, date, and time on all reports. In businesses with time-sensitive report needs, the inclusion of these controls is important.

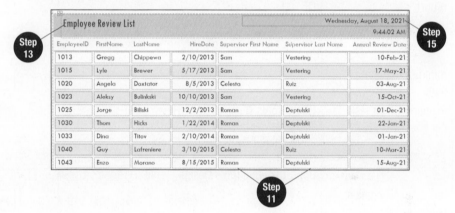

**16** Click the total amount at the bottom of the *EmployeeID* column, press the Delete key, click the remaining bar, and then press the Delete key again.

**17** Click the page number at the bottom of the *Annual Review Date* column and then press the Delete key.

**18** Save the report, accepting the default report name of *ReviewList*.

**19** Print and then close the ReviewList report.

**20** Redisplay the Navigation pane and then close **3-WEEmployees**.

**Check Your Work** Compare your work to the model answer available in the online course.

## In Addition

### Understanding Report Sections
A report is divided into five sections, described below.

| Report Section | Description |
|---|---|
| Report Header | Controls in this section are printed once at the beginning of the report, such as the report title. |
| Page Header | Controls in this section are printed at the top of each page, such as column headings. |
| Detail | Controls in this section make up the body of the report by printing the data from the associated table or query. |
| Page Footer | Controls in this section are printed at the bottom of each page, such as the report date and page numbers. |
| Report Footer | Controls in this section are printed once at the end of the report, such as column totals. |

# Features Summary

| Feature | Ribbon Tab, Group | Button | Keyboard Shortcut |
|---|---|---|---|
| add fields to a form | Form Layout Tools Design, Tools | | |
| create query in Design view | Create, Queries | | |
| Design view | Home, Views | | |
| Form tool | Create, Forms | | |
| Form view | Home, Views | | |
| Form Wizard | Create, Forms | | |
| insert logo in form or report | Form Layout Tools Design, Header/Footer OR Report Layout Tools Design, Header/Footer | | |
| Layout view | Home, Views | | |
| minimize Navigation pane | | | |
| Property Sheet task pane | Query Tools Design, Show/Hide OR Form Layout Tools Design, Tools OR Report Layout Tools Design, Tools | | Alt + Enter |
| redisplay Navigation pane | | | |
| Report tool | Create, Reports | | |
| run a query | Query Tools Design, Results | | |
| Simple Query Wizard | Create, Queries | | |

Microsoft®

# PowerPoint®

## 365

### 2019 Brief Edition

Nita Rutkosky

Audrey Roggenkamp
Pierce College Puyallup
Puyallup, Washington

Ian Rutkosky
Pierce College Puyallup
Puyallup, Washington

PARADIGM
EDUCATION SOLUTIONS

St. Paul

**Vice President, Content and Digital Solutions:** Christine Hurney
**Director of Content Development:** Carley Fruzzetti
**Testers:** Desiree Carvel; Ann E. Mills, Ivy Tech Community College of Indiana, Evansville, IN
**Director of Production:** Timothy W. Larson
**Production Editor/Project Manager:** Jen Weaverling
**Cover and Text Design:** Valerie King
**Senior Design and Production Specialist:** Julie Johnston
**Copy Editor:** Deborah Brandt
**Indexer:** Terry Casey
**Vice President, Director of Digital Products:** Chuck Bratton
**Digital Projects Manager:** Tom Modl
**Digital Solutions Manager:** Gerry Yumul
**Senior Director of Digital Products and Onboarding:** Christopher Johnson
**Supervisor of Digital Products and Onboarding:** Ryan Isdahl
**Vice President of Marketing:** Lara Weber McLellan
**Marketing and Communications Manager**: Selena Hicks

© 2020 by Publishing, LLC
875 Montreal Way
St. Paul, MN 55102
Email: CustomerService@ParadigmEducation.com
Website: ParadigmEducation.com

Printed in the United States of America

28 27 26 25 24 23 22 21 20 19    1 2 3 4 5 6 7 8 9 10 11 12

# Contents

# PowerPoint® 365

Create colorful and powerful presentations using PowerPoint, Microsoft's presentation program that is included in the Office suite. Use PowerPoint to organize and present information and create visual aids for a presentation. PowerPoint is a full-featured presentation program that provides a wide variety of editing and formatting features as well as sophisticated visual elements such as images, SmartArt, WordArt, and drawn objects. While working in PowerPoint, you will produce presentations for the following six companies.

First Choice Travel is a travel center offering a full range of traveling services from booking flights, hotel reservations, and rental cars to offering travel seminars.

The Waterfront Bistro offers fine dining for lunch and dinner and also offers banquet facilities, a wine cellar, and catering services.

Worldwide Enterprises is a national and international distributor of products for a variety of companies and is the exclusive movie distribution agent for Marquee Productions.

Marquee Productions is involved in all aspects of creating movies from script writing and development to filming. The company produces documentaries, biographies, as well as historical and action movies.

Performance Threads maintains an inventory of rental costumes and also researches, designs, and sews special-order and custom-made costumes.

The mission of the Niagara Peninsula College Theatre Arts Division is to offer a curriculum designed to provide students with a thorough exposure to all aspects of the theatre arts.

# *In Section 1 you will learn how to*

## Prepare a Presentation

Prepare a presentation using a template provided by PowerPoint or create a presentation and apply formatting with a design theme. Preparing a presentation consists of general steps such as creating and editing slides; adding enhancements to slides; and saving, previewing, printing, and closing a presentation and running a slide show. When running a slide show, the way in which one slide is removed from the screen and the next slide is displayed is referred to as a *transition*. Interesting transitions and transition sounds can be added to slides in a presentation.

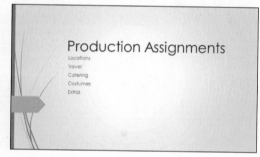

Create presentations using PowerPoint design themes and apply various slide layouts to change the appearance of slides.

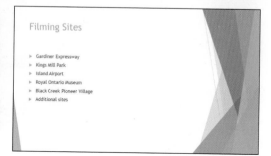

# In Section 2 you will learn how to

## Edit and Enhance Slides

Edit slides and slide elements in a presentation to customize and personalize the presentation. Editing can include such functions as rearranging and deleting slides; cutting, copying, and pasting text; changing the font, paragraph alignment, and paragraph spacing; and changing the design theme, theme color, and theme font. Add visual interest to a presentation by inserting images, pictures, and SmartArt organizational charts and graphics.

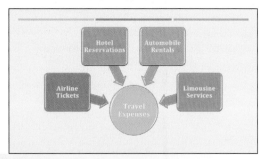

Edit slides by performing such actions as rearranging and deleting slides and changing slide size. Perform editing tasks on text in slides such as changing the font, paragraph alignment, and spacing. Enhance the visual interest of a presentation by inserting such elements as a company logo, image, an organizational chart, and a graphic.

# *In Section 3 you will learn how to*

## Customize Presentations

Customize a presentation with the WordArt feature and by drawing and formatting objects and text boxes. Additional features for customizing a presentation include using the Clipboard; inserting and formatting a table; inserting actions buttons, hyperlinks, and headers and footers; and inserting audio and video files.

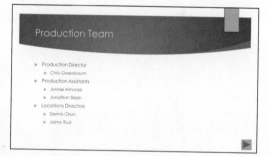

Further customize presentations with features such as headers and footers, audio and video files, WordArt, shapes, text boxes, and tables.

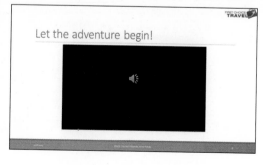

# PowerPoint

## Preparing a Presentation

 Data Files

Before beginning section work, copy the PowerPointS1 folder to your storage medium and then make PowerPointS1 the active folder.

## Skills

- Open, save, and close a presentation
- Run a slide show
- Choose a design theme
- Insert a new slide in the presentation
- Navigate in a presentation
- Change the slide layout
- Change the presentation view
- Rearrange, delete, and hide slides
- Use the Tell Me and Help features

- Check spelling in a presentation
- Use Thesaurus to display synonyms for words
- Run a slide show and use the Pen button options during a slide show
- Use ink tools
- Add slide transitions and transition sounds to a presentation
- Print and preview a presentation

## Projects Overview

Use a predesigned template to prepare a presentation about the new features in PowerPoint; prepare a movie production meeting presentation; prepare a location team meeting presentation.

Prepare an executive meeting presentation for Worldwide Enterprises.

Prepare a presentation containing information on the accommodations and services offered by The Waterfront Bistro.

Prepare a presentation on Toronto, Ontario, Canada.

Prepare a presentation for a costume meeting.

The online course includes additional training and assessment resources.

1

PowerPoint is a presentation graphics program used to organize and present information. Use PowerPoint to create visual aids for a presentation and then print copies of the aids as well as run the slide show. To open a predesigned PowerPoint template, open the PowerPoint program, click the template, and then click the Create button. The presentation screen contains a variety of features for working with a presentation, such as the Title bar, Quick Access Toolbar, ribbon, and Status bar. After creating a presentation, save the presentation so it is available for future use. Save a presentation at the Save As backstage area.

**What You Will Do**   You are an employee of Marquee Productions and Microsoft Office has just been installed on your computer. You need to prepare a presentation in the near future so you decide to open a PowerPoint file and experiment with running the slide show.

Opening a
Presentation Based
on a Template

Exploring the
PowerPoint Screen

Running a Slide Show

Saving to a Removable
Disk

Closing a Presentation
and Closing PowerPoint

**1**   At the Windows desktop, click the Start button and then click the PowerPoint tile at the Start menu.

Depending on your system configuration, these steps may vary.

**2**   At the PowerPoint opening screen, click the *Welcome to PowerPoint* template.

If this template is not visible, you will need to search for it. To do this, click in the search text box, type Welcome to PowerPoint, and then press the Enter key.

**3**   Click the Create button.

The Welcome to PowerPoint template opens in the PowerPoint window. What displays in the PowerPoint window will vary depending on what type of presentation you are creating. However, the PowerPoint window contains some consistent elements such as those identified in Figure 1.1. Refer to Table 1.1 for a description of the window elements.

**4**   Run the slide show by clicking the Start From Beginning button 🖵 on the Quick Access Toolbar.

**5** When the first slide fills the screen, read the information and then click the left mouse button. Continue reading the information in each slide and clicking the left mouse button to advance to the next slide. When a black screen displays, click the left mouse button to end the slide show.

**FIGURE 1.1** PowerPoint Window

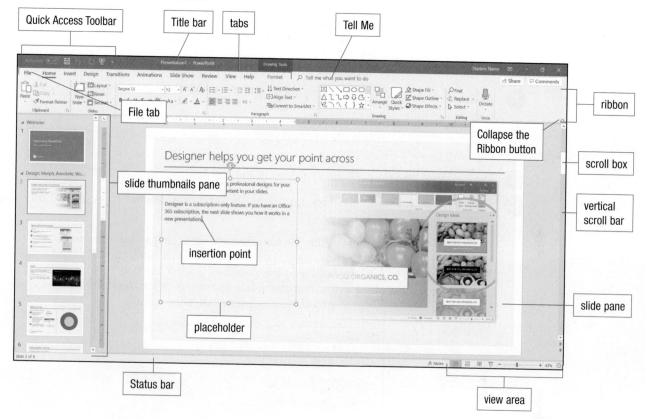

**Table 1.1** PowerPoint Window Elements

| Feature | Description |
| --- | --- |
| Collapse the Ribbon button | when clicked, removes ribbon from screen |
| File tab | when clicked, displays backstage area that contains options for working with and managing presentations |
| I-beam pointer | used to move insertion point or to select text |
| insertion point | indicates location of next character entered at the keyboard |
| placeholder | location on slide with dotted border; holds text or objects |
| Quick Access Toolbar | contains buttons for commonly used commands |
| ribbon | area containing tabs with options and buttons divided into groups |
| scroll box | used to scroll through slides in presentation; click and hold down mouse button on scroll box to indicate slide number and title |
| slide pane | displays slide and slide contents |
| slide thumbnails pane | left side of screen; displays slide thumbnails |
| Status bar | displays slide number, view buttons, and Zoom slider bar |
| tabs | contain commands and buttons organized into groups |
| Tell Me | used to look up a feature and provide options for using the feature |
| Title bar | displays presentation name followed by program name |
| vertical scroll bar | used to display specific slides |
| view area | location on the Status bar that contains buttons for changing presentation view |

**6** Save the presentation by clicking the Save button  on the Quick Access Toolbar.

**7** At the Save As backstage area, click the *Browse* option.

**8** At the Save As dialog box, click the drive in the Navigation pane that contains your storage medium.

> Press the F12 function key to display the Save As dialog box without displaying the Save As backstage area.

**9** Double-click the *PowerPointS1* folder in the Content pane.

**10** Click in the *File name* text box, type 1-MPPowerPoint, and then press the Enter key (or click the Save button).

> PowerPoint automatically adds the file extension *.pptx* to the end of a presentation name. By default, file extensions do not display. File extensions can be turned on by clicking the File Explorer button on the Windows taskbar, clicking the View tab, and then clicking the *File name extensions* check box to insert a check mark. This textbook will show file names without the extensions, since that is the default.

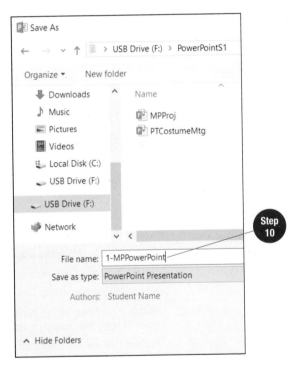

**11** At the PowerPoint window, print the presentation information in outline layout by clicking the File tab and then clicking the *Print* option.

The File tab is in the upper left corner of the screen at the left of the Home tab. When you click the File tab, the backstage area displays with options for working with and managing presentations.

**12** At the Print backstage area, click the second gallery in the *Settings* category (the gallery containing the text *Full Page Slides*) and then click *Outline* in the *Print Layout* section of the drop-down list.

**13** Click the Print button. ***Note: If working in a lab, check with your instructor before printing.***

**14** Close the presentation by clicking the File tab and then clicking the *Close* option.

If a message displays asking if you want to save the presentation, click Yes.

**15** Close PowerPoint by clicking the Close button in the upper right corner of the screen.

Check Your Work  Compare your work to the model answer available in the online course.

## In Addition

### Using Tabs

The ribbon area displays below the Quick Access Toolbar. The buttons and options in the ribbon area vary depending on the tab selected and the width of the window displayed on the screen. PowerPoint features are organized into tabs that display in the ribbon area. Commands and buttons are organized into groups within a tab. For example, the Home tab, which is the default tab, contains the Clipboard, Slides, Font, Paragraph, Drawing, and Editing groups. Hover the mouse pointer over a button to display a ScreenTip with the name of the button, a keyboard shortcut (if any), and a description of the purpose of the button.

Create a PowerPoint presentation using an installed template similar to the previous activity, or begin with a blank presentation and apply personalized formatting or a slide design theme. To display a blank PowerPoint presentation, use the keyboard shortcut Ctrl + N, or click the File tab (or the File tab and then the *New* option), and then click the *Blank Presentation* template at the backstage area. A PowerPoint presentation screen displays in Normal view with the slide pane in the center and the slide thumbnails pane at the left side of the screen.

**What You Will Do**   Chris Greenbaum, production manager for Marquee Productions, has asked you to prepare slides for a movie production meeting. You decide to prepare the presentation using a design template provided by PowerPoint.

Opening a Blank Presentation

Applying a Design Theme

Inserting and Deleting Text in Slides

Inserting a New Slide

**1**   Open PowerPoint.

**2**   At the PowerPoint opening screen, click the *Blank Presentation* template.

**3**   At the PowerPoint window, click the Design tab.

**4**   Click the More Themes button ⊡ in the Themes group.

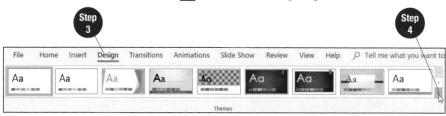

**5**   Click the *Wisp* option in the *Office* section of the drop-down gallery.

When you click the More Themes button, a drop-down gallery displays. This gallery contains the live preview feature. Hover the mouse pointer over one of the design themes and the slide in the slide pane displays with the design theme formatting applied. With the live preview feature, you can view a design theme before actually applying it to the presentation. If you are using PowerPoint 365, the Design Ideas task pane opens at the right side of the screen with additional options for the selected design theme. Apply an option by clicking the option thumbnail in the task pane. Close this task pane by clicking the Design Ideas button in the Designer group on the Design tab.

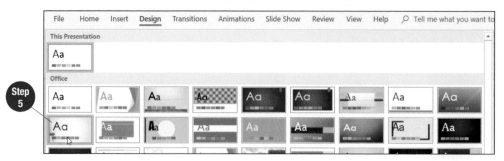

**6**   Click the second option from the left in the Variants group.

This changes the tab at the left of the slide to a dark gold color.

**7** Click in the *Click to add title* placeholder in the slide and then type Marquee Productions.

> A *placeholder* is a location on a slide that is marked with a border and holds text or an object.

**8** Click in the *Click to add subtitle* placeholder in the slide and then type Movie Production Meeting.

**9** Click the Home tab and then click the New Slide button in the Slides group.

> When you click this button, a new slide displays in the slide pane with the Title and Content layout. You will learn more about slide layouts in Activity 1.3.

**10** Click in the *Click to add title* placeholder in the slide and then type Agenda.

**11** Click in the *Click to add text* placeholder in the slide and then type Production Team.

**12** Press the Enter key and then type the following agenda items, pressing the Enter key after each item except the last one: Production Assignments, Production Schedule, Locations, and Summary.

> You can use keys on the keyboard to move the insertion point to various locations within a placeholder in a slide. Refer to Table 1.2 on the next page for a list of insertion point movement commands.

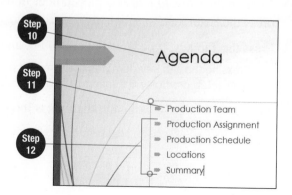

**13** Click the New Slide button in the Slides group on the Home tab.

**Table 1.2** Insertion Point Movement Commands

| To move insertion point | Press |
|---|---|
| One character left | Left Arrow |
| One character right | Right Arrow |
| One line up | Up Arrow |
| One line down | Down Arrow |
| One word to the left | Ctrl + Left Arrow |
| One word to the right | Ctrl + Right Arrow |
| To end of a line of text | End |
| To beginning of a line of text | Home |
| To beginning of current paragraph in placeholder | Ctrl + Up Arrow |
| To beginning of previous paragraph in placeholder | Ctrl + Up Arrow two times |
| To beginning of next paragraph in placeholder | Ctrl + Down Arrow |
| To beginning of text in placeholder | Ctrl + Home |
| To end of text in placeholder | Ctrl + End |

14 Click in the *Click to add title* placeholder in the slide and then type Department Reports.

15 Click in the *Click to add text* placeholder in the slide and then type the bulleted text as shown in the slide below. Press the Enter key after each item except the last one.

16 Click the New Slide button in the Slides group on the Home tab.

17 Click in the *Click to add title* placeholder in the slide and then type Locations.

18 Click in the *Click to add text* placeholder in the slide, type Studio Shoots, and then press the Enter key.

19 Press the Tab key, type Vancouver Studio, and then press the Enter key.

> Pressing the Tab key demotes the insertion point to a second-level bullet, while pressing Shift + Tab promotes the insertion point back to the first level.

20 Type Los Angeles Studio and then press the Enter key.

**In Brief**

**Choose Design Theme**
1. Click Design tab.
2. Click More Themes button.
3. Click theme at drop-down gallery.

**Insert New Slide**
1. Click Home tab.
2. Click New Slide button.
OR
Press Ctrl + M.

**21** Press Shift + Tab, type Location Shoots, and then press the Enter key.

**22** Press the Tab key, type Stanley Park, and then press the Enter key.

**23** Type Downtown Streets.

**24** Click the Save button on the Quick Access Toolbar.

**25** At the Save As backstage area, click the *Browse* option.

**26** At the Save As dialog box, click the drive in the Navigation pane that contains your storage medium.

**27** Double-click the *PowerPointS1* folder in the Content pane.

**28** Click in the *File name* text box, type 1-MPProdMtg, and then press the Enter key (or click the Save button).

**29** Close the presentation by clicking the File tab and then clicking the *Close* option.

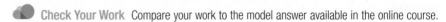

Check Your Work  Compare your work to the model answer available in the online course.

## In Addition

### Planning a Presentation

Consider the following basic guidelines when preparing content for a presentation:

- **Determine the main purpose.** Do not try to cover too many topics. Identifying the main point of the presentation will help to stay focused and convey a clear message to the audience.
- **Determine the output.** To help decide the type of output needed, consider the availability of equipment, the size of the room where the presentation will be held, and the number of people who will be attending the presentation.
- **Show one idea per slide.** Each slide in a presentation should convey only one main idea. Too many ideas on a slide may confuse the audience and cause the presenter to stray from the purpose of the slide.

- **Maintain a consistent design.** A consistent design and color scheme for slides in a presentation will create continuity and cohesiveness. Do not use too much color or too many images or other graphic elements.
- **Keep slides uncluttered and easy to read.** Keep slides simple to make them easy for the audience to understand. Keep words and other items, such as bullets, to a minimum.
- **Determine printing needs.** Will the audience members require handouts? If so, will these handouts consist of a printing of each slide? an outline of the presentation? a printing of each slide with space for taking notes?

Open an existing presentation by displaying the Home backstage area and then clicking the presentation in the Recent list or displaying the Open backstage area and then clicking the presentation in the *Recent* option list. A presentation can also be opened at the Open dialog box. Display the Open dialog box by clicking the File tab and then clicking the *Open* option. At the Open backstage area, click the *Browse* option. Navigate through slides in a presentation with buttons on the vertical scroll bar, by clicking slide thumbnails in Normal view, or by using keys on the keyboard. Insert a new slide with a specific layout by clicking the New Slide button arrow in the Slides group on the Home tab or the Insert tab and then clicking the layout at the drop-down list. Choose the layout that matches the type of text or object that will be inserted in the slide.

**What You Will Do**   Chris Greenbaum has asked you to add more information to the movie production meeting presentation. You will insert a new slide between the second and third slides in the presentation and another at the end of the presentation.

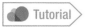

Opening from a Removable Disk

Navigating to Slides

Choosing a Slide Layout

Saving with the Same Name

1. Click the File tab and then click the *Open* option.

2. At the Open backstage area, click the *Browse* option.

3. In the Navigation pane of the Open dialog box, click the drive where your USB flash drive is located (such as *Removable Disk (F:)*).

   You can also display the Open dialog box without displaying the Open backstage area by pressing Ctrl + F12.

4. Double-click the *PowerPointS1* folder in the Content pane.

5. Double-click *1-MPProdMtg* in the Content pane.

6. With **1-MPProdMtg** open, click the Next Slide button ⬇ at the bottom of the vertical scroll bar.

   Clicking this button displays the next slide, Slide 2, in the presentation. Notice that *Slide 2 of 4* displays at the left of the Status bar.

7. Click the Previous Slide button ⬆ above the Next Slide button to display Slide 1.

   When you click the Previous Slide button, Slide 1 displays in the slide pane and *Slide 1 of 4* displays at the left of the Status bar.

8. Display Slide 2 in the slide pane by clicking the second slide in the slide thumbnails pane (the slide titled *Agenda*).

9. Insert a new slide between Slides 2 and 3 by clicking the New Slide button in the Slides group on the Home tab.

   When you select a slide in the slide thumbnails pane and then click the New Slide button, the new slide is inserted after the selected slide.

**10** Click in the *Click to add title* placeholder in the slide in the slide pane and then type Production Schedule.

**11** Click in the *Click to add text* placeholder in the slide and then type the bulleted text as shown at the right. Press the Enter key after typing each item except the last one.

**12** Click below the last thumbnail in the slide thumbnails pane. (You may need to scroll down the slide thumbnails pane to display the last slide.)

> When you click below the slide thumbnail, an orange horizontal line displays below Slide 5.

**13** Click the New Slide button arrow on the Home tab and then click the *Title Slide* layout in the drop-down list.

**14** Click in the *Click to add title* placeholder and then type Production Leader.

**15** Click in the *Click to add subtitle* placeholder and then type Chris Greenbaum.

**16** Click the Save button on the Quick Access Toolbar to save **1-MPProdMtg**.

 **Check Your Work**  Compare your work to the model answer available in the online course.

## In Addition

### Opening a Presentation from the Recent or *Recent* Option List

The Home backstage area contains a list of the most recently opened presentations. In addition to the Home backstage area, the Open backstage area with the *Recent* option selected displays a list of the most recently opened presentations. The presentations in the *Recent* option list at the Open backstage area are grouped into categories such as *Today*, *Yesterday*, and possibly *This Week* and *Older*. To open a presentation from the Recent list at the Home backstage area or the *Recent* option list at the Open backstage area, click the presentation name in the list.

# Activity 1.4  Changing Views

PowerPoint provides different viewing options for a presentation. Change the presentation view with buttons in the Presentation Views group on the View tab or with buttons in the view area on the Status bar. The Normal view is the default view, and this view can be changed to Outline view, Slide Sorter view, Notes Page view, or Reading view. Choose the view based on the type of activity being performed in the presentation. The Outline view provides another method for entering text in a slide. When Outline view is active, the slide thumbnails pane changes to an outline pane for entering text. Insert speaker's notes into a presentation using the notes pane, which can be displayed by clicking the Notes button on the Status bar.

**What You Will Do**  After reviewing the movie production presentation, Chris Greenbaum has asked you to add a new slide and edit an existing slide.

 Tutorial
Changing Views

 Tutorial
Entering Text in the Outline Pane

 Tutorial
Changing the Display Percentage

1. With **1-MPProdMtg** open, click the View tab and then click the Outline View button in the Presentation Views group.

2. Click immediately right of the text *Music* in the third slide (near the middle of the outline pane), press the Enter key, and then press Shift + Tab.

   This moves the insertion point back a level and inserts the number *4* followed by a slide icon.

3. Type Production Assignments, press the Enter key, and then press the Tab key. Type the remaining text for Slide 4 as shown at the right. Do not press the Enter key after typing *Extras*.

4. Click immediately right of the text *Location Shoots* in the third slide.

5. Press the Enter key and then type Editing.

   This inserts *Editing* between *Location Shoots* and *Dubbing*.

6. Make Slide 6 (*Locations*) the active slide in the slide pane, click in the *Click to add notes* placeholder in the notes pane (if the text is not visible, click the Notes button on the Status bar to display the notes pane), and then type Camille Matsui will report on the park location.

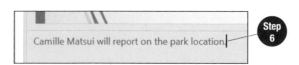

7. Display the slides in Notes Page view by clicking the Notes Page button in the Presentation Views group.

   In Notes Page view, an individual slide displays on a page with any added notes displayed below it. Notice that the note you created about Camille Matsui displays below the slide on the page.

8. Click the Previous Slide button on the vertical scroll bar until Slide 1 displays.

**9** Increase the zoom by clicking the Zoom button ⊞ in the Zoom group on the View tab, clicking *100%* at the Zoom dialog box, and then clicking OK.

**10** You can also change the zoom using the Zoom slider bar. Change the zoom by positioning the mouse pointer on the Zoom slider button at the right side of the Status bar. Click and hold down the left mouse button, drag to the right until the zoom percentage at the right of the Zoom slider bar displays as approximately *138%*, and then release the mouse button.

**11** Click the Zoom Out button ⊟ at the left of the Zoom slider bar until *70%* displays at the right of the slider bar.

> Click the Zoom Out button to decrease the zoom display and click the Zoom In button to increase the display.

**12** View all slides in the presentation as slide thumbnails by clicking the Slide Sorter button ⊞ in the view area on the Status bar.

**13** View the presentation in Reading view by clicking the Reading View button ⊞ in the Presentation Views group.

> Use Reading view to show the presentation to someone viewing the presentation on his or her own computer. You can also use Reading view to view a presentation in a window with controls that make the presentation easy to view. In Reading view, navigation buttons display in the lower right corner of the screen immediately left of the view area on the Status bar.

**14** View the slides in the presentation in Reading view by clicking the left mouse button on the slides until a black screen displays. At the black screen, click the mouse button again.

> This returns the presentation to the previous view—in this case, Slide Sorter view.

**15** Return the presentation to Normal view by clicking the Normal button ⊞ in the Presentation Views group.

**16** If necessary, close the notes pane by clicking the Notes button on the Status bar.

**17** Save **1-MPProdMtg**.

> ● **Check Your Work**  Compare your work to the model answer available in the online course.

## In Addition

### Navigating Using the Keyboard

Use the keyboard to display slides in a presentation. In Normal view, press the Down Arrow or Page Down key to display the next slide or press the Up Arrow or Page Up key to display the previous slide in the presentation. Press the Home key to display the first slide in the presentation and press the End key to display the last slide in the presentation. Navigate in Outline view and Slide Sorter view by using the arrow keys on the keyboard. Navigate in Reading view by using the Right Arrow key to move to the next slide or the Left Arrow key to move to the previous slide.

Click the New Slide button and a slide is inserted with the Title and Content layout. This default layout can be changed by clicking the Layout button in the Slides group on the Home tab and then clicking a layout at the drop-down list. Objects in a slide, such as text, charts, tables, and other graphic elements, are generally positioned in placeholders. Click the text or object to select the placeholder and a dashed border will surround the place-holder. A selected placeholder can be moved, sized, and/or deleted.

**What You Will Do**　You have decided to make a few changes to the layout of slides in the movie production presentation.

Modifying Placeholders

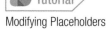

Changing a Slide Layout

**1** With **1-MPProdMtg** open, make Slide 7 active in the slide pane.

**2** Click the Home tab, click the Layout button  in the Slides group, and then click the *Title and Content* layout at the drop-down list.

**3** Click immediately right of the *r* in *Leader* (this selects the placeholder), press the Backspace key until *Leader* is deleted, and then type Team.

> Sizing handles display around the selected placeholder. Use these sizing handles to increase and/or decrease the size of the placeholder.

**4** Click immediately right of the *m* in *Greenbaum*.

**5** Type a comma (,), press the spacebar, and then type Production Manager.

**6** Press the Enter key and then type the remaining names and titles shown in the slide above. (Do not press the Enter key after typing *Josh Hart, Locations Director*.)

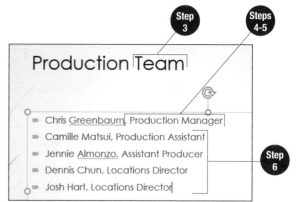

**7** Click the Previous Slide button on the vertical scroll bar until Slide 4 displays.

**8** Change the slide layout by clicking the Layout button in the Slides group and then clicking the *Title Slide* layout at the drop-down list.

**9** Click in the title *Production Assignments*.

> This selects the placeholder.

**10** Decrease the size of the placeholder by positioning the mouse pointer on the middle sizing handle at the top of the placeholder until the pointer turns into an up-and-down pointing arrow. Click and hold down the left mouse button, drag down to the approximate location shown at the right, and then release the mouse button.

**In Brief**

**Change Slide Layout**
1. Make slide active.
2. Click Home tab.
3. Click Layout button.
4. Click layout.

**Move Placeholder**
1. Click inside placeholder.
2. Drag with mouse to new position.

**Size Placeholder**
1. Click inside placeholder.
2. Drag sizing handles to increase/decrease size.

⑪ Move the title placeholder so it positions the title as shown in Figure 1.2. To do this, position the mouse pointer on the placeholder border until the mouse pointer displays with a four-headed arrow attached, click and hold down the left mouse button, drag to the approximate location shown in the figure, and then release the mouse button.

⑫ Increase the size of the subtitle placeholder (and the size of the text). Begin by clicking in the word *Locations*.

This selects the placeholder containing the text.

⑬ Position the mouse pointer on the middle sizing handle at the top of the placeholder until the pointer turns into an up-and-down-pointing arrow. Click and hold down the left mouse button, drag up approximately one inch, and then release the mouse button.

Increasing the size of the placeholder automatically increases the size of the text in the placeholder. This is because, by default, PowerPoint automatically sizes the contents to fit the placeholder. Read the In Addition at the bottom of this page for information on the AutoFit Options button.

⑭ Move the content placeholder so it positions the text as shown in Figure 1.2. To do this, position the mouse pointer on the placeholder border until the mouse pointer displays with a four-headed arrow attached, click and hold down the left mouse button, drag to the approximate location shown in the figure, and then release the mouse button.

**Figure 1.2** Slide 4

Production Assignments

Locations
Travel
Catering
Costumes
Extras

⑮ Click outside the placeholder to deselect it.

If you are not satisfied with the changes you make to a placeholder, click the Reset button 🔲 in the Slides group on the Home tab. This resets the placeholder's position, size, and formatting to the default settings.

⑯ Save **1-MPProdMtg**.

🔵 Check Your Work  Compare your work to the model answer available in the online course.

## In Addition

### Using the AutoFit Options Button

If the size of a placeholder is decreased so the existing text does not fit within it, PowerPoint will automatically decrease the size of the text so it fits in the placeholder. Click in the text that has been decreased in size and an AutoFit Options button displays at the left of the placeholder. Click the AutoFit Options button and a list of choices displays for positioning objects in the placeholder, as shown at the right. The *AutoFit Text to Placeholder* option is selected by default and tells PowerPoint to fit text within the boundaries of the placeholder. Click the middle choice, *Stop Fitting Text to This Placeholder*, and PowerPoint will not automatically

fit the text or object within the placeholder. Choose the last option, *Control AutoCorrect Options*, to display the AutoCorrect dialog box with the AutoFormat As You Type tab selected. Additional options may display depending upon the placeholder and the type of data it contains.

Editing a presentation may include such tasks as rearranging, deleting, or hiding specific slides. PowerPoint provides various views for creating and managing a presentation. Manage slides in the slide thumbnails pane or in Slide Sorter view. Switch to Slide Sorter view by clicking the Slide Sorter button in the view area on the Status bar or by clicking the View tab and then clicking the Slide Sorter button in the Presentation Views group.

**What You Will Do**   Chris Greenbaum has asked you to make some changes to the presentation, including rearranging the slides, deleting a slide, and hiding a slide.

Tutorial

Rearranging Slides

Tutorial

Deleting Slides

Tutorial

Hiding and Unhiding Slides

**1** With **1-MPProdMtg** open, click Slide 5 in the slide thumbnails pane and then press the Delete key on the keyboard.

> You can also delete a slide by right-clicking the slide in the slide thumbnails pane and then clicking *Delete Slide* at the shortcut menu.

**2** Click the Slide Sorter button in the view area on the Status bar.

**3** Click Slide 6 to make it active.

> A selected slide displays with an orange border.

**4** Position the mouse pointer on Slide 6, click and hold down the left mouse button, drag the slide (the mouse pointer will display with a square attached) to the left of Slide 3, and then release the mouse button.

**5** Click the Normal button in the view area on the Status bar.

**6** Position the mouse pointer on the Slide 5 thumbnail in the slide thumbnails pane, click and hold down the left mouse button, drag up until the slide displays immediately below the Slide 3 thumbnail, and then release the mouse button.

**In Brief**

**Delete Slide**
1. Right-click slide thumbnail.
2. Click *Delete Slide*.
OR
1. Click slide in slide thumbnails pane.
2. Press Delete key.

**Move Slide**
1. Click Slide Sorter button on Status bar.
2. Click slide.
3. Drag to new position.
OR
1. Click slide in slide thumbnails pane.
2. Drag to new position.

**Hide Slide**
1. Click slide thumbnail.
2. Click Slide Show tab.
3. Click Hide Slide button.

**7** With the Slide 4 thumbnail selected in the slide thumbnails pane (thumbnail displays with an orange border), hide the slide by clicking the Slide Show tab and then clicking the Hide Slide button ◻ in the Set Up group.

> When a slide is hidden, the slide thumbnail displays dimmed and the slide number displays with a diagonal line across the number.

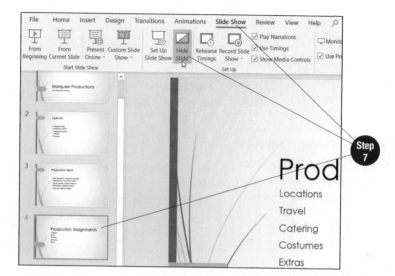

**8** Run the slide show by clicking the From Beginning button ▣ in the Start Slide Show group. Click the left mouse button to advance each slide until a black screen displays. At the black screen, click the left mouse button again.

**9** After running the slide show, you decide to redisplay the hidden slide. To do this, make sure the Slide 4 thumbnail is selected in the slide thumbnails pane and then click the Hide Slide button in the Set Up group.

**10** Save **1-MPProdMtg**.

**Check Your Work** Compare your work to the model answer available in the online course.

## In Addition

### Copying Slides within a Presentation

Copying a slide within a presentation is similar to moving a slide. To copy a slide, position the mouse pointer on the desired slide, press and hold down the Ctrl key, and then click and hold down left mouse button. Drag to the location where you want the slide copied, release the left mouse button, and then release the Ctrl key. When you drag with the mouse, the mouse pointer displays with a square and a plus symbol attached.

PowerPoint includes the Tell Me feature, which provides information and guidance on how to complete a command. To use Tell Me, click in the *Tell Me* text box on the ribbon to the right of all the tabs and then type the command. Type text in the *Tell Me* text box and a drop-down list displays with options for completing the command, displaying information on the function from sources on the web, and displaying help information on the function. The Help task pane provides another method for accessing help on a command. Display the Help task pane using the Tell Me feature, by pressing the F1 function key on the keyboard, or by clicking the Help tab and then clicking the Help button in the Help group.

**What You Will Do**   To enhance the appearance of Slide 1 in the presentation, you will change the font size of the subtitle *Movie Production Meeting*, using the Tell Me feature to complete the task. You will also use the Tell Me feature to access the Help task pane and locate articles about slide masters.

Using the Tell Me Feature

Using the Help Feature

**1** With **1-MPProdMtg** open, make Slide 1 the active slide, click in the subtitle *Movie Production Meeting*, and then click the border of the placeholder to select it.

**2** Click in the *Tell Me* text box.

The *Tell Me* text box is on the ribbon at the right of the Drawing Tools Format tab and contains the text *Tell me what you want to do*. When you click in the text box, the last five functions entered will display in a drop-down list.

**3** Type font size in the *Tell Me* text box.

A drop-down list displays with options such as *Font Size*, *Decrease Font Size*, *Font Settings*, and *Increase Font Size*.

**4** Click the arrow at the right of the *Font Size* option at the drop-down list.

When you click the arrow at the right of the *Font Size* option, a side menu displays.

**5** At the side menu that displays, click *28*.

The 28-point font size is applied to the selected subtitle. The Tell Me feature guided you through the process of changing font size without having to learn how to change font size using a button on the ribbon or an option at a dialog box.

**In Brief**

**Use Tell Me**
1. Click in *Tell Me* text box.
2. Type search phrase.
3. Click option.

**Use Help**
1. Position mouse over button.
2. Click Tell me more link.
OR
1. Press F1 function key.
2. Type search text.
3. Press Enter key.
OR
1. Click Help tab.
2. Click Help button.
3. Type search text.
4. Press Enter key.

**6** The Tell Me feature also includes access to the Help task pane. To display the Help task pane with information on slide masters, click in the *Tell Me* text box and then type slide master.

**7** At the drop-down list, point to *Get Help on "slide master"*.

**8** At the side menu that displays, click the first option.

Clicking an option in the side menu displays the Help task pane at the right side of the screen. Read the information in the task pane. You can also display the Help task pane by pressing the F1 function key or clicking the Help tab and then clicking the Help button.

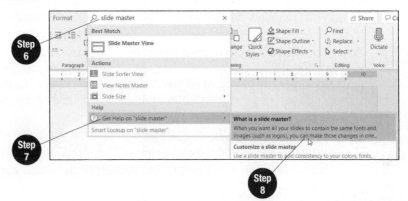

**9** Close the Help task pane by clicking the Close button in the upper right corner of the task pane.

Check Your Work  Compare your work to the model answer available in the online course.

## In Addition

### Accessing Smart Lookup

Use the Smart Lookup feature to access information on a function from a variety of sources on the web such as Wikipedia, Bing, and the Oxford Dictionary. The Tell Me feature is one way to access Smart Lookup. To use Tell Me for Smart Lookup, click in the *Tell Me* text box, type the function, and then click the *Smart Lookup* option in the drop-down list. Clicking the *Smart Lookup* option displays the Smart Lookup task pane at the right side of the screen with information on the function from a variety of locations on the internet. Smart Lookup can also be accessed with the Smart Lookup button in the Insights group on the Review tab or by selecting text, right-clicking the selected text, and then clicking *Smart Lookup* at the shortcut menu.

### Getting Help on Specific Functions

Some dialog boxes and backstage areas contain a help button that, when clicked, will display the Microsoft Office Support website with information about the functions in the dialog box or backstage area. Hover the mouse over some buttons and the ScreenTip that displays may include a help icon and the text *Tell me more*. Click this hyperlinked text and the Help task pane displays with information about the button feature. Hover the mouse pointer over a button and then press F1 to display the Help task pane with information about the button feature.

Use PowerPoint's spelling checker to find and correct misspelled words and duplicated words (such as *and and*). The spelling checker compares words in slides with words in its dictionary. If a match is found, the word is passed over. If no match is found, the spelling checker stops, selects the word, and offers possible replacements. Use the Thesaurus to find synonyms, antonyms, and related words for a particular word. To use the Thesaurus, click in a word, click the Review tab, and then click the Thesaurus button in the Proofing group. This displays the Thesaurus task pane with information about the word.

**What You Will Do**   You have decided to create a new slide in the movie production presentation. Because several changes have been made to the presentation, you know that checking the spelling of all the slide text is important. Complete a spelling check of all slides and then use the Thesaurus to replace a couple of words with synonyms.

Tutorial

Checking Spelling

Tutorial

Using the Thesaurus

**1** With **1-MPProdMtg** open, position the mouse pointer on the scroll box on the vertical scroll bar at the right side of the screen. Click and hold down the left mouse button, drag the scroll box to the bottom of the scroll bar, and then release the mouse button.

> This displays Slide 6 in the slide pane. As you drag the scroll box on the vertical scroll bar, a box displays indicating the slide number and slide title (if the slide contains a title).

**2** Click the Home tab and then click the New Slide button in the Slides group.

> This inserts a new slide at the end of the presentation.

**3** Click in the *Click to add title* placeholder and then type Summary.

**4** Click in the *Click to add text* placeholder and then type the text shown in the slide at the right.

> Type the words exactly as shown. You will check the spelling in the next steps.

**5** Complete a spelling check by moving the insertion point to the beginning of the word *Timetable*, clicking the Review tab, and then clicking the Spelling button in the Proofing group.

**6** When the spelling checker selects *Asignments* in Slide 7 and displays *Assignments* in the list box in the Spelling task pane, click the Change button.

> Refer to the In Addition for a description of the Spelling task pane buttons.

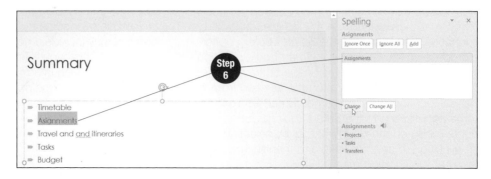

## In Brief

**Complete Spelling Check**
1. Click Review tab.
2. Click Spelling button.
3. Change or ignore highlighted words.
4. When spelling check is completed, click OK.

**Use Thesaurus**
1. Click in word.
2. Click Review tab.
3. Click Thesaurus button.
4. Position mouse pointer on replacement word in Thesaurus task pane, click down arrow at right of word, click *Insert*.

**7** When the spelling checker selects the second *and* in the slide, click the Delete button.

**8** If the spelling checker selects *Greenbaum* in Slide 3, click the Ignore All button.

> Greenbaum is a proper name and is spelled correctly. Clicking the Ignore All button tells the spelling checker to leave the name as spelled.

**9** If the spelling checker selects *Almonzo* in Slide 3, click the Ignore All button.

**10** At the message stating that the spelling check is complete, click OK.

**11** Display Slide 7 in the slide pane and then click in the word *Timetable*.

**12** Look up synonyms for *Timetable* by clicking the Thesaurus button 📖 in the Proofing group.

> The Thesaurus task pane displays at the right side of the screen and contains lists of synonyms for *Timetable*. Depending on the word you are looking up, the words in the Thesaurus task pane list box may display followed by *(n.)* for *noun*, *(v.)* for *verb*, *(adj.)* for *adjective*, or *(adv.)* for *adverb*. Antonyms may display in the list of related synonyms, usually near the end and followed by *(Antonym)*.

**13** Position the mouse pointer on the word *Schedule* in the Thesaurus task pane, click the down arrow at the right of the word, and then click *Insert* at the drop-down list.

> This replaces *Timetable* with *Schedule*.

**14** Close the Thesaurus task pane by clicking the Close button in the upper right corner of the task pane.

**15** Right-click in the word *Tasks*, point to *Synonyms*, and then click *Responsibilities*.

> The shortcut menu offers another method for displaying synonyms for words.

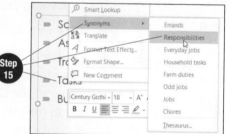

**16** Save **1-MPProdMtg**.

☁ **Check Your Work** Compare your work to the model answer available in the online course.

## In Addition

### Using Spelling Task Pane Buttons
This table displays descriptions of the Spelling task pane buttons.

| Button | Function |
|---|---|
| Ignore Once | skips that occurrence of the word and leaves currently selected text as written |
| Ignore All | skips that occurrence of the word and all other occurrences of the word in the presentation |
| Add | adds the selected word to the main spelling check dictionary |
| Delete | deletes the currently selected word(s) |
| Change | replaces the selected word with the selected word in the suggestions list box |
| Change All | replaces the selected word and all other occurrences of the word in the presentation with the selected word in the suggestions list box |

Run a slide show in PowerPoint manually, advance the slides automatically, or set up a slide show to run continuously for demonstration purposes. In addition to the Start From Beginning button on the Quick Access Toolbar, run a slide show with the From Beginning button on the Slide Show tab or the Slide Show button on the Status bar. Run the slide show beginning with the currently active slide by clicking the From Current Slide button in the Start Slide Show group or clicking the Slide Show button in the view area on the Status bar. Use the mouse or keyboard to advance through the slides. Buttons on the Slide Show toolbar can also be used. These buttons display when the mouse pointer is moved while running a slide show. Use the pen tool to emphasize major points or draw the attention of the audience to specific items in a slide. The pen tool contains options such as a laser pointer, drawing pen, highlighter, and eraser. Write and highlight on a slide in Normal view with options on the Ink Tools Pens tab. Display this tab by clicking the Start Inking button in the Ink group on the Review tab. This feature is useful when using a pen, stylus, or finger to draw on a tablet. If the Draw tab displays on the ribbon, the Start Inking button will not display on the Review tab. However, the Draw tab contains options for drawing and highlighting on a slide. (This activity assumes the Start Inking button is available.)

**MARQUEE**
PRODUCTIONS

**What You Will Do**   You are now ready to run the movie production meeting slide show. You will use the mouse to perform various actions while running the slide show and use the pen tool and ink tools to emphasize points in slides.

Navigating in a Slide Show

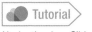
Changing the Display when Running a Slide Show

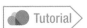
Displaying Slide Show Help and Hiding Slides during a Slide Show

Using Pen Button Options during a Slide Show

Using Ink Tools

**1**   With **1-MPProdMtg** open, click the Slide Show tab and then click the From Beginning button in the Start Slide Show group.

> Clicking this button begins the slide show, and Slide 1 fills the entire screen.

**2**   After viewing Slide 1, click the left mouse button to advance to the next slide.

**3**   At Slide 2, move the mouse pointer until the Slide Show toolbar displays dimmed in the lower left corner of the slide and then click the Previous button (displays with a left arrow) on the toolbar to display the previous slide (Slide 1).

> Use buttons on the Slide Show toolbar to display the next slide, the previous slide, or a specific slide; use the pen, laser pointer, and highlighter to emphasize text on the slide; display slide thumbnails; and zoom in on elements of a slide. You can also display the Slide Show Help dialog box, shown in Figure 1.3, which describes all the navigation options available while running a slide show. Display this dialog box by clicking the More slide show options button on the Slide Show toolbar and then clicking *Help*.

**4**   Click the Next button (displays with a right arrow) on the Slide Show toolbar to display the next slide (Slide 2).

**5**   Display the previous slide (Slide 1) by right-clicking anywhere in the slide and then clicking *Previous* at the shortcut menu.

> Right-clicking displays the shortcut menu with a variety of options including options to display the previous or next slide.

**Figure 1.3** Slide Show Help Dialog Box

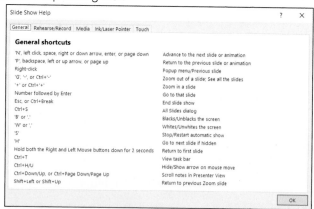

6. Display Slide 4 by pressing the number 4 key and then pressing the Enter key.

   Move to any slide in a presentation by typing the slide number and then pressing the Enter key.

7. Change to a black screen by pressing the letter B key.

   When you press the letter B key, the slide is removed from the screen and the screen displays black. This might be useful in a situation where you want to discuss something with your audience that is unrelated to the slide.

8. Return to Slide 4 by pressing the letter B key.

   Pressing the letter B key switches between the slide and a black screen. Press the letter W key if you want to switch between the slide and a white screen.

9. Zoom in on the bulleted items in Slide 4 by clicking the Zoom into the slide button (displays as a magnifying glass) on the Slide Show toolbar, hovering the magnification area over the bulleted items, and then clicking the left mouse button.

10. Right-click on the screen to display Slide 4 without magnification.

11. Display thumbnails of all the slides in the presentation while viewing the slide show by clicking the See all slides button on the Slide Show toolbar.

12. Click the Slide 3 thumbnail on the screen.

    This displays Slide 3 in the slide show.

13. Click the left mouse button to display Slide 4. Continue clicking the left mouse button until a black screen displays. At the black screen, click the left mouse button again.

    This returns the presentation to the Normal view.

14. Make Slide 1 active.

15. Display Slide 2 by clicking the Next Slide button at the bottom of the vertical scroll bar.

16. Click the From Current Slide button 🖥 in the Start Slide Show group on the Slide Show tab.

    Clicking this button begins the slide show with the active slide.

17. Run the slide show by clicking the left mouse button at each slide until Slide 5 is active (contains the title *Production Schedule*).

**18** Move the mouse to display the Slide Show toolbar, click the Pen button, and then click *Laser Pointer*.

> This turns the mouse pointer into a red, hollow, glowing circle.

**19** Practice moving the laser pointer around the screen.

**20** Click the Pen button on the Slide Show toolbar and then click *Pen*.

> This turns the mouse pointer into a small circle.

**21** Click and hold down the left mouse button and draw a circle around the text *Location Shoots*.

**22** Using the mouse, draw a line below *Dubbing*.

**23** Erase the pen markings by clicking the Pen button on the Slide Show toolbar and then clicking *Erase All Ink on Slide*.

**24** Change the color of the ink by clicking the Pen button and then clicking the *Blue* color (ninth color option).

**25** Using the mouse, draw a blue line below the word *Music*.

**26** Return the mouse pointer back to an arrow by pressing the Esc key.

**27** Click the left mouse button to advance to Slide 6.

**28** Click the Pen button and then click *Highlighter*.

**29** Using the mouse, drag through the words *Studio Shoots*.

**30** Using the mouse, drag through the words *Location Shoots*.

**31** Return the mouse pointer back to an arrow by pressing the Esc key.

**32** Press the Esc key on the keyboard to end the slide show without viewing the remaining slides. At the message asking if you want to keep your ink annotations, click the Discard button.

**In Brief**

**Run Slide Show**
Click Start From
Beginning button on
Quick Access Toolbar.
OR
1. Click Slide Show tab.
2. Click From Beginning
   button or From
   Current Slide button.
OR
Click Slide Show button
on Status bar.

**Use Pen Tool When
Running Slide Show**
1. Run slide show.
2. Move mouse.
3. Click Pen button on
   Slide Show toolbar.
4. Click *Pen* option.
5. Draw in slide with pen.

**Use Ink Tools**
1. Click Review tab.
2. Click Start Inking
   button.
3. Draw or highlight on
   slide using pen or
   highlighter options.
4. Click Stop Inking
   button.

**33** With Slide 6 displayed in Normal view, draw a circle around text to display when running a slide show. Begin by clicking the Review tab and then clicking the Start Inking button  in the Ink group.

> The Ink Tools Pens tab will display with options for writing or highlighting on a slide. This feature is particularly useful for tablets. The mouse pointer will display as a small circle. If the Review tab does not contain the Start Inking tool, remove the Draw tab from the ribbon. To do this, click the File tab and then click *Options*. At the PowerPoint Options dialog box, click the *Customize Ribbon* option in the left panel. Click the *Draw* check box in the list box at the right to remove the check mark and then click OK to close the dialog box.

**34** Click the *Dark Green Pen (0.35 mm)* option in the Pens gallery (fourth column, first row).

**35** Using the mouse, draw a rectangle around the text *Studio Shoots*.

> If you are not satisfied with the appearance of the rectangle, click the Undo button on the Quick Access Toolbar, and then draw the rectangle again.

**36** Click the *Aqua Highlighter (4.0 mm)* option in the Pens gallery (seventh column, first row).

**37** Using the mouse, drag through the words *Los Angeles Studio*.

**38** Click the Stop Inking button ⊠ in the Close group to turn off the inking feature.

**39** Click the Slide Show button in the view area on the Status bar.

**40** Notice that the green rectangle and aqua highlighting display on the slide and then press the Esc key to return the presentation to Normal view.

**41** Save **1-MPProdMtg**.

> **Check Your Work** Compare your work to the model answer available in the online course.

---

# In Addition

### Hiding and Displaying the Mouse Pointer

When running a slide show, the mouse pointer is set, by default, to be hidden after three seconds of inactivity. The mouse pointer will appear again when the mouse is moved. Change this default setting by clicking the More slide show options button on the Slide Show toolbar, clicking *Arrow Options*, and then clicking *Visible* if the mouse pointer should always be visible or *Hidden* if the mouse pointer should not display at all when running the slide show. The *Automatic* option is the default setting.

### Viewing in Presenter View

When running a slide show using two monitors, the presentation can display in Presenter view on one of the monitors. Use this view to control the slide show. For example, in Presenter view speaker notes are visible, all the Slide Show toolbar options are available, and slides can be advanced and slide timings can be set. Press Alt + F5 to display the presentation in Presenter view.

A variety of transitions and transition sounds can be applied to a presentation. When running a presentation, a transition is how one slide is removed from the screen and the next slide is displayed. Interesting transitions such as fades, dissolves, push, cover, wipes, stripes, and bar can add interest to your presentation. In addition to a transition, a transition sound can be applied that will play as one slide is removed from the screen and the next slide is displayed. Add transitions and transition sounds with options on the Transitions tab.

**MARQUEE PRODUCTIONS**

**What You Will Do**   You have decided to enhance the movie production meeting presentation by adding transitions and transition sound to the slides.

 Tutorial

Adding Slide Transitions

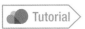 Tutorial

Adding Sound to Slide Transitions

1. With **1-MPProdMtg** open, click Slide 1 in the slide thumbnails pane and then click the Transitions tab.

2. Click the More Transitions button in the gallery in the Transition to This Slide group.

3. Click the *Ripple* option in the *Exciting* section at the drop-down list.

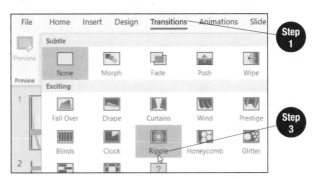

4. Click the Effect Options button in the Transition to This Slide group and then click *From Top-Left* at the drop-down list.

   The effect options change depending on the transition selected.

5. Click the *Sound* option box arrow in the Timing group.

6. Click the *Breeze* option at the drop-down list.

**In Brief**

**Add Transition to All Slides in Presentation**
1. Click Transitions tab.
2. Click More Transitions button in gallery in Transition to This Slide group.
3. Click transition.
4. Click Apply To All button.

**Add Transition Sound to All Slides in Presentation**
1. Click Transitions tab.
2. Click *Sound* option box arrow.
3. Click sound option.
4. Click Apply To All button.

**7** Apply three seconds to each slide transition by clicking in the *Duration* measurement box, typing 3, and then pressing the Enter key.

**8** Click the Apply To All button  in the Timing group.

> Notice that Play Animations star icons display below the slide numbers in the slide thumbnails pane.

**9** Click the Slide 1 thumbnail in the slide thumbnails pane.

**10** Run the slide show by clicking the Slide Show button in the view area on the Status bar.

**11** Click the left mouse button to advance each slide.

**12** At the black screen after the last slide, click the left mouse button again to return the presentation to the Normal view.

**13** Click the More Transitions button in the gallery in the Transition to This Slide group.

**14** Click the *Curtains* option in the *Exciting* section of the drop-down list.

**15** Click the *Sound* option box arrow and then click *Whoosh* at the drop-down list.

**16** Click the *Duration* measurement box down arrow until *02.50* displays.

**17** Click the Apply To All button in the Timing group.

**18** With Slide 1 active, run the slide show.

**19** Save **1-MPProdMtg**.

---

## In Addition

### Running a Slide Show Automatically

Slides in a slide show can be advanced automatically after a specific number of seconds by inserting a check mark in the *After* check box in the Timing group and removing the check mark from the *On Mouse Click* check box. Change the time in the *After* measurement box by clicking the *After* measurement box up or down arrow or by selecting the number in the measurement box and then typing the specific time. If the transition time should affect all slides in the presentation, click the Apply To All button. In Slide Sorter view, the transition time displays below each affected slide. Click the Slide Show button to run the slide show. The first slide displays for the specified amount of time and then the next slide automatically displays.

A presentation can be printed with each slide on a separate piece of paper; each slide at the top of the page, leaving the bottom of the page for notes; up to nine slides or a specific number of slides on a single piece of paper; or the slide titles and topics in outline form. Before printing a presentation, consider previewing it. Choose print options and display a preview of the presentation at the Print backstage area. Display this view by clicking the File tab and then clicking the *Print* option. Click the Back button or press the Esc key to exit the backstage area without choosing an option.

**What You Will Do** Staff members need the movie production meeting slides printed as handouts and as an outline. You will preview and print the presentation in various formats.

Previewing Slides and Printing

**1** With **1-MPProdMtg** open, display Slide 1 in the slide pane.

**2** Click the File tab and then click the *Print* option.

> Slide 1 of the presentation displays at the right side of the screen as it will when printed. Use the Next Page button (right-pointing arrow) below and at the left of the slide to view the next slide in the presentation, click the Previous Page button (left-pointing arrow) to display the previous slide in the presentation, use the Zoom slider bar to increase or decrease the size of the slide, and click the Zoom to Page button to fit the slide in the preview area in the Print backstage area. The left of the Print backstage area displays the Print button and *Copies* measurement box along with two categories—*Printer* and *Settings*. Click the Print button to send the presentation to the printer. Specify the number of copies to print with the *Copies* measurement box. Use the *Printer* gallery to specify the printer. The *Settings* category contains a number of galleries that describe how the slides will print.

**3** Click the Next Page button below and at the left of the preview slide to display the next slide in the presentation.

> This displays Slide 2 in the preview area.

**4** Click the Zoom In button ⊞ at the right of the Zoom slider bar two times.

> Click the Zoom In button to increase the size of the slide or click the Zoom Out button (displays with a minus symbol) to decrease the size of the slide.

**5** Click the Zoom to Page button ⊕ at the right of the Zoom slider bar.

> Click the Zoom to Page button to fit the entire slide in the viewing area in the Print backstage area.

**6** You decide to print the slides on two pages and you want to preview how the slides will display on the pages. To do this, click the second gallery in the *Settings* category (contains the text *Full Page Slides*) and then click *4 Slides Horizontal* in the *Handouts* section.

Notice how four slides display on the preview page.

**7** Click the Print button at the top of the Print backstage area.

**8** You want to print all slide text on one page to use as a reference during your presentation. To do this, click the File tab and then click the *Print* option.

**9** At the Print backstage area, click the second gallery in the *Settings* category (contains the text *4 Slides Horizontal*) and then click *Outline* in the *Print Layout* section.

**10** Click the Print button at the top of the Print backstage area.

With the *Outline* option selected, the presentation prints on one page with slide numbers, slide icons, and slide text in outline form.

**11** You want to print only Slide 6. To do this, click the File tab and then click the *Print* option.

**12** At the Print backstage area, click the second gallery in the *Settings* category (contains the text *Outline*) and then click *Full Page Slides* in the *Print Layout* section.

**13** Click in the *Slides* text box below the first gallery in the *Settings* category, type 6, and then click the Print button.

**14** Save **1-MPProdMtg**.

**15** Close the presentation by clicking the File tab and then clicking the *Close* option.

 **Check Your Work** Compare your work to the model answer available in the online course.

## In Addition

### Using Options at the Slide Size Dialog Box

Change slide orientation with options at the Slide Size dialog box, shown at the right. Display this dialog box by clicking the Design tab, clicking the Slide Size button in the Customize group, and then clicking *Customize Slide Size* at the drop-down list. Use options at this dialog box to specify how slides should be sized; page width and height; orientation for slides; and orientation for notes, handouts, and outlines.

# Features Summary

| Feature | Ribbon Tab, Group | Button/Option | File Tab Option | Keyboard Shortcut |
|---------|-------------------|---------------|-----------------|-------------------|
| apply transitions and sound to all slides | Transitions, Timing | | | |
| close a presentation | | | *Close* | Ctrl + F4 |
| close PowerPoint | | ✕ | | |
| display Presenter view | | | | Alt + F5 |
| Help task pane | Help, Help | | | F1 |
| hide slide | Slide Show, Set Up | | | |
| ink tools | Review, Ink | | | |
| layout | Home, Slides | | | |
| new slide | Home, Slides OR Insert, Slides | | | Ctrl + M |
| Normal view | View, Presentation Views | | | |
| Notes Page view | View, Presentation Views | | | |
| Open backstage area | | | *Open* | Ctrl + O |
| open blank presentation | | | | Ctrl + N |
| Outline view | View, Presentation Views | | | |
| Print backstage area | | | *Print* | Ctrl + P |
| Reading view | View, Presentation Views | | | |
| run slide show from current slide | Slide Show, Start Slide Show | | | Shift + F5 |
| run slide show from Slide 1 | Slide Show, Start Slide Show | | | F5 |
| save | | 💾 | *Save* | Ctrl + S |
| Save As backstage area | | | *Save As* | |
| Slide Sorter view | View, Presentation Views | | | |
| spelling checker | Review, Proofing | abc | | F7 |
| themes | Design, Themes | | | |
| Thesaurus | Review, Proofing | | | Shift + F7 |
| transitions | Transitions, Transition to This Slide | | | |
| transition duration | Transitions, Timing | | | |
| transition sound | Transitions, Timing | | | |
| Zoom dialog box | View, Zoom | | | |

# Editing and Enhancing Slides

**Data Files**

Before beginning section work, copy the PowerPointS2 folder to your storage medium and then make PowerPointS2 the active folder.

## Skills

- Increase and decrease the indent of text
- Select, cut, copy, and paste text
- Apply font and font effects
- Find and replace fonts
- Apply formatting with Format Painter
- Change alignment and line and paragraph spacing

- Change the slide size and format design themes and slide background
- Insert, size, position, and format images
- Insert and format a screen clipping
- Insert and format a SmartArt graphic
- Apply animation to objects and text in a slide

## Projects Overview

Open an existing project presentation, save the presentation with a new name, and then edit and format the presentation. Open an existing annual meeting presentation for Marquee Productions and then save, edit, and format the presentation.

NIAGARA PENINSULA COLLEGE

Open an existing presentation for the Theatre Arts Division and then save, edit, and format the presentation.

FIRST CHOICE TRAVEL

Open an existing presentation on vacation specials and then save, edit, and format the presentation.

The Waterfront BISTRO

Prepare and format a presentation on the services offered by The Waterfront Bistro.

Performance Threads

Prepare and format a presentation on company structure, policies, and benefits.

Worldwide Enterprises

Prepare and format a presentation for a planning meeting of the distribution department.

The online course includes additional training and assessment resources.

# Increasing and Decreasing Indent; Cutting, Copying, and Pasting Text

Text that is formatted as a bulleted list in a slide can have multiple levels. Click the Decrease List Level button in the Paragraph group on the Home tab or press Shift + Tab to promote text to the previous level. Click the Increase List Level button or press the Tab key to demote text to the next level. Text levels can also be promoted (decrease the text indent) and/or text levels can be demoted (increase the text indent) in the slide in Outline view. Select text in a slide and then delete the text from the slide, cut text from one location and paste it into another, or copy and paste the text. Use buttons in the Clipboard group on the Home tab to cut, copy, and paste text.

**What You Will Do**   Chris Greenbaum, production manager for Marquee Productions, has prepared a documentary project presentation and has asked you to edit the presentation by increasing and decreasing text levels and selecting, deleting, moving, copying, and pasting text in slides.

Tutorial

Increasing and Decreasing Indent

Tutorial

Selecting Text

Tutorial

Cutting, Copying, and Pasting Text

1. Open **MPProj** from your PowerPointS2 folder and then save the presentation with the name **2-MPProj**.

2. Display Slide 5 in the slide pane.

3. You decide to promote the names below *Script Authors* so that they display as second-level bullets. To do this, position the mouse pointer immediately left of the *D* in *Dana*, click the left mouse button, and then click the Decrease List Level button in the Paragraph group on the Home tab.

> Clicking the Decrease List Level button will promote text to the previous tab position, while clicking the Increase List Level button will demote text to the next tab position.

4. Position the insertion point immediately left of the *K* in *Karl* in Slide 5 and then promote the text to the previous level by pressing Shift + Tab.

5. Demote two of the names below *Script Consultants*. Begin by clicking immediately left of the *J* in *Jaime* and then clicking the Increase List Level button in the Paragraph group on the Home tab.

6. Position the insertion point immediately left of the *G* in *Genaro* and then press the Tab key.

7. Display Slide 6 in the slide pane.

**Decrease Text Level Indent**
Click Decrease List Level button or press Shift + Tab.

**Increase Text Level Indent**
Click Increase List Level button or press Tab.

**Cut and Paste Text**
1. Select text.
2. Click Cut button.
3. Position insertion point.
4. Click Paste button.

**Copy and Paste Text**
1. Select text.
2. Click Copy button.
3. Position insertion point.
4. Click Paste button.

**8** Position the mouse pointer on the bullet before *Script Rewriting* until the mouse pointer turns into a four-headed arrow and then click the left mouse button.

> This selects the text *Script Rewriting* and displays the Mini toolbar, which provides easy access to formatting options and buttons. Refer to the In Addition for additional information on selecting text.

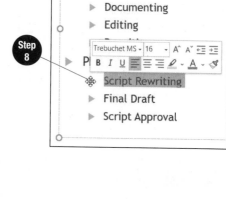

**9** Press the Delete key.

> This deletes the selected text.

**10** Display Slide 5 in the slide pane.

**11** Position the mouse pointer on the bullet before *Genaro Dufoe* until the mouse pointer turns into a four-headed arrow and then click the left mouse button.

**12** Click the Cut button ✂ in the Clipboard group on the Home tab.

> The keyboard shortcut to cut text is Ctrl + X.

**13** Position the mouse pointer immediately left of the *A* in *Allan Herron*, click the left mouse button, and then click the Paste button 📋 in the Clipboard group.

> The keyboard shortcut to paste text is Ctrl + V.

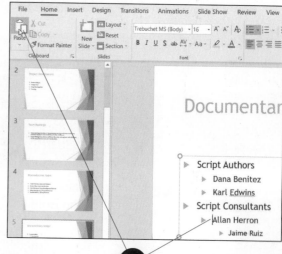

**14** Using the mouse, drag to select the text *Script Authors* and then click the Copy button 📋 in the Clipboard group.

> The keyboard shortcut to copy text is Ctrl + C.

**15** Make Slide 2 active, position the insertion point immediately left of the *S* in *Scouting*, and then click the Paste button in the Clipboard group.

> If *Script Authors* and *Scouting* display on the same line, press the Enter key.

**16** Save **2-MPProj**.

**Check Your Work** Compare your work to the model answer available in the online course.

# In Addition

## Selecting Text

| To select | Perform this action |
|---|---|
| entire word | Double-click word. |
| entire paragraph | Triple-click in paragraph. |
| text mouse pointer passes through | Click and drag with mouse. |
| all text in selected object box | Click Select button in Editing group and then click Select All; or press Ctrl + A. |

The Font group on the Home tab contains two rows of options and buttons. The top row contains options and buttons for changing the font and font size and a button for clearing formatting. The bottom row contains buttons for applying font effects such as bold, italics, underlining, text shadow, strikethrough, and character spacing, as well as buttons for changing the case and/or font color of selected text.

**What You Will Do**  Certain text elements on slides in the documentary project presentation need to be highlighted to make them stand out. You decide to apply font effects to and change the font size of specific text.

Applying Font Formatting

**1**  With **2-MPProj** open, display Slide 1 in the slide pane.

**2**  Select the title *Marquee Productions* and then click the Italic button $I$ in the Font group on the Home tab.

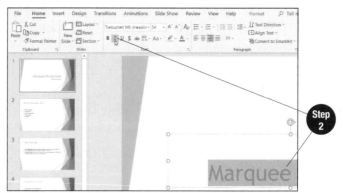

**3**  Select the subtitle *Documentary Project*, click the Increase Font Size button $A^{\wedge}$, and then click the Bold button $B$ in the Font group.

**4**  Make Slide 6 active in the slide pane, select the text *Phase 1*, and then click the Underline button $U$ in the Font group.

**5**  Select and then underline the text *Phase 2*.

**6**  Select and then underline the text *Phase 3*.

**7**  Make Slide 1 active.

**8** Select the title *Marquee Productions*, click the *Font* option box arrow in the Font group, scroll down the drop-down gallery (fonts display in alphabetical order), and then click *Cambria*.

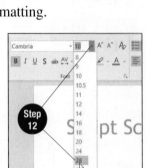

**9** Select the subtitle *Documentary Project*, click the *Font* option box arrow, and then click *Cambria* at the drop-down gallery.

> The drop-down gallery displays the most recently used fonts at the top of the gallery.

**10** Make Slide 6 active, select the text *Phase 1*, click the Underline button to remove underlining, and then click the Bold button to apply bold formatting.

**11** With *Phase 1* still selected, click *Trebuchet MS* in the *Font* option box, type cam, and then press the Enter key.

> An alternative method for selecting a font is to type the first few letters of the font name in the *Font* option box until the entire font name displays and then press the Enter key.

**12** Click the *Font Size* option box arrow and then click *28*.

**13** Select the text *Phase 2*, remove the underlining, apply bold formatting, change the font to Cambria, and then change the font size to 28 points.

**14** Select the text *Phase 3*, remove the underlining, apply bold formatting, change the font to Cambria, and then change the font size to 28 points.

**15** Print Slides 1 and 6. Begin by clicking the File tab and then clicking the *Print* option.

**16** At the Print backstage area, click in the *Slides* text box (below the first gallery in the *Settings* category) and then type 1,6.

**17** Click the second gallery in the *Settings* category (contains the text *Full Page Slides*) and then click *2 Slides* in the *Handouts* section of the drop-down list.

**18** Click the Print button.

> The two slides print on the same page.

**19** Save **2-MPProj**.

 Check Your Work  Compare your work to the model answer available in the online course.

## In Addition

### Choosing Fonts

A typeface is a set of characters with a common design and shape. PowerPoint refers to a typeface as a *font*. Fonts can be decorative or plain and are either monospaced or proportional. A monospaced font allots the same amount of horizontal space for each character, while a proportional font allots a different amount of space for each character. Fonts are divided into two main categories: serif and sans serif. A serif is a small line at the end of a character stroke. Consider using a serif font for text-intensive slides, because the serifs can help move the reader's eyes across the text. Use a sans serif font for titles, subtitles, headings, and short lines of text.

In addition to options and buttons in the Font group on the Home tab, font formatting can be applied with options at the Font dialog box. Use options at this dialog box to change the font, as well as its style and size; change the font color; and apply formatting effects such as underline, strikethrough, superscript, subscript, small caps, and all caps. To change the font for all slides in a presentation, use the Replace Font dialog box to replace all occurrences of a specific font in the presentation.

**What You Will Do** You are still not satisfied with the fonts in the documentary project presentation, so you decide to change the font for the title and subtitle and replace the Trebuchet MS font on the remaining slides.

Tutorial

Applying Font Formatting at the Font Dialog Box

Tutorial

Replacing Fonts

① With **2-MPProj** open, make Slide 1 active.

② Select the title *Marquee Productions*.

③ Display the Font dialog box by clicking the Font group dialog box launcher 🔲 on the Home tab.

④ At the Font dialog box, click the *Latin text font* option box arrow and then click *Candara* at the drop-down list.

⑤ Select the current measurement in the *Size* measurement box and then type 60.

⑥ Click the Font color button in the *All text* section and then click the *Blue, Accent 2, Darker 25%* option (sixth column, fifth row in the *Theme Colors* section).

⑦ Click OK to close the Font dialog box.

### In Brief

**Change Font at Font Dialog Box**
1. Select text.
2. Click Font group dialog box launcher.
3. Click options at Font dialog box.
4. Click OK.

**Change All Occurrences of Font**
1. Click Replace button arrow.
2. Click *Replace Fonts*.
3. Make sure appropriate font displays in *Replace* text box.
4. Press Tab.
5. Click *With* option box arrow.
6. Click new font.
7. Click Replace button.
8. Click Close button.

**8** Select the subtitle *Documentary Project*.

**9** Click the Font group dialog box launcher.

**10** At the Font dialog box, click the *Latin text font* option box arrow and then click *Candara* at the drop-down list.

**11** Click the *Font style* option box arrow and then click *Bold Italic* at the drop-down list.

**12** Select the current measurement in the *Size* measurement box and then type *30*.

**13** Click the Font color button in the *All text* section and then click the *Turquoise, Accent 1* color option (fifth column, first row in the *Theme Colors* section).

**14** Click OK to close the Font dialog box.

**15** Make Slide 2 active.

**16** You decide to replace all occurrences of the Trebuchet MS font in the presentation with the Cambria font. To begin, click the Replace button arrow  in the Editing group on the Home tab and then click *Replace Fonts* at the drop-down list.

**17** At the Replace Font dialog box, click the *Replace* option box arrow and then click *Trebuchet MS* at the drop-down list.

**18** Click the *With* option box arrow, scroll down the drop-down list and then click *Cambria*.

**19** Click the Replace button and then click the Close button.

**20** Save **2-MPProj**.

Step 10  Step 11  Step 12
Step 13  Step 14
Step 17  Step 19  Step 18

Check Your Work  Compare your work to the model answer available in the online course.

---

## In Addition

### Choosing Fonts

Choose a font for a presentation based on the tone and message the presentation should convey. For example, choose a more serious font such as Constantia or Cambria for a conservative audience and choose a less formal font such as Comic Sans MS, Lucida Handwriting, or Mistral for a more informal or lighthearted audience. For text-intensive slides, choose a serif font such as Cambria, Constantia, Garamond, or Bookman Old Style. For titles, subtitles, headings, and short text items, consider a sans serif font such as Calibri, Candara, Arial, or Trebuchet MS. Use no more than two or three different fonts in each presentation. To ensure text readability in a slide, choose a font color that contrasts with the slide background.

Use the Format Painter feature to apply the same formatting in more than one location in a slide or slides. To use Format Painter, apply formatting to text, position the insertion point anywhere in the formatted text, and then double-click the Format Painter button in the Clipboard group on the Home tab. Using the mouse, select the additional text to which the formatting is to be applied. After applying the formatting in the specific locations, click the Format Painter button to deactivate it. If formatting is to be applied in only one other location, click the Format Painter button just once. The first time text is clicked or text is selected, the formatting will be applied and the Format Painter button will be deactivated.

**What You Will Do**   Improve the appearance of slides in the documentary project presentation by applying a font and then using Format Painter to apply the formatting to other text.

Formatting with
Format Painter

1. With **2-MPProj** open, make sure Slide 2 is active.

2. Select the title *Project Development*.

3. Click the Font group dialog box launcher.

4. At the Font dialog box, click in the *Latin text font* option box, type can, and then press the Tab key.

   As you type letters, fonts that match the letters display in the option box.

5. Click the *Font style* option box arrow and then click *Bold Italic* at the drop-down list.

6. Select the current measurement in the *Size* measurement box and then type 40.

7. Click the Font color button in the *All text* section and then click the *Blue, Accent 2, Darker 25%* color option (sixth column, fifth row in the *Theme Colors* section).

8. Click OK to close the Font dialog box.

9. Deselect the text by clicking in the slide in the slide pane.

**In Brief**

**Format with Format Painter**
1. Click in formatted text.
2. Double-click Format Painter button.
3. Click in or select text to be formatted.
4. Click Format Painter button.

**10** Click in the title *Project Development*.

**11** Double-click the Format Painter button  in the Clipboard group on the Home tab.

**12** Click the Next Slide button to display Slide 3.

**13** Triple-click *Team Meetings* to select the title.

> The mouse pointer displays with a paintbrush attached. This indicates that Format Painter is active. You can also apply the formatting by clicking individual words in the title, but doing so will not format the spaces within titles that consist of more than one word. If the paintbrush is no longer attached to the mouse pointer, Format Painter has been turned off. Turn it back on by clicking in a slide title with the desired formatting and then double-clicking the Format Painter button.

**14** Click the Next Slide button to display Slide 4.

**15** Using the mouse, select the title *Preproduction Team*.

**16** Apply formatting to the titles in the remaining three slides.

**17** When formatting has been applied to all slide titles, click the Format Painter button in the Clipboard group on the Home tab.

> Clicking the Format Painter button turns off the feature.

**18** Save **2-MPProj**.

> **Check Your Work** Compare your work to the model answer available in the online course.

## In Addition

### Choosing a Custom Color

Click the Font color button at the Font dialog box and a palette of color choices displays. Click the *More Colors* option and the Colors dialog box displays with the Standard tab selected, showing a honeycomb of color options. Click the Custom tab and the dialog box displays as shown at the right. Use options on this tab to mix your own color. Click a color in the *Colors* palette or enter the values for the color in the *Red*, *Green*, and *Blue* measurement boxes. Adjust the luminosity of the current color by dragging the slider at the right side of the color palette.

The slide design theme generally determines the horizontal and vertical alignment of text in placeholders. Text may be left-aligned, center-aligned, right-aligned, or justified in a place-holder as well as aligned at the top, middle, or bottom of the placeholder. Change align-ment for specific text with buttons in the Paragraph group on the Home tab or with options from the Align Text button drop-down gallery. Use options at the Line Spacing button drop-down gallery or the *Line Spacing* option at the Paragraph dialog box to change line spac-ing. The Paragraph dialog box also contains options for changing text alignment and inden-tation as well as spacing before and after text.

**What You Will Do** Change the alignment and improve the appearance of specific text in slides by adjusting the vertical alignment and paragraph spacing of text.

Tutorial

Changing Alignment

Tutorial

Changing Line Spacing

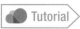

Tutorial

Changing Paragraph Spacing

**1** With **2-MPProj** open, make Slide 1 active.

**2** Click in the text *Marquee Productions* and then click the Center button ☰ in the Paragraph group on the Home tab.

> You can also change text alignment with the keyboard shortcuts shown in Table 2.1.

**3** Click in the text *Documentary Project* and then click the Center button.

**4** Make Slide 3 active (contains the title *Team Meetings*), click in the bulleted text, and then press Ctrl + A to select all of the bulleted text.

> Ctrl + A is the keyboard shortcut for selecting all text in a placeholder.

**5** Justify the text by clicking the Justify button ☰ in the Paragraph group.

**6** Click the Align Text button ⊞ in the Paragraph group and then click *Middle* at the drop-down gallery.

> This aligns the bulleted text vertically in the middle of the placeholder.

**7** With the bulleted text still selected, click the Line Spacing button ↕☰ ⌄ in the Paragraph group and then click *Line Spacing Options* at the drop-down gallery.

**8** At the Paragraph dialog box, click the *After* measurement box up arrow two times.

> This inserts *12 pt* in the *After* measurement box.

**9** Click OK to close the dialog box.

**10** Make Slide 4 active (contains the title *Preproduction Team*).

**11** Click in the bulleted text and then select all of the bulleted text by clicking the Select button in the Editing group on the Home tab and then clicking *Select All* at the drop-down list.

**12** Click the Line Spacing button in the Paragraph group and then click *1.5* at the drop-down gallery.

**13** Make Slide 7 active (contains the title *Preproduction Assignments*).

**14** Click in the bulleted text and then press Ctrl + A.

**15** Click the Line Spacing button in the Paragraph group and then click *Line Spacing Options* at the drop-down gallery.

**16** At the Paragraph dialog box, click the *After* measurement box up arrow two times.

> This inserts *12 pt* in the *After* measurement box.

**17** Click OK to close the dialog box.

**18** Print only Slide 1 of the presentation as a handout.

**19** Save **2-MPProj**.

**Table 2.1** Alignment Keyboard Shortcuts

| Alignment | Keyboard Shortcut |
|-----------|-------------------|
| left | Ctrl + L |
| center | Ctrl + E |
| right | Ctrl + R |
| justify | Ctrl + J |

**Check Your Work** Compare your work to the model answer available in the online course.

## In Addition

### Inserting a New Line

When creating bulleted text in a slide, pressing the Enter key causes the insertion point to move to the next line, inserting another bullet. Situations may occur where a blank line should be inserted between bulleted items without creating another bullet. One method for doing this is to use the New Line command, Shift + Enter. Pressing Shift + Enter inserts a new line that is considered part of the previous paragraph. Press the Enter key to continue the bulleted list.

By default, the slide size in PowerPoint is Widescreen (16:9), but slide size can be changed with options in the Slide Size button drop-down list in the Customize group on the Design tab. Change the design theme applied to slides in a presentation or change the color, font, or effects of a theme with options on the Design tab. Format the slide background with options in the Format Background task pane. Display this task pane by clicking the Format Background button in the Customize group on the Design tab.

**What You Will Do**   You are not pleased with the design theme for the documentary project presentation and decide to apply a different theme and then change the colors and fonts for the theme.

Changing Slide Size

Modifying Design Themes

Formatting the Slide Background

**1** With **2-MPProj** open, click the Design tab.

**2** Click the Slide Size button ⬚ in the Customize group and then click *Standard (4:3)* at the drop-down list.

**3** At the Microsoft PowerPoint dialog box, click the Maximize button.

> Click the Maximize button to maximize the size of the content on the new slide. Click the Ensure Fit button to scale down the contents of the slide to fit on the new slide.

**4** Run the slide show beginning with Slide 1 and notice any changes to the layout of the slides.

**5** Click the Slide Size button and then click *Custom Slide Size* at the drop-down list.

**6** At the Slide Size dialog box, click the *Slides sized for* option box arrow and then click *Widescreen* at the drop-down list.

**7** Click OK.

**8** Click the More Themes button in the Themes group.

**9** Click *Dividend* at the drop-down gallery.

**10** Click the More Variants button in the Variants group.

**11** Point to *Colors* and then click *Yellow Orange* at the side menu.

**In Brief**

**Change Slide Size**
1. Click Design tab.
2. Click Slide Size button.
3. Click slide size.

**Change Design Theme**
1. Click Design tab.
2. Click More Themes button.
3. Click theme.

**Change Theme Colors**
1. Click Design tab.
2. Click More Variants button.
3. Point to *Colors*.
4. Click option.

**Change Theme Fonts**
1. Click Design tab.
2. Click More Variants button.
3. Point to *Fonts*.
4. Click option.

**Format Slide Background**
1. Click Design tab.
2. Click Format Background button.
3. Make changes in task pane.

**12** Make Slide 2 active.

**13** Click the More Variants button in the Variants group.

**14** Point to *Fonts*, scroll down the side menu, and then click *Cambria*.

**15** Apply a background style by clicking the More Variants button in the Variants group, pointing to *Background Styles*, and then clicking *Style 9* at the side menu (first column, third row).

**16** Run the slide show beginning with Slide 1.

**17** Customize the background by clicking the Format Background button  in the Customize group on the Design tab.

> This displays the Format Background task pane with a number of options for customizing slide backgrounds.

**18** At the Format Background task pane, if necessary, click *Fill* to display fill options.

**19** Click the *Solid fill* option, click the Color button, and then click the *Light Yellow, Background 2* color option (third column, first row in the *Theme Colors* section).

**20** Click the Apply to All button at the bottom of the task pane.

**21** Close the task pane by clicking the close button in the upper right corner.

**22** Save **2-MPProj** and then print Slide 1 of the presentation.

**Check Your Work** Compare your work to the model answer available in the online course.

# In Addition

## Inserting an Image as a Slide Background

Insert an image as the background of an entire slide by clicking the Design tab and then clicking the Format Background button in the Customize group. At the Format Background task pane, click *Fill* to display fill options, and then click the *Picture or texture fill* option.

Click the File button in the *Insert picture from* section, navigate to the folder containing the image, and then double-click the image. The image will automatically be inserted as the current slide's background.

Add visual interest to a presentation by inserting an image such as a logo, picture, or clip art in a slide. Insert an image from a drive or folder with the Insert Picture dialog box. Display the Insert Picture dialog box by clicking the Pictures button on the Insert tab or clicking the picture image in the content placeholder. At this dialog box, navigate to the drive or folder containing the image and then double-click the image. The image is inserted in the slide and the Picture Tools Format tab is selected. Use buttons on the Picture Tools Format tab to recolor the image, apply a picture style, arrange the image in the slide, and size the image. An image can also be sized using the sizing handles that display around the selected image and an image can be positioned using the mouse.

**What You Will Do** Chris Greenbaum has asked you to insert the company logo on the first slide of the presentation and insert and format an image on a new slide at the end of the presentation.

Inserting, Sizing, and Positioning an Image

Formatting an Image

① With **2-MPProj** open, make sure Slide 1 is active.

② Click in the title *Marquee Productions*, click the title placeholder border (border turns into a solid line when selected), and then press the Delete key.

> The title text will be deleted but the placeholder will not.

③ Delete the title placeholder by clicking the title placeholder border again and then pressing the Delete key.

④ Complete steps similar to those in Steps 2 and 3 to delete the subtitle text and placeholder.

⑤ Insert the company logo in the slide as shown in Figure 2.1. To begin, click the Insert tab and then click the Pictures button 🖾 in the Images group.

Step 5

⑥ At the Insert Picture dialog box, navigate to your PowerPointS2 folder and then double-click the *MPLogo* image file.

> The image is inserted in the slide, selection handles display around the image, and the Picture Tools Format tab is active. If the Design Ideas task pane displays at the right side of the screen, close the task pane by clicking the Close button in the upper right corner of the task pane.

⑦ Increase the size of the logo by clicking in the *Width* measurement box in the Size group, typing 6.5, and then pressing the Enter key.

> When you change the width of the logo, the height automatically adjusts to maintain the proportions of the logo. You can also size an image using the sizing handles that display around the selected image. Use the middle sizing handles to change the width of an image. Use the top and bottom handles to change the height, and use the corner sizing handles to adjust both the width and height of the image at the same time.

Step 7

**8** Move the logo so it is positioned as shown in Figure 2.1. To do this, position the mouse pointer on the image until the pointer displays with a four-headed arrow attached, click and hold down the left mouse button, drag the image to the position shown in the figure, and then release the mouse button.

**9** With the image selected, click the Color button in the Adjust group and then click the *Saturation 200%* option (fifth option in the *Color Saturation* section).

**10** Click the Corrections button in the Adjust group and then click the *Brightness: +20% Contrast: -40%* option (fourth column, first row in the *Brightness/Contrast* section).

**11** Click the *Drop Shadow Rectangle* option in the Picture Styles gallery (fourth option).

**12** Click the Picture Effects button in the Picture Styles group, point to *Glow*, and then click the *Glow: 5 point; Orange, Accent color 1* option (first column, first row in the *Glow Variations* section).

**13** Click outside the logo to deselect it.

**Figure 2.1** Slide 1

**14** Make Slide 7 active.

**15** Insert a new slide by clicking the New Slide button in the Slides group on the Home tab.

**16** Click in the *Click to add title* placeholder and then type Travel Arrangements.

**17** Click in the *Click to add text* placeholder and then type the bulleted text shown in Figure 2.2.

**18** Click the Insert tab and then click the Pictures button in the Images group.

**19** At the Insert Picture dialog box, navigate to your PowerPointS2 folder and then double-click the *Airport* image file.

**20** Click in the *Height* measurement box in the Size group on the Picture Tools Format tab, type 3.5, and then press the Enter key.

> When you change the height measurement, the width measurement changes automatically to maintain the proportions of the image.

**21** Using the mouse, drag the image so it is positioned as shown in Figure 2.2.

**22** Click the Color button in the Adjust group on the Picture Tools Format tab and then click the *Brown, Accent color 2 Light* option (third column, third row in the *Recolor* section).

Step 22

**23** Click the Corrections button in the Adjust group and then click the *Brightness: 0% (Normal) Contrast: +40%* option (third column, fifth row in the *Brightness/ Contrast* section).

**24** Click the Picture Effects button in the Picture Styles group, point to *Shadow*, and then click the *Offset: Top Right* option (first column, third row in the *Outer* section).

Step 24

**In Brief**

**Insert Image**
1. Click Insert tab.
2. Click Pictures button.
3. At Insert Picture dialog box, navigate to folder.
4. Double-click image file.

**25** Click the Rotate button  in the Arrange group and then click *Flip Horizontal* at the drop-down gallery.

**26** Make Slide 7 active and then click the Home tab.

**27** Click in the title *PREPRODUCTION ASSIGNMENTS* and then click the Format Painter button in the Clipboard group.

**28** Make Slide 8 active and then select the entire title *TRAVEL ARRANGEMENTS*.

This applies 40-point Candara bold italic formatting in a brown accent color.

**29** Save **2-MPProj**.

**Figure 2.2** Slide 8

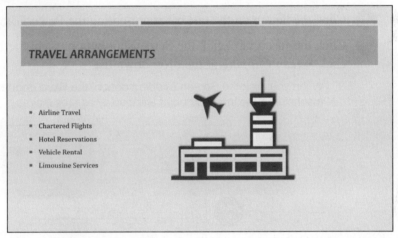

Check Your Work  Compare your work to the model answer available in the online course.

# In Addition

## Formatting with Buttons and Options on the Picture Tools Format Tab

Format images in a slide with buttons and options on the Picture Tools Format tab. Use buttons in the Adjust group to adjust the brightness and contrast of the image; change the image color or change to a different image; reset the image to its original size, position, and color; and compress the image. (Compress an image to reduce the resolution or discard extra information to save room on a hard drive or to reduce download time.) Use buttons in the Picture Styles group to apply a predesigned style, insert a picture border, or apply a picture effect. The Arrange group contains buttons for positioning the image and aligning and rotating the image. Use options in the Size group to crop the image and specify the height and width of the image.

## Inserting an Online Image

Click the Online Pictures button on the Insert tab and the Online Pictures window displays. Use options in this window to search for images using Bing. At the window, click a category or type a category in the search text box and then press the Enter key. In the list of images, double-click the desired image. The image is inserted in the slide and the Picture Tools Format tab is active.

The Images group on the Insert tab contains the Screenshot button, which can be used to capture all or part of the contents of a screen as an image. Format a screenshot with options on the Picture Tools Format tab.

**What You Will Do**   Chris Greenbaum has asked you to include a screen clipping of the title page of a script document in a slide.

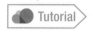

Inserting and Formatting Screenshot and Screen Clipping Images

**1** With **2-MPProj** open, make Slide 6 active.

**2** Insert a screenshot image from a Word document into the slide. Begin by opening Word and then opening **MPScript** from your PowerPointS2 folder.

> Make sure 2-MPProj and MPScript are the only open files.

**3** Click the Zoom Out button at the left of the Zoom slider bar until *50%* displays at the right of the slider bar.

**4** Click the button on the taskbar representing the PowerPoint presentation **2-MPProj**.

**5** Click the Insert tab, click the Screenshot button in the Images group, and then click *Screen Clipping* at the drop-down list.

> When you click the *Screen Clipping* option, the Word document will display in a dimmed manner and the insertion point will display as crosshairs.

**6** With the Word document displayed in a dimmed manner, position the crosshairs in the top left corner of the Word document and then drag down and to the right to select the entire document.

> Once you have created a screenshot of the Word document, the image will be inserted into Slide 6 of 2-MPProj.

**7** With the screenshot selected, click in the *Shape Height* measurement box in the Size group on the Picture Tools Format tab, type *5*, and then press the Enter key.

**8** Click the Picture Border button arrow [✎] in the Picture Styles group and then click the *Orange, Accent 1* option at the drop-down list (fifth column, first row in the *Theme Colors* section).

**9** Position the screenshot in the slide as shown in Figure 2.3.

**10** Click the Word button on the taskbar, close the document, and then close Word.

If a message displays asking if you want to save changes made in the document, click the Don't Save button.

**11** Save **2-MPProj**.

**Figure 2.3** Slide 6

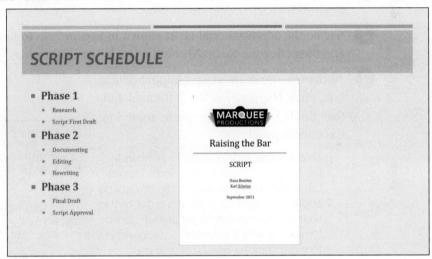

🔵 Check Your Work  Compare your work to the model answer available in the online course.

## In Addition

### Inserting a Screenshot

To capture the entire screen, open a file, click the Insert tab, click the Screenshot button in the Images group, and then click the screen thumbnail at the drop-down list. The currently active file does not display as a thumbnail at the drop-down list—only any other files that are open.

Use the SmartArt feature to create a variety of graphic diagrams, including process, cycle, relationship, matrix, and pyramid diagrams. SmartArt can also be used to visually illustrate hierarchical data in an organizational chart. To display a menu of SmartArt choices, click the Insert tab and then click the SmartArt button in the Illustrations group. This displays the Choose a SmartArt Graphic dialog box. At this dialog box, click the type of organization chart or graphic in the left panel and then double-click the graphic in the middle panel. This inserts the organizational chart or graphic in the slide. Some SmartArt graphics are designed to include text. Type text in a graphic shape by selecting the shape and then typing text in the shape. Use buttons on the SmartArt Tools Design tab and the SmartArt Tools Format tab to customize a graphic.

Tutorial

Inserting, Sizing, and Positioning SmartArt

Tutorial

Formatting SmartArt

**What You Will Do**   Chris Greenbaum has asked you to create a slide containing an organizational chart that illustrates the hierarchy of the people involved in production and a slide containing a SmartArt graphic of travel expenses.

**1**   With **2-MPProj** open, make Slide 2 active and then click the New Slide button in the Slides group on the Insert tab.

**2**   Create the organizational chart shown in Figure 2.4. To begin, click the Insert tab and then click the SmartArt button 📭 in the Illustrations group.

**3**   At the Choose a SmartArt Graphic dialog box, click *Hierarchy* in the left panel and then double-click the *Hierarchy* option in the middle panel.

> This displays the organizational chart in the slide with the SmartArt Tools Design tab active. Use buttons on this tab to add additional boxes, change the order of the shapes, choose a different layout, apply formatting with a SmartArt style, or reset the formatting of the organizational chart.

**4**   If a *Type your text here* window displays at the left of the organizational chart, close it by clicking the Text Pane button 🔲 in the Create Graphic group.

> You can also close the window by clicking the Close button in the upper right corner of the window.

**5**   Delete one of the boxes in the organizational chart. Begin by clicking the border of the second text box from the top at the left side of the chart.

> Make sure the box containing the *[Text]* placeholder is selected.

**6**   Press the Delete key.

**7**   With the second box from the top at the right selected, click the Add Shape button 🔲 in the Create Graphic group.

> This inserts a box to the right of the selected box.
> Your organizational chart should contain the same boxes shown in Figure 2.4. (The new box does not contain a *[Text]* placeholder, but you can still type text in the box.)

**8** Click the *[Text]* placeholder in the top box, type Chris Greenbaum, press the Enter key, and then type Production Manager. Click in each of the remaining boxes and type the text as shown in Figure 2.4.

**9** Click the Change Colors button 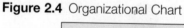 in the SmartArt Styles group on the SmartArt Tools Design tab and then click the *Colorful Range - Accent Colors 4 to 5* option (fourth option in the *Colorful* section).

**10** Click the More SmartArt Styles button at the right of the gallery in the SmartArt Styles group.

**11** Click the *Inset* option at the drop-down gallery (second option in the *3-D* section).

**12** Click the SmartArt Tools Format tab.

**13** Click inside the SmartArt graphic border but outside any shape.

**14** Click in the *Height* measurement box in the Size group, type 5, click in the *Width* measurement box, type 10, and then press the Enter key.

**15** Move the graphic so it is positioned in the slide as shown in Figure 2.4. Do this by positioning the mouse pointer on the graphic border until the pointer displays with a four-headed arrow attached, clicking and holding down the left mouse button, dragging the graphic to the specific location, and then releasing the mouse button.

**16** Click in the *CLICK TO ADD TITLE* placeholder and then type Team Structure.

**Figure 2.4** Organizational Chart

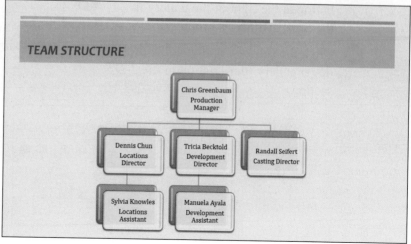

**17** Make Slide 2 active, click in the title *Project Development*, click the Home tab, and then click the Format Painter button in the Clipboard group.

**18** Make Slide 3 active and then select the entire title *Team Structure*.

**19** Make Slide 9 active.

**20** Click the New Slide button arrow in the Slides group on the Home tab and then click the *Blank* layout at the drop-down list.

**21** Create the SmartArt graphic shown in Figure 2.5. To begin, click the Insert tab and then click the SmartArt button in the Illustrations group.

**22** At the Choose a SmartArt Graphic dialog box, click *Relationship* in the left panel and then double-click the *Converging Radial* option in the middle panel. (This option may be the first option from the right in the sixth row or the first option from the left in the seventh row.)

**23** If necessary, close the *Type your text here* window by clicking the Close button in the upper right corner of the window.

**24** Click the Add Shape button in the Create Graphic group.

**25** Click in each of the shapes and insert the text shown in Figure 2.5.

**26** Click the Change Colors button in the SmartArt Styles group and then click the *Colorful - Accent Colors* option (first option in the *Colorful* section).

**27** Click the More SmartArt Styles button at the right of the gallery in the SmartArt Styles group.

**28** Click the *Cartoon* option at the drop-down gallery (third option in the *3-D* section).

**29** Click the SmartArt Tools Format tab.

**30** Click inside the SmartArt graphic border but outside any shape.

> This deselects the shapes but keeps the graphic selected.

**31** Click the More WordArt Styles button at the right of the gallery in the WordArt Styles group and then click the option in the fourth column, second row (white fill with orange outline).

**32** Click in the *Width* measurement box in the Size group, type 9.5, and then press the Enter key.

**33** Click the Align button ⊟ in the Arrange group and then click *Align Center* at the drop-down list.

**34** Save **2-MPProj**.

**Figure 2.5** SmartArt Graphic

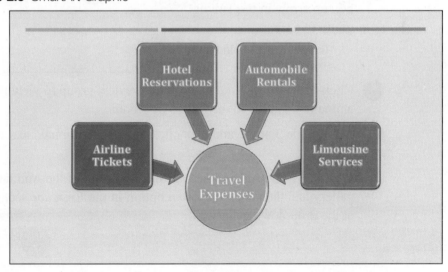

Check Your Work  Compare your work to the model answer available in the online course.

## In Addition

### Inserting Text in the Text Pane

Enter text in a SmartArt shape by clicking in the shape and then typing the text. Text can also be inserted in a SmartArt shape by typing text in SmartArt's text pane. Display the text pane by clicking the Text Pane button in the Create Graphic group on the SmartArt Tools Design tab.

Animate individual objects and text in a slide with options on the Animations tab. Click the Animations tab and the tab displays with a variety of animation styles and with options for customizing and applying times to animations in a presentation. Click the More Animations button at the right of the gallery in the Animation group and a drop-down gallery of animation styles displays that can be applied to objects and text as they enter a slide, exit a slide, and/or follow a motion path. Animations can also be applied to emphasize objects in a slide. If the same animation is to be applied to other objects in a presentation, use the Animation Painter button in the Advanced Animation group on the Animations tab.

**What You Will Do**   To finalize the presentation, Chris Greenbaum has asked you to apply animation to objects and text in the presentation.

 Tutorial
Applying and
Removing Animations

 Tutorial
Modifying Animations

**①** With **2-MPProj** open, make sure Slide 10 is active and the SmartArt graphic is selected.

**②** Click the Animations tab and then click the *Fly In* option in the Animation gallery in the Animation group.

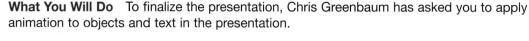

**③** Click the Effect Options button in the Animation group and then click *One by One* in the *Sequence* section at the drop-down gallery.

**④** Click the *Duration* measurement box up arrow in the Timing group two times.

> This inserts *01.00* in the measurement box.

**⑤** Click the Preview button in the Preview group to view the animation applied to the SmartArt graphic.

**⑥** Make Slide 3 active and then click the organizational chart to select it.

**⑦** Click the More Animations button at the right of the Animation gallery and then click the *Zoom* option in the *Entrance* section at the drop-down gallery.

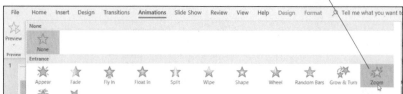

**⑧** Click the Effect Options button in the Animation group and then click *One by One* in the *Sequence* section at the drop-down gallery.

**In Brief**

**Apply Animation to Object**
1. Click object.
2. Click Animations tab.
3. Click animation option.

**9** Click Slide 2 to make it active and then click in the bulleted text to select the placeholder.

**10** Click the *Fly In* option in the gallery in the Animation group.

> Applying this animation creates a *build* for the bulleted items. A build displays important points in a slide one point at a time and is useful for keeping the audience's attention focused on the point being presented rather than reading ahead.

**11** Click the *Duration* measurement box up arrow in the Timing group two times.

> This inserts *01.00* in the measurement box.

**12** Apply the same animation to the bulleted text in Slides 4 through 9. To begin, click in the bulleted text to select the placeholder and then double-click the Animation Painter button ☆ in the Advanced Animation group.

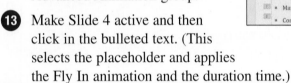

**13** Make Slide 4 active and then click in the bulleted text. (This selects the placeholder and applies the Fly In animation and the duration time.)

**14** Make Slide 5 active and then click in the bulleted text.

**15** Make Slide 6 active and then click in the bulleted text. Repeat this action for Slides 7–9.

**16** Click the Animation Painter button to turn off the feature.

**17** Make Slide 1 active and then run the slide show. Click the mouse button to advance slides and to display the individual organizational chart objects, bulleted items, and SmartArt graphic objects.

**18** Print the presentation as handouts with six slides displayed horizontally on one page. To do this, click the File tab and then click the *Print* option.

**19** At the Print backstage area, click the second gallery (contains the text *Full Page Slides*) in the *Settings* category and then click *6 Slides Horizontal* at the drop-down list.

**20** Click the Print button.

**21** Save and then close **2-MPProj**.

**Check Your Work** Compare your work to the model answer available in the online course.

## In Addition

### Applying Custom Animation

Apply custom animation to selected objects in a slide by clicking the Animation Pane button in the Advanced Animation group on the Animations tab. This displays the Animation task pane at the right of the screen. Use options in this task pane to control the order in which objects appear on a slide, choose animation direction and speed, and specify how objects will appear in the slide.

# Features Summary

| Feature | Ribbon Tab, Group | Button | Keyboard Shortcut |
|---------|-------------------|--------|-------------------|
| align left | Home, Paragraph | | Ctrl + L |
| align right | Home, Paragraph | | Ctrl + R |
| align vertically | Home, Paragraph | | |
| animation effect options | Animations, Animation | | |
| bold | Home, Font | B | Ctrl + B |
| center | Home, Paragraph | | Ctrl + E |
| copy selected text | Home, Clipboard | | Ctrl + C |
| cut selected text | Home, Clipboard | | Ctrl + X |
| decrease font size | Home, Font | | Ctrl + Shift + < |
| decrease list level | Home, Paragraph | | Shift + Tab |
| font | Home, Font | | |
| font color | Home, Font | | |
| Font dialog box | Home, Font | | Ctrl + Shift + F |
| font size | Home, Font | | |
| format background | Design, Customize | | |
| Format Painter | Home, Clipboard | | |
| increase font size | Home, Font | | Ctrl + Shift + > |
| increase list level | Home, Paragraph | | Tab |
| insert image | Insert, Images | | |
| insert screenshot | Insert, Images | | |
| insert SmartArt | Insert, Illustrations | | |
| italic | Home, Font | I | Ctrl + I |
| justify | Home, Paragraph | | Ctrl + J |
| line spacing | Home, Paragraph | | |
| paste selected text | Home, Clipboard | | Ctrl + V |
| preview animation | Animations, Preview | | |
| slide size | Design, Customize | | |
| underline | Home, Font | U | Ctrl + U |

# Integrating Programs

# Word, Excel, Access, and PowerPoint

 **Data Files**

Before beginning section work, copy the IntegratingBrief folder to your storage medium and then make IntegratingBrief the active folder.

## Skills

- Export Access data to Excel and Word
- Import Excel data to a new table in Access
- Export a PowerPoint presentation to Word
- Export a Word outline to a PowerPoint presentation
- Link an Excel chart with a Word document and PowerPoint presentation

- Edit a linked object
- Embed and edit a Word table in a PowerPoint slide
- Link data to a new Access table and edit linked data
- Embed an Excel worksheet in a Word document

## Projects Overview

 **NIAGARA PENINSULA COLLEGE**

Export grades from an Access table to an Excel worksheet; import grades from an Excel worksheet into an Access database table; send a college division PowerPoint presentation to a Word document; and link grades between an Excel worksheet and an Access database table.

 **Worldwide Enterprises**

Export data on US distributors from an Access report to a Word document; prepare a presentation for the Distribution Department of Worldwide Enterprises using a Word outline; copy an Excel chart and link it to both the Distribution Department meeting

presentation and to a Word document and then edit the linked chart; copy a Word table containing data on preview distribution dates, embed it in a PowerPoint slide, and then edit the table.

 **FIRST CHOICE TRAVEL**

Create and format a Word document containing information on vacation specials using data in a PowerPoint presentation.

 **Performance Threads**

Copy data in an Excel worksheet on employee payroll, embed the data in a Word document, and then update the payroll hours for the employees for the next week.

 The online course includes additional training and assessment resources.

1

One of the advantages of a suite like Microsoft Office is the ability to exchange data between programs. Access, like other programs in the suite, offers a feature to export data into other programs—in this case, Excel and Word. Export data to Excel using the Excel button in the Export group on the External Data tab. An Access object such as a table, form, or query can be exported.

**NIAGARA PENINSULA COLLEGE**

**What You Will Do**  You are Katherine Lamont, Theatre Arts Division instructor at Niagara Peninsula College. You want to work on your grades for your AC-215 class over the weekend and you do not have Access installed on your personal laptop. You decide to export your Access grading table to Excel.

**1** Open **IB-NPCStudentGrades** and then enable the content.

**2** Click the down arrow in the upper right corner of the Navigation pane and then click *Object Type* at the drop-down list.

**3** Click the *StudentGradesAC215-03* query.

**4** Click the External Data tab.

**5** Click the Excel button in the Export group.

**6** At the Export - Excel Spreadsheet dialog box, click the Browse button.

**7** At the File Save dialog box, navigate to the IntegratingBrief folder on your storage medium.

The name of the query is automatically inserted in the *File name* text box.

**8** Click the *File name* text box, press the Home key to move the insertion point to the beginning of the file name, type IB- (the file name should appear as **IB-StudentGradesAC215-03**), and then click the Save button.

**9** At the Export - Excel Spreadsheet dialog box, click the *Export data with formatting and layout* check box to insert a check mark.

**10** Click the *Open the destination file after the export operation is complete* check box to insert a check mark and then click OK.

Excel opens and the grades from the query are displayed in cells in a worksheet in the workbook.

**11** If Access is not active, click the Access button on the taskbar.

**12** Click the Close button at the Export - Excel Spreadsheet dialog box.

**13** Close **IB-NPCStudentGrades**.

**14** Click the Excel button on the taskbar.

**15** In **IB-StudentGradesAC215-03**, insert the following grades in the specified cells in the worksheet:

| D4: | C |
| D8: | B |
| D10: | F |
| D14: | A |
| D16: | C |
| D18: | B |

**16** Save, print, and then close **IB-StudentGradesAC215-03**.

**Check Your Work** Compare your work to the model answer available in the online course.

## In Addition

### Exporting Limitations

A table, form, or query can be exported to Excel but not a macro, module, or report. If a table contains subdata-sheets or a form contains subforms, each subdatasheet or subform must be exported to view them in Excel.

Data can be exported from Access to Word in a manner similar to exporting data to Excel. To export data to Word, open the database, select the object, click the External Data tab, click the More button in the Export group, and then click *Word* at the drop-down list. At the Export - RTF File dialog box, make changes and then click OK. Word automatically opens and the data displays in a Word document that is automatically saved with the same name as the database object. The difference is that the file extension *.rtf* is added to the name rather than the Word document extension, *.docx*. An RTF file is saved in rich-text format, which preserves formatting such as fonts and styles.

**Worldwide Enterprises**

**What You Will Do**   Sam Vestering, the manager of North American Distribution for Worldwide Enterprises, needs information on US distributors for an upcoming meeting. He has asked you to export the information from an Access database to a Word document.

**1** Open **IB-WEDistributors** and then enable the content.

**2** Click *US_Distributors* in the Tables group in the Navigation pane.

**3** Click the External Data tab, click the More button 🔲 in the Export group, and then click *Word* at the drop-down list.

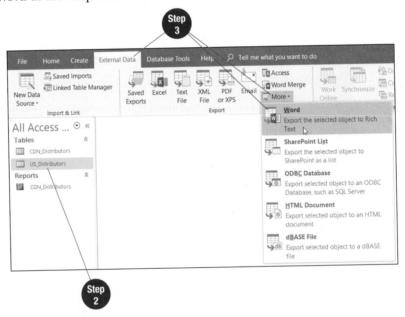

**4** At the Export - RTF File dialog box, click the Browse button.

**5** At the File Save dialog box, navigate to your IntegratingBrief folder.

**6** Click the *File name* text box, press the Home key to move the insertion point to the beginning of the file name, type IB- (the file name should appear as **IB-US_Distributors**), and then click the Save button.

In Brief

Export Access Table
to Word
1. Open database.
2. Click table in
   Navigation pane.
3. Click External Data
   tab.
4. Click More button in
   Export group.
5. Click *Word*.
6. At Export - RTF File
   dialog box, click
   Browse button.
7. At File Save dialog
   box, navigate to
   folder.
8. Click Save button.
9. Click options at
   Export - RTF File
   dialog box.
10. Click OK.

**7** At the Export - RTF File dialog box, click the *Open the destination file after the export operation is complete* check box and then click OK.

Microsoft Word opens and the information for US distributors displays in a document.

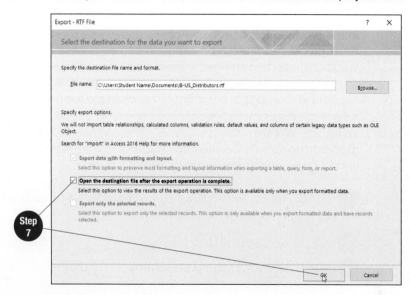

**8** If Access is not active, click the Access button on the taskbar.

**9** Click the Close button at the Export - RTF File dialog box.

**10** Close **IB-WEDistributors**.

**11** Click the Word button on the taskbar.

**12** Change the layout to landscape orientation by clicking the Layout tab, clicking the Orientation button in the Page Setup group, and then clicking *Landscape* at the drop-down list.

**13** Click in any cell in the table.

**14** Autofit the contents by clicking the Table Tools Layout tab, clicking the AutoFit button in the Cell Size group, and then clicking *AutoFit Contents* at the drop-down list.

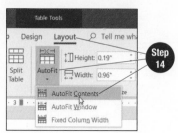

**15** Save, print, and then close **IB-US_Distributors**.

**Check Your Work** Compare your work to the model answer available in the online course.

# In Addition

## Adjusting a Table

In this activity, the Word table was adjusted to the cell contents. The table AutoFit feature contains three options for adjusting table contents as described at the right.

| Option | Action |
|---|---|
| *AutoFit Contents* | adjusts table to accommodate table text |
| *AutoFit Window* | sizes table to fit within window or browser; if browser changes size, table size automatically adjusts to fit within window |
| *Fixed Column Width* | adjusts each column to fixed width using current widths of the columns |

In the previous two activities, Access data was exported to Excel and Word. Data from other programs can also be imported into an Access table. For example, data from an Excel worksheet can be imported to create a new table in a database file. Data in the original program is not connected to the data imported into an Access table. If changes are made to the data in the original program, those changes are not reflected in the Access table.

**What You Will Do**  You are Gina Simmons, Theatre Arts instructor. You have recorded grades in an Excel worksheet for students in the Beginning Theatre class. You want to import those grades into a database.

1. Make Access active and then open **IB-NPCStudentGrades**. If necessary, enable the content.

2. Click the External Data tab.

3. Click the New Data Source button in the Import & Link group, click *From File* at the drop-down list, and then click *Excel* at the side menu.

4. At the Get External Data - Excel Spreadsheet dialog box, click the Browse button.

5. At the File Open dialog box, navigate to your IntegratingBrief folder and then double-click **NPCBegThGrades**.

6. At the Get External Data - Excel Spreadsheet dialog box, click the OK button.

7. At the first Import Spreadsheet Wizard dialog box, insert a check mark in the *First Row Contains Column Headings* check box and then click the Next button.

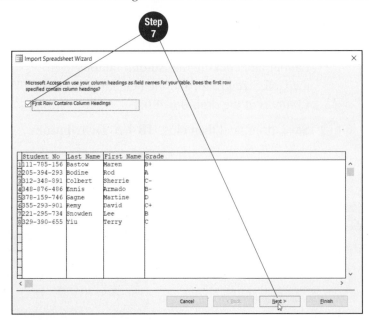

8. At the second Import Spreadsheet Wizard dialog box, click the Next button.

**In Brief**

**Import Data to New Table**
1. Open database.
2. Click External Data tab.
3. Click New Data Source button in Import & Link group.
4. Click *From File* option.
5. Click *Excel* option.
6. Click OK at Get External Data - Excel Spreadsheet dialog box.
7. Follow Import Spreadsheet Wizard steps.

9  At the third Import Spreadsheet Wizard dialog box, click the *Choose my own primary key* option (this inserts *Student No* in the text box at the right of the option) and then click the Next button.

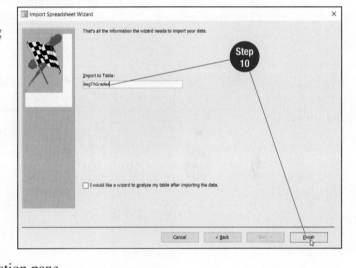

10  At the fourth Import Spreadsheet Wizard dialog box, type BegThGrades in the *Import to Table* text box and then click the Finish button.

11  At the Get External Data - Excel Spreadsheet dialog box, click the Close button.

12  Open the new table by double-clicking *BegThGrades* in the Tables group in the Navigation pane.

13  Print and then close BegThGrades.

14  Close **IB-NPCStudentGrades**.

**Check Your Work**  Compare your work to the model answer available in the online course.

# In Addition

## Importing or Linking a Table

Data from another program can be imported into an Access table or the data can be linked. Choose the method depending on how the data will be used. Consider linking an Excel file instead of importing to keep data in an Excel worksheet but use Access to perform queries and create reports. In Access, linked data can only be updated in one direction. Once an Excel table is linked to Access, the data cannot be edited in the Access table. The data in the Excel file can be updated and then changes are reflected in Access, but the data cannot be updated within Access.

One of the benefits of a suite like Microsoft Office is that data in one program can be sent to another program. For example, send PowerPoint content to a Word document. To send presentation content to a document, click the File tab, click the *Export* option, click the *Create Handouts* option, and then click the Create Handouts button. At the Send to Microsoft Word dialog box, specify the layout of the content in the Word document and whether to paste content or link content and then click OK. One of the advantages to sending PowerPoint presentation content to a Word document is that the content can be formatted using the Word formatting options.

**What You Will Do**   Create a Word document handout that contains slides from a PowerPoint presentation on the Theatre Arts Division at Niagara Peninsula College.

1. Open PowerPoint and then open **NPCDivPres**.

2. Save the presentation with the name **IB-NPCDivPres**.

3. Click the File tab, click the *Export* option, click the *Create Handouts* option, and then click the Create Handouts button.

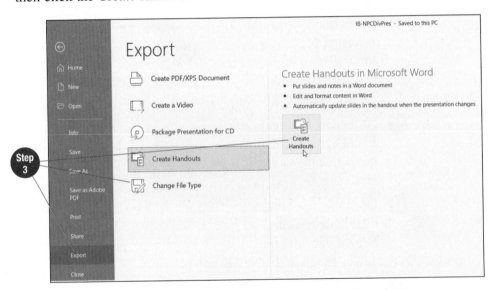

4. At the Send to Microsoft Word dialog box, click the *Blank lines next to slides* option.

5. Click the *Paste link* option in the *Add slides to Microsoft Word document* section and then click OK.

6. Click the Word button on the taskbar.

   The slides display in a Word document as thumbnails followed by blank lines.

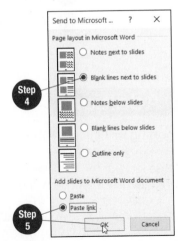

In Brief

Export PowerPoint
Presentation to Word
1. Open presentation.
2. Click File tab.
3. Click *Export* option.
4. Click *Create Handouts*
   option.
5. Click Create Handouts
   button.
6. Choose options at
   Send to Microsoft
   Word dialog box.
7. Click OK.

**7** Save the Word document in the IntegratingBrief folder on your storage medium and name it **IB-NPCDivPresHandout**.

**8** Print and then close **IB-NPCDivPresHandout**.

**9** Click the PowerPoint button on the taskbar.

**10** Make Slide 3 active and then change *$750* to *$850*, *$350* to *$450*, and *$250* to *$300*.

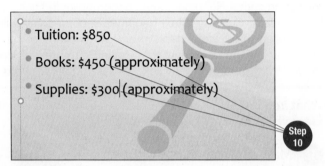

**11** Save **IB-NPCDivPres**.

**12** Click the Word button on the taskbar and then open **IB-NPCDivPresHandout**. At the message asking if you want to update the document with the data from the linked files, click the Yes button.

**13** Scroll through the document and notice that the amounts in Slide 3 reflect the changes you made to Slide 3 in the PowerPoint presentation. (If you do not see the updated amounts, right-click Slide 3 in the document and then click *Update Link* at the shortcut menu.)

**14** Save, print, and then close **IB-NPCDivPresHandout**.

**15** Make PowerPoint active and then close **IB-NPCDivPres**.

**Check Your Work**  Compare your work to the model answer available in the online course.

## In Addition

### Pasting and Linking Data

The *Paste* option at the Send to Microsoft Word dialog box is selected by default and is available for all of the page layout options. With this option selected, the data inserted in Word is not connected or linked to the original data in the PowerPoint presentation. If the data in the presentation is updated and the data should be updated in the Word document as well, select the *Paste link* option at the Send to Microsoft Word dialog box. This option is available for all of the page layout options except the *Outline only* option.

Create text for slides in a Word outline and then export that outline to PowerPoint. PowerPoint creates new slides based on the heading styles used in the Word outline. Text formatted with a Heading 1 style becomes slide titles. Heading 2 text becomes first-level bulleted text; Heading 3 text becomes second-level bulleted text, and so on. If styles are not applied to outline text in Word, PowerPoint uses tabs or indents to place text on slides. To export a Word document to a PowerPoint presentation, first add the Send to Microsoft PowerPoint button to the Quick Access Toolbar in Word.

**Worldwide Enterprises**

**What You Will Do**   Prepare a presentation for the Distribution Department of Worldwide Enterprises using a Word outline.

1. Make sure both Word and PowerPoint are open.

2. Make Word active and then open **WEOutline**.

   Text in this document has been formatted with the Heading 1 and Heading 2 styles.

3. Add a Send to Microsoft PowerPoint button to the Quick Access Toolbar. Begin by clicking the Customize Quick Access Toolbar button ⏷ at the right of the Quick Access Toolbar in Word.

4. Click *More Commands* at the drop-down list.

5. Click the *Choose commands from* option box arrow and then click *All Commands* at the drop-down list.

Step 3

Step 4

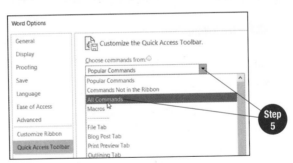

Step 5

6. Scroll down the list box below the *Choose commands from* option box and then double-click *Send to Microsoft PowerPoint*.

   Items in the list box display in alphabetical order.

7. Click OK to close the Word Options dialog box.

   Notice the Send to Microsoft PowerPoint button added to the Quick Access Toolbar.

8. Send the outline to PowerPoint by clicking the Send to Microsoft PowerPoint button ▣ on the Quick Access Toolbar.

Step 8

**9** When the presentation displays on the screen, make sure Slide 1 is the active slide. (If the presentation does not display, click the PowerPoint button on the taskbar. If necessary, click the Enable Editing button at the top of the PowerPoint window.)

The presentation is created with a blank design template.

**10** With Slide 1 active, change the layout by clicking the Layout button 🔲 in the Slides group on the Home tab and then clicking the *Title Slide* option at the drop-down list.

**11** Make Slide 4 active and then apply the Title Only layout. Apply the Title Only layout to Slides 5 and 6 as well.

**12** Apply a design theme by clicking the Design tab, clicking the More Themes button ⏷ at the right of the gallery in the Themes group, and then clicking the *Retrospect* option (shown below).

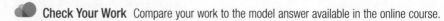

**13** Save the presentation and name it **IB-WEDistDeptMtg**.

**14** Close **IB-WEDistDeptMtg**.

**15** Click the Word button on the taskbar.

**16** Right-click the Send to Microsoft PowerPoint button on the Quick Access Toolbar and then click *Remove from Quick Access Toolbar* at the shortcut menu.

**17** Close **WEOutline** without saving changes.

⬤ **Check Your Work** Compare your work to the model answer available in the online course.

# In Addition

## Applying a Style in Word

Heading styles were already applied to the text in **WEOutline**. If an outline is created in Word that is to be exported to PowerPoint, apply styles using options in the Styles group on the Home tab. A Word document contains a number of predesigned formats grouped into style sets. Click the Design tab to display the available style sets in the Document Formatting group. Choose a style set and the styles visible in the Styles group on the Home tab change to reflect the selection. To display additional available styles, click the More Styles button ⏷ at the right of the gallery in the Styles group on the Home tab. To apply a heading style, position the insertion point in the text, click the More Styles button, and then click the specific style at the drop-down gallery.

An object, such as a table or chart, can be copied and linked to files created in other programs. For example, copy an Excel chart and link it to a Word document and/or a PowerPoint presentation. The advantage to copying and linking over copying and pasting is that when an object is edited in the originating program, called the *source program*, the object is automatically updated in the linked file in the other program, called the *destination program*. When an object is linked, it exists in the source program but not as a separate object in the destination program. Since the object is located only in the source program, changes made to the object in the source program will be reflected in the destination program. An object can be linked to more than one destination program or file.

**Worldwide Enterprises**

**What You Will Do** In preparation for a company meeting, you will copy an Excel chart and link it to both the Worldwide Enterprises Distribution Department meeting presentation and to a Word document.

1. Make sure Word and PowerPoint are open and then open Excel.

2. Make Word active and then open **WERevDoc**. Save the document with the name **IB-WERevDoc**.

3. Make PowerPoint active, open **IB-WEDistDeptMtg**, and then make Slide 6 active.

4. Make Excel active and then open **WERevChart**. Save the workbook with the name **IB-WERevChart**.

5. Copy and link the chart to the Word document and the PowerPoint presentation by clicking in the chart to select it.

> Make sure you select the chart and not a specific chart element. To do so, try clicking just inside the chart border.

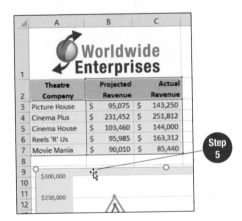

6. With the chart selected, click the Copy button in the Clipboard group on the Home tab.

7. Click the Word button on the taskbar.

8. Press Ctrl + End to move the insertion point to the end of the document.

9. Click the Paste button arrow and then click *Paste Special* at the drop-down list.

**Link Object between Programs**
1. Open source program, open file containing object.
2. Select object, click Copy button.
3. Open destination program, open file into which object will be linked.
4. Click Paste button arrow, click *Paste Special*.
5. At Paste Special dialog box, click *Paste*.
6. Click object in *As* list box.
7. Click OK.

**10** At the Paste Special dialog box, click the *Paste link* option, click the *Microsoft Excel Chart Object* option in the *As* list box, and then click OK.

**11** Select the chart and then center it by clicking the Center button in the Paragraph group on the Home tab.

**12** Save, print, and then close **IB-WERevDoc**.

**13** Click the PowerPoint button on the taskbar.

**14** With Slide 6 the active slide, make sure the Home tab is selected, click the Paste button arrow, and then click *Paste Special*.

**15** At the Paste Special dialog box, click the *Paste link* option, make sure *Microsoft Excel Chart Object* is selected in the *As* list box, and then click OK.

**16** Increase the size of the chart so it better fills the slide and then center it on the slide.

**17** Click outside the chart to deselect it.

**18** Save the presentation, print only Slide 6, and then close **IB-WEDistDeptMtg**.

**19** Click the Excel button on the taskbar and then click outside the chart to deselect it.

**20** Save, print, and then close **IB-WERevChart**.

Step 10

Step 15

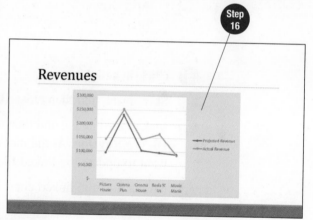

Step 16

**Check Your Work** Compare your work to the model answer available in the online course.

## In Addition

### Linking Data or an Object within a Program

In this activity, an object was linked between programs using the Paste Special dialog box. An object can also be linked in Word using options at the Object dialog box. To do this, click the Insert tab and then click the Object button in the Text group. At the Object dialog box, click the Create from File tab. At the dialog box, type the file name in the *File name* text box or click the Browse button and then select the file from the appropriate folder. Click the *Link to file* check box to insert a check mark and then click OK.

The advantage to linking an object over simply copying it is that editing the object in the source program will automatically update the object in the destination program(s) as well. To edit a linked object, open the file containing the object in the source program, make edits, and then save the file. The next time the document, workbook, or presentation is opened in the destination program, the object will be updated.

**Worldwide Enterprises**

**What You Will Do**   Edit the actual and projected revenue numbers in the Worldwide Enterprises Excel worksheet and then open and print the Word document and PowerPoint presentation containing the linked chart.

1  Make sure Word, Excel, and PowerPoint are open.

2  Make Excel active and then open **IB-WERevChart**.

3  You discover that one theatre company was left out of the revenues chart. Add a row to the worksheet by clicking in cell A6 to make it the active cell. Click the Insert button arrow 🔲 in the Cells group on the Home tab and then click *Insert Sheet Rows* at the drop-down list.

4  Insert the following data in the specified cells:
   - A6:   Regal Theatres
   - B6:   69550
   - C6:   50320

5  Click in cell A3.

6  Save, print, and then close **IB-WERevChart**.

7  Make Word active and then open **IB-WERevDoc**. At the message asking if you want to update the linked file, click the Yes button.

8  Notice how the linked chart is automatically updated to reflect the changes you made to the chart in Excel.

Step 5

Step 4

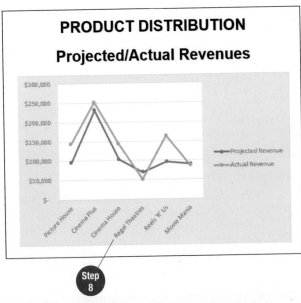

**PRODUCT DISTRIBUTION**

**Projected/Actual Revenues**

Step 8

**9** Save, print, and then close **IB-WERevDoc**.

**10** Make PowerPoint active and then open **IB-WEDistDeptMtg**.

**11** At the message stating that the presentation contains links, click the Update Links button.

**12** Make Slide 6 the active slide and then notice how the linked chart is automatically updated to reflect the changes you made to it in Excel.

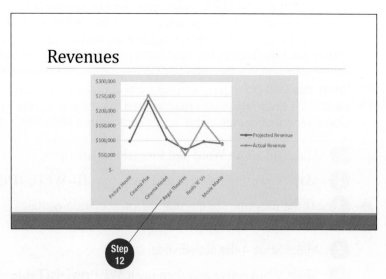

Step 12

**13** Save the presentation and then print only Slide 6.

**14** Close **IB-WEDistDeptMtg**.

**Check Your Work** Compare your work to the model answer available in the online course.

## In Addition

### Updating a Link Manually

A link can be updated in the destination program. To do this, open a Word document containing a linked object. Right-click the object, point to *Linked (type of object) Object*, and then click *Links*. At the Links dialog box, click the *Manual update* option and then click OK. With *Manual update* selected, the link will only be updated by right-clicking the linked object and then clicking *Update Link* or at the Links dialog box by clicking the link in the list box and then clicking the Update Now button.

An object can be copied and pasted, copied and linked, or copied and embedded from one file into another. A linked object resides in the source program but not as a separate object in the destination program. An embedded object resides in the source program as well as in the destination program. If a change is made to an embedded object in the source program, the change will not be made to the object in the destination program. The main advantage to embedding rather than simply copying and pasting is that an embedded object can be edited in the destination program using the tools of the source program.

**Worldwide Enterprises**

**What You Will Do**   Copy a Word table containing data on preview distribution dates for Worldwide Enterprises and then embed the table in a slide in a PowerPoint presentation. Update the distribution dates for the embedded table.

1. Make sure both Word and PowerPoint are open.

2. Make PowerPoint active and then open **IB-WEDistDeptMtg**.

3. At the message stating that the presentation contains links, click the Update Links button.

4. Make Slide 4 the active slide.

5. Make Word active and then open **WEPrevDistTable**.

6. Click in a cell in the table and then select the table. To do this, click the Table Tools Layout tab, click the Select button in the Table group, and then click *Select Table* at the drop-down list.

7. With the table selected, click the Home tab and then click the Copy button in the Clipboard group.

8. Click the PowerPoint button on the taskbar.

9. With Slide 4 the active slide, click the Paste button arrow and then click *Paste Special* at the drop-down list.

10. At the Paste Special dialog box, click *Microsoft Word Document Object* in the *As* list box and then click OK.

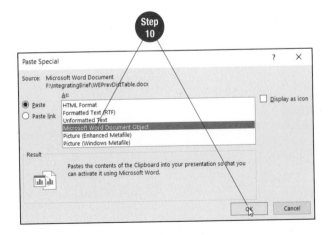

**11** With the table selected in the slide, use the sizing handles to increase the size and position of the table so it displays as shown below.

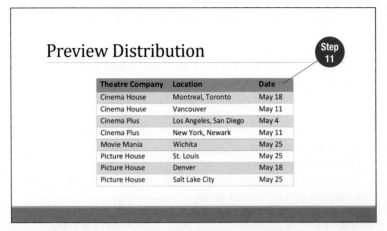

**12** The distribution date to Picture House in St. Louis has been delayed until June 1. Edit the date by double-clicking the table in the slide.

Double-clicking the table displays the Word tabs and ribbon at the top of the screen. A horizontal and vertical ruler also display around the table.

**13** Using the mouse, select *May 25* in the *St. Louis* row and then type June 1.

**14** Click outside the table to deselect it.

Clicking outside the table deselects it and also removes the Word tabs.

**15** Print Slide 4 of the presentation.

**16** Delete Slide 5.

**17** Apply a transition and transition sound of your choosing to all slides in the presentation.

**18** Run the slide show.

**19** Save and then close **IB-WEDistDeptMtg**.

**20** Click the Word button on the taskbar and then close the document.

**Check Your Work** Compare your work to the model answer available in the online course.

## In Addition

### Display an Embedded Object as an Icon

An embedded object displays in the destination program as it appears in the source program. Embed an object as an icon in the destination program representing the object. To change the embedded object to an icon, right-click the object, point to *Document Object*, and then click *Convert*. At the Convert dialog box, click the *Display as icon* check box and then click OK. To view the embedded object in the source program, double-click the icon in the destination program. Notice that the title bar in the source program identifies the program in which the object is embedded.

Imported data is not connected to the source program. If the data will only be used in Access, import it. However, if the data will be updated in a program other than Access, link the data. Changes made to linked data are reflected in both the source and the destination programs. For example, an Excel worksheet can be linked with an Access table and, when changes are made in the Excel worksheet, the same changes will be reflected in the Access table.

**NIAGARA PENINSULA COLLEGE**

**What You Will Do**   You are Cal Rubine, Theatre Arts instructor at Niagara Peninsula College. You record students' grades in an Excel worksheet and link the grades to an Access database file. With the data linked, changes you make to the Excel worksheet are reflected in the Access table.

**1**  Make Excel active and then open **NPCTRA220**.

**2**  Save the workbook with the name **IB-NPCTRA220**.

**3**  Print and then close **IB-NPCTRA220**.

**4**  Make Access active and then open **IB-NPCStudentGrades**.

**5**  Click the External Data tab, click the New Data Source button in the Import & Link group, click *From File* at the drop-down list, and then click *Excel* at the side menu.

**6**  At the Get External Data - Excel Spreadsheet dialog box, click the Browse button.

**7**  Navigate to the IntegratingBrief folder on your storage medium and then double-click *IB-NPCTRA220*.

**8**  At the Get External Data - Excel Spreadsheet dialog box, click the *Link to the data source by creating a linked table* option and then click OK.

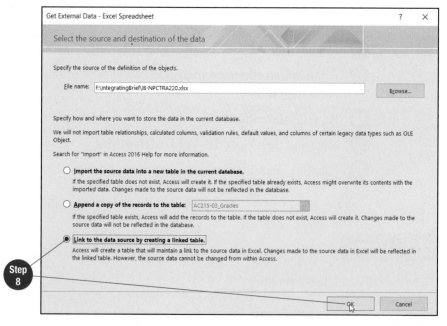

**9**  At the first Link Spreadsheet Wizard dialog box, make sure the *First Row Contains Column Headings* check box contains a check mark and then click the Next button.

In Brief

**Link Data to New Table**
1. Open database.
2. Click External Data tab.
3. Click New Data Source button in Import & Link group.
4. Click *From File* option.
5. Click *Excel* option.
6. At Get External Data - Excel Spreadsheet dialog box, click Browse button.
7. Navigate to folder, then double-click file.
8. At Get External Data - Excel Spreadsheet dialog box, click *Link to the data source by creating a linked table* option, then click OK.
9. Follow Link Spreadsheet Wizard steps.

**10** At the second Link Spreadsheet Wizard dialog box, type LinkedGrades in the *Linked Table Name* text box and then click the Finish button.

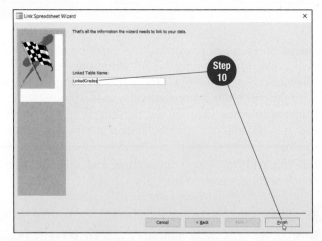

**11** At the message stating the link is finished, click OK.

Access uses different icons to represent linked tables and tables that are stored in the current database. Notice the icon that displays before the LinkedGrades table.

**12** Open the new LinkedGrades table in Datasheet view.

**13** Close the LinkedGrades table.

**14** Make Excel active and then open **IB-NPCTRA220**.

**15** Make cell E2 active, click the AutoSum button arrow $\Sigma$, click *Average* at the drop-down list, and then press the Enter key.

This inserts *3.00* in cell E2.

**16** Copy the formula in cell E2 down to the range E3:E9.

**17** Save, print, and then close **IB-NPCTRA220**.

| | A | B | C | D | E |
|---|---|---|---|---|---|
| 1 | Student No | Student | Midterm | Final | Average |
| 2 | 111-785-156 | Bastow, M. | 3.25 | 2.75 | 3.00 |
| 3 | 359-845-475 | Collyer, S. | 1.50 | 1.00 | 1.25 |
| 4 | 157-457-856 | Dwyer, B. | 3.50 | 3.50 | 3.50 |
| 5 | 348-876-486 | Ennis, A. | 2.25 | 2.00 | 2.13 |
| 6 | 378-159-746 | Gagne, M. | 3.00 | 3.50 | 3.25 |
| 7 | 197-486-745 | Koning, J. | 2.75 | 2.50 | 2.63 |
| 8 | 314-745-856 | Morgan, B. | 3.75 | 3.00 | 3.38 |
| 9 | 349-874-658 | Retieffe, S. | 4.00 | 3.50 | 3.75 |
| 10 | | | | | |

Step 16

**18** Click the Access button on the taskbar and then open the LinkedGrades table and notice the worksheet contains the average amounts.

**19** Print and then close the table.

**20** Close **IB-NPCStudentGrades** and then close Access.

 **Check Your Work** Compare your work to the model answer available in the online course.

## In Addition

### Deleting the Link to a Linked Table

To delete the link to a table, open the database and then click the table in the Navigation pane. Click the Home tab and then click the Delete button in the Records group. At the question asking if you want to remove the link to the table, click Yes. Access deletes the link and removes the table's name from the Navigation pane. When a linked table is deleted, the information Access uses to open the table is deleted, not the table itself. The same table can be linked again, if necessary.

As learned in a previous activity, an object can be copied and then linked or embedded between files in a program. An embedded object resides in the file in the source program as well as in the destination program. If a change is made to an embedded object in the source program, the change is not made to the object in the destination program. The advantage to embedding rather than simply copying and pasting is that an embedded object can be edited in the destination program using the tools of the source program.

**What You Will Do**   Copy data in an Excel worksheet on employee payroll for Performance Threads and then embed the data in a Word document.

1. Make Word active and then open **PTWordNov8Pay**.

2. Save the document with the name **IB-PTWordNov8Pay**.

3. Make Excel active and then open **PTExcelNov8Pay**.

4. Save the workbook with the name **IB-PTExcelNov8Pay**.

5. Embed cells into the Word document. Start by selecting the range A3:D8.

6. Click the Copy button in the Clipboard group on the Home tab.

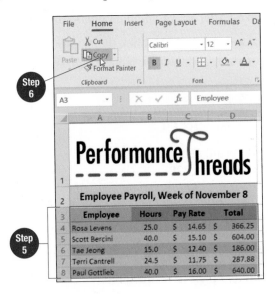

7. Click the Word button on the taskbar.

8. Press Ctrl + End to move the insertion point to the end of the document. (The insertion point is positioned a double space below *Week of November 8, 2021.*)

9. Click the Paste button arrow and then click *Paste Special* at the drop-down list.

## In Brief

**Embed Data**
1. Open programs and files.
2. Select data in source program.
3. Click Copy button.
4. Click button on taskbar representing destination program.
5. Click Paste button arrow.
6. Click *Paste Special*.
7. Click object in *As* list box.
8. Click OK.

**10** At the Paste Special dialog box, click *Microsoft Excel Worksheet Object* in the *As* list box and then click OK.

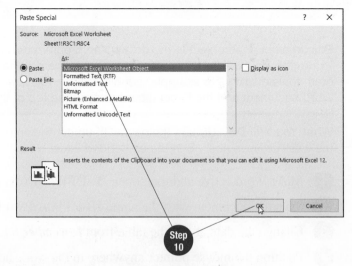

Step 10

**11** If necessary, click outside the table to deselect it.

**12** Save, print, and then close **IB-PTWordNov8Pay**.

**13** Click the Excel button on the taskbar.

**14** Press the Esc key to remove the moving marquee around the range A3:D8.

**15** Click in cell A2 to make it the active cell.

**16** Save and then close **IB-PTExcelNov8Pay**.

**Check Your Work** Compare your work to the model answer available in the online course.

---

# In Addition

### Inserting an Embedded Object from an Existing File

An Excel worksheet can be embedded in a Word document using the Copy button and options at the Paste Special dialog box. Another method is available for embedding an object from an existing file. In the destination program document, position the insertion point where the object is to be embedded and then click the Object button in the Text group on the Insert tab. At the Object dialog box, click the Create from File tab. At the Object dialog box with the Create from File tab selected, type the file name in the *File name* text box or click the Browse button and then select the file from the appropriate folder. At the Object dialog box, make sure the *Link to file* check box does not contain a check mark and then click OK.

Edit an embedded object in the destination program using the tools of the source program. To do this, double-click the object in the file in the destination program and the source program tools display. For example, double-click an Excel worksheet that is embedded in a Word document and the Excel tabs display at the top of the screen.

Performance Threads

**What You Will Do**  Update the payroll hours for the employees of Performance Threads for the week of November 15 in the embedded Excel worksheet.

**1**  Make Word active and then open **IB-PTWordNov8Pay**.

**2**  Save the document with the name **IB-PTWordNov15Pay**.

**3**  Change the date above the table from *November 8* to *November 15*.

**4**  Position the mouse pointer anywhere in the worksheet and then double-click the left mouse button.

  In a few moments, the worksheet displays surrounded by column and row designations and the Excel tabs.

**5**  To produce the ordered costumes on time, the part-time employees worked a full 40 hours for the week of November 15. Make cell B4 the active cell and then change the number to *40.0*.

**6**  Make cell B6 the active cell and then change the number to *40.0*.

**7**  Make cell B7 the active cell and then change the number to *40.0*.

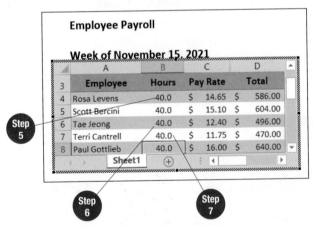

**8**  Bobbie Sinclair, business manager, wants to know the payroll total for the week of November 15 to determine the impact it has on the monthly budget. Add a new row to the table by making cell A8 the active cell and then pressing the Enter key.

**9** With cell A9 the active cell, type Total.

**10** Make cell D9 the active cell and then click the AutoSum button in the Editing group on the Home tab.

**11** Make sure *D4:D8* displays in cell D9 and then press the Enter key.

**12** Increase the height of the worksheet by one row by positioning the mouse pointer on the bottom middle black sizing square until the pointer turns into a double-headed arrow pointing up and down. Click and hold down the left mouse button, drag down one row, and then release the mouse button.

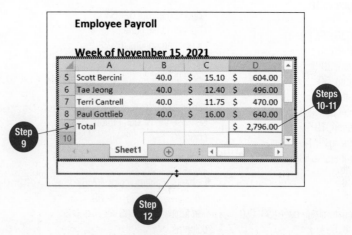

**13** Using the arrow keys on the keyboard, make cell A3 the active cell and position cell A3 in the upper left corner of the worksheet. (This will display all cells in the worksheet containing data.)

**14** Click outside the worksheet to deselect it.

**15** Save, print, and then close **IB-PTWordNov15Pay**.

The gridlines do not print.

**Check Your Work** Compare your work to the model answer available in the online course.

## In Addition

### Troubleshooting Linking and Embedding Problems

If a linked or embedded object is double-clicked and a message appears indicating that the source file or source program cannot be opened, consider the following troubleshooting options. Check to make sure that the source program is installed on the computer. If the source program is not installed, convert the object to the file format of a program that is installed. Check to make sure the source program does not have any dialog boxes open and, if it is a linked object, check to make sure someone else is not working in the source file.

# INDEX

## WORD

### A

*Account* option, 5
Add Field dialog box, 115
Address Block button, 112
Add Shape button, 96
Align button, 95
Align Center button, 102
aligning
  paragraphs, 38–39, 80–81
  vertically, 80–81
Align Left button, 39
Alignment button, 50
Align Right button, 38
Align Top Center button, 103
Arrange All button, 19
AutoCorrect, using, 3, 14–15
automatic numbers/bulleting, turning off, 47

### B

background, customizing page, 68–69
backstage area, 3–4
  options, 5
backstage view, 26, 27
Bibliography button, 78
*Blank document* template, 2
blank page, inserting, 71
Blank Page button, 71
Bold button, 34
borders
  adding to tables, 104
  adding to text, 54–55
  applying to page, 68–69
  changing options, 69
Borders and Shading dialog box, 54–55
Borders button, 54
boxes, enclosing text within, 92, 93, 95
Breaks button, 106
bullets
  inserting, 46–47
  turning off automatic, 47
Bullets button, 46

### C

cells
  changing size, 102–103
  changing width, 102–103
  creating, 100–102
  described, 100
  keyboard shortcuts for selecting, 103
  moving insertion point, 100
  word wrap feature, 100
Center button, 38
center tab symbol, 50
certificate of appreciation template, 28–29

Change Case button, 34
Change Colors button, 97
changing width, 102–103
characters, inserting special, 48–49
Check Document button, 12
citations
  creating work cited page, 78–79
  inserting, 74–77
Clear All Formatting button, 50, 51
Click and Type, aligning paragraphs using, 80–81
Clip Art, inserting, sizing and moving, 81–83
Clipboard group, 62–63
Clipboard task pane
  choosing options, 65
  using, 64–65
Close button, 7
*Close* option, 5, 7
closing document, 6, 7
Collapse the Ribbon button, 2, 3, 21
color
  adding in WordArt, 90
  changing, 97, 99
  changing theme color, 57, 67
  customizing page, 68–69
  in tables, 104–105
columns
  changing size, 102–103
  changing width, 102–103, 107
  creating, 100–101
  formatting text in, 102–103
  newspaper, 106–107
Columns button, 107
Columns dialog box, 107
Column Width button, 17
company logos, creating and modifying using WordArt, 90–91
continuous section breaks, inserting, 106
Copy button, 62
copying text, 62–63
Corrections button, 82
cover page, inserting/deleting, 70–71
Cover Page button, 70
curve, drawing, 95
Customize Address List dialog box, 115
Customize Columns button, 115
Cut button, 62
cutting text, 62–63

### D

data source file
  described, 110
  editing, 114–115
  inserting new field, 115
  for mail merge, 110
decimal tab, setting, 51
default document formatting
  changing, 56–57
  elements, 5
deleting
  tabs, 51

text, 8–9, 10–11
Design tab, 56
display percentage, changing, 18–19
document. *See also* text
  changing
    default formatting, 56–57
    display percentage, 18–19
    line and paragraph spacing, 42–43
    views, 16–17
  closing, 6, 7
  creating, 2–4
  creating using template, 28–29
  default formatting, 5
  formatting with Font group and Mini toolbar, 34–35
  insert one document into another, 106–107
  main, 110
  merging with envelopes, 110–113
  MLA style, 74–79
  naming, 7
  navigating in, 10–11
  opening, 8–9
  previewing, 27
  printing, 4–5, 26–27
  readability, 106
  resuming reading or editing, 11
  saving, 4, 6–7
    in different format, 30–31
    in PDF format, 108–109
    as web page, 109
  scrolling in, 10–11
  section break, 106–107
  spelling and grammar check, 12–13
document icon, 30
Draft button, 16
Draft view, 16
Drawing Tools Format tab, 91
Drop Cap button, 92
drop caps, creating, 92–93

### E

Edit Data Source dialog box, 114–115
editing
  data source file, 114–115
  PDF file, 31
  resuming, and insertion point, 11
  while checking spelling and grammar, 13
Editor task pane, 12, 13
Edit Recipient List button, 114
envelopes
  customizing, 85
  merging documents and, 110–113
  preparing, 84–85
Envelopes button, 84
errors, correcting
  spelling and grammar check, 12–13
  using AutoCorrect, 3
  words not in Spelling dictionary, 5
*Export* option, 5
Extend mode, 10

AutoSum button, 14
AVERAGE function, 58–59

## B

Backstage view
  Close button, 5
  print area, 24
  Print option, 4
  Save as button, 4
bar chart
  creating, 68–69
  modifying, 74–75
bold, 36
bold italic, 36
borders
  adding, 42–43
  creating custom, 43
Break Link button, 111

## C

calculations, performing using formulas,
    12–13
Cancel button, 7
cell address, 2
  including in formula, 12
cell pointer, 2, 3
cells, 2
  active, 2, 3, 6
  aligning data in, 20–21, 40–41
  changing font size, style, and color,
    36–37
  clearing, 28–29
  copying, 32–33
  deleting, 31
  editing, 28–29
  editing data in, 18–19
  entering data, 3, 6–7
  entering formulas into, 12–13
  fill options, 10–11
  formatting numeric, 38–39
  formatting options, 20–21
  going to specific, 8
  indentation changes, 40–41
  inserting, 31
  inserting line break, 7
  keyboard movement commands, 6
  linking, 32–33, 88–89
  moving, 32–33
  range, 6, 7
  range name, 64–65
  rotating text, 21
  selecting, 6–7
  wrapping text within, 41
cell styles
  applying, 44–47
  creating new, 47
  described, 44
Center button, 40
chart elements, 75
charts
  bar, 68–69, 74

chart elements, 75
column, 68–69
hierarchy, 70–71
line, 72–73
linking Excel, with Word document,
    112–113
modifying and formatting, 74–75
pie, 71
Recommended Charts button, 69
Sparklines group, 71
Clear button, 28
clip art, inserting, moving and resizing,
    52–53
clipboard, 16, 17, 32–33
Close button, 5
Collapse the Ribbon button, 2, 3
colon (:), 14
color
  adding shading, 42–43
  adding to cells, 42–43
  fill, 42–43
  font, 36–37
  format sheet tabs, 82–83
column chart
  creating, 68–69
  modifying, 74–75
columns
  adjusting width of, 34–35
  deleting, 30–31
  inserting, 30–31
  letters for, 2
  printing headings on multiple pages, 77
  sorting by multiple criteria, 94–95
  sorting by single criteria, 94–95
  width default setting, 34
  width of, 34–35
Column Width dialog box, 35
comma style, 38
Comma Style button, 38
comments
  deleting, 98–99
  described, 98
  editing, 98–99
  inserting, 98–99
  printing, 98–99
Content pane, 4
Copy and Paste
  cells, 32–33
  copying formulas, 16–17
  versus fill handle, 17
  linking cells, 32–33, 88
Copy button, 16
Copy dialog box, 85
copying
  cells, 32–33
  formats, 42–43
  formulas, 16–17
  relative, 16
  Word data into worksheet, 106–107
  worksheet, 84–85
COUNT function, 58–59

currency style, 38
custom borders, creating, 43
Cut and Paste, cells, 32–33
Cut button, 32
cycling between open programs, 107

## D

data
  alignment of, in cells, 40–41
  copying and pasting Word data into
    worksheet, 106–107
  editing, 18–19
  editing linked data, 110–111
  entering into cell, 3, 6–7
  filtering, not formatted as table, 97
  formatting, as table, 92–93
  linking between programs, 108–109
  linking within program, 109
date function, 60–61
dates, default alignment of, 40
Date & Time button, 60
decimals, adjusting, 38–39
Decrease Decimal button, 39
Decrease Indent button, 40
default font, 36
deleting
  cells, 31
  columns, 30–31
  comments, 98–99
  page break, in normal view, 91
  rows, 30–31
  worksheet, 83
destination cell, 16
  copy and paste cell contents, 32
destination program, 106
dialog box launcher, 2, 3
division (/), 12, 13
document, linking worksheet with Word
    document, 108–109
dollar symbol ($), 56
drag and drop, 33
drawing shapes, 72–73

## E

editing
  cells, 28–29
  comments, 98–99
  data in cells, 18–19
  embedded object, 114, 115
  linked data, 110–111
  proofing tools, 28–29
  undo and redo, 18–19
Effects option, 37
embedded object, 114
  inserting, from existing file, 116
embedding
  Excel worksheet into Word document,
    114–116
  troubleshooting problems, 116
Enter button, 7, 10
equals sign, 12, 13
exponentiation (^), 12, 13

# Photo Credits